A Handbook of International Human Rights Terminology, Second Edition

A · HANDBOOK · OF · INTERNATIONAL HUMAN · RIGHTS · TERMINOLOGY ·

SECOND EDITION

H. Victor Condé

UNIVERSITY OF NEBRASKA PRESS

Lincoln and London

∞

Library of Congress Cataloging-in-Publication Data
Condé, H. Victor, 1947–
A handbook of international human rights terminology / H. Victor Condé.—2nd ed.
p.   cm. — (Human rights in international perspective ; v. 8)
Includes bibliographical references.
ISBN 0-8032-1534-7 (cloth : alk. paper) — ISBN 0-8032-6439-9 (pbk. : alk. paper)
1. Human rights—Dictionaries.   I. Title.   II. Series.
K3239.6.C66   2004
341.4′8′03—dc22   2003067182

• CONTENTS •

Appendix C:

Appendix D:

SINCE THE writing of the initial Handbook the author has had the opportunity to observe his students in the United States and in Europe test-driving it in class and using it in term papers. He has received many favorable comments from around the world of those who have been helped by it. The feedback has been positive enough to let him know that the thousands of hours put into its writing were not in vain. The Handbook has helped students, lawyers, human rights activists, government agents, and the average citizen increase the understanding of that body of human knowledge known as human rights.

As anticipated, the author also received constructive criticism, well taken and valid corrections, and suggestions for new terms not found in the original edition. Thanks to all those who cared enough about human rights to give the author their valuable input.

The need for this second edition came about because the world of human rights law, politics, and institutions has been slowly evolving since the initial edition, and some terms have had to be changed to reflect a change in accepted terminology or the name of a particular forum or procedure.

On top of all that, 9/11 occurred. This launched the "war on terrorism," which gave rise to or brought back again such terms as terrorism, enemy combatant, unilateralism, anticipatory self defense, material breach, and national security. In the interpretation and application of these terms rests the lives of many human beings and a potential for billions of dollars of destruction caused by terrorism and the armed conflict that may ensue to combat it. Many see the present world as a more dangerous place for human rights and fundamental freedoms than ever before. The international community has said that the solution to the world's problems is human rights education at all levels, for everyone, so that the world transforms from a planet of violence and hostile use of force into one characterized by a culture of human rights and peace in a rule of law society.

This second edition picks up where the first ended and is an attempt to again further the understanding of human rights by increasing the understanding of the terms used therein. Many new human rights texts of all varieties are appearing on bookshelves, and still, few of them will define the human rights terms they use, so as to assure full understanding and comprehension. Would that we all understood the language of human rights well enough that that would not be a problem. May this book help in that regard.

The Handbook has now been translated into several foreign languages, and it is the author's intention that it be translated into still others. In addition, it is the author's intention that a more portable and paperback edition of this second edition be produced so as to see its use expand.

What the world needs now is not more soldiers trained to kill or destroy in order to stop others from killing or destroying, but more humans educated in human rights, who are capable and willing to challenge governments to abide by the human rights norms that are the birthright of all human beings and were painfully birthed in the crucible of the holocaust. No justice, no peace. Let us all work together for the promotion and protection of human rights by first learning them ourselves at school or online or elsewhere. And let us teach them to our children, the future of this planet. The time for war should be no more. Let us promote justice and peace through increase in the knowledge of and action for human rights.

· ACKNOWLEDGMENTS ·

DEEPEST THANKS again to my patient wife Jean who again put up with me during this endless process; and to my precious daughter, Simone Thérèse Condé, who inspired the first edition and now the second, and who makes this work all worthwhile. Je t'aime.

Special Thanks to Rita Cartwright, Robert Savage, Bob and Monique Gibbs, Steven Kennedy, Morton Winston, Jean Bernard Marie, Elena Ipollitti, Msgr. Wm. McLaughlin, John Wanvig, John Felcyn, Paula Lizano Van der Laat, and all the staff of the International Institute of Human Rights in Strasbourg, France.

I give thanks and glory and praise to God for the freedom and knowledge to be able to write this book.

In thankful memory of Marie Therese Condé, my mother, who gave me the model, guidance, strength, and faith to struggle for the rights of other human beings as a human rights lawyer, advocate, and professor.

In memoriam: Sergio Vieira de Mello, Joan Fitzpatrick, Arthur C. Helton, 2003.

· INTRODUCTION ·
Civilization Is a Race between Education and Catastrophe

HUMAN RIGHTS is becoming the language of the entire world in the realm of politics, international relations, and law. To many scholars it is now deemed the dominant discourse of our day, and it is becoming more broadly so daily.

So important has human rights become in the eyes of the global community that the United Nations (UN) has declared the years 1995–2004 as the UN Decade of Human Rights Education. Human rights education is expanding both within and outside of the United States, with courses and terminal degree programs being established everywhere. The present is only the beginning stage of the study of human rights as an academic discipline that is available not only to law faculties but to other disciplines as well, such as political science, international relations, history, philosophy, social studies, and even religion, to name just a few.

The study of human rights should not be undertaken for mere intellectual stimulation or pleasure. It should be undertaken by all persons at appropriate levels and in both academic and nonacademic contexts so that a culture of human rights is inculcated in the learner. The learner (whether a student or not) is the bearer or holder of internationally recognized human rights. Human rights are the birthright of humanity, and their protection is the first responsibility of all states. They are inherent attributes of the human personality, and their purpose is the legal protection of the inherent human dignity of each individual human being. Life itself can be at stake if they are not preserved.

With the burgeoning of human rights studies, the need has arisen for academic tools with which to present this critical area of study. Textbooks are being written, articles published, and reports and statistics disseminated. Conferences, seminars, workshops, and institutes are beginning to proliferate. This book is intended to provide to the student of human rights an important tool for understanding the meaning of terms used in the field of international human rights and the words that will unlock the meaning of concepts and theories, law and procedures, institutions, and means of interpreting human rights.

This work was born out of my past twenty years of experience as a student, lawyer, and professor of international and comparative human rights in both the United States and Europe. When I began to study this field in depth for the first time, in the early 1980s, I had been a lawyer for ten years. Yet I struggled to understand lectures and texts unaccompanied by any, or at best few, definitions of words and terms, leaving me with serious gaps in my knowledge or with misunderstandings. Some words I had never before learned, *jus cogens*, for example. Others I had learned, but with different meanings, *protocol*, for example.

As a professor teaching the "Introduction to Human Rights" course for the past twelve years, I became convinced of the value of defining a sufficient number of terms for students at the beginning of the course so that they would understand the texts and lectures they would subsequently seek to digest, analyze, and understand. The results were clear and positive.

Furthermore, as I taught students from other countries who had already studied human rights in their native (non-English) language, I observed their inability to relate, or at least difficulty in relating, the terms they had learned in their own language with the equivalent term in English, for example, *Amparo* and *habeas corpus*. Once they learned the meaning of the English term, they could relate it to what they had learned in their native language and thus were better able to understand the subject matter in English and in their native tongue.

Most students of human rights today must learn the subject from a "baptism in a million words." This means that they must read texts, articles, laws, and reports, ad nauseam, and must try to discern and infer the meaning of terms by themselves through a sort of deductive synthesis. I hope that using this book prior to commencing study or as a tool during study and lectures will help students to maximize their understanding of the subject matter and minimize any misunderstandings.

The following list of terms has been culled from written materials in the field of human rights, though some obviously originate from other disciplines, such as history (e.g., *Holocaust*), political science (e.g., *totalitarianism*), and international relations (e.g., *Third World*). These are the terms that constitute the flesh and blood of human rights discourse and implementation. Here they will be defined only in the ways they are used and understood in the context of human rights. The body of terms used in international human rights discourse is a hybrid of terms from public international law, common law, and the civil law tradition, with a few from other systems and traditions. When used in relation to human rights they acquire particular meanings. This book is intended to convey these meanings at a basic intellectual level.

Some of the terms defined are not specific to human rights literature, such as *mutatis mutandis*: Although these words have no special meaning or nuance in relation to human rights, they nonetheless appear in the literature and discourse of human rights with frequency, and often without definition.

This reference work is meant primarily for those beginning their exposure to human rights literature and discourse. Many terms found in this work, however, are ones that even seasoned scholars have never encountered (e.g., *lex ferenda*) or have encountered but passed by for lack of a definition. It is hoped that scholars, too, may find this work useful.

Readers can use this book not merely as a reference tool for specific definitions but also as a sort of ongoing textbook for increasing their human rights vocabulary and general knowledge. This can be done by browsing through the List of Terms Defined and choosing a few interesting words to look up and learn. Teachers of human rights and related subjects would do well to assign certain terms for students to study in addition to regular reading assignments. And as indicated earlier, I have found that defining certain basic terms before giving a lecture is very beneficial to students, especially those gaining their first exposure to human rights terminology.

The choice of terms included in this work is purely that of the author, who recognizes that there are many other terms deserving inclusion, and even other definitions worth adding, but not included here.

METHODOLOGY

This work defines terms commonly found in human rights discourse, primarily in the legal and political realms. Terms are listed in alphabetical order. Words that appear in parentheses within or after the term being defined, for example, "Absolute (Human) Rights," give the main context in which the term often appears or its nature. One sees both the terms *absolute human rights* and simply *absolute rights*, with *human* implied.

When a word has several different meanings, depending on the context, the different meanings will be numbered.

A solidus (/) between words means "and/or," that is, that the term applies to either or all of those words. For example, "Abuse of Rights (Principle/Clause)" refers to the "abuse of rights principle" or to an "abuse of rights clause" found in a treaty.

Some of the terms defined in this work are in fact acronyms. Acronyms are words made up of the first or key letters of the words of a multiword term. For example, NGO stands for "Nongovernmental Organization." Sometimes the acronym is set forth itself as a separate term. Sometimes it is set forth in parentheses, for example, "Most Favored Nation (Trading) Status (MFN):" Only those acronyms that are most prominent in human rights literature and discourse are used.

Words in italics are foreign-language words, usually Latin or French. Such terms will be followed by the literal meaning of the term in brackets, for example, "*Erge Omnes* [Latin, lit.: toward everyone/all]:" This means that the term is a Latin-language term whose literal ("lit.") meaning is "toward everyone/all." This is done to give the best sense of the literal meaning of the term in hopes that it may aid in understanding the meaning in the human rights context.

Whenever the words *he/his/him* are used, they will also mean "she/hers/her." No gender bias is intended. Whenever *vs.* (an abbreviation for *versus*) appears in the contextual parentheses after the term, it indicates an opposite. That is, the term following vs. is the opposite of the term defined or is a term usually seen in contrast with the defined term. For example, "Universality (vs. Cultural Relativism):" Almost always, the word *state* means a country, a state in the international legal or political relations sense, such as the United States or Germany, not a federal subunit such as Texas or Hawaii.

I have chosen not to define most of the substantive human rights themselves because it is too problematic and because other adequate references exist. See the Bibliography.

A list of your substantive human rights found in the "International Bill of Rights" is included in Appendix A. The reader is strongly encouraged to read and become familiar with his or her own human rights.

There is no single, established, official scholarly source of definitions for all of the following terms. One can consult dictionaries of international law and the few dictionaries and encyclopedias of human rights to find some of them defined in the international context. And one can consult legal dictionaries, glossaries, thesauri, and references on Latin legal and nonlegal terms that are applicable in particular domestic (national) legal systems. But none are written specifically for the field of international human rights from an up-to-date, human rights-oriented perspective for persons who are not scholars or legal specialists. Hence the present work.

This book is a start, designed to help beginners and scholars alike on the path to a meaningful and fruitful understanding of human rights, especially their own human rights, as a step toward creating a human rights culture for the whole strife-torn world.

The following definitions are not intended as official or legally authoritative definitions and do not purport to be binding as definitive in any legal matter in any national or international forum, whether political, administrative, quasi-judicial, or judicial. These definitions are for academic purposes only.

• ABBREVIATIONS AND • SPECIAL TERMS

SOME ENTRIES will direct readers to certain major international human rights instruments for examples. These examples should be examined in order to gain the fullest sense of the term defined and to see the term in full context or in actual use.

*ACHR	American Convention on Human Rights (Organization of American States, 1969)
*ACHPR	African Charter on Human and Peoples' Rights (Organization of African Unity, 1981)
*ECHR	European Convention on Human Rights (Council of Europe, 1950)
GC (I II III IV)	Geneva Conventions of 1949 (ICRC)
ICRC	International Committee of the Red Cross
*ICCPR	International Covenant on Civil and Political Rights (UN, 1966)
*ICCPR-OP	First Optional Protocol to the International Covenant on Civil and Political Rights (UN 1966, "First OP")
*ICESCR	International Covenant on Economic, Social and Cultural Rights (UN, 1966)
P I, P II	Protocol I and Protocol II to the 1949 Geneva Conventions (ICRC, 1977)
*UDHR	Universal Declaration of Human Rights (UN, 1948)
UNCH	United Nations Charter (UN, 1945)
Vienna Convention of 1969	Vienna Convention on the Law of Treaties (UN, 1969)

The full or excerpted texts of the instruments marked with an asterisk are in Appendix B.

The following special terms are employed throughout the text:

aka   "also known as." Used to indicate a synonym or a roughly synonymous term. Example: "Collective Rights (aka Group Rights)."

caveat   *Caveat* is a Latin word meaning "let him or her be aware" or "be careful." It is a warning to the reader to watch out for something possibly misleading or confusing. Where the word *caveat* appears in a definition it usually calls the reader's attention to possible confusion between the term defined and another one, or refers to an instrument that is sometimes mistaken for another. Example: "Caveat: The term 'Servitude' has a unique meaning generally in international law."

complaint*   The asterisk refers to *complaint* and all its synonyms—*petition application, communication.* Example: "Individual Complaint*." This means that the definition applies to individual complaints, individual petitions, individual applications, individual communications.

LOAC   "Law of Armed Conflict," which covers the field of humanitarian law and the law of war, also known as the *jus ad bellum* and the *jus in bello.* The acronym follows a term with a peculiarly armed conflict-related meaning.

(Principle)   Indicates that the term is the name of a principle of law, such as in the term "Proportionality (Principle)," which refers to the Principle of Proportionality.

Ratification*/ Ratify*   Refers to all forms of a state's formal approval of a treaty*, such as succession, adhesion, approval, or succession, by which the state becomes bound as a state party. Example: "Under the principle of *Pacta Sunt Servanda,* states must obey treaties* that they have ratified*." This means that states must obey all treaties, covenants, conventions, pacts, agreements, charters, and protocols to which they have submitted instruments of ratification, accession, adhesion, approval, or succession. ("Approval" is the generic term covering all these acts indicating a state's consent to be bound.)

Treaty*   Means that the definition applies alike to the terms *treaty/treaties* and their synonyms: *covenant, convention, agreement, charter, pact, protocol* Example: "Reservation (to Treaty*)." This means that the definition of the term *reservation* will apply equally to reservation to a covenant, to a convention, to an agreement, to a charter, to a pact, and to a protocol.

• LIST OF TERMS DEFINED •

1235 Procedure
1503 Procedure
Abduction
Ab Initio
Absolute (Human) Right
Abstract Rights
Abuse of Right of Petition/Submission
Abuse of Rights
Abuser Solidarity
Acceptable Collateral Damage
Acceptance
Acceptance of Jurisdiction
Accession/Accede
Accomplice Liability
Accountability/Accountable
ACHR
Acquis Conventionnel
Acta Jure Gestionis
Acta Jure Imperii
Actio Popularis
Activism
Activist
Act of Commission
Act of Omission
Act of State Doctrine
Actus Reus
Adequately Accessible
Adhesion/Adherence
Ad Hoc

ADHR
Administrative Detention
Administrative Practice
Admissibility/Admissible
Admission of Guilt
Adoption
Ad Referendum
Advisory Jurisdiction
Advisory Opinion
Advisory Services
Affirmative Action
Affirmative Obligation
African Charter on Human and
    Peoples' Rights
Aggression
Agreement
Aid Conditionality
Alien
Alien Tort Claims Act
American Convention
Amicus Curiae
Amnesty
Amparo
Anarchy
Animus Belligerandi
Anonymous Complaint
Anthropology/Anthropological
    Foundations/Basis
Anticipatory Self-Defense

Code
Code of Conduct
Code of Crimes against the Peace and
  Security of Mankind
Codification/Codify
Cold (Human) Rights
Collateral Damage
Collective Complaint
Collective Enforcement
Collective (Human) Rights
Collective Intervention
Collective Punishment
Collective Self-Defense
Colonialism
Combatant
Comity
Command Responsibility
Commentary
Commission
Commission on Human Rights
Committee
Committee against Torture
Committee for the Prevention of
  Torture
Committee on Economic, Social and
  Cultural Rights
Committee on NGOs
Committee on the Elimination of
  Discrimination against Women
Committee on the Elimination of
  Racial Discrimination
Committee on the Rights of the Child
Common Article 3
Common Crime
Common European Values
Common Standard of Achievement
Communication
Communication/Complaint Procedures
Communitarian
Community-Based Organization
Compatible/Compatibility
Compensation/*ex Gratia* Compensation
Competence/Competence-Competence
Complaint
Complementarity

Compliance
Complicitous Guilt
Composition of the Court
Compromissory Clause
Compulsory Jurisdiction
Conciliation
Concluding Observations
Conclusion
Concrete Rights
Concurrent Jurisdiction
Conditionality
Condone/Condoning Violation
Conference on Security and
  Cooperation in Europe
Conscience
Conscienticization of Human Rights
Conscientious Objection
Consensus
Consensus Principle
Consent
Consideranda
Consideration
Consistent Pattern
Consolidated (Draft) Text
Constant Jurisprudence
Constituent Instrument
Constitution
Constitutionalism
Consult/Consultation
Consultative Status
Contentious Jurisdiction
Continuing (Human Rights) Violation
Contrario
Control Council Law No. 10
Convention
Conventional (International) Law
Convention(al) Mechanism/Procedure
Copenhagen Guidelines
Core (Human) Rights
Corporal Punishment
Corporate Code of Conduct
Corpus
Country of Particular Concern
Country Reports
Country Situations

Country Specific (Human Rights)
  Legislation
Country Specific Procedure/Report/
  Mechanism
Coup d'Etat
Court
Court of Fourth Instance
Covenant
CRC
Crime against Humanity
Crimes against Peace
Crimes of Concern to the International
  Community
Cross-Cultural Human Rights
Cruel Treatment/Punishment
Crystalize
CSCE
Cultural/Culture
Cultural Diversity
Cultural Genocide
Cultural (Human) Rights
Cultural Imperialism
Cultural Relativism
Culture of Human Rights
Culture of Impunity
Culture of Peace
Cumulative Incrementalism
Custodial State
Customary *Erge Omnes*
Customary International Law
Damages
Dangerous Forces
Death Penalty
Decade
Decision
Declaration
Declaration of Independence
Declaration on Human Rights
  Defenders
Declaratory
De Facto
De Facto Refugee
Defenders
Degrading Treatment/Punishment

Dehumanization
De Jure
Démarche
De Martens Clause
Democracy–Development–Human
  Rights Triad
Democratic Deficit
Democratic Governance
Democratic Necessity
Democratization
Demonize/Demonization
Denial of Justice
Denunciation
De Plano
Deportation
Deposit/Depository
Derogable (Human) Rights
Derogation
Descent
Desiderata
Désistement
Desuetude
Detaining Power
Detention
Developing Country/State/Nation
Development
Dictatorship
Dictum
Differential Treatment
Dignity
Disadvantaged Group
Disappearance
Discrimination
Dissemination
Distinction
Diversity
Doctrine
Document
Domestic/Internal Affairs
Domestic Law
Domestic Remedy
Double/Dual Criminality
Double/Dual Standard
Double Jeopardy

Draft Code of Crimes
Draft Convention
Draft Text
Drittwirkung
Droit d'Ingerence
Drop/Reject a Communication
Dual Criminality
Dualist Legal System
Dual Standard
Due Process
Durban Declaration and Programme of
  Action
Duress
Duty
Duty-Holder
Duty to Prosecute
Dynamic Interpretation
Early Action
Early Warning Mechanisms/
  Procedures/Methods
ECHR
Economic (Human) Rights
ECOSOC
Education
Effective Control/Command and
  Control
Effective Investigation
Effectiveness
Effective Remedy
EIF
Election Monitoring/Observance
Elements of Crime
Emergency Reports
Emerging Global Moral Culture
Emerging Norm
Empower/Empowerment
Enemy Combatant
Enforced Disappearance
Enjoyment of Human Rights
Enslavement
Ensure Human Rights
Enter/Entry into Force
Entitlement
Equality

Equality before the Law
Equality of Arms
Equitable Geographical Distribution/
  Representation
Equity Feminism
Erge Omnes
Estoppel
Ethics
Ethnic
Ethnic Cleansing
Ethnocentric/Ethnocentrism
European Convention on Human
  Rights
Ex Aequo et Bono
Examination
Exceptional Diligence
Exceptionalism
Excessive Force
Exclusion/Exclusive
Executive Agreement
Executive Order
Ex Gratia Payment/Compensation
Exhaustion of Domestic Remedies
Ex Officio
Expel/Expulsion
Ex Post Facto Law
Expression
Expressis Verbis
Expropriation
Extermination
Extraconvention(al)
  Mechanism/Procedure
Extradition
Extrajudicial Execution
Extralegal
Extraterritorial Application
Extraterritorial Effect
Extraterritorial Jurisdiction
Fact-finding
Failure to Act
Fair Balance
Fair Trial
Fascism
Federal Clause

Female Circumcision
Female Genital Mutilation
Field Presence
First Generation Human Rights
Forced Assimilation
Forced Disappearance
Foreign Sovereignty Immunity Act
Forum
Forum Internum
Forum of Shame
"Four Freedoms"
Fourth Instance
Framework Convention
Free and Fair Elections
Freedom
Freedom of Expression
Freedom of Religion
French Declaration
Friendly Settlement
Friendship, Commerce, and Navigation
Fulfill Human Rights
Full Enjoyment
Full Powers
Fundamental Freedoms
Fundamentalism/Fundamentalist
Fundamentally Adequate System of
    Justice
Fundamental Standards of Humanity
Gemeinschaft
Gender
Gender Bias
Gender Crime
Gender Discrimination
Gender Feminism
Gender Mainstreaming
Gender Racism
General Assembly
General Comments
General Consultative Status
General Human Rights Legislation
General International Law
General Participation Clause
General Principles of International
    Criminal Law

General Principles of Law
General Recommendations
General Treaty
Generating Effect
Geneva Convention(s)
Geneva Law
Genocide
Genocide Convention
Gesellschaft
Ghetto
Girl Child
Global Compact
Globalization
Good Faith
Good Governance
Good Offices
Governmental-Nongovernmental
    Organization
Government-Appointed
    Nongovernmental Organization
Grave Breach
Grosso Modo
Gross Violations(s)
Group (Human) Rights
Guerrilla War(fare)/Soldier
Guidelines
Habeas Corpus
Hague Law
Hague Regulations
Hard Core (Human) Rights
Hard Law
Harmonizing Domestic Legislation
Hate Crime
Hate Speech
Hegemonic Stability Theory
Helsinki Accords
Helsinki Final Act
Helsinki Process
High Commissioner for Human Rights
High Commissioner for Refugees
High Contracting Party
Holder
Holding
Holocaust

Hominum Causa Omne Jus
  Constitutum Est
Homophobia
Horizontal Effect/Horizontality
Hors de Combat
Hostis Humani Generis
House Arrest
Human Dignity
Human Dimension Mechanism
Humane Treatment
Humanitarian
Humanitarian Assistance
Humanitarian Intervention
Humanitarian Law
Humanity
Human Rights
Human Rights Abuses
Human Rights Approach
Human Rights Committee
Human Rights Education
Human Rights Imperialism
Human Rights Monitor
Human Rights Movement
Human Rights NGO
Human Rights Officer
Human Rights Reports
Human Rights Violation
Human Security
Human Shield
ICC
ICCPR/CCPR/CPR
ICESCR/CESCR/ESCR
ICJ
ICRC
ICTR
ICTY
Ideology
IFI
IGO
Illegal Alien
Illegal Combatant
Ill-Founded
ILO
Immediate (Human) Right

Immigrant
Immunity
Immunity Claims/Rights
Immunity/Impunity Agreements
Impartiality
Imperfect Obligations
Imperialism
Implement/Implementation
Implementing Legislation
Implied Rights
Imprescriptability
Imprisonment
Impunity
In Absentia Trial/Prosecution
In Abstracto
Inadmissible/Inadmissibility
Inalienable Rights
In Camera
Incendiary Weapons
Inclusion/Inclusive
Incommunicado Detention
Incompatible/Incompatibility
Incompatible Reservation
In Concreto
Incorporation
Indemnification
Indemnity/Indemnities
Independent and Impartial Judiciary
Independent Experts
Independent Monitor
Indictment
Indigenous People(s)/Population
Indiscriminate Attack/Force
Individual Capacity
Individual Complaint
Individual Criminal Responsibility
Individualism
Individual Right
Indivisibility
In Extenso
In Fine
Infra
INGO
Inherent

Just Satisfaction
Just War
Labor Rights
Lacuna
Latu Sensu
Law
Lawful Interference
Law-Making Treaty
Law of Armed Conflict
Law of Nations
League of Nations
Legal Integrity
Legality
Legal Positivism
Legal Rights
Legislative History
Legitimacy
Legitimate Aim
Lèse Humanité
Lex Ferenda/de Lege Ferenda
Lex Gentium
Lex Lata/de Lege Lata
Lex Specialis
Liberalism
Liberty
Liberty and Security of Person
Lieber Code
Life Plan
Limburg Principles
Limitation
Linguistic Minority/Group
Linkage/Link
Locus Classicus
Locus Standi
Lodge
London Charter
Lustration Laws
Maastricht Guidelines
Mainstreaming
Malta Declaration
Mandate
Mandate System
Mandatory Coercive Measures
Manifestly Ill-Founded

Manifesto Rights
Marginalize(d)
Margin of Appreciation
Margin of Discretion
Martens Clause
Martial Law
Massacre
Mass Exodus/Migration
Material Application/Scope
Material Breach
Material Damage
Means of Implementation
Mechanism
Mediation
Megacrimes
Member State
Memorandum of Understanding
Memorial
Mens Rea
Mercenary
Merits
Metaright
Methods and Means of Combat
Military Commission
Military Necessity
Minimum Humanitarian Standards
Minimum (International) Standard
Minorities Treaties System
Minority
Minority Rights
Mistreatment
Mitigation
Mixed Armed Conflict
Mobilization of Shame
Mobilizing Principles
Model Treaty
Monism/Monist Legal System
Monitor/Monitoring
Moral Authority
Moral Damages
Moral Integrity
Moral Rights
Morals
Most-Favorable-to-the-Individual

Occupied Territory
Official Languages
Ombudsman
On-Site Investigation / Fact-Finding
Opinio Juris
Opinion
Oppression
Optional Clause
Optional Protocol
Oral Intervention
Ordinary Crime
Ordinary Meaning of Terms
Ordre Public
Organization of American States
Organization on Security and
    Cooperation in Europe
OSCE
Other
Outrages upon the Personality
Pact
Pacta Sunt Servanda
Pact of San Jose
Pari Materia
Pari Passu
Paris Minimum Standards
    of Human Rights Norms
    in a State of Emergency
Participatory (Human) Rights
Particularities
Particular Situations
Party
Passim
Passive Personality Principle
Peacekeeping
Peacemaking
People / Peoples
Peoples' Rights
Peremptory Norm
Perfect Obligation
Perfidy
Permanent Normal Trade Relations /
    Status
Permissive Jurisdiction
Perpetrator

Per Se
Persecution
Persistent Objector Rule
Personal Jurisdiction
Persons in the Power of the Enemy
Petition
Petition-Information System
Petition-Redress System
Petition System
Physical Integrity
Pillage
Plausible Deniability
Plenipotentiary
Plunder
Pluralism
Pogrom
Police Brutality
Police Power
Police State
Political Asylum
Political Correctness / Politically Correct
Political (Human) Rights
Politically Motivated Prosecution
Political Offense
Political Will
Popular Pluralism
Popular Sovereignty
Positive International Law
Positive Obligation
Positive Right
Positivism
Postmodern / Postmodernity
Preamble
Precautionary Measures
Preemptive Self-Defense
Prejudice
Preliminary (*in Limine Litis*) Objections
Preparatory Commission
Preparatory Committee
Preparatory Works
Prep. Com.
Prescribed by Law
Pressing Social Need
Presumption of Innocence

Reject/Drop a Communication
Relativism
Relief Operation
Religion
Religious Discrimination and
   Intolerance
Reparations
Reports/Reporting
Representative Capacity
Repression
Reprisal
Reservation
Res Judicata
Resolution
Resolution 728
Resolution 1235
Resource Claims/Rights
Respect Human Rights
Restitution
Restriction
Restrictive Sovereign Immunity
Retaliation
Retorsion
Reverse Discrimination
Revised 1503 Procedure
Revised European Social Charter
Revision
Right(s)
Right of Initiative
Right of/to (Humanitarian)
   Intervention
Right of/to Return
Rights and Freedoms of Others
Rights-Based Approach
Rights of the Accused
Right to Know the Truth
Right to Reply
Right to Truth
Ripen
Riyadh Guidelines
Roma
Rome Statute
Roster
Rule

Rule of Law
Rules of Engagement
Rules of Procedure
Ruse
Safeguards
Sanctions
Savings Clause
Secondary Rules
Second Generation (Human) Rights
Sectional (Human Rights) Instrument
Sectorial (Human) Rights
Secure
Security
Security Council
Segregation
Seize/Seized
Selectivity
Self-Defense
Self-Determination
Self-Executing
Self-Help
Self-Incrimination
Servitude
Sign/Signature
Signatory
Signature/Signatory *ad Referendum*
Sine Qua Non
Sinti
Si Omnes Clause
Siracusa Principles
Slavery
Slice Instrument
Social Clause
Social Contract
Social (Human) Rights
Socialism
Social Justice
Soft Law
Soft Power
Solidarity
Sovereign Equality
Sovereign Immunity
Sovereignty
Sovereignty Proviso

Special Consultative Status
Special Procedures / Mechanisms
Special Rapporteur
Specialty
Specificities
Standard
Standard Minimum Rules
Standard-Setting
Standard-Setting Mandate
Standing
Stare Decisis
State
State Consent
Stateless Person
State of Emergency
State of Exception
State of Nationality
State of Siege
State Party
State Practice
State Responsibility for the Treatment
  of Aliens
Statute
Stereotype
Stocktaking
Strasbourg Proof
Strict Interpretation / Construction
Stricto Sensu
Strike / Stricken from the List / Roll
Strong Cultural Relativism
Structural Adjustment Program
Structural Violence
Sub-Commission on Prevention of
  Discrimination and Protection
  of Minorities
Sub-Commission on Promotion and
  Protection of Human Rights
Subject
Subjective (Human) Rights
Subsidiarity
Subsidiary
Subsistence (Human) Rights
Substantive Rights / Norms

Succession
Sui Generis
Sullivan Principles
Summary Execution
Superfluous Injury
Superior Orders
Supervision
Supervisory Mechanisms
Supervisory Role
Supplementary Means of Interpretation
Suppression
Supra
Suspension Clause
Systematic Attacks / Violations
Systematic Human Rights Education
Technical Cooperation
Ter
Termination of Treaty
Terms of Reference
Territorial Application / Scope
Territorial Integrity
Territorial Principle
Territorial Sovereignty
Territorial State
Terrorism
Textual Mandate
Thematic Procedures / Reports /
  Mechanisms
Third Generation (Human) Rights
Third-Party Effect
Third World
Threshold
Tokyo Rules
Tolerance
Torture
Totalitarianism
Trafficking in Human Beings / Persons
Transformation
Transformative Human Rights
  Education
Transnational Activists
Transnational Corporation
Transnational Crime

Transnational Human Rights Network
Transnational Human Rights
  Obligations
Transparence / Transparent
Travaux Préparatoires
Treaty
Treaty-Based
Treaty *Erge Omnes*
Treaty (Monitoring/Supervising) Body
Trial Monitoring/Observation
Truth Commission
Tu Quoque
Turku Abo Principles
Tyranny/ Tyrant
UDHR
Ultra Vires
Unalienable Rights
UN Charter
Understanding
Undertake
Unilateral Intervention
Unilateralism
Unipolar Moment
Universal
Universal Declaration of Human Rights
Universality
Universalization of Human Rights
Universal Jurisdiction
Universal Suffrage
Unlawful Combatant
Unnecessary Suffering

Unprivileged Belligerent/Combatant
Urgent Action
Usage
Utility
Vel Non
Victim
Vienna Convention on Consular
  Relations
Vienna Convention on the Law of
  Treaties
Vienna Declaration and Programme of
  Action
Views
Violation
Violence against Women
Vis-à-Vis
Void ab Initio
Voluntary Trust
War
War Crimes
Weak Cultural Relativism
Weapons of Mass Destruction
Weltanschauung
Widespread Attacks/ Violations
Women's (Human) Rights
Working Group
Working Languages
World Trade Organization
Worldview
Xenophobia
Zeitgeist

A Handbook of International Human Rights Terminology, Second Edition

• DEFINITIONS OF TERMS •

1235 PROCEDURE (UN)

Based on the ECOSOC Resolution No. 1235 (1967), this UN human rights procedure is the basis of public international debate within the Commission on Human Rights, focusing on gross violations of human rights in a number of states. Both state governments and NGOs can, to a certain degree, participate in this debate at the annual meeting of the Commission on Human Rights, aimed at identifying country-specific situations to which they believe the commission should give attention. This procedure may also involve the commission and subcommission studying and investigating particular situations of gross violations through whatever means the commission chooses, e.g., studies, reports, on-site investigation.

1503 PROCEDURE (UN)

The procedure established by ECOSOC Resolution No. 1503 (1970) that was built on the ECOSOC Resolution No. 1235 (1967) (see 1235 Procedure, supra). It is a non-treaty-based human rights procedure/mechanism for investigation by the UN Sub-Commission on the Promotion

and Protection of Human Rights of specific "situations" of gross and systematic human rights violations.

This resolution authorizes the Sub-Commission to consider written "communications" received from a nongovernmental source, such as a group/NGO/individual, claiming to be a victim of violations or having direct and reliable knowledge of violations. In the words of the resolution, these communications, received initially by the UN Secretary General, "appear to reveal a consistent pattern of gross and reliably attested violations of human rights and fundamental freedoms within the terms of reference of the Sub-Commission." Thus, even if submitted by an individual victim of a violation, these communications must not be about only one violation or concerning one victim, but must be systematic, manifold, and about many people and many violations. Moreover, these violations must constitute what are called "gross violations," a term that is not clearly defined, but which refers to the most serious human rights violations, such as genocide, apartheid, summary executions, torture, and slavery.

When the Sub-Commission determines the existence of such a consistent pattern of violations, it refers the "situation" to the Commission on Human Rights, which in turn considers it and determines the next course of action.

These proceedings may be filed against any state in the world and are confidential and dealt with in closed private sessions.

The 1503 Procedure was significantly revised in 2000. *See* Revised 1503 Procedure, infra.

Abduction (of Person)

A forcible, surprise, secret capture and taking away of an individual against his will, such as when secret police abduct an opposition dissident or union leader to silence him. When committed by government agents, abduction is usually a human rights violation and may entail the violation of several different human rights, such as freedom of movement; liberty and security of person; freedom from torture or cruel, inhuman, or degrading treatment; or even the right to life. Often referred to as a "forced disappearance" when the authorities hold the victim incommunicado and deny holding him.

Ab Initio

See Void ab Initio, infra.

Absolute (Human) Right (vs. Prima Facie [Human Right])

A right that continues to exist at all times and can be asserted regardless of the intervening circumstances. It cannot be limited or restricted. It is nonderogable, meaning that it cannot be suspended in time of public emergency. Freedom from torture is an example of an absolute human right. It is contrasted

with prima facie human rights, which can be limited, or derogated. Example: ICCPR article 16 is an absolute right, whereas article 12 is a prima facie human right.

Abstract Rights (vs. Concrete Rights)

General political aims. These are aims that serve political interests but cannot be considered legal or hard human rights because their material scope, methods of realization, and duty-holders have not been defined and generally accepted. The claimed human right to peace is an example.

Abuse of Right of Petition / Submission (Clause)

Describes a clause in a treaty* that declares, as a grounds of inadmissibility and rejection of a complaint* in a judicial or quasi-judicial forum, that in submitting the complaint* the author was motivated by reasons and for goals other than the good faith vindication of human rights treaty* norms; e.g., for using profanity or solely for "political reasons." It is akin to "abuse of rights," supra. It involves the use of legal processes (i.e., filing a complaint* to harm a person or state rather than to pursue a just human rights violation claim via a complaint* process). *See* ECHR, article 35.3; ICCPR-OP, article 3.

Abuse of Rights (Principle / Clause)

Describes a principle / clause in a treaty* that provides that a state or other person / group will be in violation of that treaty* if it exercises rights or fulfills obligations under that treaty* in such a way as to prejudice / violate the rights of others or in a way that prevents others from exercising or respecting human rights under the treaty*. It prevents anyone from acting under a treaty* in a way that would result in a violation of human rights. This is a general principle of international law. *See* ICCPR, article 5; ECHR, article 17.

ABUSER SOLIDARITY

The action and attitude of states that are regarded as consistent human rights violators whereby such states work together to fend off and defend each other against accusations by other states, international, intergovernmental organizations, or NGOs of violating human rights.

This occurs especially in international, intergovernmental organizations such as the UN where certain well-known human rights violator states will work in concert with each other to stop any resolutions, studies, or other action aimed at bringing to light and dealing with violations. It is most typically seen in the actions of certain member states of the UN Commission on Human Rights.

ACCEPTABLE COLLATERAL DAMAGE (LOAC)

Collateral damage is the term used in humanitarian law to euphemistically express the damage caused by military attack, offensive or defensive, to nonmilitary civilians and civilian objects. For example, if an armed force launches a missile or drops bombs from an airplane on an enemy military target, and if there are civilian persons in the vicinity where the bomb/missile explodes and they are too close to the explosion, the civilians might be injured or killed. Their injury or death would be considered collateral damage. In such cases the civilian persons and objects are damaged "collaterally" to the military target. Under humanitarian

law it is never legally permissible to intentionally target civilians in an attack.

All of the Law of Armed Conflict is a balance between the military needs (military necessity) of the fighting parties on one hand and the principle of humanity on the other. In most armed conflicts collateral damage occurs sometimes accidentally, sometimes negligently, and sometimes purposefully. The idea of "acceptable" collateral damage is a subjective value judgment that the amount of civilian casualties and property damage should not be so much greater (disproportionate) than the military necessity so as to no longer be tolerable. It means an amount of collateral damage a party or organization can live with as being the unfortunate price to pay for achieving a military objective.

This term may also be used to refer to collateral damage that is within the legal limits of international humanitarian law standards. The fact that collateral damage is acceptable to a belligerent or its friends does not means it is legally acceptable and legitimate. Whether collateral damage is legally permissible depends on whether it is consistent with the principles of distinction/discrimination and proportionality.

ACCEPTANCE (OF TREATY*/ INSTRUMENT OF) (AKA APPROVAL)

An international act whereby a state expresses at the international level, with or after treaty* signature, its formal intent to, or consent to, be bound by/become a party to the treaty*. Such acceptance is contained in a written international, legal instrument, similar in meaning to an instrument of ratification*, approval, adhesion, or accession. Sometimes states sign a treaty* "subject to acceptance," meaning that the signature is still subject to ratification*. Submission or deposit of an unqualified Instrument of Acceptance at the time of signature legally obligates that state to obey the terms of the treaty*. Otherwise, the subsequent instrument of ratification* does so.

ACCEPTANCE OF JURISDICTION (CLAUSE) (ICC)

A clause in an international treaty-statute, such as the ICC Statute, which sets forth the extent to which a ratifying* state is accepting to be bound by the elements constituting the subject matter jurisdiction of a court/tribunal, e.g., war crimes, genocide, and all crimes within the "inherent jurisdiction" or the forum.

ACCESSION/ACCEDE (TO TREATY*/INSTRUMENT OF)

An international act whereby a state expresses at the international level its formal consent to be bound by/become a party to a treaty*. Such act of accession is contained in a written international legal instrument, similar to an instrument of ratification*, approval, adhesion, or accession. Accession is the term used when the acceding state was not signatory to the original treaty* that has been sufficiently ratified* by other states and already entered into force. By such instrument a state is said to "accede" to the treaty* obligations. It means roughly the same as "Adhesion," infra.

Submission/deposit of an instrument of accession legally obligates that state to obey the terms of the treaty*.

ACCOMPLICE LIABILITY (CRIMINAL LAW)

In criminal law, including international criminal law, this principle holds that it is a secondary form of criminal responsibility for a crime. It connotes complicity in a crime without being a perpetrator. One who aids and abets a crime is responsible for the crime under accomplice liability. An example is one who only drives a getaway car in a bank robbery. That driver is criminally responsible for the crime of robbery as an accomplice under the theory of accomplice liability.

ACCOUNTABILITY/ACCOUNTABLE (PRINCIPLE) (VS. IMPUNITY)

The obligation, condition, or willingness to accept and hold legal, political, or moral responsibility of one to society for one's own actions. It also includes responsibility to society for the wrongful acts of those under one for whom one is legally responsible. It means having one's actions subject to public examination and possibly suffering legal or political consequences for one's own or one's subordinate's wrongdoing, whether by commission or omission. For persons in government it means having to be answerable to the people for how they fulfill their public duties.

Human rights violations are violations of the inherent human dignity of members of a society. Such violations are committed by those who represent or act on behalf of the government and are violations of the law. No one in government has the right to commit human rights violations. Therefore, if someone in government commits such violations, he must be held accountable, that is, personally responsible to society for abusing his power and position. This applies to all branches of government. It means, for example, that legislators, policemen, judges, soldiers, generals, prison guards, defense ministers, interior ministers, and even presidents, kings, and prime ministers, all have some type of accountability for human rights violations. This accountability is to the society they serve, such as a city, county, state, or country. It can even involve accountability to all of humanity, all humankind, such as for commission of war crimes or genocide, as was seen in the Nuremberg Trials after World War II.

This is an essential, basic principle in human rights law. It is meant to preserve the rule of law, which means that no one is above the law or exempt from it in regard to respect for human rights. In theory, persons in government will not commit violations if they know that they will have to answer for such acts. Civilians are also accountable to society for their actions, usually under criminal laws.

As to legal responsibility for human rights violations, the opposite of accountability is impunity.

ACHR (IACHR)

Abbreviation for the American Convention on Human Rights, commonly known as the American Convention or the Pact of San Jose and sometimes abbreviated IACHR. This is a binding general human rights instrument of the Organization of American States, adopted in 1969.

ACQUIS CONVENTIONNEL
[French, lit.: that which is acquired by the convention]

All those things that are added by the actual practice and experience to the text of a human rights treaty* subsequent to its entry into force through its implementation, interpretation, and application. It is that which is added by all that the convention experiences. It includes, for example, the jurisprudence of cases decided under the treaty and any doctrines or principles developed over the course of its interpretation.

ACTA JURE GESTIONIS (vs. ACTA JURE IMPERII)
[Latin, lit.: acts by the law of business]

A term found most often in relation to the question of the sovereign immunity of a state from being sued by or in another state. The classical rule was that a state has legal immunity from being sued for injuries caused by acts that it commits under its official power of governance as a state within the territory of the state. There was an exception where the state was not engaged in official acts of governance but of commercial acts, such as the international sale of goods (e.g., oil or grain) or the operation of airlines. If a state harms an individual from another state while engaged in commercial acts, it does not enjoy immunity from suit in another state. Such commercial acts are referred to in legal language as *acta jure gestioni*.

These acts are contrasted with *acta jure imperii*, which are state acts that are normal acts of official governance.

ACTA JURE IMPERII (vs. ACTA JURE GENTIONIS)
[Latin, lit.: acts by the Law of Governance]

A term found most often in relation to the question of the sovereign immunity of a state from being sued by or in another state. The classical rule was that a state has legal immunity from being sued for injuries caused for acts that it commits under its official power of governance as a state within the territory of the state. Such normal official government acts are referred to in legal language as *acta jure imperii*. There was an exception where the state was not engaged in official acts of governance but of commercial acts, such as international sale of goods (e.g., oil or grain) or the operation of airlines. If a state harms an individual from another state while engaged in commercial acts, it does not enjoy immunity from suit in another state. Such commercial acts were known as *acta jure gentionis*.

ACTIO POPULARIS (COMPLAINT*)
[Latin, lit.: lawsuit of the people]

A Latin phrase seen most commonly in the ECHR system to describe a written petition (complaint*) that alleges a potential violation by a state based on a statute/ law or regulation that has not yet been applied. It is somewhat akin to a class action lawsuit that is filed on behalf of all persons similarly situated. It is like filing a complaint* on behalf of everyone who might be affected by the application of the law. This term is seen when the commission/court discusses admissibility as to standing to bring the claim, whether or not the petitioner is a victim of a violation of a right. *Actio popularis* complaints* are not generally admissible under contentious jurisdiction. They are inadmissible under the ECHR system, where one most often sees this term.

ACTIVISM (HUMAN RIGHTS)

The activity of persons or groups, such as nongovernmental organizations, actively engaged in seeking the respect for, protection against, or remedy for the violation of human rights, whether a particular human right, multiple rights, or all human rights. The work of those who are actively supportive of some part of the body of human rights while not being actively opposed to another part of that body of rights.

ACTIVIST (HUMAN RIGHTS)

A person, or the quality of being, actively engaged in seeking the respect for, protection against, or remedy for the violation of human rights, whether a particular human right, multiple rights, or all human rights. Those who are actively supportive of some part of the body of human rights while not being actively opposed to another part of that body of rights.

An activist may be an individual acting alone, or as part of an organization, or the organization itself.

ACT OF COMMISSION (vs. ACT OF OMISSION)

A violation of a human right or criminal liability for committing human rights violations, which can be done either by committing an act that interferes with another's exercise of human rights or by failing to act when there is an affirmative duty and opportunity to do so. If, for example, a policeman pulls out a gun and shoots an unarmed suspect with no justification, this would be an affirmative act of commission of a human rights violation against the victim.

ACT OF OMISSION (vs. ACT OF COMMISSION)

A violation of a human right or criminal liability for committing human rights violations, which can be done either by committing an act that interferes with another's exercise of human rights or by failing to act when there is an affirmative duty and opportunity to do so. If, for example, a policeman sees someone about to shoot another person and the officer has the power and authority to protect the intended victim, but for no reason the policeman refuses or fails to act without justification, then the policeman has committed a human rights violation against the victim by his act of omission to protect the victim.

ACT OF STATE DOCTRINE

A judicial doctrine that holds that acts carried out as part of a nation's exercise of sovereign powers are not attributable to individuals and thus cannot be the subject of a lawsuit in another state against the state or its agents without the consent of the offending state. It is a doctrine of justiciability that seeks to avoid judicial interference in the relations between the forum state and the alleged offender state by requiring/promoting a political/diplomatic solution rather than a judicial one. It is the deferring of the court to the executive branch in the exercise of foreign policy.

ACTUS REUS (CRIMINAL LAW)
[Latin, lit.: guilty act]

The conduct for which a person may be criminally responsible and liable for punishment. It may consist of an act or a failure to act (by omission), or a combination of both. One of two necessary parts of a crime: the criminal act (*actus reus*) and the criminal state of mind (*mens rea*). For most crimes, it must be proved that the alleged perpetrator had a certain *mens rea* (state of mind, e.g., knowledge or in-

tent) at the time he committed the *actus reus* (criminal act or omission, e.g., taking property).

ADEQUATELY ACCESSIBLE (PRINCIPLE OF LEGALITY)

The principle of legality states that all laws, such as criminal laws and laws restricting the exercise of human rights, must be clear, specific and detailed, and duly promulgated and accessible to everyone in order to be legally legitimate. They must also be enacted by a proper authority ("provided by law"). Accessibility refers to the ability of the individual to find out and know what the law says, so that persons can conduct their lives consistent with them. Laws must be made known to the people by the government in ways that allow everyone to know them and comply with them.

ADHESION/ADHERENCE (TO TREATY*/INSTRUMENT OF)

An international act whereby a state expresses at the international level its formal consent to be bound by/become a party to a treaty*. Such adhesion/adherence is contained in a written international legal instrument, similar to an instrument of ratification*, approval, or accession. "Adhesion" is a term used when the adhering state was not signatory to the original treaty* that had been sufficiently ratified* by other states and had already entered into force. By such instrument a state is said to "adhere" to the treaty* obligations. Roughly the same as "Accession," supra.

Submission/deposit of an Instrument of Adhesion legally obligates that state to obey the terms of the treaty*.

AD HOC (WORKING GROUP/
TRIBUNAL/JUDGE)
[Latin, lit.: to this thing]

Generally means "pertaining to a particular limited purpose or time period only."

1. Ad Hoc Working Group: An auxiliary body set up within an organization for the purpose of dealing with a specific limited issue, and no other.

2. Ad Hoc Tribunal: A judicial forum (court/tribunal) set up to handle legal cases involving a specific limited matter, e.g., war crimes. The 1945 International Military Tribunal at Nuremberg was an ad hoc tribunal dealing only with Nazi Germany's international crimes in World War II.

3. Ad Hoc Judge: A judge specially appointed to sit for a particular case, either alone or as one of a group of judges adjudicating a matter.

ADHR

Abbreviation for the American Declaration of the Rights and Duties of Man, commonly known as the American Declaration of Human Rights. This is a nonbinding regional human rights instrument of the Organization of American States, adopted in 1949 and applicable to most North, Central, and South American States.

ADMINISTRATIVE DETENTION
(AKA PREVENTATIVE DETENTION)

The compulsory incarceration of a person following a perceived threat adjudicated by a public executive official without the appearance of the detainee before an ordinary court of law pursuant to a formal criminal charge and without any objective finding as to the guilt of the detainee or the correctness of the executive perception. Usually the basis for such detention is the government's fear that the person detained may be part of some organization, movement, or criminal conspiracy that may engage in unlawful violent acts. The justification often given for such detention is the protection of public safety, or even national security, by preventing such persons from committing any of the feared acts, e.g., terroristic bombing. It is substantially the same as "Preventative Detention."

ADMINISTRATIVE PRACTICE
(OF VIOLATIONS)

An accumulation of identical or analogous breaches of a certain human rights treaty norm, which are sufficiently numerous and interconnected to amount not merely to isolated incidents or exceptions but to a pattern or system. A consistent, continuous pattern of officially sanctioned government activity done domestically pursuant to law or policy and not an isolated incidence of such activity by government.

This concept arises in human rights complaint* procedures when the international forum is determining whether the complainant has exhausted domestic remedies before filing with the international forum. The rule of exhaustion of domestic remedies does not apply in some systems where an applicant complains of the existence of an administrative practice by the government, with the aim of preventing its continuation or recurrence. This exception was established in the Council of Europe Human Rights system where the commission in one case stated: "Where there is a practice of nonobservance of certain [treaty] provisions, the remedies prescribed will of necessity be sidestepped or rendered inadequate. Thus, if there was an administrative practice norm of torture or ill treatment, judicial remedies prescribed would tend to be rendered ineffective by the difficulty of securing probative evidence, and administrative inquiries would either not be instituted, or, if they were, would be likely to be half-hearted or incomplete."

Admissibility/Admissible (Complaint*) (vs. Inadmissibility/ Inadmissible)

The criteria upon which a written complaint* alleging human rights violations by a state is accepted for consideration/ adjudication by a human rights forum such as a court or commission. If a complaint* fulfills all of the criteria of "admissibility" set forth in a given convention system's statute or rules, the complaint* is deemed "admissible" and the court or commission will consider itself as "seized" of the case. If not, it is deemed "inadmissible" or "nonadmissible." It also refers to the grounds of admissibility. *See* ECHR, articles 34–35.

Admission of Guilt

The formal voluntary confessing of criminal guilt by a person suspected of commission of a crime, made to a criminal court in response to a specific criminal charge. In common law jurisdictions it is known as a "guilty plea." It is made usually prior to completion of a criminal trial.

Adoption (of Treaty* Text)

The formal act by resolution expressing the agreement of the states negotiating a treaty* as to what the form and content (text) of the treaty* shall be. Adoption takes place after the drafting of a treaty* text is complete and is accomplished by a vote by way of institutional resolution to determine the consent of all negotiating states. It sets the official text of a treaty*. The date of "adoption" of a treaty* is usually found below the title of a treaty*, along with the date the treaty* enters into force.

Ad Referendum (Signatory)

See Signature/Signatory *ad Referendum*.

Advisory Jurisdiction (vs. Contentious Jurisdiction)

The power or competence of a court or tribunal upon the request of a state or intergovernmental organ to issue an advisory opinion on the interpretation or application of a treaty* norm when no actual adversarial case exists. Contrast this term with "Contentious Jurisdiction," which is an adversarial matter concerning a particular alleged violation of a treaty* norm. *See* ACHR, article 64.

Advisory Opinion

A legal opinion rendered by a court or tribunal as to the interpretation or application of an international norm requested by a state or an organ of an international intergovernmental organization, and not as a judgment in a contentious case where an actual controversy exists. Advisory opinions are usually not binding as a matter of law but may serve to establish principles of law. The party requesting an advisory opinion must be legally authorized (i.e., they must have standing) to make such a request of the court in order for the court or tribunal to have the competence to render such an opinion. *See* ACHR, article 64.

ADVISORY SERVICES (AND TECHNICAL ASSISTANCE/COOPERATION)

The function of an office of an international intergovernmental organization whereby it assists a member state having human rights problems or trying to strengthen its national infrastructures (such as a legal system: constitution, laws, regulations judiciary, prosecutor), which are essential for implementation of international human rights standards. Such office is staffed with experts in the field of human rights who advise the states on how to set up and run their national systems to best comply with international standards. The best example is the United Nations' Office of the High Commissioner for Human Rights, Geneva, Switzerland, which has an Office of Advisory Services and Technical Assistance. It may include seminars, training courses, or fellowship grants. It offers its services to states that request it or sometimes upon referral where a state is under scrutiny by the UN for human rights violations.

AFFIRMATIVE ACTION

Action taken as a matter of policy, principle, administrative rule, or law by government or business to make up for past discrimination in education, work, and promotions against women and certain races, ethnic groups, religions, or disabilities by granting certain preferences or giving special consideration to those persons possessing such characteristics so as to undo the effects of past discrimination. Affirmative action attempts to make things the way they would have been had there been no previous discrimination.

AFFIRMATIVE OBLIGATION (VS. NEGATIVE OBLIGATION)

An obligation of the state to take some positive action under a treaty* norm and not merely to refrain from acting. Example: The right to education imposes an affirmative obligation upon a state to build schools and provide teachers.

AFRICAN CHARTER ON HUMAN AND PEOPLES' RIGHTS (OAU, BANJUL— 1981) (AKA AFRICAN CHARTER/ BANJUL CHARTER) (ACHPR)

A general human rights treaty adopted by the Organization of African Unity (OAU), an African Regional IGO, in Banjul, Gambia in 1981. The ACHPR is the principal human rights treaty of the OAU, and treaty implementation is supervised by the African Commission on Human and Peoples' Rights. A court is in the process of being added by a protocol to allow for judicial implementation in this OAU human rights regime.

A "charter" is an international legal instrument, a treaty, creating legal obligations under international law. This human rights treaty applies only to States in Africa that have ratified* it. This charter is unique in that it contains what had commonly been known as first, second, and third generation human rights. It is particularly these so-called third generation rights that constitute the "peoples' rights," which are of a collective/group rights nature. This reflects the African anthropology with its unique social traditions and structures.

Sometimes this treaty is referred to as

the African Charter or as the Banjul Charter because of its adoption in Banjul. Often treaties and protocols to treaties are commonly known by the place where they were adopted, such as the "Pact of San Jose" (Costa Rica), which is an alternate name for the ACHR.

AGGRESSION (INTERNATIONAL CRIME OF) (AKA CRIMES AGAINST PEACE)

A crime included within the Nuremberg/London Charter under the term "crimes against peace." Aggression generally means an internationally criminal act of starting unlawful hostilities against the sovereignty, territorial integrity, or political independence of another state. It includes the acts of planning, preparing, ordering, initiating, or carrying out such acts.

Simply stated, aggression is the starting of an armed attack against another state without international legal justification. It is a hostile military act intentionally initiated by government or military persons of one state against another state, one that rises to the level of severity of an international crime, harming all of humankind. The *locus classicus* of this international crime was the Nuremberg/London Charter, which set forth the basis of certain crimes charges against Nazi war criminals in the Nuremberg Trials. In one of its decisions the Nuremberg Court stated, "To initiate a war of aggression, therefore, is not only an international crime, it is the supreme international crime, differing only from other war crimes in that it contains within itself the accumulated evil of the whole." The international crime of aggression continues to exist as a norm of customary international law in the body of inter-

national criminal law. It is binding on all states and all persons.

The definition of aggression is very controversial and evolving. The most common post Nuremberg definition is found in UN Resolution 3314 of 1974. That Resolution defined aggression as "the use of armed force by a state against the sovereignty, territorial integrity, or political independence of another state, or in any manner inconsistent with the Charter of the UN."

The states parties to the 1998 Rome Statute of the International Criminal Court included aggression as a crime in article 5 of the ICC Statute. They intended to eventually define the term aggression in article 5 in the context of an international criminal law act engaging individual criminal responsibility. It would then become one of the core crimes of the ICC system. One of many suggested compromise definitions in the ICC, offered as an example of the difficulty in arriving at a definition, was offered by Benjamin Ferencz, a former Nuremberg prosecutor. His proposed definition reads:

(1) For purposes of this [ICC] Statute, aggression shall be defined as set forth in General Assembly Resolution 3314 (xxix) on December 14, 1974. Particular attention is drawn to the reaffirmations contained therein of "the duty of states not to use armed force to deprive peoples of their right to self determination, freedom and independence, or to disrupt territorial integrity" and that "the territory of a State shall not be violated by being the object even temporarily of military occupation taken by another State in contravention of the [UN] Charter." Furthermore, "any

annexation by the use of force of the territory of another state or part thereof may qualify as an act of aggression. Nothing can prejudice the above rights particularly of "peoples under colonial and racist regimes or other forms of alien domination."

The key issue in the definition process is defining the role of the UN Security Council, which is the organ of the UN charged with determining politically the existence of an act of aggression.

AGREEMENT (TREATY* INSTRUMENT)

A treaty*. An international legal instrument between two or more states or legal entities, more commonly used for bilateral instruments, usually in a single instrument, and differing from a convention in that it usually deals with less permanent or narrow subject matter, e.g., the 1995 Dayton Agreement (Bosnia). Agreements are often less formal than other treaty* forms but are still legally binding under international law.

AID CONDITIONALITY (FOREIGN AID)

The practice/policy of linking the granting of financial/material foreign aid to the recipient state's changing or maintaining certain standards of human rights practice. Fulfillment of such standards is a precondition for receipt of the aid.

ALIEN (VS. CITIZEN) (AKA NONNATIONAL)

A foreign born resident of a state who has not been naturalized and is still a subject or citizen and owes allegiance to a different state. In the 1985 UN "Declaration on the Human Rights of Individuals Who are Not Nationals of the Country in Which They Live," an alien is defined as "any individual who is not a national of the state in which he or she is present."

An alien may be residing in the other country legally or illegally, or may only be present temporarily, such as a tourist, and still be considered an alien. The major human rights issues involving aliens is discrimination based on nationality and political rights such as the right to vote or run for public office and equality before the law.

Under most human rights instruments such as the ICCPR, aliens present in a state are holders of, and can fully exercise, all human rights under such instruments, except as are explicitly excepted in the text of the instrument. *See,* e.g., ICCPR, article 25.

ALIEN TORT CLAIMS ACT (AKA ALIEN TORT STATUTE, ATCA, OR A "1350" ACTION/CASE)

A U.S. federal statute enacted in 1789, and found in section 1350 of Title 28 of the *United States Code*. It gives power (subject matter jurisdiction) to federal district courts to hear judicial cases filed by a foreigner (plaintiff) against another foreigner (defendant) for acts, committed by the defendant, which constituted "torts in violation of international law," such as torture, disappearances, slavery, and summary executions. The text itself reads:

> The District Courts shall have original jurisdiction of any civil action an alien for a tort only, committed in violation of the law of nations or a treaty of the United States.

Violations of internationally recognized human rights are meant to be remedied in national courts and other bodies before resorting to international systems. International human rights are properly the concern of all states. Many states such as the U.S. allow their courts to be used for lawsuits filed for human rights violations that occur in other states and where neither the victim nor the violator are U.S. citizens. The intent of the U.S. Congress in 1789 was to provide our courts as a judicial forum for those injured by certain violations of international law, thus helping to enforce international law.

Many lawsuits have been filed in U.S. federal courts using this as the basis for court jurisdiction. They are sometimes referred to as "1350" cases or actions, and abbreviated ATCA.

AMERICAN CONVENTION (ON HUMAN RIGHTS) (OAS–SAN JOSE 1969)

Usually refers to the American Convention on Human Rights, adopted in San Jose, Costa Rica, by the Organization of American States (OAS) in 1969. This general human rights treaty* is binding on OAS member states parties from North, Central, and South America that have ratified*. The treaty* is supervised within the OAS by the American Commission on Human Rights and the American Court of Human Rights, a forum created by the convention itself.

AMICUS CURIAE (BRIEF / MEMORIAL)
[Latin, lit.: friend of the court]

A person or group who has no right to appear in a legal proceeding as a party but who is allowed by the court to offer a legal argument or factual information on a given issue that will assist the court in understanding an unusually complicated or novel legal issue. An amicus, as the person or organization is called by the court, will usually file a written legal brief / memorial setting forth his position. In international cases, an amicus curiae can ask to be allowed to participate at trial or appeal stages, but only with the prior permission of the court. The plural is *amici curiae.*

AMNESTY (GRANT OF, LAW / DECREE)

An act of a government authority by executive grant/decree, or by parliamentary/congressional legislation, by which an official legal pardon is given by the state to anyone who has committed human rights violations in an internal conflict, such as a revolution or insurgency. It results in the legal impunity of such violators.

AMPARO
[Spanish, lit.: Protection / Defense]

The Spanish word for the legal /judicial procedure roughly equivalent to habeas corpus in common law. It is a writ or legal process used to challenge the constitutionality or legal basis of any laws or administrational acts, such as an arrest or detention. It can be used to force the state to produce the person and to prove to the court that its seizure and detention is legal or constitutional, or to release him. The term is used primarily in Spanish speaking states of the Western hemisphere.

ANARCHY

A condition of political chaos, disorder, and lawlessness in a state caused by an absence of government, failure of governmental authority, or lack of respect for the rule of law. A lack of any restraints on the conduct of government or individuals. A belief that government and law should be abolished and replaced by mutual human cooperation.

ANIMUS BELLIGERANDI (LOAC)
[Latin, lit.: state of mind/attitude of making war]

The subjective intent of a state necessary for entering into a formal legal status of war (state of war). It means the mental intent to wage war against another state, as opposed to an accident or random act of violence.

ANONYMOUS COMPLAINT*

"Anonymous" means without a name, of unknown or unnamed origin, or hiding/not disclosing the name of its author. A complaint* or other denominated, written communication (petition/application) submitted to a quasi-judicial or judicial human rights forum by an individual or group in which the identity of its author(s) is not disclosed is an anonymous complaint*. In most human rights systems, e.g., ICCPR, ECHR, complaints*, etc., that are anonymous are generally inadmissible and will not be considered. Some systems may in certain situations provide for some anonymity when disclosure might jeopardize the life of the complainant.

ANTHROPOLOGY/ANTHROPOLOGICAL FOUNDATIONS/BASIS (OF HUMAN RIGHTS)

Human rights have been studied from the perspective of many different academic disciplines. This includes from the perspective of anthropology. The study of the anthropology of human rights, or the anthropological foundation or basis of human rights involves: 1) the study of human rights cross-culturally, that is, the study of what peoples in various societies regard as human rights and how these conceptualizations compare with each other; 2) the search for the origins of human rights in various societies.

ANTICIPATORY SELF-DEFENSE (LOAC)

A proposed legal doctrine meant to serve as a legal justification by a state for the use of military force against another state in international relations. Under this proposed doctrine a state would be justified in using force against another state if it has clear and convincing evidence to believe that the other state intends to and is planning to make an armed attack against the target state in the immediate future. This would fulfill the LOAC principle of military necessity.

This justification is built on the argument that a state need not wait until another state is actually attacking it before it can respond, but may use force to neutralize the threat before the attack is even launched. An example of where this defense was claimed is the 1984 attack by Israel on the unfinished nuclear reactor in Iraq, which Israel believed would be used to create nuclear weapons to be used against Israel in the future. This asserted defense was rejected by the international community.

Under international law a state may only engage in the use of hostile force against another state if it is a response to an actual armed attack. The idea of anticipatory self-defense is an attempt to ideologically justify an attack where an armed attack is more remote, not immediate or imminent or even certain. Under the famous *Caroline* case, self-defense is permitted under international law only if it is "instant, overwhelming and leaving no choice of means, and no moment for deliberation."

Anticipatory self-defense is not accepted by the weight of scholars in international law because it could too easily be misused. It could allow a state to violate the letter and spirit of the UNCH as to the use of force in nonactual self-defense situations, and offers too much room for abuse by a state conjuring up a belligerency that may never happen. Individual and collective self-defense is an inherent state right and is expressly authorized under article 51 of the UNCH. However, self-defense refers only to force used to repel an actual attack and ends once the armed attack has been stopped. It does not allow a state to do whatever it feels will prevent any possible future attack. An attack must be actually being mounted and on its way. Moreover, the right to self-defense ends once the Security Council becomes seized of the conflict issue.

This defense has been used in the context of the war on terrorism by the U.S. and other states to seek out and eradicate Al-Qaeda terrorists, and to feel legally justified in entering and acting militarily in any state harboring such persons. It is similar to the proposed George Bush doctrine of preventative self-defense, also called preemptive self-defense. The whole U.S. war on terrorism is based on this prevention of future terrorism justification by going out to find terrorists and "take them out" so as to prevent them from ever being able to mount an attack. If a state launched an armed conflict and did not have a valid legal defense, which this one is not, it would arguably constitute the international crime

of aggression, a crime against peace, as well as a violation of article 2(4) of the UNCH, and possibly constitute a breach of a relevant UN Security Council resolution. *See also* Preemptive Self-Defense

ANTILOCUTION (OF PERSONS/GROUPS)

Privately or publicly speaking negatively about a person or group. Antilocution can be the cause of human rights violations. Sometimes applied in the sense of the "in" and the "out" person/group.

ANTI-SEMITISM

A hostile, intolerant, or discriminatory attitude against Jews as a racial or religious group. Also used to characterize the acts or statements manifesting such attitude, usually in a hateful and injurious manner. Actually, the true and full meaning of the word refers to such attitude against anyone of Semitic origin, which includes Arabs as well as Jews, since both groups are Semites. In the United States and many other states, however, most people associate this attitude specifically with those of Jewish origin.

Anti-Semitic attitudes by themselves may not be human rights violations, because they are part of personal beliefs. However, certain actions manifesting anti-Semitic attitudes can be characterized as hate crimes, and if committed by a government or its agents, can be violations of human rights. Such anti-Semitic actions might include: defacing synagogues, desecrating cemeteries, or physically beating or killing a Semitic person because of that characteristic. Anti-Semitic speech can be considered hate speech. Under article 20 of the ICCPR, "any advocacy of national, racial or religious hatred that constitutes incitement to discrimination, hostility or violence shall be prohibited by law." This would include hatred based on anti-Semitic motives.

APARTHEID

A system of racial, religious, and ethnic discrimination and social separation, usually with the majority group dominating the minority. It is usually characterized by physical and territorial separation of races and the discriminatory distribution of public benefits and services. Apartheid imposes slaverylike practices on an entire segment of the population based on a distinguishing characteristic, such as race. It is a human rights violation and arguably an international crime. An example is the former state racial ideology/segregation practiced in South Africa.

A POSTERIORI (HUMAN) RIGHTS (VS. A PRIORI)
[Latin, lit.: from after or following something]

A philosophical term describing a claim or belief that human rights exist based on information derived from human sensory experience. This is contrasted with *a priori* rights. (*See* infra.) An example of an a posteriori right is the right to a nationality. It does not exist by virtue of reason alone but because of the human experience perceived as to the effects of statelessness on certain people, giving rise to a desire to create that right to solve their problem.

APPEALS CHAMBER (COURT/TRIBUNAL)

That part of a court whose judges sit in determination of appeals from decisions, judgments, and orders of the Trial Chambers. An appeal is a review of the legal correctness of a judicial act of the trial court for purpose of determining whether the judicial act should be declared invalid, or whether the Trial Chamber must make a different or new decision/ judgment/ order.

APPLICABLE LAW (OF A JUDICIAL FORUM)

The bodies/sources of law, whether from national or international sources, which a judicial or quasi-judicial forum is authorized to apply, whether in enforcement or interpretation, in a given treaty* regime context. It is most often set forth in a specific provision within the statute of an international court.

APPLICATION

1. A Complaint: A written adversarial complaint presented to an international human rights forum alleging a violation of human rights by a state. Some systems use the term "application" instead of "petition," "complaint," or "communication." They are all roughly the same. It is submitted to an international judicial or quasi-judicial organ to seek a finding or judgment that a violation of human rights has occurred. It can be filed by individuals, NGOs, or states, depending on the system in which it is handled (i.e., the United Nations or the Council of Europe).

2. Implementation of Norms: The actual practice and use of human rights norms by a state—going from words in a text to reality in practice. Sometimes used to refer to the actual practice of a state judged by the applicable norm. A state is primarily obligated to apply the

norms in its day-to-day public life so as to harmonize its conduct with international standards. "Application" is the actual actions of a state in a way that fulfills its human rights obligations. It also refers to how a state applies the norms.

APPROVAL (OF TREATY*/INSTRUMENT OF)

See Acceptance.

A PRIORI (HUMAN) RIGHTS (VS. A POSTERIORI)
[Latin, lit.: from before or prior to something]

A philosophical term describing a claim or belief that human rights exist by virtue of reason and do not depend on sensory or other forms of human experience for their justification. An a priori human right is one we know is true because our reason says it is true. An example would be freedom of thought and opinion, because to think that it is or is not a right presupposes this right (freedom to think or believe such right exists). This is contrasted with *a posteriori* rights. (*See* supra.) Some views on the divine origin of human rights are really a priori justifications for the basis of human rights.

Some people argue that human rights are a priori rights and can all be justified by reason alone. Some say they are deduced from human experience and are thus a posteriori.

ARBITRARY ARREST/DETENTION

Arbitrary arrest occurs when a person is taken into custody by the government authorities (federal, state, or local) without a proper, well-founded, lawful basis for doing so. Arbitrary detention means keeping a person in detention or custody without taking steps to prosecute or release. Thus, the victim of arbitrary detention appears to be in the position of being held indefinitely, without charges and criminal prosecution.

In general, arbitrary arrest or detention denies the person his or her right to the "liberty and security of person" and "due process of law." Government may only deprive a person of physical liberty if it is done pursuant to law.

Under international human rights law, everyone has a right to liberty and security of person. That means that everyone has a right to go around freely, believing that government will not interfere with their freedom without having a legal ground to do so, such as evidence that the person committed a crime.

Under article 9 of the ICCPR, "Everyone has the right to liberty and security of person. No one shall be subjected to arbitrary arrest or detention." This article sets forth the procedural human rights of arrested and detained persons. Arbitrary arrests and detentions are not done only where the victim is suspected of having committed a crime. It may apply, for example, in the case of a mentally ill street person being institutionalized against his will, or in a so-called administrative detention, wherein police round up and detain people more for fear of possible future criminal activity, without any legitimate factual basis, than for having committed a crime. Any type of depriving a person of physical liberty can bring into play this human rights norm. Where detention lasts an unjustifiably and unreasonably long time, it is referred to as "Prolonged Arbitrary Detention" (*see* infra).

Armed Conflict (LOAC)

Hostile military engagement between two or more states that may or may not constitute a state of "war" (*see* Internationalized Armed Conflict, infra) or a civil war characterized by hostilities between the state and an opposing faction or factions, or between opposing factions (*see* Internal Armed Conflict).

For purposes of the LOAC there is a fivefold classification of conflicts:

1. Traditional international armed conflicts between two or more states;

2. Those between a state and organized armed groups in the state and under a responsible command;

3. Those waged as part of a conflict against racist or colonial regimes, or alien occupation;

4. Those internal conflicts falling under common article 3 of the 1949 Geneva Conventions;

5. Riots, internal disorders, and tension; internal strife. This type is not an armed conflict subject to the classical LOAC.

Armed Forces (LOAC)

Used in the Law of Armed Conflict (LOAC) with slightly different meanings depending on the normative system (custom versus Geneva Conventions) to which it refers. The four GCs and Protocol I (P I) are now the locus classicus for the definition of this term. Normally it means the state military personnel who are authorized to engage in armed conflict on behalf of the state and who have the right to be treated as prisoners of war when captured by their adversary. It refers to the state's military agents who exercise the right to engage in hostilities, i.e., who hold the *jus ad bellum*. See P I, article 43.

Armistice (LOAC)

An agreement between belligerent parties to suspend military hostilities against each other. Armistice stops hostilities, but it does not mean the armed conflict or war is legally terminated.

Arrest

Any physical denial of freedom of movement by the government for purposes of detaining a person who is suspected of having committed a crime. An arrest begins the process of a person being brought physically before law enforcement authorities and courts so as to read and face charges of criminal conduct, and, if found guilty, to be punished for such crimes.

Arrest is government conduct primarily covered by the human right to liberty and security of person. *See* ICCPR, article 9. An arrest that does not comply with the human right to liberty and security of the arrested person is not a lawful arrest and would constitute a violation of human rights.

Arrest Warrant

A legal instrument, an order or writ, issued by a competent legal authority, usually a judge of a court, that orders that a person or persons be deprived of their liberty and that the appropriate agencies of government, such as police or sheriff or marshal, capture, seize, and take the person or persons into custody and detain them, usually to appear before a court on a criminal charge.

Article(s) (of a Treaty*) (abbrev.: art./arts.)

A distinct numbered section or clause of a legal or political instrument, such as a treaty* or a declaration. Articles set apart the distinct parts of a treaty*/declaration after the preamble and usually identify separate clauses setting forth one or more distinct substantive or procedural rights. For example, UDHR, article 18: Freedom of Thought, Conscience, and Religion.

Asian Values

A description of the conceptual defense raised by Asian states when they are charged with acting inconsistent with or having laws not in harmony with the generally accepted human rights norms and their interpretation. It in essence says that in Asia there are certain distinct values, specificities, or particularities, such as a communitarian social construct or a certain status of persons such as women or children, that do not permit a so-called "Western" interpretation or application of their domestic norms or practices. This is one variation of the defenses often raised to the claim of the universality of human rights in the global debate over whether human rights are universal or culturally relative.

Generally speaking, such a claim or defense is not valid as a matter of generally accepted international human rights law.

Assassination

By dictionary definition assassination is commonly defined as "a murder by surprise for political reasons."

A murder is a crime. Since murder is *per se* an illegal act, this definition defeats any reasoned advancement of the proposition that murder can somehow be made lawful if it is against a certain type of person, such as a terrorist leader. In other words, all murder is a violation of both domestic law and international law. An assassination cannot be legally justified under any circumstances, even in an armed

conflict situation. A killing in an armed conflict situation permitted by the LOAC would not be an assassination.

Under international human rights law an assassination is a violation of the human rights to life, to liberty and security of person, to due process of law with all procedural safeguards, to freedom of movement, to freedom of association, and cruel and inhuman treatment or punishment. Human rights law only permits a state to seek the arrest, prosecution, and punishment of the target person, unless it is an armed conflict situation and the killing is fully justified under the LOAC.

Assembly of States Parties (ASP) (ICC)

Those states that have ratified the Rome Statute for an International Criminal Court (1998) make up the Assembly of States Parties, a body that is charged with establishing the administration of the court, choosing judges, and seeing that the court performs its job within its mandate and terms of reference. The Assembly of States Parties was formally established when the ICC Rome Statute entered into force in July 2002.

Asylum (Right of)

The claimed right of a person who flees from his country and seeks to stay and is allowed to remain in a country not his own because he fears being persecuted if returned to his own country or country of last residence. Asylum is, in effect, a surrogate legal protection offered by the asylum state to protect that person from persecution by his own state, usually on the basis of the asylum seeker's race/ ethnicity, religion, nationality, political opinion, or membership in a particular social group. *See* UDHR, article 14.

ASYLUM SEEKER

A person fleeing from his state of citizenship or last residence and who is trying to enter into, or is already inside, a state not his own to obtain legal protection by that other state because of past persecution or a well-founded fear of future persecution. The asylum seeker fears a harmful violation of his human rights and is unwilling or unable to seek protection from his own state.

ATROCITY

An act or series of acts usually committed by humans against humans that is particularly and utterly brutal, wicked, barbaric, and revolting; usually characterized by physical violence, such as a mass murder or an act of torture.

ATROCITY LAW

A proposed description of that part of the body of international law that brings into play the arrest, prosecution, and punishment of individuals who have committed serious crimes of concern to the whole of mankind, such as war crimes, crimes against humanity, and genocide. Although normally such crimes are dealt with under the headings of international humanitarian law or international criminal law, this new description seeks to identify a body of international legal norms aimed at deterring and punishing those who commit the human atrocities one reads and hears about all over the world, and which impact the global community and its sense of human security.

The basic elements of this proposed description are

1. Such crimes are of significant magnitude, such as those that are widespread, or large-scale, or systematic, or particularly gross, such as to create a grave concern to the whole international community;

2. Such crimes can occur in peacetime or wartime and in international and noninternational armed conflict;

3. Such crimes must already be identified as international crimes under international law, such as war crimes, aggression, crimes against humanity, or genocide;

4. Such crimes are perpetrated by or committed under the responsible command or orders by rulers or an elite group in a society;

5. Such crimes under customary international law hold individuals criminally responsible regardless of official position or status.

ATTACK

1. Military: In the LOAC it is defined as an act of violence committed against an adversary, whether in offense or in defense. *See* P I, article 49.1.

2. Crimes against humanity: In the context of crimes against humanity, which are defined as a widespread or systematic attack against a civilian population, the term attack has been defined as conduct that results in violence, but not limited to conduct by use of armed force. In this context an attack encompasses, *inter alia*, situations in which persons not taking part in a particular hostility are mistreated, or a situation in which noncombatants or the civilian population are targeted.

AUDIATUR ET ALTERA PARS
[Latin, lit.: and may the other side be heard]

A general principle of law, which states that a judicial body must allow and make way for a party to present evidence and be heard about allegations/issues raised by the other party to a case. *See* OPI, article 5(1).

AUT DEDERE AUT JUDICARE (PRINCIPLE)
[Latin, lit.: either hand over or adjudicate]

A principle of international criminal law that applies to the extradition of international criminal suspects/fugitives. This principle states that when a person is a suspect accused of committing certain international crimes in one state and that person is found in another state, the state where the defendant is found is under a legal obligation either to arrest and prosecute the accused or must apprehend and surrender/extradite that person to any requesting state having jurisdiction for prosecution. This obligation is set forth in some treaties* such as the Convention against Torture and the four GCs. *See* GC IV, article 146. In English it is sometimes called the "prosecute or extradite" principle.

AUTHENTICATION (OF TREATY*)

The international legal treaty* process whereby the definitive text of a treaty* is established. This procedure may be set out in the treaty* text itself or by the signatures ad referendum set to a text by state representatives. It also sets the official languages in which the text is deemed authentic (e.g., French, English, or Russian).

AUTHENTIC TEXT (OF TREATY* INSTRUMENT)

The text of a treaty* as adopted by the negotiating states in the languages that have been chosen as acceptable official languages for such text. A treaty* may be translated into many different languages, but only authentic texts can be used in the international interpretation and implementation of a given treaty*. A treaty* usually contains a specific provision in its final clauses setting forth the languages of authentic texts. *See*, e.g., ICCPR, article 53.

AUTHORITY AND CONTROL (OVER PERSON) (JURISDICTION)

A formula used by certain systems of international human rights law to determine whether the legal obligation of a state applies as regards certain individuals particularly as to acts occurring outside of the subject state. In such systems, such as the Inter-American human rights system, the Inter-American Commission and Court will find that the human rights norms do apply to persons over whom a member state actually exercises authority and control.

This issue arose in the case of the Al-Qaeda/Taliban prisoners held by the U.S. in Guantanamo, Cuba in 2002. In a case before the Inter-American Commission on Human Rights, the commission found that the legal obligations under the ADHR arose because the U.S. was actually exercising sole legal authority and control over these prisoners. This was so even though the victim prisoners were not technically within the sovereign territory of the United States. The commission decided it had jurisdiction over the matter for purposes of requesting precautionary measures against the U.S. The commission ruled that no person under the authority and control of a state, regardless of his or her circumstances, is devoid of legal protection for his or her fundamental and nonderogable human rights, such as access to a competent impartial legal tribunal to determine basic human rights.

AUTOMATIC JURISDICTION (AKA INHERENT JURISDICTION) (ICC)

Used in the context of the Rome Statute for the International Criminal Court, adopted in July 1998, entered into force July 2002, to refer to the subject matter jurisdiction (i.e., which international crimes are handled by the court) that is given to the court automatically upon a state party's ratification* of the ICC Statute. As to ratifying states, the court has automatic jurisdiction over genocide, war crimes, and crimes against humanity, and will have jurisdiction over the crime of aggression once that crime is adequately defined. It is substantially the same as "Inherent Jurisdiction."

AUTONOMY/AUTONOMOUS

1. Political: The act or status of a society or group, entity, or self-governing territory, at least in terms of its internal administration, to govern itself without being detached from the state or other entity of which it is a part. It remains to some degree under the ultimate sovereignty/jurisdiction of the overlying state government.
2. Juridical: When used in relation to the applicability of a norm in a given case analysis, it may sometimes be said that the norm has or does not have any autonomous role, meaning that the norm can function by itself, or if it cannot that

the norm must be applied in conjunction with another norm to have any legal applicability. For example: Article 14 of the ECHR has no autonomous applicability. It must be read and interpreted in conjunction (*juncto*) with another norm of that convention.

AUTONOMY REGIME

A legal, political, administrative structure established within a state to accommodate minority groups, such as national, racial, religious, ethnic, cultural, or linguistic groups. Such a regime allows them a certain amount of legal right to govern themselves and to feel that their particular differences (particularities/specificities) can continue to exist and be developed. This may be done, for example, by allowing the group to have governance and jurisdiction over a specific territory within the state in which it exists, or exclusive governance over the group's own members within the larger state, or jurisdiction over certain areas of life, such as education, religious observance, and culture.

AVAILABLE RESOURCES (ICESCR)

The ICESCR requires that a state party to that human rights treaty undertake the legal obligation to take progressive steps "to the maximum of its available resources" toward the realization of the economic, social, and cultural rights in that instrument. The term "its available resources" in the context of the ICESCR refers to both the resources within a state, and equally to those available from the international community through international cooperation and assistance. A state party has a legal obligation to see to the equitable and effective use and access to both of these resource sources, to be used toward the progressive realization of such rights.

AWARD (OF COURT/TRIBUNAL)

Relief or damages provided to the winning party in an adjudicated dispute; usually monetary.

BANJUL CHARTER (AKA AFRICAN CHARTER ON HUMAN AND PEOPLES' RIGHTS)

The commonly used short title given to the African Charter on Human and Peoples' Rights. The African Charter was adopted by the Organization of African States in Banjul, Gambia, in 1981. Often treaties and protocols to treaties are commonly known by the place where they were adopted, such as the "Pact of San Jose" (Costa Rica), which refers to the ACHR.

See African Charter on Human and Peoples' Rights, supra.

BANTUSTAN

A geographical political area in South Africa, which was reserved for forced occupation by a group of Black African people with limited self-government. Its official name was a homeland. A bantustan was the so-called homeland that the ruling Afrikaners set up for the Blacks in the process of establishing apartheid. There were several of these bantustans. The Afrikaners granted the inhabitants of a bantustan titular sovereignty over the area, while keeping real power and control unto themselves. It was similar to an American Indian reservation. The bantustans did not possess territorial contiguity to each other and were kept apart to minimize their political power and threat to the apartheid system. They were purely legal fictions. The bantustan system in South Africa was abolished in 1993.

While this term was peculiar to South Africa and has largely come into disuse there, it is still employed to refer to state systems of forced segregation of a people deemed a threat to a ruling majority or minority in order to fractionalize, disempower, and physically confine and control the target group. It has been used, for example, to refer to the situation in Palestine in 2003 in reference to the Road Map for Peace, the so-called Israeli "Security Wall," and the proposed map cutting up Palestinian territory.

BASIC HUMAN RIGHTS

This term refers to those human rights that are generally considered most necessary or essential to the well being and human dignity of the individual person. In concept, when basic human rights are guaranteed, they help to assure the primary material and nonmaterial needs of human beings, so that they can lead a dignified life.

Basic human rights are the most fundamental needs of human beings to live a life consistent with their human dignity. Because of this, these rights are given absolute precedence (priority) in both national and international law and policy. There is no universally accepted list of these rights, as they vary somewhat according to different cultural contexts. However, they would include, for example, the right to life, food, shelter, medical treatment, freedom from torture, cruel, degrading, and inhuman treatment and punishment, and freedom of religion, freedom of expression, and freedom from slavery. All human rights are considered equal, interdependent, interrelated, and indivisible in theory. However, the term basic human rights is used to designate certain human rights that are simply too basic *not* to be respected.

Basic human rights are set forth in the following international human rights instruments: UDHR, ICCPR, and ICESCR, although the term basic human rights is narrower than all of the substantive rights set forth in them. It is an abstract concept and not easy to define clearly, but is often used in human rights discourse.

BASIC PRINCIPLES (UN)

A written set of general principles drafted by an organization such as the UN to serve as a general guide to state government authorities to allow them to harmonize their government conduct with their international human rights legal obligations. For example, in 1985 the UN issued its Basic Principles on the Independence of the Judiciary, aimed at helping states protect the due process/fair trial rights of persons appearing before state courts. These principles are drafted with consideration of all legal and political systems in the world. They are not legally binding, though their implementation in domestic law and practice is encouraged.

BEARER (OF RIGHTS) (AKA HOLDER)

The legal personality, whether a state, group, or individual, who is the subject of rights in international law is known as the "bearer" or "holder" of rights. A holder and a bearer of rights are the same thing. It is the one who holds, possesses, or can claim to have the right and to as-

sert it legally. It also refers to one who has the right to defend such rights. Human beings are the principal bearers of human rights, not states.

BEIJING DECLARATION AND PLATFORM OF ACTION (1995 FOURTH WORLD CONFERENCE ON WOMEN)

The official title of the document that was issued by the states present and participating in the 1995 UN Fourth World Conference on Women, held in Beijing, China. This conference was held for reexamining the status and condition of women in the world, and how protection of women was being implemented in national and international human rights law. The fundamental principle of the Declaration and motto of the conference was that "human rights are women's rights."

BEIJING RULES (JUVENILE JUSTICE)

A name used for the 1985 United Nations Minimum Rules for the Administration of Juvenile Justice, adopted in Beijing, which sets forth extensive principles and rules for the treatment of juveniles to protect their human rights when they are within a state's juvenile justice system.

BELGRADE MINIMUM RULES OF PROCEDURE FOR INTERNATIONAL HUMAN RIGHTS FACT-FINDING MISSIONS (BELGRADE RULES)

A set of nonbinding rules formulated by the International Law Association at a conference in Belgrade in 1980 for purposes of rendering fact-finding missions most credible, reliable, efficient, and effective. They include, for example, rules on the selection of fact finders, on site investigation, and the manner of collection of evidence.

BELLIGERENCE / BELLIGERENCY (LOAC)

An armed conflict of a noninternational or international character that is governed by international law. When applied to noninternational armed conflict, it means that the level of conflict has risen to the point where the state recognizes a state of belligerency, as opposed to mere insurgency or rebellion. When applied to international armed conflict, it means that the states involved have recognized the conflict as having risen to the level of belligerency, thus engaging the applicability of international law.

BELLIGERENT (LOAC)

A party to an armed conflict controlled by the international law of war/armed conflict. The state of being at war or in armed conflict, specifically the status of a legally recognized belligerent state, nation, or group.

BIGOT / BIGOTRY

The attitude and perception of being strongly and openly biased and prejudiced against another person or group on the basis of a certain distinguishing characteristic or set of beliefs that the bigot does not like. Bigotry is an intolerance of such differences. Such an attitude is seen as a danger to respect for human rights and fundamental freedoms, because it looks at another as being unacceptable, or less than equal, or rightly to be discriminated against.

Bigotry is an attitude inconsistent with respect for human dignity and an attitude that human rights education seeks to root out and replace with an attitude of tolerance and respect. Although it is permissible to hold opinions reflecting bigotry, bigotry can lead to harmful acts of intolerance, and those acts can be prevented or punished by society. According to the international community, the best remedy for bigotry is education in human rights.

BILATERAL (vs. MULTILATERAL) TREATY*

A bilateral treaty* is an international legal agreement, however titled, between two states only, such as the United States and Canada. Bilateral treaties* establish rights and obligations *inter se* ("between each other") that are governed by international law. When there are more than two state parties it is called a multilateral treaty*.

BILL OF RIGHTS (U.S.)

The popular title and description of the first ten amendments to the U.S. Constitution, which establish, in an indirect way, legal protection of certain basic rights of individuals somewhat similar to human rights. There is also an "International Bill of Rights" found in the field of international human rights. *See* International Bill of Rights, infra, and appendixes A and B.

BINDING (TREATY*/DECLARATION/ RESOLUTION/NORM/OBLIGATION) (vs. NONBINDING)

A legal term that describes the nature of a norm (treaty*, custom, etc.) as a standard of conduct with which a state must legally comply. It is a mandatory, obligatory requirement. This term is used to describe a treaty* that has been ratified* by a state. If a state has ratified* a treaty*, and if the instrument has entered into force, the instrument is "binding" upon the state and it must comply with the treaty* under the principle of *pacta sunt servanda* (i.e., agreements must be kept).

A binding treaty* must nevertheless be considered along with any reservations, declarations, and understandings (RDUS) submitted upon ratification*. Only if a treaty* is binding is a state bound to comply with it. A state's noncompliance leads to a breach/material breach or violation of the treaty*.

BIOETHICS

The science of morality as concerns human life and the human body. The acceptable conduct of mankind as regards its treatment of human life and the human body. A field of knowledge, discourse, and study concerned with the philosophical and ethical implications of certain biological and medical procedures, and certain technologies, affecting human life. Examples are cloning, stem cell research and human genome mapping, and treatment of the terminally ill. Every bioethical issue implicates one or more human right.

The major conceptual difference between human rights and bioethics is that bioethical issues/debates are based mostly on differences in underlying value systems, whereas human rights constitute a common standard of conduct accepted by all nations as binding legal standards (norms) for all humankind, although there are issues as to interpretation and application of human rights.

BIS (DRAFT ARTICLES: BIS, TER, QUATER)
[Latin, lit.: second/twice]

1. Draft Treaty* Articles: A Latin numerical adverb used to identify a certain proposed draft article of a proposed treaty*. In the drafting of an international instrument often different parties will submit various draft articles or alternative wordings for consideration. Each of these drafts is accorded a sequential Latin designation. The second proposed draft is given the designation "bis," meaning the second proposed draft, e.g., "article 5 bis." The next proposed article 5 is designated ter (third); the next is quater (fourth). The drafting states will negotiate and deliberate over which proposal to adopt as the authentic treaty* text. This helps identify the various proposals for correctness and ease of negotiation.

2. Generally: Bis can also be used generally in other contexts to refer to a second one of something. Example: "Trial Chamber 1 bis" refers to a second trial court chamber, such as when one chamber has been divided into two separate chambers, resulting in the designation of Trial Chamber 1 and Trial Chamber 1 bis.

BLACK LETTER LAW

In the context of human rights, black letter law stands for treaty law and domestic legislation enacted to implement those treaty norms. These are also part of what is known as hard law. This is contrasted with sources of human rights norms such as customary international law and general principles of law. It is a positivistic law with express written norms.

BODY OF PRINCIPLES (UN)

A set of written general principles drafted by the UN to assist states in conforming their national institutions to international human rights standards in a particular area, such as with respect to prisoners; e.g., the UN Body of Principles for the Protection of All Persons under Any Form of Detention or Imprisonment.

BOGOTA DECLARATION (AKA AMERICAN DECLARATION OF HUMAN RIGHTS)

An alternative title given to the American Declaration of the Rights and Duties of Man, which is commonly referred to as the "American Declaration of Human Rights." This general human rights declaration was adopted by the Organization of American States at its meeting in Bogota, Columbia, in 1948. Many instruments of the OAS are referred to by the place where they were adopted.

BONA FIDES (AKA GOOD FAITH) (INTERPRETATION AND APPLICATION OF TREATY NORMS)
[Latin lit.: Good Faith]

Used as a noun, bona fides refers to the mental attitude exhibited by a person, state, or group of persons, who acts according to what is believed to be the morally/ethically right way to accomplish a right result. It connotes fairness, openness, and honesty in a relationship. It is a principal obligation of international law/relations whereby a state acts consistent with the reasonable expectations of the international community or another state with whom it has dealings, in an honest and open manner to promote stability, peace, and harmonious international relations. This usually means that the state will act consistent with its treaty* obligations.

The implied obligation of good faith as to fulfillment of treaties* is set forth in article 26 of the Vienna Convention of 1968 and UN Charter article 2(2). Under article 31(1) of the Vienna Convention, a state that has signed a treaty* or has expressed its consent to be bound by it accepts an obligation to refrain from acts that would defeat the object and purpose of that treaty*, even though it may not be formally legally obligated to obey that treaty*, as it would upon ratification. Thus, when a state signs a treaty*, it does accept this Vienna Convention (a treaty* now deemed binding on all states, as a matter of customary international law) obligation of Bona Fides/Good Faith, to act in a way that shows to all states/parties the sincerity of its intention to become bound by the treaty* until it finally ratifies it. For example, the U.S. has signed but not ratified the Convention on the Rights of the Child (CRC). Even though the U.S. is not formally bound, de jure, to obey the treaty under the doctrine of *pacta sunt servanda*, it should act domestically consistent with the terms of the CRC as a sign of its good faith to eventually become so legally bound.

Generally speaking, when used as an adjective, bona fide means made in good faith without fraud or deceit; something that is actually genuine and what it purports to be.

BREACH (OF INTERNATIONAL NORM) (AKA VIOLATION)

The failure of a state to comply with an international norm is a breach of its legal obligation. A state is said to breach its normative obligation under treaty* or customary law when its conduct is not in harmony with the norm. "Breach" is most properly used in the context of the law of armed conflict, especially under the GCs of 1949, which established vio-

lations of those four treaties as being either regular breaches or, for certain enumerated more serious violations, grave
breaches. The latter constitute international crimes. *See* GC IV, articles 146–147.

A breach entails the international responsibility of the offending state and its
agents, depending on the source of the
norms violated (treaty* versus custom).
The breach can be of a specific treaty*
norm or a norm of customary international law. The breach can be by a state's
action or inaction and can occur when
nonstate/governmental actors commit
the acts with the state's collusion or
complicity or its failure to prevent or
stop such acts. If a breach is considered
a "Material Breach" (*see* infra), it means
that the state has either repudiated a
treaty* or violated a provision essential to
accomplishing the object and purpose of
the treaty*. The word "Violation" is also
used somewhat interchangeably.

BRICKER AMENDMENT
(U.S. CONGRESS)

A series of proposed amendments to the
U.S. Constitution in the 1950s, which
would have amended the treaty power in
the Constitution to prevent the president
from entering into any self-executing
human rights treaties or using executive
agreements on human rights, and requiring larger Senate action on international human rights treaty making by
the executive.

From 1952–57, this series of proposed
amendments was part of a strenuous debate over whether and how the new human rights treaties under the UN would
apply in U.S. law. This debate was
sparked by the political conservatives in
reaction to several court decisions, such
as the cases of *Sei Fuji vs. California* and

Oyama vs. California. In these cases the
courts dealt with the applicability of human rights provisions of international
treaties, such as the UN Charter, which
would have invalidated some state laws allowing state racial discrimination against
aliens.

The amendments would have prohibited the executive from entering into any
self-executing human rights treaties by
declaring all such treaties to be non-self-
executing; would have required congressional legislation to implement them;
and would have limited the use of executive agreements. The proposals were the
result of the fears in Congress that the
U.S. would be criticized for human rights
violations before international bodies and
sued for violations in U.S. courts. They
were also meant to reverse the effect of
the 1920 U.S. Supreme Court case *Mis-
souri vs. Holland*. In that decision the Supreme Court held that the 10th Amendment did not limit the treaty making
power of the federal government.

The term has come to be associated
with any strong political contention for
limiting U.S. entry into any human
rights treaties that would become part of
U.S. law and would become binding on
both federal and state governments, and
would serve as a basis for claims of international human rights violations.

BROAD-MINDEDNESS (PLURALISM,
TOLERANCE AND)

A term meaning the capacity to have
an open and tolerant mind, not being
narrow-minded or intolerant, even when
another person's ideas or expressions are
found to be unpleasant, or intolerable. It
is a word often seen in the phrase "pluralism, tolerance, and broad-mindedness,"
found in some ECHR jurisprudence—

largely in cases involving freedom of expression. This capacity to think broadmindedly about all others as being equal despite differences and as having individual human dignity is deemed a necessary social element for the success of a democratic society.

CAPITAL PUNISHMENT (AKA DEATH PENALTY)

The criminal sentence of punishment by being put to death for the commission of a capital criminal offense. Also commonly known as the "Death Penalty."

CASUS BELLI (LOAC)
[Latin, lit.: an occurrence of war]

An act by one state that offends another to the extent that the second state is justified in declaring war.

CASUS FOEDERIS
[Latin, lit.: a cause of an alliance]

An international act or event, the occurrence of which invokes or triggers the application of a mutual/collective defense treaty* (alliance), such as when a third party attacks one of the parties to such treaty*; e.g., an attack on a NATO member.

CAT

An acronym for the Convention against Torture (1984); also used to refer to the Committee against Torture. Also seen as CT.

CATEGORY I, II, III (ROSTER) (NONGOVERNMENTAL ORGANIZATION OR NGO)

In the United Nations's system prior to 1996, all nongovernmental organizations (NGOs) were characterized by their nature and relationship to the UN. They were given a certain category status. (*See* ECOSOC resolution 1996/31.) The new system describes them as having "General Consultative Status," "Special Consultative Status," or "Roster Status." Category I is now Special Consultative Status, Category II is now General Consultative Status, and Category III is still Roster. The category determines the nature of the NGO's consultative status.

Category I: The ECOSOC description formerly given to NGOs that have, on the basis of their own mandate, a special interest in all of the human rights activities of the ECOSOC.

Category II: The ECOSOC description formerly given to NGOs that have a special mandate, were interested only in some human rights activities of the ECOSOC, and could make essential contributions to the ECOSOC's activities.

Category III: Also known as "Roster." The ECOSOC description of NGOs that have been placed on the roster, a residual list of all other NGOs; they can be consulted by ECOSOC organs, such as the Commission on Human Rights, on an ad hoc basis. *See* Roster; Consultative Status.

CAUTIO JUDICATUM SOLVI (BAIL BOND)
[Latin, lit.: court-determined bail bond for release]

A payment or posting of a bond by a person detained upon accusation of having committed a crime in order to allow the accused to leave detention by assuring the court that the accused will attend all hearings or forfeit the bond. Money posted to secure release of a prisoner; a bail bond.

CEDAW

An acronym for the United Nations Convention on the Elimination of All Forms of Discrimination against Women (1979). It can also refer to the Committee on the Elimination of All Forms of Discrimination against Women, the UN body that implements this treaty.

CENTRE FOR HUMAN RIGHTS (UN)

The former name of the administrative offices of the Secretariat of the United Nations in Geneva, Switzerland, that dealt with human rights. It is now known as the Office of the High Commissioner for Human Rights. It was sometimes also referred to as the "Human Rights Centre."

CERD

An acronym for the United Nations Convention on the Elimination of Racial Discrimination (1965).

It can also refer to the Committee on the Elimination of Racial Discrimination, the body that implements this treaty.

CESCR (AKA ICESCR/ESCR)

Acronym for the United Nations (International) Covenant on Economic, Social and Cultural Rights.

CHAIRMAN'S STATEMENT

In the political administrative context of the UN Commission on Human Rights and its Sub-Commission, a chairman's statement is an informal procedural statement made officially by the chairman of a session, stating certain action that should be taken regarding a particular human rights situation, often action agreed upon by the state under scrutiny under the public procedures. Such a statement is different from a resolution or a decision of the forum. Such statements are mostly made for largely political reasons as a compromise chosen instead of a resolution, when the members cannot agree on the terms of a resolution.

CHALLENGES TO JURISDICTION

A formal motion seeking a formal judicial determination by a court/tribunal as to whether that forum has subject matter jurisdiction to engage in the judicial determination of a particular case. It must normally be filed by a party with standing to challenge whether or not that forum can be seized of the case.

CHAMBERS (OF COURT/TRIBUNAL)

That part of a court or tribunal in which the judges operate, either as pretrial, trial, or appeals chambers judges. A case is handled by a certain designated chambers, which is composed of one or more judges. A court/tribunal may have more than one chamber at each level.

CHARITY (PRINCIPLE) (LOAC)

The principle of international humanitarian law that requires a belligerent to treat adversaries in its power the way it would wish itself to be treated, i.e., humanely and with compassion.

CHARTER (TREATY INSTRUMENT)

A type of treaty by which states establish an international intergovernmental organization, or sometimes a human rights treaty system. It is usually a formal and solemn international legal instrument—a treaty—and thus is legally binding on states/parties. An example is the United Nations Charter. A charter establishes global or regional intergovernmental organizations, and as their constituent instrument defines their authority. It designates its own principal organs and may set forth certain basic purposes and principles. Some charters, such as the Arab Charter on Human Rights (1994) and the African Charter on Human and Peoples' Rights (1981), are actually international human rights treaties that are binding upon the states that are parties to them. They create a human rights system by setting forth substantive human rights norms and establishing a supervisory mechanism to ensure implementation.

CHARTER-BASED (ORGAN/PROCEDURE/BODY/MECHANISM) (AKA NON-TREATY-BASED ORGAN, ETC.)

An organ, procedure, body, or mechanism that is based on, set up within, or set forth in the constitution or charter of an intergovernmental organization—or is based on decisions taken by the assembly or representative body of an IGO to so establish it. The United Nations Commission on Human Rights is a charter-based body established pursuant to article 68 of the UNCH. Known as a "non-treaty-based" organ, it is distinguished from a "treaty-based" organ, which is set forth in a human rights treaty* as a means of implementing/supervising the treaty* and whose terms of reference are defined by that particular treaty*.

CHILDREN'S (HUMAN) RIGHTS

The totality of those norms of conventional and customary international law that seek to protect children through the establishment of specific child-related normative standards that are accepted in international law and within the systems that seek to implement those norms. The locus classicus of children's human rights is the 1989 United Nations Convention on the Rights of the Child.

CHIVALRY (PRINCIPLE) (LOAC)

The principle of humanitarian law that embodies the code of bravery and courtesy among soldiers, prohibiting treacherous or dishonorable conduct or fighting unfairly. Otherwise stated, dishonorable (treacherous) means that dishonorable expedients and dishonorable conduct during armed conflict are forbidden as a principle of the law of armed conflict.

CITIZEN (VS. ALIEN/NONCITIZEN)

A legal status whereby an individual has both privileges/rights and responsibilities as a full member of a state society. This status is obtained usually through birth within the territory of the state (jus soli); by blood relationship, usually by being born to a citizen (jus sanguinis); or by naturalization, which is the administrative process of requesting the state government to grant citizenship.

CIVIL HUMAN RIGHTS

Generally relating to or involving the general public, their activities and their needs or ways or civic affairs as distinguished from special (such as military or religious) affairs.

A term describing a category of human rights that are rights held by individuals to enjoy freedom within a civil society and equality with others. Civil human rights are individual freedoms, such as freedom of privacy, expression, religion, and movement; nondiscrimination; due process of law; freedom from torture; and the right to life, liberty, and the security of the person.

These are not the same as "Civil Rights," as utilized in the United States, even though some civil rights are also civil human rights. Examples of the former include racial equality and non-discrimination.

CIVILIAN (vs. COMBATANT) (LOAC)

An inhabitant of a state or territory who is not engaged in an armed conflict going on in that state/territory. *See also* Non-combatant. A civilian or noncombatant does not have the legal right to engage directly in hostilities. This term is important in the Law of Armed Conflict (LOAC), and especially the "Humanitarian Law," in determining who has the right to engage in hostilities (*jus ad bellum*) and who can or cannot be held as a prisoner of war. Civilians and civilian objects normally cannot be attacked and enjoy certain protections of the *jus in bello*, "Humanitarian Law," not afforded to combatants. *See* P I, articles 50–51.

CIVILIAN OBJECT (vs. MILITARY OBJECT) (LOAC)

A term used to describe all physical objects found in a territory where an armed conflict is occurring, although by their nature, location, purpose, or use these objects do not contribute to the military activity or ability of any party. The capture or destruction of such objects, in whole or in part, would not result in a definite, concrete military advantage for either side. A term used in the Law of Armed Conflict (LOAC) to distinguish a civilian "object" from a military "object." It is permissible under the LOAC to attack military objects but not to attack civilian objects. *See* P I, articles 48, 52.

CIVILIAN POPULATION (vs. COMBATANTS) (LOAC)

A term used to describe all persons who are not combatants, found in a territory where an armed conflict is occurring. In the Law of Armed Conflict (LOAC) this term is used to distinguish such persons from combatants, who can legally be attacked. It is permissible under the (LOAC) to attack combatants and military objects, but not permissible under the principle of distinction/discrimination to attack the civilian population, which enjoys general legal protection against the dangers of military operations. *See* P I, articles. 48–51.

CIVIL LIBERTIES

Legal guarantees established by the governed of a democratic society that are assurances that the basic freedom of individuals will not be curtailed by government. Freedom of expression, freedom of peaceable assembly, and the right to a fair criminal trial are examples of civil liberties. They are usually found in a constitution/bill of rights.

CIVIL RIGHTS (U.S. LEGISLATION) (vs. HUMAN RIGHTS)

As commonly used in the United States, this term refers to the nonpolitical rights of citizens and certain others to liberty and equality of treatment found in the Constitution's Bill of Rights and in the so-called Civil Rights Acts.

Civil rights are rights whose purpose is

to ensure the respect of such persons in a civil society and are rights granted by the sovereign through legislation, e.g., as the U.S. Congress's passage of the Civil Rights Acts. The object of civil rights is to create a harmonious, peaceful, and stable society. The sovereign who grants civil rights can also repeal or amend such civil rights legislation.

In contrast, human rights inhere in all human beings by nature. Human rights are not granted by state sovereigns but are actually only recognized by them in human rights instruments (treaties*, such as the ICCPR) as already existing in humans as humans. Human rights are thus not subject to alienation, termination, annulment, or modification by a sovereign, though some can be limited and/or suspended in public emergency situations. This term is also sometimes used in a general sense to refer to "Civil Human Rights" (*see* supra).

CIVIL SOCIETY

The local, national, and international network of individuals, movements, and organizations of nonprofit interest groups that form in the private sector to assert interests, identities, or causes outside of state-based and controlled political institutions. They organize to impact and change the public sector, especially governments and intergovernmental organizations. For example, NGOs such as Amnesty International and the League of Women Voters are part of civil society.

CIVIL WAR (AKA NONINTERNATIONAL ARMED CONFLICT/INTERNAL ARMED CONFLICT) (LOAC)

A public armed conflict either between rival entities, none of which are states, or between the state and an armed opposition group or groups, wherein all of the hostilities occur within the territory of only one state.

CLASSICAL (HUMAN) RIGHTS (vs. SOCIAL [HUMAN] RIGHTS)

A term used to refer to the categories of "civil and political" human rights. These are historically the first rights to be recognized, and they protect the individual from the action of the state. These are contrasted with "social" (human) rights, which, as used in this sense, refer to economic, social, and cultural rights as a group. *See* Social (Human) Rights.

CLAUSE (OF A TREATY*)

A distinct article in a treaty* instrument. A clause contains a separate and distinct substantive or procedural norm. Examples include a freedom-of-expression clause or a limitation clause, a derogation clause, or a denunciation clause.

CLAWBACK CLAUSE (OF A TREATY*) (AKA LIMITATION/RESTRICTION CLAUSE)

A term referring to a "Limitation" or "Restriction" clause (*see* infra) in a human rights treaty*. Heard mostly in the parlance of the United Kingdom. A limitation/restriction clause is a "clawback" from the substantive right. Example: ICCPR article 12.3 is a clawback clause.

CODE

A systematic collection or compendium or revision of laws, rules, and regulations, usually by subject. (*Black's Law Dictionary* 7th Ed.)

CODE OF CONDUCT

See Corporate Code of Conduct, infra.

CODE OF CRIMES AGAINST
THE PEACE AND SECURITY
OF MANKIND (DRAFT 1996)

An alternative term referring to the draft UN instrument entitled the "Code of Offenses against the Peace and Security of Mankind." This is an instrument researched and drafted by the International Law Commission of the United Nations, begun in the early 1950s, put off for many years, and finally completed in full draft in 1996. This Code seeks to define those international crimes, which served as the basis of the Nuremberg Trials: principally aggression (planning/starting and aggressive war), war crimes, and crimes against humanity.

These are all considered legal norms of international law binding on all states on the basis of customary international law on genocide. It also sets forth the so-called "Nuremberg Principles," such as that providing for individual criminal responsibility regardless of an accused acting in any official position, or command responsibility of superior officers or officials for certain acts of their subordinates.

CODIFICATION/CODIFY (OF NORMS)

The process of collecting and arranging systematically, usually by subject, the laws of a state or country, or the rules and regulations covering a particular area or subject or law. The rational, systematic ordering of legal norms in a logical order, transforming them into a whole body of law applicable to a particular subject, such as war crimes or crimes against humanity. To reduce, classify, or systematize various norms into a code of laws. The process of reducing customary laws or other rules of international conduct to a written form, which is then adopted as a treaty by nations. The systematization and formulation of rules of international law where there has already been extensive state practice, precedent, and doctrine.

Codification in the area of public international law began in the eighteenth century. The major antecedents to human rights norms, which are part of codifications of existing norms for armed conflicts, are the Hague Conventions of 1899 and 1907, which were a codification of existing customary law of armed conflict. Modern examples of codifications include the Geneva Conventions of 1949, which are, in great part, a codification of the then existing norms of international humanitarian law applicable to such subjects as prisoner of war.

COLD (HUMAN) RIGHTS

A description of human rights that do not meet the immediate physical, sensory, and psychological needs of persons. These do not provide warmth, friendship, food, family, charity, or sanctity.

COLLATERAL DAMAGE (LOAC)

Damage to civilian persons or civilian objects during an armed conflict attack, where a military objective was targeted, but the damage that actually resulted went beyond the military target. Damage to noncombatants and nonmilitary objects from an armed attack.

In armed conflict there is a level of collateral damage that is considered legally acceptable under the LOAC, and beyond that level it would be a violation of the LOAC and a potentially a war crime. This brings into play the principle of proportionality. All attacks must be proportionate to the military advantage anticipated from a particular armed attack. The standard of proportionality is not gauged by the military advantage gained in relations to the whole armed conflict. *See* P I, article 51.5.

The U.S. Department of Defense defines collateral damage as "unintentional or accidental injury or damage to persons or objects that would not be lawful military targets in the circumstances ruling at the time. Such damage is not unlawful so long as it is not excessive in light of the overall military advantage anticipated from the attack."

COLLECTIVE COMPLAINT (PROCEDURE/SYSTEM)

A complaint system or procedure for dealing with allegations of multiple violations of human rights, not merely isolated individual cases. Collective complaints focus more on a series and practice of failures of the state to meet its normative human rights obligations.

In some systems these complaints can be filed by NGOs, such as under the European Social Charter, which allows collective complaints of "unsatisfactory application of the [ES] Charter."

COLLECTIVE ENFORCEMENT

The political concept that a human rights treaty* system is a sort of collective effort of all states parties to the treaty* to work toward the full enjoyment of all the fundamental rights in the treaty* in all those states. This term is actually used in the preamble to the European Convention on Human Rights, which sets such collective enforcement of human rights norms as the object and purpose of the ECHR. The international enforcement mechanism created by that treaty adds a supplemental and ultimate remedy beyond that offered by national systems.

COLLECTIVE (HUMAN) RIGHTS (AKA GROUP RIGHTS) (VS. INDIVIDUAL RIGHTS)

These are human rights that are said to be either

1. Held by the collective/group for the benefit of the individual members of the collective/group, or
2. Held by each individual member of the collective/group, but collectively for the benefit of the whole collective/group.

These rights are generally contrasted with individual rights, which are held by each individual person regardless of his or her belonging to a group. Some rights, such as minority or indigenous rights, are said to be "collective" or "group" rights. The concept of collective/group rights is controversial and is not accepted by all.

COLLECTIVE INTERVENTION (AKA MULTILATERAL INTERVENTION) (VS. UNILATERAL INTERVENTION)

The act of an organized group of states without prior UN authorization but with arguable tacit approval of the UN Security Council to forcibly intervene in the internal affairs or on the territory of another state to stop breaches of the peace, threats to the peace, or acts of military aggression. This is contrasted with a multilateral intervention, which is one authorized by the Security Council under Chapter VII, and with Unilateral Intervention.

COLLECTIVE PUNISHMENT (LOAC)

The punishment of persons who are not guilty of committing wrongful acts for the purpose of generally punishing a group or population of people for acts committed by only one or some of them. Collective punishment, the punishment of persons without regard to their individual culpability, is usually meted out to frighten the people punished into revealing which members of the group have committed wrongful acts (e.g., sabotage) against those doing the punishing or to prevent further wrongful acts. Collective punishment is unlawful under international humanitarian law (LOAC) as it violates the principle of individual criminal responsibility and the right to fundamental judicial guarantees. *See* GC IV, article 33.

COLLECTIVE SELF-DEFENSE (LOAC)

The customary international legal right (*jus ad bellum*) of every state to enter into agreements and to act in collective concert with other states, bilaterally or multilaterally, to defend a state or states from an armed attack. Every state has the inherent legal right to defend itself and to ask other states to come to its defense. Self-defense is valid only when the necessity for doing it is instant, overwhelming, and leaves no choice of means or moment for deliberation. The acts of self-defense must be proportionate to the attack. Collective self-defense is provided in article 51 of the UNCH.

COLONIALISM

The control of one state by another state, usually distant and possessing a different culture, by transplanting people from the colonizing state to the colony to politically and economically run the colony. An example would be Indonesia, which was formerly a colony of The Netherlands.

COMBATANT (VS. NONCOMBATANT) (LOAC)

Persons legally authorized by their government or other authority to participate in the operation of hostilities in a war or other armed conflict. This term is found in the Law of Armed Conflict (LOAC, especially the "Humanitarian Law," and is used primarily to distinguish between those who have the right to engage in hostilities (*jus ad bellum*) and civilians, who do not have such right. Combatants can be attacked unless they are "*Hors de Combat*" (*see* infra); noncombatants (civilians) cannot be attacked. The former can be taken as prisoners of war; the latter cannot. *See* P I, articles 43–44.

COMITY

Acts or practices of states based on goodwill and mutuality rather than on the strict application and enforcement of rules of law.

COMMAND RESPONSIBILITY (LOAC)

The legal principle of international humanitarian law and international criminal law that establishes the individual criminal responsibility of commanding officers for the war crimes and crimes against humanity committed by those under their command, where the commander had the required mental awareness of the acts of their subordinates.

The international law applicable in armed conflicts, known as international humanitarian law, establishes individual criminal responsibility of military commanders for the acts of soldiers under their command in certain situations. Normally, the rule is that a commander will be responsible for the crimes of his soldiers where he "knew or should have known under the circumstances" that the wrongful acts of subordinates were occurring and he did not take steps when he had the power and authority to do so to stop and to punish such acts; the commander failed or refused to act to suppress or repress violations of humanitarian law. It is a vicarious liability of commanding officers for the acts of soldiers under their command. This places a burden on commanders to know what their troops are doing and to prevent all war crimes and crimes against humanity, which the troops may try to commit.

If a commanding officer orders troops to commit such acts as war crimes or crimes against humanity, that commander will be directly criminally responsible as a perpetrator of such international crimes. But command responsibility applies when the commander fails to control acts of those subordinates where the commander did not plan or order the acts, but failed to stop them when able to do so.

This principle can also be applied in international criminal law to nonmilitary government agents to impose international criminal responsibility upon government officials and personnel for acts of their governmental subordinates.

Criteria for finding individual criminal liability under this principle of international law include:

1. Existence of a superior-subordinate relationship;

2. That persons under the defendant's effective command had committed, were committing, or were about to commit criminally unlawful acts such as torture, war crimes, or crimes against humanity;

3. The defendant knew, or owing to the circumstances at the time, should have known that persons under his effective command had committed, were committing, or were about to commit such acts;

4. The defendant failed to take all necessary and reasonable measures within his power to prevent or repress the commission of such acts, or failed to investigate the events in an effort to punish the perpetrators.

COMMENTARY (TO TREATY*)

A written scholarly reference work that explains the background, history, and intended meaning of provisions of a particular treaty* with reference to the legislative history. Commentaries are often written by experts in the field pertaining to that treaty*, who were likely close to the treaty's* formative process. Example: *Pictet's Commentary to the Geneva Conventions of 1949.*

COMMISSION

A group of persons appointed by a body to investigate an internal dispute and to propose a settlement, to deal with complaints* of human rights violations, or to initiate studies and reports on human rights issues as to a certain state or issue/

theme. An example is the United Nations Commission on Human Rights (*see* infra).

COMMISSION ON HUMAN RIGHTS (UN)

The United Nations commission established as a subsidiary body under ECOSOC for the purpose of dealing with human rights situations and promoting the setting of standards by drafting treaties* and establishing other human rights standards. It is the most important human rights body of the UN and is a very political forum. The commission is composed of fifty-three member states representing all regions of the world. The commission's members sit in their representative capacity, promoting the interest of their respective states.

COMMITTEE

A person or an assembly of persons on a board to whom the consideration, determination, or management of any matter is referred, as by an international organization, a commission, a court, or a legislature delegating a particular duty. For example, in article 28 of the ICCPR, the treaty establishes the Human Rights Committee, a team of experts who monitor and supervise the implementation of that treaty by states who are legally bound to obey it. A committee can be a quasi-judicial body if the source of its authority so establishes, as in the case of the UN Human Rights Committee.

COMMITTEE AGAINST TORTURE (CAT)

A UN treaty-based body established in article 17, et seq., of the Convention against Torture, and other Cruel, Inhuman or Degrading Treatment or Punishment, to supervise and monitor the implementation of that multilateral treaty by the states parties to that legal instrument.

Sometimes the acronym CAT is also used to refer to the Convention itself.

COMMITTEE FOR THE PREVENTION OF TORTURE (CPT)

The supervisory body of the 1987 European Convention for the Prevention of Torture.

COMMITTEE ON ECONOMIC, SOCIAL AND CULTURAL RIGHTS (CESCR)

A UN body established by ECOSOC in 1987 to supervise and monitor the implementation of the International Covenant on Economic, Social and Cultural Rights (ICESCR) by the states parties to that multilateral treaty instrument. Unlike most UN treaty-based bodies, this body was not created by the terms of the ICESCR, but by ECOSOC after this treaty entered into force. It receives reports from states parties and can issue general comments.

COMMITTEE ON NGOS (ECOSOC)

That subsidiary organ of ECOSOC that meets biannually to review applications made by NGOs seeking to be granted a certain status that will allow the NGOs to act in relation to the UN. *See* Consultative Status, infra.

COMMITTEE ON THE ELIMINATION OF DISCRIMINATION AGAINST WOMEN (CEDAW)

A UN treaty-based body established in article 17, et seq., of the Convention on the Elimination of Discrimination against Women to supervise and monitor the implementation of that multilateral treaty by the states parties to that legal instrument.

Sometimes the acronym CEDAW is also used to refer to the Convention itself.

COMMITTEE ON THE ELIMINATION OF RACIAL DISCRIMINATION (CERD)

A UN treaty-based body established in article 8, et seq., of the Convention on the Elimination of All Forms of Racial Discrimination to supervise and monitor the implementation of that multilateral treaty by the states parties to that legal instrument.

Sometimes the acronym CERD is also used to refer to the Convention itself.

COMMITTEE ON THE RIGHTS OF THE CHILD (CRC)

A UN treaty-based body established in article 42, et seq., of the Convention on the Rights of the Child to supervise and monitor the implementation of that multilateral treaty by the states parties to that legal instrument.

Sometimes the acronym CRC is also used to refer to the Convention itself.

COMMON ARTICLE 3 (OF 1949 GCS) (LOAC)

Refers to article 3 of each of the four Geneva Conventions (GCs) of 1949, all four of which say exactly the same thing, i.e., they all have the same wording and shared application. Common Article 3 applies to cases "of armed conflict not of an international character." They establish, inter alia, a minimum standard of humane treatment without discrimination, including protection of the physi-

cal and moral integrity and due process rights of civilians and combatants who have laid down their arms or are *hors de combat*, and they call for the collection of and caring for the sick and wounded in noninternational armed conflicts. The rest of the provisions of the four GCs only apply to international armed conflicts.

COMMON CRIME (AKA ORDINARY CRIME) (VS. INTERNATIONAL CRIME)

An act or failure to act in a manner that constitutes a crime under the domestic (national or local) law of a state. This is contrasted with an international crime, which is prohibited by the international community, such as genocide. Some acts can constitute both a common crime and an international crime at the same time. For example, if someone kills another person, the killer has committed an act that would constitute an act of murder under national law. That same murder could also constitute the crime of genocide or a war crime if that act were committed as part of a larger genocidal act or military attack. Sometimes the same act can be prosecuted before an international criminal tribunal and a national criminal tribunal.

COMMON EUROPEAN VALUES (ECHR)

Values which are common to all member states of the Council of Europe. A term used within the ECHR system, found in the case law of the European Court of Human Rights.

In seeking to render a decision in a contentious case filed with the Court where the Court finds itself faced with a new issue, it will review the domestic practice and attitude of the various members states, national laws, other European and international instruments, and the court's own case law to see if there is some common way or consensus between them on the issue. If there is such a common value, the Court will resolve the case in a way that best upholds and protects the "common European values."

COMMON STANDARD OF ACHIEVEMENT (UDHR)

A phrase in the preamble to the Universal Declaration of Human Rights that states how the UDHR is to be viewed by all states of the world. As an aspirational or hortatory document, it was not initially intended to be a legally binding standard of conduct of government under international law. It was meant to be a goal to be strived for, a nonbinding standard to be followed by all governments and by all people of all states.

COMMUNICATION (AKA PETITION / APPLICATION/COMPLAINT)

A formal written document through which an individual, group (e.g., an NGO), or state may submit to the attention of some international organ, such as a human rights commission or court or to another offending state, an alleged breach/violation of some conventional or other normative obligation by that state.

The words "petition," "application," or "complaint*" generally have the same meaning as "communication" in this context, and each human rights system uses one or the other of these terms.

COMMUNICATION / COMPLAINT PROCEDURES

A set of formal legal procedures through which an individual, group, or state (or states) may submit, for consideration and decision by some international human rights organ, a formal written document alleging a breach or violation by the named state of some treaty or other legal norm binding on that state for the protection of human rights. One of the ways human rights are implemented (a word used in place of "enforced") in a human rights system is by means of a procedure or mechanism for filing formal written complaints against a state believed to have violated the legal norms of that system. Such complaints (also referred to as communications, applications, or petitions) can be filed in international human rights systems such as the UN Human Rights Committee and the Inter-American Commission on Human Rights. Usually this requires that the state has accepted the jurisdiction (competence) of the particular organ to which the complaint is submitted.

Such international procedures are a backup to domestic procedures and usually require the exhaustion of all available and accessible domestic remedies before filing a complaint* at the international level.

COMMUNITARIAN (SOCIETY)

A type of society that gives ideological and practical priority to the community (sometimes called the state) over the individual. It does not recognize individual autonomy and human rights as more important than the needs of the community.

COMMUNITY-BASED ORGANIZATION (CBO)

A local grassroots organization rising up in a community in order to deal with issues affecting that particular community, such as development or the environment.

COMPATIBLE/COMPATIBILITY (OF CLAIM/COMPLAINT*/ ALLEGATION WITH NORMS)

The state of something being capable of being associated and consonant with another thing. Used in the context of human rights complaint* procedures to describe the condition of a written complaint* that is admissible because it is consistent/in accordance with the requirements of the norms/rule/procedures of the treaty*, such as regards the person who has filed the complaint*, the time when the events occurred, the place the acts occurred, or whether the allegations state a valid claim of a violation of a substantive right in the treaty*.

If a complaint* is compatible with the underlying treaty*, there are grounds for the forum finding the complaint* admissible and the forum properly "seized" of the matter, and for the forum to continue to examine and give it consideration and proceed to determine the merits of the complaint*.

This determination of compatibility is usually made by a commission in the ECHR and ACHR contexts at the admissibility stage. *See* ECHR, article 35.3.

This term can also be applied generally to the relation of an argument or claim or even a proposed norm to an existing accepted human rights norm.

COMPENSATION/*EX GRATIA* COMPENSATION

Money ordered to be paid by a judicial or quasi-judicial body to extinguish a state's legal obligation by the payment of monetary damages to those whose human rights have been found to have been violated under international law. An *ex gratia* compensation payment is one agreed to in good faith by the state after negotiation, to be paid to a complainant although the state does not admit to a violation or has not yet been found to have committed a violation.

COMPETENCE/COMPETENCE-COMPETENCE (OF A JUDICIAL/ QUASI-JUDICIAL FORUM)

1. Competence: The authority of a court or commission to handle a specific case/ matter brought before it. It is a concept akin to "subject matter jurisdiction" as found in common law countries. A body may only deal with cases or issues that it has been legally and expressly, or by implication, authorized/mandated to handle.

2. Competence-Competence: A juridical term referring to the judicial principle that a court has inherent jurisdiction to render a decision as to whether it can exercise its jurisdiction in a given case. It is the court's power to determine the scope of its own power and the cases it can adjudicate.

COMPLAINT (AKA PETITION/ APPLICATION/COMMUNICATION/ DENUNCIATION)

A formal written document through which an individual, group, or state (or states) may submit for consideration by an international organ, such as a human rights commission or court, an alleged breach or violation by a state of a conventional or other normative obligation to protect human rights.

The words "petition," "communication," and "application" generally mean the same thing and are synonymous with "complaint." Each human rights system uses one of these terms to mean the same thing. The term "denunciation" (*see* infra) is also sometimes used.

COMPLEMENTARITY (OF JUDICIAL SYSTEMS/JURISDICTIONS)

A principle describing the relationship between two normative/legal/judicial systems whereby one system is meant to complement the other in a way that assures the achievement of an ultimate goal, such as the implementation of international legal obligations for criminal justice. Used in the context of the permanent UN International Criminal Court (ICC) to describe the relationship between this international tribunal and domestic (national) criminal court jurisdictions.

Application of this principle to the ICC means that the permanent tribunal is competent to prosecute cases not tried by, or not seriously and diligently prosecuted by, national courts.

COMPLIANCE (WITH NORMS) (VS. NONCOMPLIANCE)

Compliance with norms means that a state or other international actor is acting in a manner consistent with, and according to, the terms of a human rights legal norm as contained in a treaty* or in customary international law. The goal of the international human rights movement is to establish worldwide norms based on the inherent dignity of each human being that will be recognized and upheld by all the governments of the world and, indeed, by everyone.

If a state party ratifies* a legal instrument and thereby agrees to uphold those norms, it is therefore expected to stay in compliance with the guidelines to which it has become bound. The state in this way is agreeing to become accountable to the international community for the respect of the norms.

When state conduct is not in accordance with a human rights norm, the state is said to be in a status of "noncompliance" with its normative obligation. This also applies to obligations under both treaty* and customary international law. One can also speak of compliance with soft law norms where applicable, even though these are not hard law obligations.

COMPLICITOUS GUILT

The basis of vicarious criminal responsibility of persons who did not actually commit the acts of a crime, the *actus reus*, but who acted in a way either before, during, or after the criminal activity in such a way and with such a state of mind as to become legally criminally responsible for the crime and subject to criminal prosecution. Those who aid or abet or in any way facilitate the commission of the crime are subject to prosecution by the concept of complicitous guilt. In the area of international criminal law for prosecution or war crimes, crimes against humanity, or genocide and the like, those subject to national or international prosecution will be both the perpetrators who committed the criminal act and those responsible by complicitous guilt.

Sometimes also known as "accomplice liability." *See* supra.

COMPOSITION OF THE COURT

The number and qualifications of judges for a particular judicial forum, such as the European Court of Human Rights. The composition of the court is spelled out in an article of the treaty* that establishes that legal forum. In the ECHR the composition of the court is set forth in articles 20–21.

COMPROMISSORY CLAUSE

A treaty* clause that provides for submission of a legal dispute to a particular court specified in the treaty*. For example, article IX of the Genocide Convention states, "Disputes between the contracting parties relating to the interpretation, application, or fulfillment of the present Convention, . . . shall be submitted to the International Court of Justice at the request of any party to the dispute."

COMPULSORY JURISDICTION (COURT / TRIBUNAL)

The mandatory right, power, and authority of a court/tribunal to adjudicate a claim against a certain party, such as a state, where the party has previously expressly agreed to accept the court/tribunal's jurisdiction (competence) over it. If a party is bound by a treaty* provision accepting the compulsory jurisdiction of a judicial forum, it has no choice but to accept and submit to the exercise of jurisdiction over it in a particular case. It is a legal obligation to do so.

CONCILIATION

A method of peaceful settlement of a dispute whereby the parties to the dispute refer it to a commission of persons whose task is to make findings of fact and attempt to bring the parties to an agreement, making nonbinding proposals for settlement usually contained in a report.

For example, the Council of Europe and the Inter-American Human Rights systems contain procedures for conciliation where a written complaint has been submitted alleging a state party violation of a convention norm. *See* ECHR, article 38; *see also* ACHR, article 48.) An agreement reached by the parties through conciliation is called a "Friendly Settlement."

CONCLUDING OBSERVATIONS (TREATY-BASED BODIES)

Written remarks made by a treaty-based body, such as the UN Human Rights Committee, concerning its opinions as to a state's formal report, after that body's review of the state report and any statements by the state at a hearing before that body. These will involve the conclusion of the body as to the adequacy of the report, and whether the state has made any notable changes in its application or interpretation of the treaty* norms. These are sometimes made with recommendations as to how the state could improve its compliance with the treaty* or the reporting requirement itself. These are made to help the state best comply with the treaty* and indicate how the body will report to its higher-up organs as to state party compliance.

CONCLUSION (OF TREATY*)

Refers to the process of the adoption of a text, authentication of the text, and indication by the states parties of their consent to be bound.

CONCRETE RIGHTS (VS. ABSTRACT RIGHTS)

Dworkin stated that such a concept refers to political aims that are more precisely defined than abstract rights, so as to express more definitely the weight such aims have against other political aims on particular occasions. According to him only concrete rights can spell out the trade-offs with other objectives that would be essential to specify what needs to be done by society to make such rights possible to be realized in fact.

Concurrent Jurisdiction (of Courts/Tribunals)

A judicial situation where two or more courts or tribunals at the same time all have the subject matter and personal jurisdiction to handle certain similar cases. For example, an international court and a national court may both have concurrent jurisdiction to try a war crimes case. In such a situation it is permissible for either court to prosecute those responsible for such crimes.

Conditionality (Political/ Legal/Policy)

The status of political/legal/foreign policy of a state/international organization/international institution conditioning/tying the grant of benefits, or relief from a burden such as international debt, to the servient state's compliance with a specified obligation on its part, usually as a precondition to receiving the benefit.

Condone/Condoning Violation

The attitude and action/inaction of a state in a way that allows human rights violations to occur, most commonly as applies to the acts of private individuals and groups. This usually happens through the state failing to take any action when it becomes aware that viola-

tions may occur or have occurred, and by failing to take any steps to prevent or remedy them. Failing to take any action, such as such as police protection, condones human rights violations by implicitly saying that the states does not care about such acts and will take no action to deter or punish them. Condoning such acts leads to the state being held legally responsible by omission for the human rights violation of its own agents or private parties. Some states consider a human rights violation to occur only where such condoning is a matter of state policy to so act or not act.

Conference on Security and Cooperation in Europe (csce) (changed to: Organization on Security and Cooperation in Europe [osce])

A post–World War II political organization made up of thirty-one European states plus the United States and Canada to deal with issues of security, cooperation, and human rights in Europe in the postwar period. It now has approximately fifty-four state members, and in 1994 it changed its name to the Organization on Security and Cooperation in Europe (osce). Its activities are based on the Helsinki Final Act of 1975, which led to its establishment of the "Helsinki Process" and its "Human Dimension Mechanism" (*see* infra), both of which deal with certain human rights issues in member states, e.g., minority rights.

Conscience (Freedom of)

The internal dictates of the human mind, heart, and spirit, by which a human being makes a decision about how to see the world and how to rightly act in it. It is the activity of a person's internal forum, the *forum internum*. It is often found in connection with the concepts of thought, opinion, religion, or belief.

Under international human rights law, everyone has the human right to freedom of thought, conscience, and religion or belief. *See* UDHR and ICCPR articles 18, ECHR article 9, and ACHR article 13. This means that everyone has the legal right to form their conscience as they want and to act according to one's conscience. One cannot be forced by the state or anyone else to act a certain way contrary to one's conscience; however, the state may limit a person's acting according to their conscience in certain circumstances, particularly under limitations or restriction clauses, for a legitimate aim, such as public safety, public health, or national security. This freedom does not allow a person to act any way he wishes.

An example would be a person whose conscience says it is all right to commit suicide and tries to jump off a tall building. A state could prevent such an act for such reasons as to protect others and the suicidal individual from injury.

CONSCIENTICIZATION OF HUMAN RIGHTS

The process of educating individuals in and for human rights in a way that transforms their minds to see the reality of the world in light of individual human rights and fundamental freedoms for the protection of human dignity. It is more than just cognitive awareness of human rights. It is, in a way, the development of an individual culture of human rights in the human conscience. The conscience becomes conformed to automatically apply

human rights standards to every human activity.

CONSCIENTIOUS OBJECTION (TO MILITARY/CIVIL OBLIGATION)

The refusal to serve in the military or civil service of one's country because such service violates one's religious or philosophical beliefs; one's conscience tells one it is wrong. Generally, conscientious objection means the refusal to do anything because it violates the dictates of one's conscience (e.g., paying a war tax). It is usually made in reference to government demands.

CONSENSUS (ORGANIZATIONAL VOTE)

A term describing the process of coming to a decision by member voting in which no party or member of the body voices a substantial objection to the decision. This is contrasted with other decisions made, e.g., by a majority or two-thirds vote. It is close to the sense of *unanimous* or at least to "without substantial objection."

CONSENSUS PRINCIPLE

In the European Court of Human Rights this principle means that the court will look to the different states parties' laws to determine to what extent there is a consensus in a certain area of law, for example, the age of consent for same sex consensual acts. This is done where the court is trying to determine how wide or narrow to set the margin or appreciation accorded to states in determining the validity of a limitation. The greater the consensus of laws (similarity between the different state laws) the narrower the margin of appreciation accorded to the alleged violating state.

Consent (Medical Intervention/ Treatment/Experiment)

The conscious assent of a person to allow another person or persons to do a medical treatment or intervention, or the assent of a person to be the subject of a medical or scientific experiment. In order for such consent to be legally valid under international human rights and humanitarian law, it needs to be free, informed, and voluntary consent before such acts can be done to the person/subject. There can be certain acts done for medical or scientific purposes that would never be legally valid, even if the person-subject expressly consents.

Consideranda (of Treaty*/ Declaration/Resolution)
[Latin, lit.: things which must be kept in mind]

The collective phrases found in the beginning or preamble of an international instrument such as a treaty*, declaration, or resolution, wherein the reasons for adopting that instrument are recited. Some examples of *consideranda* language would be the following:
   "*Considering* the obligations of States to protect children . . ."
   "Recalling the horrors of past wars . . ."
   "Whereas recognition of the inherent dignity . . ."
   "Conscious of the complexity of the problems . . ."
   See Appendix B, ICCPR, preamble.

Consideration (of Complaint*, by a Forum)

The process of an international judicial or quasi-judicial body examining a complaint*, after determining its admissibility, as to the applicable law and facts alleged by the complainant concerning the subject human rights violations. Only if a complaint* is found admissible will the forum then proceed to examine the law and facts (merits) of the complaint*.

Consistent Pattern (of Gross and Reliably Attested Violations)

The term of reference/criteria for the admissibility/handling of human rights complaints under the 1503 Procedure in the UN Commission on Human Rights. The commission is empowered under ECOSOC Resolution 1503 to deal with situations of human rights violations, but only if they meet all the elements of this jurisdictional term.

Consolidated (Draft) Text

In the process of negotiating and drafting a treaty* many different proposals are made regarding the contents and wording of the various parts of the text. When all of the proposals are put into one document for purposes of working on the text in all its proposed parts to that point in time, one prepares the "consolidated" draft text.

Constant Jurisprudence (French: "Jurisprudence Constante")

Usually seen in the ECHR to refer to a settled practice of a court/commission as to how it decides cases on a given issue. It is akin to the common law principle of stare decisis but not the same. Simply stated, it means the way the court or commission normally decides an issue in a given fact situation. Courts and commissions normally follow the constant jurisprudence, prior decisions, and judgments but are not legally obligated to do so, as would happen in a stare decisis system where precedents must be followed.

CONSTITUENT INSTRUMENT (OF A BODY/FORUM)

The legal instrument that establishes a body or a forum. It is an agreement of those parties, usually states, to create a body/forum with a specific mandate and terms of reference to accomplish a certain goal and purpose. Examples: The Rome Statute of 1998 is the constituent instrument of the International Criminal Court; the U.S. Constitution is the constituent instrument of the United States of America.

CONSTITUTION

The basic law by which a state or organization is established and governed. A system or body of fundamental principles according to which a nation, state, or body politic is constituted or governed.

A constitution usually sets out the reasons for establishing the state or organization, its purposes, and its constituent organs (e.g., state legislature, executive offices, judicial system, organization, general assembly, secretariat or court). It sometimes sets forth basic principles and rights upon which the state or organization is based, and sometimes even sets forth specific human rights. It usually specifies or limits the scope of power and duties of government.

A constitution is an act of people antecedent to a government, and a government is the only creature of a constitution. It is not an act of government but of a people constituting a government. It is the body of elements to which one can refer and quote, which contains principles on which government is established; the manner in which it shall be organized; the powers it shall have; the mode of elections; duration of representatives and officials; powers that the executive and other branches have; everything that relates to the complete organization of a civil government; and the principles upon which it shall act and by which it is bound.

Increasingly one sees modern constitutions including reference to specific international human rights norms or referring to international human rights instruments

CONSTITUTIONALISM

The concept of a system of government in which power and authority are distributed and limited in a written constitution, through a system of laws in which everyone is subject to the rule of law, even those who govern/rule the society.

CONSULT/CONSULTATION (NGO WITH IGO)

The function of NGOs in relation to international intergovernmental organizations such as the United Nations. This function is one in which the NGO provides information, materials, and reports, and the IGO sometimes allows interventions and other submissions to the IGO regarding matters with the NGO's competence in order to assist the IGO in dealing with human rights issues, either thematically or in reference to a particular state.

IGOs can establish a relationship with NGOs for the purpose of benefiting the IGO in its work. NGOs are not states and thus normally not a functioning member of the IGO and thus cannot participate in its operations and deliberations. To allow the NGO to have a positive input and assist the IGO, the process of consultation was established.

The idea and description of the IGO-NGO relationship as one of consultation came about through article 71 of the UN Charter. That article said that "ECOSOC may make suitable arrangements for consultation with nongovernmental organizations which are concerned with matters within its competence." Some systems such as the UN have set up a formal system of consultative status with different levels of consultation and relationship. *See also* Consultative Status, infra.

CONSULTATIVE STATUS (NGO)

The status held by a nongovernmental organization (NGO) in the context of the United Nations ECOSOC that allows ECOSOC to "consult" with such an NGO on matters under consideration by its bodies, such as the Commission on Human Rights. Consultative status allows an NGO to submit written or sometimes oral intervention statements about a certain human rights issue or implementation mechanism.

NGOs in categories I and II possess consultative status. The former have general consultative status; the latter have special consultative status, i.e., only within a few fields of interest of ECOSOC. All other NGOs are considered as roster NGOs and may be consulted by ECOSOC and its organs on an ad hoc basis.

CONTENTIOUS JURISDICTION (VS. ADVISORY JURISDICTION)

The jurisdiction of a court/tribunal where an actual case or controversy has arisen between two or more parties who seek judicial resolution of the matter. It is engaged when a complaint* has been submitted alleging human rights violations by a state. The complaint* may be filed by an individual or a group (e.g., an NGO) or by a state or states against another state, depending on which system is involved.

Contentious jurisdiction is contrasted with "Advisory Jurisdiction," in which a state or organ requests the court to issue an advisory opinion on the interpretations or application of a law when no actual adversarial case exists. Contentious jurisdiction is exercised in an adversarial legal proceeding before a court.

CONTINUING (HUMAN RIGHTS) VIOLATION

A doctrine seen in the jurisprudence of some international human rights fora, such as the ECHR organs and United Nations Human Rights Committee, to satisfy the requirements of admissibility of a complaint*. Refers to situations in which the action of a state creates results that continue for a long time beyond the initial acts and continue to constitute a violation.

It means that a violation of a substantive human rights norm will be deemed to exist if the acts of a respondent state occurred before a state was bound by a treaty* norm if the effects of those state acts continue to exist during the time the state does in fact later become bound.

CONTRARIO (A CONTRARIO)

Same as "*A Contrario,*" supra.

CONTROL COUNCIL LAW NO. 10 (PROSECUTIONS/TRIALS)

A term designating the legal basis of a certain system set of war crime prosecutions arising out of the Nazi atrocities of World War II, which took place parallel to the Nuremberg Trials. Whereas the Nuremberg Trials were aimed at the high-level military and civilian Nazi war criminals, the Control Council 10 trials were aimed at the lower echelons of war criminals and were held in different tribunals in different countries in Europe. This law served to provide a uniform basis for all Nazi prosecutions for such international crimes wherever committed in Europe and wherever prosecuted. It set up the same three part sets of crimes known as War Crimes, Crimes against Peace, and Crimes against Humanity.

The full title of the law was Control Council Law No. 10, Punishment of Persons Guilty of War Crimes, Crimes against Peace and against Humanity, December 20, 1945.

Convention (Treaty Instrument)

A binding, multilateral legal agreement between states governed by international law for the regulation of matters affecting all of them.

A term used in the title of a particular treaty, e.g., Convention on the Rights of the Child.

The name "convention" means roughly the same as "treaty," "covenant," "pact," or "agreement," all of which are international legal instruments. Conventions are now mostly multilateral, meaning between more than two states, and set forth human rights (or other) norms that are legally binding obligations of the states parties who ratify them. There is little actual meaningful significance between the various names "covenant," "convention," "treaty," or "agreement." In the semantic sense "convention"

means "coming together" (Latin: *conventus*). These instruments establish norms for the conduct of states as they deal with human rights, and they are normally open to all states for the participation of the whole international community.

This term is also used in the general sense to refer to positive treaty law, sometimes as "conventions," a term used instead of treaties to distinguish them from other sources of international law, such as customary law and general principles of law.

Conventional (International) Law

Refers to international law as found in international treaties (covenant, convention, charter pact, agreement, statute, protocol) as opposed to customary international law or general principles of law. Conventional law refers to the source of the norms as coming from treaties (conventions) as opposed to nontreaty* sources. It is also called "black letter" law or "positive international law."

Convention(al) Mechanism/ Procedure (aka Treaty*-Based Mechanism/Procedure) (vs. Nonconvention[al]/Charter-Based Mechanism/Procedure)

A human rights mechanism/procedure that is established in and by a human rights treaty* instrument, e.g., the interstate complaint* procedure of the UN Human Rights Committee is a "conventional procedure" of the ICCPR.

Copenhagen Guidelines (European Union)

Guidelines adopted by the European Union at a 1993 summit establishing criteria for new member state candidates. The guidelines state, in part, that "the candidates must achieve stability of institutions guaranteeing democracy, the rule of law, human rights, and respect for the protection of minorities."

CORE (HUMAN) RIGHTS

A term not specifically defined as to which human rights are "core." These rights would include, e.g., the right to life, to freedom of speech, to legal personality, and to freedom from torture. The idea is that these are the absolutely essential rights for basic human existence with dignity. This approximates the idea of "Hard Core Human Rights" and is roughly equivalent to "Nonderogable" rights.

CORPORAL PUNISHMENT

Any physical hitting or touching of a person imposed as a consequence of some type of misconduct, criminal or otherwise. An example would be spanking a child as an act of discipline.

CORPORATE CODE OF CONDUCT

A set of agreed upon guidelines for a corporation's actions and activities in its operations, made to assure that it acts consistent with international human rights norms itself, and that it does not encourage or incite or collude with government in the latter's commission of human rights violations.

Corporations, especially large and powerful transnational corporations (TNCs, formerly called Multinational Corporations [MNCs]), are considered to be "nonstate actors" in the international arena. They have sometimes engaged in acts that would be considered human rights violations if committed by government, such as slavery, inhuman treatment, and sex discrimination. They have also acted in collusion with governments or encouraged or incited human rights violations by governments in order to facilitate their corporate operations. As a result of such actions committed by TNCs around the world, the international community, largely aided and acting through NGOs, has sought to expose such harmful action and has pushed corporations and international intergovernmental organizations to try to pressure such corporations to voluntarily adopt such codes of conduct and to operate according to their guidelines. Generally these corporate codes of conduct are not legally binding upon the corporation under international or national law. Some corporations have drafted and adopted their own codes of conduct.

CORPUS (OF LAWS/NORMS/RULES)
[Latin, lit.: body]

A Latin word meaning the entire collection (body) of all laws/norms/rules of a particular kind or concerning a particular topic. Example: The Geneva Conventions of 1949 form part of the corpus of international humanitarian law.

COUNTRY OF PARTICULAR CONCERN (CPC)

A characterization of a state under certain general human rights legislation in the U.S. An example is the 1998 International Religious Freedom Act, which ties U.S. foreign policy to a foreign state's compliance with international human rights norms regarding religious freedom. Under this legislation the U.S. government seeks to identify states that engage in or tolerate particularly severe or systematic violations of international religious freedom norms. If a state engages in or tolerates such violations, the U.S. government designates and lists it as a "country of particular concern" and begins action to persuade the violating state to cease such violations. It does this by taking measures such as cutting off foreign aid or assistance to such states.

This term can be used in other human rights systems and contexts.

Country Reports

A title for the U.S. Department of State's annual work entitled "Country Reports on Human Rights Practices," which is a detailed report prepared by the U.S. Department of State, Bureau of Human Rights, Democracy and Labor, and presented to the Senate Foreign Relations Committee and the House Committee on Foreign Affairs to assist those law making bodies in U.S. foreign policy and foreign aid. It is updated and presented each year. It is a report of the human rights record of almost every country in the world.

A country report is prepared from information supplied to the Department of State by American Consulates and Embassies, which have human rights officers compiling such information from various sources, such as newspapers, churches, NGOs, and labor unions. It serves as a primary source for many federal departmental bodies, such as immigration courts. The level of U.S. military and foreign economic development aid is based largely upon each state's human rights record. It is important that these reports be made and kept up-to-date because they directly affect the ongoing relationship of the United States with

other countries in the world whose human rights conditions may be changing for better or worse. These reports are always critiqued and criticized by certain NGOs and some states as being biased or incomplete, or reflecting a dual standard.

This term can also be used in other human rights systems and contexts pertaining to reports about the human rights situation in a particular state.

Country Situations (un)

An alleged human rights violation situation, which has risen to the level of seriousness and severity in a particular state so that the UN Commission on Human Rights and its Sub-Commission can study and take certain action on in order to stop or remedy or prevent such violation.

Country Specific (Human Rights) Legislation (vs. General Human Rights Legislation)

A law passed by a legislative authority, aimed at one particular state/country in response to reports of that state's human rights violations, and aimed at causing some shame or negative impact or denying some benefit to that state to encourage it to improve its human rights record.

Country Specific Procedure / Report / Mechanism (vs. Thematic Procedure etc.)

A term describing an international, intergovernmental organization procedure, report, or mechanism for the implementation of human rights norms that focuses on particular countries and not themes or subject matters. Country specific reports are an in-depth study of the human rights situation in a specific country. A country specific implementation mechanism is set up as a suborgan to monitor a situation in a specific country. Country specific reports are usually done by special rapporteurs who are given a mandate to prepare an in-depth study of the country's situation. These reports or procedures are contrasted with "thematic reports" or procedures, which cover a specific topic/theme as opposed to a specific state.

COUP D'ETAT

A forcible overthrow of a government from within the state, often by members of the existing government or by the military. It brings into power a new government or interim leadership, which seeks to bring about a transition to a new government. *Coups d'Etat* are often violent and accompanied by a summary execution of leaders and other human rights violations, such as exile or forcible expulsion.

COURT (AKA TRIBUNAL)

A court is a judicial body for the transaction of judicial business such as deciding contentious cases and issuing advisory opinions. It is presided over by judges who apply and interpret law and decide the merits of contentious cases, applying the law to the facts proven by evidence. Some courts render judgments that are legally binding upon the parties. Some courts are known as "tribunals," a word that has the same meaning as "court."

COURT OF FOURTH INSTANCE

An appeals court in a European civil law system that reviews the correctness of a lower court decision under national law. It is sometimes referred to by human rights quasi-judicial and judicial bodies in determining the admissibility of a complaint*.

One usually sees the phrase used such as "This commission/court will not sit as a court of fourth instance over domestic legal decisions." It means that the international forum is not to act as a sort of appellate court as to the correctness of a national court's judgment under its national law. This fourth instance formula states briefly that the international forum will not second-guess the national forum's findings of fact nor whether the national court has applied the national law properly. The international forum will not review judgments issued by national courts acting within their competence and with due judicial guarantees unless it considers that a violation of the subject international human rights treaty* is involved. This is because the international forum's only purpose is to ensure compliance with the international human rights treaty* obligation, and not how the national court has complied with its own national law or legal procedures.

COVENANT (TREATY INSTRUMENT)

A binding international legal agreement between states governed by international law for the regulation of matters affecting all of them. A term used in the title of a treaty, e.g., International Covenant on Civil and Political Rights (ICCPR). The name "covenant" means roughly the same as "treaty" (the generic word), "convention," "agreement," "pact," "charter," or "statute," all of which are international legal instruments.

Covenants are usually multilateral and set forth human rights (or other) norms of conduct that are legal obligations of the state parties who ratify*/accede to/ succeed to them. Covenants are by definition legal instruments and are intended to be binding on states. In the semantic sense, a covenant means a promise or an agreement.

CRC

Acronym for the UN Convention on the Rights of the Child (1989).

CRIMES AGAINST HUMANITY

An inhumane act committed in the context of a widespread or systematic attack against civilian populations, where the perpetrator is aware of the connection between his act and the wider attack.

A term describing a group of international crimes. The international community has criminalized acts such as murder, extermination, genocide, enslavement, deportation, or other serious inhuman acts against civilians or the civilian population before or during an armed conflict. Classically, there needed to be a nexus between these crimes and an armed conflict. Now the law seems to no longer require such a nexus; that is, there need not be an armed conflict. Note that the definition may still be in a state of evolution.

These criminal norms create international criminal responsibility on individuals under international law. This class of international crime was first established as such in the Nuremberg Charter (London Charter) 1945, which also set forth crimes against peace and war crimes. These served as the basis for prosecution of Nazi war criminals in the Nuremberg Trials and other similar trials. They serve as a legal basis of crimes under the recent International Criminal Tribunals for the Former Yugoslavia and for Rwanda and are now considered to be binding as customary international law.

These crimes have been included within the jurisdiction of the International Criminal Court, in the Rome ICC Statute, article 5, and defined in article 7. (*See* Appendix C.) They require no nexus to an armed conflict but have the threshold requirement of being either widespread or systematic attacks against any civilian population.

CRIMES AGAINST PEACE
(AKA CRIME OF AGGRESSION)

A term describing a group of international crimes, which consist of the planning, ordering, preparation, conspiring, initiating, and waging of an unjustified aggressive armed conflict against another state.

This is usually known as the Crime of Aggression. (*See* Aggression, supra.) It was articulated as an international crime at the 1945 Nuremberg Trials and was based on international customary law set forth in article 6 of the London Charter, which served as the basis of the Nuremberg Trials. Under it, certain Nazi military and civilian leaders were prosecuted and punished under international law for the Nazi military action against other countries. The international community has not been able to more fully define this crime.

It establishes individual criminal responsibility under international law regardless of any official position and gives rise to universal jurisdiction, meaning that any state in the world has jurisdiction to prosecute the perpetrators.

It was alleged that NATO countries in their bombing of Yugoslavia in early

1999, regarding Kosovo, were committing acts of aggression constituting international crimes. The UN Charter, article 2.4 prohibits the use or threat to use force against the political independence or territorial integrity of other states and is seen as the prohibition against aggression (Crimes against Peace) in the UN Charter.

The international crimes of aggression will also be one of the crimes within the jurisdiction of the proposed International Criminal Court. By this court the international community hopes to prevent such crimes for fear of prosecution and punishment.

Crimes against Peace are violations of the *jus ad bellum*.

Crimes of Concern to the International Community (International Criminal Law)

Under international law there have evolved certain acts, which, wherever they are committed, are considered international crimes. This means that they are crimes whose impact harms the interests of the whole human race and which are thus considered criminal acts under international law. Genocide is a crime of concern to the international community as is a crime against humanity or a crime against peace (aggression). Crimes of concern to the international community form part of the body of law known as international criminal law. Most crimes of concern to the international community give rise to universal jurisdiction, meaning that every state in the world can prosecute a person who committed such an act.

The International Criminal Court was established in 2003 to prosecute crimes of concern to the international community.

Cross-Cultural Human Rights (Issues/Study)

The study or involvement in human rights from the perspective of different human cultures, with a view to seeing and understanding how different societies and cultures interpret and apply human rights. The more different cultures understand each other, the less tension and more harmony there will be and the less chance of human rights violations.

Cruel Treatment/Punishment

Describes the infliction of pain or suffering by the state in a manner devoid of human feeling and causing injury, pain, or grief. Usually seen in human rights treaty* norms along with acts of torture, inhumane, or degrading treatment or punishment. These all represent different levels of severity of treatment/punishment:

1. Cruel treatment: If the cruel acts are not being done for the purpose of punishing the victim for a prior act, such as for a criminal or other violation, then the term "cruel treatment" is used;

2. Cruel punishment: If the cruel acts were done for the purpose of punishing the victim for his prior conduct, such as for a criminal conviction, then the term "cruel punishment" is used.

Both "Cruel Treatment" and "Cruel Punishment" are inconsistent with a victim's inherent human dignity and are human rights violations. *See* ICCPR, article 7.

Crystalize (into Customary Norm) (aka Ripen)

A term describing the process and point at which a certain international practice has evolved into a binding legal norm under customary international law. Customary international law requires a consistent state practice over the course of time (usage) and the subjective element of legality known as *opinio juris*. When a practice has become a consistent matter of international usage, and the *opinio juris* of the international community is evidenced, a practice is said to have "crystallized" into a new customary legal norm, creating binding obligations upon all states. Sometimes one hears the similar term "ripen" to describe such legal phenomenon; that is, a practice "ripens" into a binding legal norm.

CSCE (AKA OSCE)

Acronym for the Conference on Security and Cooperation in Europe (*see* supra). Since 1994 it has become known as the Organization on Security and Cooperation in Europe (OSCE) (*see* infra).

CULTURAL/CULTURE

The integrated pattern of human knowledge, belief, and behavior that depends upon humanity's capacity for learning and transmitting knowledge to succeeding generations. The customary beliefs, social forms, language, art, and material traits of a racial, religious, or social group. The set of shared attitudes, values, goals, and practices that characterizes a society.

CULTURAL DIVERSITY

The character of a society having more than one accepted culture, usually many different cultures.

CULTURAL GENOCIDE

The process of one group of people or state engaging in acts that result in the destruction or elimination of the cultural particularities of another group of people.

CULTURAL (HUMAN) RIGHTS

A category of human rights that in general protects a human being's right to participate in the cultural life of a society; to share in scientific advancement; to protect his own moral and material interests in scientific, literacy, or artistic productions; to obtain an education and to maintain his cultural identity, language, and customs. It assures a human being of his right to obtain information, training, and knowledge for the enjoyment of cultural values and cultural property. One of the major cultural rights is the right to education. *See* ICESCR, article 13.

There is no widely accepted definition of cultural human rights. They are part of what were formerly "Second Generation (Human) Rights" along with economic and social human rights.

CULTURAL IMPERIALISM

The imposition of a foreign viewpoint or culture upon another people. It is often heard that imposing a universalistic view of human rights upon certain countries, especially developing countries, by the West is a form of cultural imperialism.

CULTURAL RELATIVISM (VS. UNIVERSALITY) OF HUMAN RIGHTS

A theory of human rights that holds that all human rights must be looked at, applied, and interpreted according to different cultures and cultural values. It is contrasted with the theory of "universality" of human rights, which says that human rights are the same everywhere regardless of culture, religion, customs, or ideology. "Cultural Relativism" is a theory raised as a defense mostly by developing and third-world countries who claim that the international human rights regime must be applied relative to a given culture, whose actions would be a violation in one culture but not in another. Cultural relativism is based on the existence of cultural particularities or specificities, i.e., differences in language, religion, and customs, or even of regional particularities.

CULTURE OF HUMAN RIGHTS

A generally held social attitude that sees all members of society, indeed all human beings in all societies, as possessing inherent human dignity and, as a result, as holding inalienable human rights, which society must respect and protect in a rule of law system.

In a culture of human rights every human activity is seen in its human rights implications and judged by internationally accepted human rights norms. It is seen in relation to how a given act impacts human dignity: if negatively, it probably constitutes a violation of human rights; if positively, it probably does not do so.

This term was initially used in the 1990s in relation to the UN Decade for Human Rights Education, 1995-2004. In that context the concept of a culture of human rights, or human rights culture, was said to be the desired goal of all human rights education. Creating a culture of human rights necessarily requires human rights education of all members of society and is the primary duty of the state.

CULTURE OF IMPUNITY

An attitude or perception held by most persons that someone can commit human rights violations, even on a massive and systematic scale, and suffer no legal or other negative consequence for their acts. It also refers to the attitude of those persons committing such violations, who believe that they will never be caught and held accountable either in their own country or in an international forum for committing such acts, and who then believe it is all right to do them.

Human rights violations very often happen because those who commit them believe that they will never be caught and held accountable and punished for committing them. They believe that either since they are part of the government that the government will shield them from personal responsibility, or they believe that there is no political will or ability of the state or the legal system or of the international community to come after them to hold them accountable.

The human rights movement, both governmental and nongovernmental, has been seeking to establish legal standards and institutions for eliminating the culture of impunity so that no one will think they can commit violations with impunity. The international community has determined that the greatest way to combat the culture of impunity is to educate people about human rights. Human Rights Education is aimed at replacing the culture of impunity with the so-called "culture of human rights," where there is a rule of law society with accountability of everybody and punishment and reparation for violations.

Slowly the culture of impunity is giving way to a growing culture of human rights that breeds a culture of accountability of everyone for their actions affecting human rights. Much of this change has been fostered and promoted by human rights NGOs.

CULTURE OF PEACE

A generally held social attitude that accepts that all disputes at any level should be resolved peacefully, without resort to violence or causing harm, according to prevailing law that is consistent with international human rights standards.

The twentieth century was characterized by extensive destructive violence between and within many countries. The goal of the human rights system is to provide limitations on the conduct of government in all countries so that armed conflicts and violent rebellions and other conflicts do not occur, to the end that peace will become the norm. Respect for human rights is said to be "the foundation of freedom, justice, and peace in the world." (UDHR Preamble) The international legal community is seeking to educate the world about human rights so as to help eliminate the causes of violence and promote peace. This involves reprogramming societies from a more militaristic or belligerent attitude, which seeks to resolve disputes by force, to a society where rule of law prevails and disputes are resolved by judicial organs applying law.

A culture of peace is deemed to be the most conducive to respect for human rights and vice versa. It is most commonly heard within the UN context.

CUMULATIVE INCREMENTALISM
(UN HUMAN RIGHTS SYSTEM)

A description of the political and institutional evolution of the human rights processes of the United Nations. Over the course of UN history of dealing with human rights, the UN would have to address an issue and would often create a procedure or a body for handling that issue thereafter. As various working groups,

special rapporteurs, and other mechanisms continued to be added without much rationalization in a sort of ad hoc manner, the description of such a human rights system as one of "cumulative incrementalism" was heard and used mostly by critics. This brought a call for stock-taking and rationalization of the procedures.

The 1993 Vienna Conference on Human Rights was attended by almost all states for purposes of arriving at an updated look at human rights within the UN system and how to best rationalize all organs, procedures, and mechanisms. This conference issued the Vienna Declaration and Programme of Action, which would serve as the blueprint for stopping the cumulative incrementalism trend and lead to rationalization.

More than anything from this conference there eventually came the establishment of the Office of the UN High Commissioner for Human Rights, which was created to help coordinate and bring rationalization to the whole UN human rights system.

CUSTODIAL STATE
(ICC JURISDICTION)

The state that has the actual physical custody of a person criminally accused by the ICC and that holds that person in the state's legal custody. In the context of the Rome Statute of the International Criminal Court, one of the originally proposed bases for ICC jurisdiction was whether the custodial state had ratified the ICC Statute. This basis for jurisdiction was not accepted and did not become part of the Rome Statute. Only where the territorial state or the state of nationality of the alleged violators had ratified the Statute could the ICC exercise its complementary jurisdiction. *See* Appendix C, ICC Statute, article 12.

CUSTOMARY *ERGE OMNES* (OBLIGATION) (VS. TREATY *ERGE OMNES*)

Erge omnes obligations are those that bind all states and give all states the rights to respond to human rights violations regarding violations of customary international human rights norms by any state. This is compared with the "treaty *erge omnes*" obligations, which are obligations between only those states that are states parties to a particular treaty*.

CUSTOMARY INTERNATIONAL LAW (SOURCE OF NORMS)

In international law this term refers to a source of internationally recognized legal norms that is based on the consent of sovereign and equal states. Customary international legal norms are created by the existence of two elements, one quantitative (usage) and one qualitative (*opinio juris*):

1. Consistent Practice (Usage): The consistent, continuous, and uniform usage or practice of states in a certain matter falling within the domain of international relations over a considerable (but unspecified) period of time.

2. *Opinio Juris*: The states must always perform such acts because they deem it an obligation of international law, which is the subjective element of customary law known as the *opinio juris*. It is not done by the state out of necessity or comity, but out of a sense of legal obligation in the international arena. When a general consistent state practice is done with the *opinio juris* of most civilized states in the world, then the practice is said to "ripen" or "crystallize" into a norm of customary international law that is binding on every country in the world. It is a second source of human rights legal norms after conventional norms.

DAMAGES (INTERNATIONAL LEGAL WRONG)

Loss or harm to persons or property resulting from wrongful international acts that should be remedied by reparations.

DANGEROUS FORCES (LOAC) (WORKS AND INSTALLATION)

A term of international humanitarian law describing works and installations or places that by their nature, use, or purpose contain highly dangerous forces such as in nuclear power plants, dams, or dikes. These objects are such that their destruction or even damage may unleash the dangerous forces and destroy indiscriminately both military and civilian persons and objects. It is generally prohibited under LOAC to attack places containing dangerous forces.

DEATH PENALTY (AKA CAPITAL PUNISHMENT)

The judicial sentence of a criminal court ordering a person convicted of a capital (most serious) criminal offense to be put to death as punishment for his crime. It is also known as "Capital Punishment."

DECADE (INTERNATIONAL: UN)

A ten-year-long UN publicity/education campaign on a particular topic or group of people. A ten-year program that is declared by a resolution of the UN General

Assembly to be dedicated to the awareness and advancement of certain matters of concern to the UN, e.g., the ten-year period of 1995–2004 has been declared by the UN to be the UN "Decade for Human Rights Education."

DECISION (OF A COMMISSION/ COMMITTEE)

A determination made by a commission or committee after consideration of a complaint* alleging a human rights violation. The decision can be about the "admissibility" of the complaint* (i.e., whether it meets the various prerequisites for consideration) or about the "merits" (i.e., the application of the law to the facts).

"Decisions" are not legally binding, whereas "Judgments" of the court are.

DECLARATION (INSTRUMENT)

1. Political Instrument: A written instrument of expression of general principles by an intergovernmental organization, the principles of which are not meant to be legally binding but may have considerable moral and political authority and may constitute the terms of reference of an organ. These principles may, over the course of time, become binding as a matter of customary international law when there has been consistent state practice (usage) and evidence of the states' belief that it is acting as a matter of law (*opinio juris*) and not as a matter of comity or necessity. A declaration is not intended to be a legal instrument. It is drafted and adopted by the resolution of an international, intergovernmental organization, etc. An example is the UDHR.

2. Treaty* Instrument: An instrument submitted by a state at the time of its rat-

ification* of a treaty*, wherein the state declares the extent to which it will be bound to apply a certain provision as to, e.g., geographical or temporal scope, or it may relate to acceptance of the competence of an implementation body to handle complaints* against the state. This type of declaration is a legal instrument. It is often filed with "Reservations" and "Understandings," which together are abbreviated RDU/RUD to a treaty*.

DECLARATION OF INDEPENDENCE (U.S. JULY 4, 1776)

The founding document of the establishment of the United States, which was a declaration by the thirteen colonies that they were terminating their relationship with Britain and governing themselves. It explained to Britain and the whole world the reasons they were doing this, and proclaimed the concept of the inherent, universal, and unalienable human rights of all. This document was based on natural law concepts and served as one of the two major historical/philosophical documents on which modern human rights is based. The other document is the 1789 French Declaration of the Rights and Duties of Man and of Citizen.

DECLARATION ON HUMAN RIGHTS DEFENDERS (UN)

Another name for the UN document officially titled the "Declaration on the Right and Responsibility of Individuals, Groups, and Organs of Society to Promote and Protect Universally Recognized Human Rights and Fundamental Freedoms." This declaration was adopted by the UN General Assembly in 1999 and seeks to articulate the rights and responsibilities of all those who seek to defend human rights from being violated. Its primary purpose was to protect defenders of human rights.

This is not a legally binding instrument, but one of strong moral and political weight, which took a long time for the international community to hammer out and officially adopt. It includes a duty of states to provide human rights education.

DECLARATORY (HUMAN RIGHTS/OF CUSTOM)

Declaratory Rights are human rights that are set forth in a declaration or sometimes in a resolution adopted by an authoritative body, such as an IGO, like the UN, and that are not meant to create legally binding norms, but only to declare what the body thinks human rights should be. Declaratory rights serve as a basis for drafting legal norms for treaties*, e.g., Declaration on the Rights of Children. The key to this definition is that they are not legally binding.

When used with the term "Customary International Law" or simply "custom," in relation to treaty* law, it usually deals with whether a particular treaty* could give rise to customary international law. It can also mean that a particular treaty* was in fact drafted with the intention of codifying existing customary law norms. Such treaty* is said to be "declaratory of customary international law" or "declaratory of existing custom."

DE FACTO (VS. DE JURE)

Actually, in reality, in fact. Something that happens in fact, in reality, as opposed to happening as a matter of law,

e.g., de facto discrimination is discrimination that occurs not as a matter of law but as a matter of fact by human action whether intended or not. This would be in contrast to de jure discrimination, which would mean that it is done as a matter of law, such as a law prohibiting a certain race from using public facilities. It connotes something that is, as it is, as a matter of fact of reality and not because a law caused it to be that way.

DE FACTO REFUGEE (VS. CONVENTION[AL] REFUGEE)

A person fleeing from his country to another country who is unable or unwilling to seek legal recognition as a conventional refugee or who is unable or unwilling for valid reasons to return to his country of origin.

DEFENDERS (HUMAN RIGHTS)

Human rights defenders are persons who, based on the principles of universality and indivisibility of human rights, defend the civil, political, economic, social, and cultural human rights of other persons, including their own. Human rights defenders, whether working for women's rights, land rights, the protection of the environment, or the defense of civil liberties, play a vital role in the promotion and protection of human rights and fundamental freedoms.

They are the individuals and organizations involved in the multi-dimensional work of human rights; in civic education, advocacy, investigation, reporting of violations, and the legal defense of victims.

Their work aims at the domestic implementation of human rights law and international obligations, holding government authorities responsible for the full promotion and protection of all human rights. (Definition from International Service for Human Rights, Geneva)

The protection of human rights defenders from interference and persecution principally by governments led to the adoption in the UN in 1998 of the "Declaration on the Right and Responsibility of Individuals, Groups and Organs of Society to Promote and Protect Universally Recognized Human Rights and Fundamental Freedoms." There is now a UN Special Rapporteur who is mandated to report on compliance with this declaration.

DEGRADING TREATMENT / PUNISHMENT

Describes ill-treatment or punishment designed to arouse in victims feelings of fear, anguish, and inferiority capable of humiliating and debasing them and possibly breaking their physical or moral resistance. It is usually found / proscribed in a human rights treaty* norm in an article including torture or cruel and inhuman treatment or punishment. These all represent different levels of severity of treatment / punishment:

1. Degrading Treatment: If the degrading acts are not being done for the purpose of punishing the victim for a prior act, such as for a criminal or other violation, then the term "Degrading Treatment" is used.

2. Degrading Punishment: If the degrading acts were done for the purpose of punishing the victim for his prior conduct, such as for a criminal conviction, then the term "Degrading Punishment" is used.

Both degrading treatment and punishment are inconsistent with the victim's inherent human dignity and consti-

tute human rights violations. *See* ICCPR, article 7.

DEHUMANIZATION

The treatment of an individual or group of individuals as though they were divested of all human dignity or personality; treating someone as if they were less than human. Human rights are based on the premise that every human being has inherent human dignity and legal personality, and is fully equal in worth and rights as everyone else. In many situations giving rise to human rights violations, there was created a dehumanization of the victim person or persons, which in turn created a general attitude that the target humans were not really human and do not have the same rights as others, so to harm them is not wrong. Human rights are the legal protection of the inherent and inalienable human dignity of every human being. Dehumanization of any human being is in complete opposition to respect for human rights. There is never any justification for dehumanization of anyone.

DE JURE (VS. DE FACTO)

By operation of law, as a matter of law. Something that happens as a matter of law and not as a matter of fact or happenstance. Compare de facto, which means "as a matter of fact," and de jure, which means it is so because the law so requires it or it happens by operation of law.

DÉMARCHE
[French, lit.: to take steps to obtain something]

A French word used in international law / relations to signify a diplomatic procedure to address and resolve an issue or particular problem vis-à-vis another state. A diplomatic move or maneuver, a diplomatic representation of views to a public official of another state.

DE MARTENS CLAUSE (LOAC)

See Martens Clause.

DEMOCRACY–DEVELOPMENT–HUMAN RIGHTS TRIAD

A human rights doctrine that states that democracy, development, and human rights are absolutely necessary to create a good society and that each is an indispensable prerequisite to the other. All of these must be put into effect by a state.

DEMOCRATIC DEFICIT

The characteristic of an organization or institution not run according to democratic principles and policies, and not reflective of the will of the majority of the people affected by its decisions and actions. The UN Security Council is an example of a body with a democratic deficit. Although there are many procedural norms reflective of democratic deliberation and action in the Council, the whole process in its most critical functions is ruled by the veto power of the five permanent members of the UN Security Council, not by the majority of sovereign, equal member states of the General Assembly.

DEMOCRATIC GOVERNANCE (RIGHT TO)

A proposed theory that states that there exists a human right of individuals to be governed by a democratically elected system of government based on the premises that the will of the governed is the best source of legal authority for a state and that the first duty of a state is the protection of human rights. It includes principles of democratic accountability, respect for rule of law, transparency of government, and open public participation in governance. This right is exercised, e.g., by voting, running for elected office, participating in public debate and information gathering (especially by persons who are most affected by government action), and seeking redress for grievances against government.

DEMOCRATIC NECESSITY (PRINCIPLE)

A principle applicable to limitations/restrictions of substantive human rights that says that for any limitation of a substantive human right to be legitimate and thus legally permissible, the limitation measure must be deemed "necessary in a democratic society." This means that such measure must be used to meet a pressing social need that is supportable by specific evidence and that the limitation measure is proportional to the aim pursued (e.g., public health or safety) and is the least restrictive means of achieving that aim. A limitation that does not conform with this principle is not valid.

See also Necessary in a Democratic Society.

DEMOCRATIZATION

The political and legal process of transforming a society into one in which political power comes to be placed in all the people of society, or at least in the citizenry.

DEMONIZE/DEMONIZATION (PEOPLE/GROUP)

The act/process of someone mobilizing a person or group of persons to hate another person/group by making negative, derogatory statements about the other's characteristics, character, or the history between them. Usually members of one group try by written and/or oral statements to make an intended audience, usually of their own people, believe that the disparaged group is inherently evil, unjust, untrustworthy, less than human, not worthy of living, and even deserving of extermination or banishment. This hatred then leads to a feeling that the warring against/expelling/exterminating/discriminating against "the (demonized) other" is justified or even a national duty. The Bosnia conflict of the early 1990s was characterized by all sides attempting to demonize the other so as to cause the members of the disparaging group to want to kill or ethnically cleanse or otherwise do evil to the demonized group. Most often heard regarding such acts by or against racial/ethnic/religious/ or national groups.

DENIAL OF JUSTICE

The legal effect of a ruling (decision, judgment, order) of a judicial, quasi-judicial, or administrative forum, which resolves an actual case and controversy in a way that does not fully comply with procedural and substantive standards under any international human rights legal norms binding on the state and under national law consistent with such international norms and applicable to the particular case.

In a general sense, a denial of justice can occur in either civil or criminal legal cases. It includes but is broader than the concept of denial of due process of law.

It is a violation of customary international law for a state to deny an alien the right to access a minimally adequate system of justice to vindicate his rights against harm to his person or property within that state. This is known as a denial of justice.

DENUNCIATION (OF TREATY*, COMPLAINT)

Denunciation has two meanings, one concerning treaties* and one concerning complaints of violations of human rights:

1. Treaty*: An act of a state whereby it declares in an international instrument that it thereby no longer recognizes itself to be bound by a treaty* to which it was a state party. The procedure for a state to denounce a treaty* is by submitting an Instrument of Denunciation. This procedure is found in the "denunciation clause" of a treaty*. *See* ECHR, article 58.

2. Complaint: A word used to describe a written or sometimes oral complaint* alleging that a state is in violation of human rights norms. The denunciation may be made by an individual, a group, or state, but most often is made by the latter two. It is a "denouncing" of a state for its noncompliance with its human rights obligations.

DE PLANO (JUDICIAL PROCEDURE)

A judicial term used to describe a legal procedure whereby an action is taken on a complaint* by a forum (court/commission/tribunal) without further formality and without any prerequisites.

DEPORTATION

The act of a state in removing and sending back an alien to the country from which he came because his presence is found to be unlawful or is prejudicial to the public welfare or national security.

Deposit / Depository (of Treaty*)

The act of, or place for, a state submitting its written legal instruments, such as an instrument of ratification*. Deposit is normally necessary for such instruments to take legal effect. The act of depositing the instrument officially makes that instrument effective in the international legal realm. In the instance of an instrument of ratification*, the deposit of the instrument with the person or organ or state designated in the treaty* brings into play the entry into force of the treaty* as to the depositing state. Often the treaty* will specify that the treaty* enters into force at a certain time after such deposit. A ratifying state may also deposit an instrument containing its reservations, declarations, and understandings to the treaty* along with its instrument of ratification*.

See iccpr, article 48.2, as an example of a depository clause in a human rights treaty*.

Derogable (Human) Rights

Derogable human rights are those that are capable of being suspended in time of public emergency by the declaration of a state pursuant to a human rights treaty* and so long as the emergency continues. Treaties* specify which rights are "Nonderogable," the rest being considered derogable.

Derogation (of Human Rights/Clause)

The act of a state suspending the application and enjoyment of certain human rights upon its declaration of a state of public emergency affecting the life of a whole nation. Derogation allows the state to take measures to deal with the emergency without fear of violating human rights norms during the derogation period. A "derogation clause" is a treaty* clause wherein it sets forth the right and criteria for a state to derogate from its obligations under a treaty*. iccpr article 4 is a derogation clause. Derogations are subject to supervision by the international organ charged with their implementation.

Descent

A basis of characterizing or classifying human beings according to heritage, lineage, or parentage. It is a classification based on one's social origin and sometimes serves as the basis of human rights violations, such as discrimination or expulsion.

Descent is a term found in the un Convention on the Elimination of all Forms of Racial Discrimination. It is included within the meaning of "racial discrimination" as defined in article 1, paragraph 1, of that convention.

Desiderata
[Latin, lit.: things desired]

A Latin word used to describe things wished for or desired, such as world peace, a clean environment, and friendly international relations. It generally refers to things that one wants to achieve in law but that are not yet normative. Desirable goals as opposed to reality.

Désistement
[French, lit.: withdrawal]

A French term meaning to cease proceeding with a complaint* filed in a human rights forum (commission, tribunal, or court). This often happens when a friendly settlement between the petitioner and responding state has been agreed on and the petitioner does not wish to proceed forward to have the complaint* adjudicated. Somewhat like failing or refusing to prosecute a civil action. It results in the complaint* being dismissed.

DESUETUDE (OF TREATY* USE) (PRINCIPLE)

A French term of international law meaning the state of a treaty* as obsolescent and no longer binding, such as when compliance has become impossible for a long time or states have merely not in fact complied with it for a long time and without objection. Desuetude is a ground for terminating a treaty* without formally terminating or denouncing it when states have long acted as though it did not exist. See also *Rebus sic Stantibus*.

DETAINING POWER (LOAC)

In an international armed conflict, a detaining power refers to the state or non-state entity holding wounded, sick, and shipwrecked members of the armed forces, medical and religious personnel, civilian internees and prisoners of war, belonging to the adverse party, the "enemy."

DETENTION (OF PERSON)

A period of deprivation of personal liberty from the moment of arrest up until the time when the person concerned is either imprisoned as a final result of conviction for a criminal offense or released.

DEVELOPING COUNTRY/ STATE/NATION

A country/state/nation in which the average income is much lower than in the industrial world and in which the economy is based primarily on a few export crops, like coffee. Also referred to as "underdeveloped" country/state/nation.

The name implies that the country/state/nation is in the process of developing itself to raise the standard of living.

DEVELOPMENT (PROCESS/RIGHT TO)

Development is a complex, controversial, and difficult concept to define, both generally as a process and as a specific substantive human right.

As a process development has been defined in the 1986 UN Declaration on the Right to Development as meaning a "comprehensive economic, social, cultural, and political process, which aims at the constant improvement of all individuals in a society on the basis of their active, free, and meaningful participation in development, and in the fair distribution of the benefits resulting therefrom." As a human right, the "Right to Development" is a subjective human right of groups of individuals to have the freedom, cooperation, methods, and means to develop themselves economically, socially, culturally, and politically as a civil society, and to achieve the goals of human rights: the fullest possible development of the human personality of every individual in society. According to the 1986 Declaration, "the right to development is an inalienable human right by virtue of which every human person and all peoples are entitled to participate in, contribute to, and enjoy economic, social, cultural, and political development, in which all human rights and fundamental freedoms can be realized."

The claimed right to development was formerly classified as a "Third Generation" human right under that no longer used classification system. It is commonly referred to in the collective/group right sense. Its scope and content are very disputed and many do not even accept it as being a human right.

DICTATORSHIP

Government by a single person, junta, or other group that is not accountable, responsible, or responsive to the people or their elected representatives.

DICTUM (vs. HOLDING)
(aka OBITER DICTUM)
[Latin, lit.: a thing said]

A pronouncement of a judicial body, such as a court or tribunal, stated in the course of its decision, judgment, or ruling in a case, which pronouncement was not part of the holding of the case and not technically binding upon the parties to a subsequent case.

In a common law legal system the legal precedent that binds the parties to a lawsuit, and all subsequent parties under like legal issues, is set forth in the "holding" of that forum. The holding is that narrow particular ruling in that case. *Dictum* (pl. *dicta*) are not legally binding as precedent on subsequent cases, although sometimes other parties will refer to a *dictum* in legal briefs or pleadings to support their arguments in other similar cases. A *dictum* is a passing statement made by the judge or judges but not necessary for the ruling in that case. Judges in subsequent cases are not obliged to follow a *dictum*.

Also known by the fuller term *Obiter Dictum*.

DIFFERENTIAL TREATMENT
(OF INDIVIDUAL OR GROUP)

The government's treatment of individuals or groups in a different way from that of other individuals or groups and doing so on the basis of a particular characteristic of that individual or group, such as race ethnicity, religion, or color.

DIGNITY (HUMAN)

See Human Dignity, infra.

DISADVANTAGED GROUP
(OF PERSONS)

A social group such as women, refugees, or disabled poor persons who are most frequently subjected to discriminatory practices, whether intentional or systematic, and whose opportunities in education, employment, social advantages, or access to justice are still limited.

DISAPPEARANCE (OF PERSONS)
(aka ENFORCED DISAPPEARANCE)

The taking of a person into custody by or with the approval of authorities who hold the victim secretly and incommunicado and who deny that the victim is being held. Such act is a violation of human rights. In the Statute of the International Criminal Court it has been defined as an international crime in certain situations under the rubric of "enforced disappearances," wherein it is defined as "the arrest, detention, or abduction of persons by, or with the authorization, support, or acquiescence of a State or a political organization, followed by a refusal to acknowledge that deprivation of freedom or to give information on the fate or where-abouts of those persons, with the inten-tion of removing them from the pro-tection of the law for a prolonged period of time."

Discrimination (Principle)

A principle of human rights that is pri-marily used in two different senses, that is, two very different meanings within the context of human rights:

1. Generally, this term is most often used concerning the government or the private sector treatment of persons in dif-ferent ways based on some characteristic of the victim. It is treating people differ-ently because of their race, religion, eth-nic group, color, creed, political opinion, or other status or characteristic, where there is no reasonable and objective jus-tification for doing so.

A definition found in the UN *Conven-tion on Elimination of Racial Discrimi-nation* defines "racial discrimination" as ". . . any distinction, exclusion, restric-tion or preference based on race, etc. . . . which has the purpose or effect of nulli-fying or impairing the recognition, en-joyment or exercise, on an equal footing of human rights and fundamental free-dom." (CERD, article I).

There are many different types of dis-crimination and many laws that seek to prohibit discrimination that is unaccept-able as a matter of law. It is also true that not all types of discrimination are a vio-lation of human rights. Examples are distinctions between adults and chil-dren, citizens and noncitizens, men and women. Some distinctions may be made by society, but only so long as there exist, in human rights law terms, a "reasonable and objective justification" for such dis-

crimination; there must be no alternative measure that could be taken that would not be inconsistent with human dignity and human rights. All discrimination must comply with basic human rights.

2. Humanitarian Law: A second con-text involves a principle of humanitarian law, which states that combatants (sol-diers) must at all times distinguish, that is, "discriminate," between the civilian population and enemy combatants and between civilian objects and military ob-jectives, and accordingly to direct any armed attack only against enemy com-batants and military objectives. With re-spect to the humanitarian law principle of discrimination, soldiers may only attack enemy combatants. Failure to discrimi-nate between civilians and combatants makes an armed attack an "indiscrimi-nate attack" and a violation of humani-tarian law. This is called the "Principle of Discrimination" in the Law of Armed Conflict (LOAC). This is also called the principle of distinction. If, for example, a belligerent force were to bomb a town that had mostly civilians and only a few soldiers, and no measures were taken to only target and destroy the enemy sol-diers, this attack would most likely be considered an indiscriminate attack and a violation of humanitarian law.

Dissemination (Regular and loac)

In the LOAC, the obligation of states to make the principles of the law known to its armed forces and the civilian popula-tion by teaching them in military train-ing programs and encouraging the civil-ian population to study them. *See* GC I article 47.

In the regular sense dissemination refers to the broad communication of human rights norms and principles; rules, procedures, and studies intended to inform every member of society about their human rights; situations of human rights violations; and what can or is being done about such human rights problems. It is the process of human rights education by taking steps to communicate knowledge about human rights to everyone.

DISTINCTION (BETWEEN COMBATANTS AND CIVILIAN POPULATION) (PRINCIPLE) (AKA PRINCIPLE OF DISCRIMINATION)

See Discrimination, supra.

DIVERSITY

The literal definition of the word is "the condition of being different." In the context of human rights, it has come to mean having persons of differing race, color, gender, language, religion, ethnic background, or culture all coexisting in the same place or society in mutual acceptance, tolerance, and harmony.

Human beings differ from one another in many ways. Historically, many societies have tried to create a homogeneous society where everyone is the same. Experience and reality have proven that this does not work, because some group of people will end up trying to make all others like them, as though they themselves were the ultimate criteria of how human society should be. No person or group can claim to be that model. Modern societies tend to be democratic and egalitarian. There is however, very often a tension between persons who want all others to be more like the main population group, calling for unity and a common shared identity, and others who

want to allow everyone to be as different as they like, regardless of the impact on social harmony and cohesiveness. This can lead to one usually dominant group becoming intolerant and restricting the rights of "the other"; that is, those who are not like them. Under human rights principles, everyone has the right to be different and to express that difference so long as it is done within the law and consistent with human rights norms.

The key concept in diversity is that a variety of peoples maintain and develop their own unique and publicly accepted identity and characteristics. They also maintain an autonomous participation in the development of the common civilization. Diversity is the result of a society characterized by equality of all members and nondiscrimination in the enjoyment of all human rights. By its very nature, the concept of diversity presents challenges in creating a legal and social environment where different worldviews, religions, and lifestyles can *all* exercise their basic human rights.

Diversity is often the claimed goal of affirmative action programs, which seek to remedy certain areas of society where discrimination has led to the exclusion of certain groups. Such remedies to past discrimination can result in claims of reverse discrimination.

Where diversity leads to the fractionalization of society into too many opposing factions, it creates a situation where demagogues can rush in, demonize opposing groups, and create social crisis, which can lead to violence and result in human rights violations.

Human rights principles such as nondiscrimination, freedom of expression, and equality before the law in articles 2, 19, and 26 of the ICCPR, and treaties such as the Convention on Elimination of All

Forms of Racial Discrimination are examples of how human rights aim at protecting diversity among members of a society, such that everyone's human dignity is respected.

Doctrine

A principle or position, or the body of principles or assumptions, in a branch of knowledge or system of relief; a principle of law established through past decisions; a program of action of a state or group of states in diverse areas of international relations elevated to the rank of a political doctrine (e.g., Brezhnev Doctrine).

Document

An original or official paper relied upon usually in an administrative, political, or judicial matter as a basis, proof, or support of something or some contention. Occasionally, international human rights treaties* are known as "Documents" in certain contexts. The term also may be used interchangeably with the term "Instrument." An example is the Universal Declaration of Human Rights, which is a human rights document.

Domestic/Internal Affairs (vs. International Affairs)

Matters within a state that are not regulated by international law. Such matters are regulated solely by domestic (national or municipal) law, and no other state or international organization may interfere with them or exercise jurisdiction over them.

Domestic Law (aka Municipal Law) (vs. International Law)

Generally refers to the national law of a state applicable within the territory of a given state. "Domestic" and "Municipal" are terms used to distinguish the law from international law, which applies to states in the international arena. Note that it does not refer specifically to family law or to city government law.

Caveat: International human rights norms found in treaties* can be incorporated into or transformed into municipal/domestic law via constitutional law and thus become binding within a state or national legal system as municipal/domestic law.

Domestic Remedy (vs. International Remedy)

A legal or administrative remedy or procedure provided within a national administrative or legal system, which, if resorted to, provides real protection of a person's human rights. This is contrasted with international remedies. Domestic means within domestic or municipal law. States are generally obligated in human rights treaties* to provide a domestic remedy to implement their treaty* obligations in the state system if it does not already so provide. Failure to provide a domestic remedy will itself be a violation of a treaty* obligation under most human rights treaties*.

Double/Dual Criminality (Extradition) (Principle)

A legal principle of extradition by which a state will not allow for the extradition of a requested person to face criminal charges in a requesting state, unless the crime for which the person will be tried is a crime in both the requesting state and the requested state. A state will only extradite in situations where its own law would have permitted it to prosecute the person for the very same crime under its domestic criminal law. Sometimes also referred to as the principle of double criminality.

DOUBLE/DUAL STANDARD

The application by a state of a certain standard of conduct as to human rights by one state, but not applying the same standard to other states for committing the very same acts constituting human rights violations. Not applying the same human rights standards (norms) the same way to everybody or every state. It can also mean applying a human rights standard to other states but not to your own state for committing the very same acts constituting human rights violations

The double standard approach to honoring human rights norms defeats the purpose of the entire movement worldwide. When the world was compelled to deal with the atrocities of World War II, the concept was that there were human rights that were *basic* to the dignity of all human beings, and that governments must be made to recognize that in spite of whatever political or economic reasons might compel them otherwise.

If a state practices a double standard in, for example, its trade negotiations with other countries, allowing trade with more lucrative markets with bad human rights records, but condemning smaller countries for the same kinds of abuses, it is hypocritical. Understandably, the government of a state tries to balance its decisions in many arenas, such as economically, politically, and socially. The bottom line of human rights law, however, is for fairness and equity to all people; the other considerations must take a back seat to this principle if the establishment of human rights in the world is to work. In the preceding scenario, that state may decide to trade with *all* countries, contingent on human rights records; that would be a fair and equitable approach.

More difficult for states than even this scenario is the temptation to apply a double standard where one's *own* human rights record is concerned. If a state condemns the violations of another state, yet commits the same kind of violation, the temptation is to excuse its own behavior because of "extenuating circumstances."

DOUBLE JEOPARDY (PRINCIPLE OF CRIMINAL LAW)

The generally accepted principle of criminal law that says that a person may not be convicted for the same criminal offense twice. This principle is expressed in the Latin term *Ne Bis in Idem*.

DRAFT CODE OF CRIMES (AGAINST THE PEACE AND SECURITY OF MANKIND) (UN 1996)

See Code of Crimes against the Peace and Security of Mankind, supra.

DRAFT CONVENTION

The text of a treaty* written up as a model to be used in a process aimed at creating a binding legal treaty*. Often an NGO or a certain office of an IGO, or sometimes a state will draft a text of a treaty* to serve as a starting point for the states that will negotiate the text of a treaty*. A draft convention is not legally binding. It is only a starting point of a treaty* process. For a treaty* to become binding, it must be fully negotiated, adopted by vote, be signed and ratified* by states, and enter into force before it creates legal obligations.

DRAFT TEXT

A text of an international instrument prepared to be used as a starting point as a suggested and proposed, acceptable text for states to use in negotiating a human rights treaty* or declaration. It is sometimes prepared by an organ of an international intergovernmental organization, by a state, or by an NGO. A draft text is not legally binding until it is fully negotiated, adopted, open for signature, ratified*, and entered into force.

DRITTWIRKUNG (EFFECT OF NORMATIVE OBLIGATION) (AKA HORIZONTAL EFFECT/ HORIZONTALITY/THIRD-PARTY EFFECT)
[German, lit.: third-party effect]

A German word concerning the so-called third-party or horizontal effect of human rights obligations. A theory of the nature of human rights obligations that says two different things concerning the effects of the obligation.

First, the obligation is binding not only upon the states (a vertical obligation) and the rights existing between states and individuals, but also between individuals. Therefore, individuals can complain of human rights violations committed by other individuals (a horizontal effect).

Second, the state is responsible not only for seeing that it does not commit any violations itself, but it also has the obligation to take steps (such as by enacting legislation or passing regulations to protect in the area of private acts) to assure that private individuals do not commit acts harmful to the human rights of others.

The full term is actually *Drittwirkung der Grundrechte*.

DROIT D'INGERENCE
[French, lit.: right of intervention]

A claimed international law right of the international community and possibly of individual states to intervene in the domestic affairs of states wherein serious and systematic human rights violations are occurring, and the state cannot or is unwilling to stop them. This is related to the concept of humanitarian intervention.

Talk of a "right of intervention" has naturally alarmed many people, especially those in the developing world who see it as another guise of the old imperialism and an invitation to unilateral intervention by major powers into developing countries. The right to intervention arises in another era than the past one of colonial-style invasions. Humanitarian intervention will never be the action of a single country or of a national army playing policeman to the world, as the U.S. did in Latin America or France did in Africa. Humanitarian intervention should be carried out by an impartial, multinational force acting under the authority of international organizations and controlled by them.

It was said by some who advocated such a right that the international community needed to establish a forward-looking right of the world community to actively interfere in the affairs of sovereign nations to prevent an explosion of human rights violations.

DROP/REJECT A COMMUNICATION

The procedure of an international judicial or quasi-judicial forum whereby it refuses to handle a complaint* alleging human rights violations, filed/lodged with that forum for resolution. Communication is the same as complaint*. If the communication does not meet the legal criteria for admissibility to be handled by the forum, it may reject the communication. Sometimes complaints* are rejected even before determinations of admissibility due to defects in the complaint* such as an anonymous filing.

In the UN Commission on Human Rights, it refers to the option of the Working Group on Communications to decide to take no further action on a communication presented under the 1503 Procedure.

DUAL CRIMINALITY (EXTRADITION) (PRINCIPLE)

See Double/Dual Criminality, supra.

DUALIST LEGAL SYSTEM (VS. MONIST)

A philosophy that international law is superior to municipal law in international disputes, and municipal law is superior to international law in municipal/domestic disputes. It sets up law as existing in two separate systems: domestic and international. Compare to Monism/Monist Legal System, infra.

DUAL STANDARD

See Double/Dual Standard, supra

DUE PROCESS (OF LAW)

A course of formal proceedings (as legal proceedings) carried out regularly and in accordance with established rules and principles—also called "procedural due process."

A judicial requirement that enacted laws may not contain provisions that result in the unfair, arbitrary, or unreasonable treatment of an individual—also called "substantive due process."

Procedural due process is the one most referred to in the field of human rights and generally means fairness or fundamental fairness for defendants in criminal actions or for all parties in a civil action. Examples include the right to a lawyer, the right to notice of a hearing date, the right to adequate time to prepare a defense, the right to examine witnesses, and the right to be heard in a proceeding by an independent and impartial tribunal. *See* Appendix B, ICCPR, article 14.

DURBAN DECLARATION AND PROGRAMME OF ACTION (UN 2001)

The final document issued at the World Conference against Racism, Xenophobia and Related Intolerances in 2001, negotiated and arrived at by the states attending the conference. It sets out the view of the international community about human rights as applied to the issues of racism, xenophobia, and the duty of states and nonstate actors regarding such human rights.

DURESS

Generally, the state of mind of a person acting under external coercion by being compelled by another person under threat of force or use of force or other serious adverse consequences directed against him or someone close to him, such as a spouse, child, or relative, to engage in acts that the threatened person would not otherwise engage in, such as a war crime.

As per the LOAC, a "plea of duress" is sometimes raised as a defense to a charge of war crimes when the accused asserts that he acted as he did because of a threat against him if he refused to carry out an order. Duress is also known as "coercion." Example: The threat to a soldier of being killed if he does not carry out a military superior's unlawful command to kill civilians. It is not, however, the same as "Superior Orders" (*see* infra), which is purely a defense for carrying out the orders of a military superior officer.

Duress is seldom a complete defense to criminal responsibility; however, it may constitute a factor in mitigation of a sentence. Generally, the acts/threats giving rise to duress must be imminent, real, and inevitable, and the coerced conduct must not have produced greater harm than what could have been suffered for the failure to act and must not have resulted in death.

DUTY (VS. RIGHT) (CLAUSE)

The obligation owed by individuals and groups to the community (state), local society, family, and other individuals to act in a way that promotes the interests of the totality of the social and political context in which one lives and acts. Duties are obligatory tasks, conduct, service, or functions that arise from one's position as a citizen or legal resident of a society. To every human right there is an express or implicit correlative human duty owed. In theory everyone cannot fully enjoy their human rights unless everyone fulfills their duties.

Some human rights instruments have a "duty clause" setting forth the duties of citizens and others to their society. *See* UDHR, article 29.1; ACHPR, articles 27–29.

For example, the right to marry and found a family (have children) carries with it the correlative duty to support one's spouse and one's children. Paying taxes and obeying the criminal laws are also examples of typical duties.

DUTY-HOLDER

The person, group, organization, or political entity such as a state, which hold the particular duties that are correlative to a particular human right. Every human right has correlative duties, and those duties are born by someone, particularly the state, which is in theory supposed to be the ultimate protector of human rights.

As an example, the right to have children, to "found a family," makes the parent a duty-holder with respect to the support, nurture, protection, and provision for a child he or she brings into the world. The parent would be the duty-holder. If, for example, the parents were killed and there were no other relatives, the state would become a duty-holder with respect to the child to see that the child found the level of support needed for the child's own human rights to be realized.

DUTY TO PROSECUTE (PRINCIPLE)

A principle of international criminal law that there is an affirmative duty of a state to seek, arrest, and prosecute those who have committed international crimes. It also relates to the principle of *aut dedere aut judicare/punire*, which means that where an accused international criminal is found in a state, and a request is made for the accused to be extradited to another state to be prosecuted, the requested state has an affirmative legal obligation either to hand over the accused to the requesting state, or to itself arrest and prosecute the accused.

DYNAMIC INTERPRETATION (OF TREATY*)

A judicial doctrine of the human rights system of the Council of Europe that allows for the interpretation of the European Convention of Human Rights in a way that reflects the present historical context. Under this doctrine, the ECHR must be interpreted in accordance with present-day conditions in law and society, not with past conditions. This requires the European Court of Human Rights, the main supervising organ of the ECHR, to examine the laws and practices of the respective states members of the Council of Europe, to determine any present common values and domestic norms, and determine if there is a European consensus on a particular issue, such as cloning, the age of consent for sexual acts between persons of the same sex, or the rights of children born out of wedlock.

Such an interpretation must be in an objective and dynamic manner, taking into account social conditions and developments, but not going so far as to constitute a revision of the treaty text. Interpretation must respect the text of the treaty.

Early Action (Prevention)

Engaging in action to prevent conditions from arising or deteriorating to the point where human rights violations will occur. Too often human rights violations occur with little or no attempt by government to stop them. The international community has been seeking to improve prevention of human rights atrocities, massacres, and genocides by engaging in early action, such as injecting human rights monitors or an international civil presence at the places where problems may occur. It is an interventionist concept but comes from a realization that it is much more costly and problematic to try to remedy such horrors after the fact than to deter them from happening in the first place.

Early Warning Mechanisms / Procedures / Methods

Mechanisms, procedures, and methods for identifying and alerting the appropriate authorities of the possible or imminent outbreak of conditions that may give rise to human rights violations. They are related to the concept and process of early action. Field presences and human rights monitors are examples.

ECHR

Abbreviation for the European Convention on Human Rights, a human rights instrument of the Council of Europe adopted in 1950.

Economic (Human) Rights

A category of human rights whose purpose is to assure that human beings have the ability to obtain and maintain a minimum decent standard of living consistent with human dignity. The particular rights include the right to food, health care, social security, work, and leisure and the right to form trade unions.

Economic rights are considered programmatic or progressive rights.

ECOSOC (UN)

Acronym for the Economic (ECO) and Social (SOC) Council of the United Nations, an organ under which one finds the UN Commission on Human Rights and its Subcommission on Promotion and Protection of Human Rights, where most UN activity in the field of human rights takes place.

EDUCATION (HUMAN RIGHTS)

Human rights education (HRE) refers to education at all age, status, and occupation appropriate levels, both formal and informal, academic and nonacademic, aimed at communicating to all society the knowledge of human rights and calling for individual and collective action aimed at respect for, and protection of, human rights.

Many other definitions have been proposed. One well-known definition is that HRE is all learning that develops the knowledge, skills, and values of human rights. Some have defined education as the entire process of social life by means of which individuals and social groups learn to develop consciously within, and for the benefit of the national and international community, the whole of their personal capacities, attitudes, aptitudes, and knowledge.

For the purposes of the UN Decade for Human Rights Education, the term human rights education shall be defined as training, dissemination, and information efforts aimed at the building of a universal culture of human rights through the imparting of knowledge and skills, and the molding of attitudes directed to:

(a) The strengthening of respect for human rights and fundamental freedoms;

(b) The full development of the human personality and the sense of its dignity;

(c) The promotion of understanding, tolerance, gender equality and friendship among all nations, indigenous peoples and racial, national, ethnic, religious and linguistic groups;

(d) The enabling of all persons to participate effectively in a free society;

(e) The furtherance of the activities of the United Nations for the maintenance of peace.

There are conceptually two types of HRE: education *in* human rights and education *for* human rights. Education in human rights is the imparting of cognitive knowledge of human rights so that one knows what his rights are and how to defend his full exercise. Education *for* human rights refers to understanding and embracing the principles of human dignity and equality and the commitment to respect and protect the rights of all people, and to have the organs and institutions of society that are engaged in formal or informal education for human rights to reflect in reality and practice those very same human rights. Education for human rights is more about how we act rather than what we know.

EFFECTIVE CONTROL / COMMAND AND CONTROL (COMMAND RESPONSIBILITY)

An element of proof to establish the criminal responsibility of military commanders for the criminal acts of their subordinates under the doctrine of command responsibility.

Military commanders can become criminally responsible for the acts of their subordinates, generally, if it is proven that a superior-subordinate relationship existed, that the subordinates committed the criminal acts, and that the commander knew or should have known that the subordinates were committing or about to commit the alleged acts, and the commander failed to take necessary and reasonable measures to prevent or punish such acts.

Effective control may be defined as holding that the military commander had the actual ability to control his subordinates and to prevent their criminal acts, or to punish the subordinates accused of having committed them. Article 28 of the Rome ICC Statute uses the expression a commander's "effective command and control."

EFFECTIVE INVESTIGATION

A thorough, complete, independent, impartial, and technically competent investigation by the government of the facts and circumstances of an incident alleged to involve human rights violations. It is made for the purpose of gathering evidence to be used to determine whether violations have occurred and who and where the perpetrators and other responsible parties are, and then submitting the evidence to the appropriate governmental authorities for them to take appropriate action to remedy the violation and assure against its recurrence.

EFFECTIVENESS (PRINCIPLE OF INTERPRETATION)

A general principle of international law that is usually invoked in the interpretation and application of a norm. This principle states that a treaty* norm should be interpreted and applied in such a way as to give maximum effect to the treaty* and thus that best achieves the treaty's* object and purpose. Expressed in Latin as *ut res magis valeat quam pereat*, which means "so that the thing may be more effective, rather than be wasted/lost."

EFFECTIVE REMEDY

A legal or administrative remedy capable of producing the result for which it was designed, to compel the government to comply, not presenting a danger to those who invoke it, and to be applied impartially. A state obligation in most human rights treaties to implement treaty* obligations at the national level by establishing domestic remedies for violations. These remedies must also be "effective" remedies in that they are both accessible and capable of accomplishing the purpose of assuring compliance with the norms. It means a domestic remedy that really works. It can be either a legal or administrative remedy. An "effective remedy clause" in a treaty* is one that sets forth this obligation. *See* ICCPR article 2.3(a).

EIF (TREATY* INSTRUMENT)

Abbreviation for "Enter/Entry into Force" (*see* infra).

ELECTION MONITORING/ OBSERVANCE

Provision of the presence of neutral persons or groups from outside a state to be present in a state undergoing an election process in order to gather information on the conduct of the election and to observe the process so as to assure that it is a "free and fair election," i.e., an election in which voters were in fact free to vote by secret ballot according to their own wishes and there was no artificial manipulation of the outcome of the voting. This is a type of fact-finding process. The goal is to assure democratic participation by the exercise of the human right to vote and to assess the legitimacy of the government as the expression of the will of the people.

ELEMENTS OF CRIME

The various subjective and objective factors, which, if proven beyond a reasonable doubt, would constitute the commission of a crime and would lead to a finding of guilty in a criminal forum.

Usually, these are identified under the headings of the *Mens Rea*, the mental element (e.g., intentional, reckless) and the *Actus Reus*, the act or omission (e.g., beating, killing). Different crimes have different elements.

EMERGENCY REPORTS

A description of a type of report, which is requested by a treaty* supervising body such as the UN Human Rights Committee outside the normal reporting period provided in the treaty.

Normally, most human rights treaties* require that states parties to a treaty* submit reports of their compliance with the treaty* and do so at certain specified time intervals. These are sometimes referred to as periodic reports. Emergency reports can in some treaty-based regimes be requested by a supervising body such as the HRC when recent or current events indicate that the enjoyment of the rights in the treaty have been seriously, negatively affected.

EMERGING GLOBAL MORAL CULTURE

Description of the process of international development of a global and regional international morality, which is gradually becoming part of the culture of all states of the world. This global moral culture is articulated primarily in international human rights norms, transforming moral principles into binding legal norms so as to make them obligatory upon governments. International human rights are a canon of moral principles made binding in international law for the protection of individuals and preservation of global and regional peace and order.

The international community believes

that development of such culture, first proclaimed in the UN Charter and UDHR, is required by the increasing globalization and emergence of a global village of peoples who are all equal. The moral culture is ultimately based and grounded in the inherent human dignity of each individual human being.

EMERGING NORM (OF INTERNATIONAL LAW)

A new consistent pattern and practice of states actions in the international arena, with an apparent and increasing sense of states that the practice is becoming legally binding in International Law, as evidence of *opinio juris generalis*, possibly eventually ripening into a norm of customary international law. In the late 1990s one spoke of an emerging norm of humanitarian intervention in relation to Kosovo. This was not accepted by all states.

Whether a particular practice constitutes an emerging norm must be judged under the principles of customary public international law. One often uses the description that a norm "ripens" or "crystalizes" into a new legal norm. An emerging norm is not the same as an accepted established norm. An emerging norm is a *lex ferenda* and not yet a *lex lata*. Whether a state practice is even an emerging norm is a legal question, not political or ideological.

EMPOWER/EMPOWERMENT

The process of bestowing or imparting power on someone or making him/her more powerful for a particular end. The activation and actualization of individuals by teaching them in human rights, particularly in what their own human rights are and how to exercise and defend them. Imparting knowledge about human rights empowers individuals regardless of their occupation or level of education. Human rights education is a tool to empower human beings concerning the legal protection of their human dignity and that of the rest of humankind.

ENEMY COMBATANT (U.S.)

Used particularly by the U.S. government to describe a person who, in its opinion, does not have the legal right to engage in armed conflict covered by the LOAC but who does so. It is a U.S. determination that the individual does not have or has lost the *jus ad bellum*, the international legal right to wage war, to legally engage in armed conflict. This distinction is important because if a person does not have the international legal right to engage in combat, the *jus ad bellum*, he can be treated as a common criminal and needs to be accorded only such rights as national law accords a criminal.

In the LOAC the legal protections that arise to combatants include the right to lawfully engage in harmful, deadly, and destructive hostile activities, which would otherwise be the commission of common crimes under national law. If captured, a lawful combatant normally has all the rights of a POW status under Geneva and Hague law. If the combatant is found to have lacked the legal status as having the *jus ad bellum*, that person is deprived of the much of the protection of the LOAC accorded to prisoners of war and can be prosecuted for all his belligerent acts. However, even if a person is an illegal combatant, he or she still retains all his or her internationally recognized and applicable human rights plus a mini-

mum core of rights under the LOAC. Actually, under the LOAC persons found in the context of an armed conflict can only be either civilians or combatants. Legally speaking, if one is not a combatant, one is a civilian. Therefore, a person designated as an "enemy combatant" would legally be deemed a civilian and entitled to the LOAC protection of civilians, e.g., under GC IV, although he could be prosecuted for wrongful acts committed.

Under the U.S. position on enemy combatants, as soon as the U.S. designates a person as an enemy combatant, that person has no legal rights as a POW, has no right to due process and access to courts to determine his legal status, has no right to an attorney, and can be held indefinitely at the whim of the president.

The U.S. use of this term comes from a Supreme Court case decision (*Ex Parte Quirin*) from the Second World War, prior to much of the norms of LOAC and international human rights law. This term/designation does not exist is not accepted in the LOAC and is inconsistent with the LOAC in its legal implications for persons captured by the U.S. It is not accepted and strongly contested by the international legal community.

Under international law it is not the chief executive but the courts who have ultimate say in whether one is or is not an unlawful combatant and thus not entitled to POW legal status and protection. Normally under the LOAC, if there is any doubt as to the legal status of a combatant, article 5 of the Third Geneva Conventions of 1949 (on POWs) and customary international law would require the state to allow the person involved access to a court or tribunal to have his status determined in a court of law. International human rights law is totally against any person being deemed stripped of any basic due process rights, legal personality, or access to courts to determine the legality of his detention. Human rights are inalienable.

In the present state of the LOAC and international human rights law basically only spies, saboteurs, mercenaries, and those who do not meet the treaty definition of "combatant" (*see* GC III, article 4), and who engage in armed conflict, can possibly be declared and designated as unlawful combatants. Everyone else is a civilian. *See also* Illegal Combatant/Unlawful Combatant/Unprivileged Belligerent.

ENFORCED DISAPPEARANCE (OF PERSONS)

See Disappearance.

ENJOYMENT OF HUMAN RIGHTS

The actual, real, and full ability of an individual to act legally in a manner consistent with one's human rights. It is the transformation from human rights theory to reality. Human rights can be declared by a state and even put into law or the constitution and still not be able to be enjoyed in fact. Having a right and enjoying a right are not the same thing. There should be no legal or social or any other obstacle to one enjoying one's human rights.

ENSLAVEMENT

The destruction of the juridical personality of a person or persons as a result of exercising any or all of the powers of ownership over them. Taking control of a person as though he were an item of property and using him as one pleases.

This is a violation of the human rights of the person or persons so enslaved. It violates several individual rights, such as individual liberty and security of person, the right to juridical personality, equality before the law, inhuman treatment, and the prohibition of slavery.

ENSURE HUMAN RIGHTS (OBLIGATIONS)

One of four obligations of states as to the implementation of human rights. The other three are obligations to fulfill, to protect, and to respect.

An expression found in some human rights treaties* that describes the nature of the states parties' obligations regarding respect for and realization of the human rights norms in the treaty*. It means to render sure, certain, or safe, and to guarantee by a pledge or declaration. The obligation to ensure requires that states do all they can to see that all other states, organizations, and individuals act in a way as to allow full enjoyment of human rights.

Usually found following the preamble of a treaty*. In the context of the GCs of 1949 and P I, the phrase "ensure respect" found in article 1 of those instruments means that each state party will see to it that other states parties, and indeed all others, individuals and groups, will respect these humanitarian norms as well.

ENTER/ENTRY INTO FORCE (EIF) (TREATY* INSTRUMENT)

The process, point of time, etc., whereby a treaty* becomes operative and fully binding upon the contracting state parties who have ratified* it. Usually "Entry into Force," abbreviated EIF, happens pursuant to a specific treaty* provision upon the deposit of a certain number of state ratifications*. When the appropriate number of ratification* instruments are deposited, the treaty* "enters into force." There are usually two identifying dates to a treaty* citation: (1) date of adoption and (2) date of entry into force. Example: ICCPR was adopted in 1966; EIF was in 1976.

Entitlement

A claim upon the state to have the means to exercise and protect a right. Some definitions of human rights are based on the concept of entitlement. One definition states that a human right is a claim or entitlement of a person against a state to do something or refrain from doing something to the individual to protect human dignity. A human right may be seen as a claim upon the state to have the means to exercise one's human rights as set forth in all the various human rights instruments.

The proposition that human rights are not a gift or concession or a privilege granted by the state is indisputable. Entitlement comes from the fact that human dignity is inherent in human beings, and the rights that flow from that dignity are attributes of the human personality. Thus, this entitlement to the means to exercise and defend those rights is entirely justified.

Equality (Principle)

A general principle of elementary justice applicable to all human rights, meaning that whatever level may be reached in the realization of those rights in a particular state, they should apply to every individual residing in the state without discrimination of any kind.

The principle of equal dignity and worth of every individual in society, which must be reflected and applied in law and public policy, so that all persons are treated equally except where reasonable and objective legal bases exist for different treatment (e.g., aliens, children, prisoners). Equality is one of the key principles enshrined in all human rights instruments.

See UDHR article 7, ICCPR article 26.

Equality before the Law

The right of an individual to equal treatment in the administration or application of the law by law enforcement authorities and by the ordinary courts of the land.

Equality of Arms (French: *Égalité d'Armes*) (Principle)

A principle of human rights that says that in legal proceedings, particularly criminal proceedings, individuals have a procedural human right to obtain what they need to have a fair hearing vis-à-vis the state, such as documentary evidence and access to witnesses, so that each party has in fact the opportunity to fully and fairly present its case and neither has a substantially unfair advantage over the other. It is related to the notion of procedural due process of law.

Equitable Geographical Distribution/Representation (of Members)

Selecting persons to be members of UN human rights bodies from persons who represent the different continents of the world so that all type of states from all types of political and social systems are represented. Human rights bodies, such as the UN Commission on Human Rights, which deal with human rights situations from all over the world, are required to elect members so that all areas and cultures of the world are represented.

Equitable geographical representation is the required goal of the selection process so that the body represents the broadest scope of human particularities.

Equity Feminism (vs. Gender Feminism)

A term used by women's rights activists to describe the struggle for basic equality between men and women in society and for the right to prove their worth on an equal playing field.

Human rights theory and law calls for equality between men and women and nondiscrimination between men and women in the enjoyment of all human rights. The reality in the world is that such equality and nondiscrimination does not yet exist in many societies. Equity feminism seeks to remove the historical and legal barriers that have kept the playing field in employment (equal pay for equal work), education, property ownership, voting, and political power, uneven for women.

Also known as first wave or mainstream feminism.

Erge Omnes (Obligations)
[Latin, lit.: toward everyone/all]

A right (*jus*) or obligation (*obligatio*); "*erge omnes*" is an absolute right or obligation binding upon all states, the violation of which is of rightful concern to all states. It is the right or obligation that is said to exist toward the whole international community as a community

because it affects the whole community so detrimentally, e.g., genocide, crimes against humanity.

Estoppel (Principle)

An Anglo-Saxon legal principle allowing for self-exclusion from acquiescence during probative proceedings as a result of one's statements used in international jurisdiction in accordance with the rule of "Bona Fides." Usually an argument/issue raised in a court case by a party who is trying to bring to the forum's attention that the opposing party previously said or did something that contradicts what it is saying at the present time. A state may not subsequently contradict the veracity of statements made previously by an authorized state representative.

Ethics

A system of moral principles by which one judges the rightness or wrongness of an act in a philosophical sense. It is the relation of values to human conduct. A branch of philosophy. Ethics does not necessarily tell us whether an act is legal or not, just whether it is morally permissible or not. Ethics is not, strictly speaking, about what is legally right, but only what is morally right.

Human rights are legal rights that create legal obligations with which states and some other persons must comply. They tell us what must be done or not done in relation to the individual.

Ethnic (Minority)

Of or relating to large groups of people classed according to common racial, national, tribal, religious, linguistic, or cultural origins. This definition is not universally accepted. Various definitions of this word exist.

ETHNIC CLEANSING

A term first coined in the context of the Bosnian conflict in the early 1990s to signify the forcible removal by fear or threat or actual physical removal or destruction of an ethnic group from a specified territory so as to render the territory ethnically homogeneous. It is one group's removal of all members of all other ethnic groups.

ETHNOCENTRIC/ETHNOCENTRISM

The belief that one's ethnic group is superior to all others and that the interests of other groups are secondary to the interests of one's own group.

EUROPEAN CONVENTION ON HUMAN RIGHTS (COUNCIL OF EUROPE 1950) (AKA EUROPEAN CONVENTION)

Often also referred to as the European Convention, this refers to the Convention for the Protection of Human Rights and Fundamental Freedoms, adopted in Rome in 1950 by the Council of Europe, a regional IGO of most west European and now also many central and east European states. It is a regional human rights treaty and is supervised within the Council of Europe by the European Court of Human Rights. Formerly there was a European Commission on Human Rights as well as the court, but this was removed under Protocol II, which reorganized the whole ECHR system. *See* Appendix C.

Ex Aequo et Bono (JURISDICTION/COMPETENCE)
[Latin, lit.: from the fair and the good]

A court/tribunal's competence/jurisdiction to adjudicate cases on the basis of what is right and fair, i.e., equitable, as opposed to deciding on the basis of strict and express application of specific legal norms. The International Court of Justice under article 38 of the court's statute can make decisions on an *ex aequo et bono* basis if the parties to the case so allow.

EXAMINATION (OF A COMPLAINT*)

The process of judicial or quasi-judicial scrutiny of a formal written complaint after it has been determined to be admissible. In human rights complaint* systems, such as the European Court of Human Rights, written complaints are first submitted to the registrar of the court. If the court finds the complaint to be receivable, as containing all the proper matters and complying with clerical formalities, it will then make a determination as to whether the complaint is admissible; whether, for example, all domestic remedies have been exhausted; whether it was filed within the specified time period after exhaustion; and whether it states a *prima facie* case as to time, place, and state involved in the alleged violation. If the complaint is determined to be admissible, the forum can proceed to examine the case as to the facts and the law, and make a decision on the merits of the case or seek a friendly settlement.

EXCEPTIONAL DILIGENCE

An affirmative standard applicable to state organs, which is a higher than the

usual and normal standard, to do everything in their power to expedite resolution of a proceeding or matter because of
a certain urgency, such as a matter relating to abandoned or mistreated children
or HIV patients. This is a standard seeking to optimally protect human rights in
exceptional circumstances.

EXCEPTIONALISM

The attitude of a state that certain international human rights standards do not
apply to that country or a certain actions
of the state, such as the international military peacekeeping. It is the attitude of a
state that it should be recognized as enjoying a special exception or exemption
to the applicability of certain human
rights/humanitarian law norms because
of a unique set of circumstances.

This term is seen particularly in the
area of armed conflicts or peacekeeping
and is usually used to describe the attitude and actions of the United States of
America in the context of the International Community as regards the applicability of international human rights and
criminal law, as to war crimes, genocide,
crimes against humanity, and aggression.
This attitude of the U.S. came into play
most conspicuously and controversially
as to whether the U.S. would ratify the
Statute of the International Criminal
Court. That statute was adopted in 1998
with the U.S. voting against its adoption.
The U.S. has, since its adoption, stated
that the U.S. would ratify the ICC statute
only if official U.S. government acts and
the actions of U.S. military personnel
would be immune from prosecution by
the ICC. The U.S. felt that it should enjoy such immunity because of the extent

of its military personnel engaged in peacekeeping and to avoid "politically motivated prosecutions." The U.S. eventually
signed the ICC statute then shortly thereafter tried to "unsign" it. It has not ratified it and has stated it has no intent to
ratify.

An attitude of exceptionalism is inconsistent with the international law principles of rule of law, accountability, and
the equality of states.

EXCESSIVE FORCE
(VS. REASONABLE FORCE)

The use of more physical force than is
permitted by law, or more than is reasonable under the circumstances, by government agents.

Excessive force is the use of force to a
level that violates human rights norms. It
is force that cannot be justified by law,
giving the victim a right to make a claim
against the government for damages or
injuries suffered. It is force that crosses
the line from reasonable and lawful use.

It could theoretically also be used in
reference to government acts against the
property of a person. It is usually committed by law enforcement agents, especially the police, but could be applied
to other government agencies. It most
often occurs in the attempt to apprehend
and search for a person sought for by law
enforcement.

Human rights violations are the use of
power by government in a manner exceeding its lawful powers. It is an abuse
of power. When excessive force is used
against a human being, it violates his dignity and hence his human rights, engaging the responsibility of state under both
national and likely international law.

The use of excessive force could, depending upon the circumstances, motives, and degree of force used, violate, for example, ICCPR, article 7 as to torture, cruel, and inhuman treatment or punishment; or if the person dies, article 6, the right to life. It may, if torture occurs, constitute a violation of the Convention against Torture, articles 1, 2, and 4.

The beating of Rodney King in the mid 1990s in Los Angeles was considered a classic example of the use of excessive force. Another example, which many claimed was excessive force, was the armed force used by the NATO allies in the bombing of Yugoslavia in 1999. This claim was based on the belief that the force used by NATO in bombing attacks was more than was necessary to get the Yugoslav government to cease its alleged atrocities and ethnic cleansing in Kosovo.

Whether any use of force is excessive is often a hotly debated issue, with government usually defending its reasonableness. Reasonableness in such situations brings into play the overarching international law principle of proportionality. All use of force must be proportional to the ends sought in a way that most minimizes damage and injury to humans and their property.

EXCLUSION/EXCLUSIVE (AKA
NONINCLUSION/INCLUSIVE)
(VS. INCLUSION/INCLUSIVE,
NONEXCLUSION/EXCLUSIVE)

That which leaves out and does not accept everyone without exception, and does not include them as an equal part of a society, or as covered by a law, or as beneficiaries of a program or project or system, such as education. It is keeping them out of something they are entitled to be included in and is a discriminatory act that violates the principle of equality. The opposite is inclusive. Human rights requires, with certain exceptions, the inclusion of all human beings in all parts of society, not exclusion.

The nondiscrimination and equality provisions of international human rights instruments are legal measures aimed at preventing exclusion. *See* ICCPR, articles 2.1 and 26.

EXECUTIVE AGREEMENT (EA) (U.S.)

A political instrument of agreement between the president of the United Sates and another state. A formal agreement entered into by the president as head of state with another country's leader. These instruments look much like a treaty but are arguably not subject to the treaty requirement of the Constitution, article II, section 2 (2/3 majority Senate vote). Such agreements normally cover matters not deemed to be the normal subject of treaties.

The president can enter into executive agreements with other countries that affect the human rights of Americans in foreign countries or of aliens in the United States. Access to the courts, ownership of property, criminal jurisdiction, and due process rights are all examples. A Status of Forces agreement would be an example of an executive agreement that could affect not only people in the military, but also people harmed by them. Executive agreements cannot violate human rights norms. They cannot change existing U.S. domestic law, but must operate within the bounds of that law.

The president must act consistent with

U.S. international human rights obligations to the extent that those obligations are consistent with the Constitution.

EXECUTIVE ORDER (EO)(U.S.)

In the context of U.S. law, this refers to a formal legal statement issued by the president of the United States concerning the operation of the executive branch of the government. Such orders may concern international law, such as international human rights law and humanitarian law and U.S. policy regarding human rights. Such instruments have been issued and used by U.S. presidents in relation to the U.S. government's human rights policy and practice.

These orders sound like laws but are not enacted by Congress. Their historical source, scope, and legal effect have been rather controversial. Executive orders may in no case violate the U.S. Constitution. They are binding, if at all, only on the executive branch of the federal government, as they are issued by the president in his or her capacity as the chief executive of the United States.

EX GRATIA PAYMENT/COMPENSATION

Payments or compensation that a state agrees to pay to a person or group to resolve and settle an alleged violation of human rights in a case filed before an international forum. It is a payment offered by the state without an admission of responsibility or stipulation as to a violation. It is given in good faith to put the matter to rest.

EXHAUSTION OF DOMESTIC REMEDIES (PRINCIPLE)

A general principle of international law that requires that a person who wishes to make a complaint* against a state under international law must first seek recourse to all available and effective domestic remedies before resorting to an international judicial or quasi-judicial forum, such as human rights commissions or courts. There are some exceptions under treaty* law and custom or general principles to the exhaustion requirements, such as when the recourse is fruitless or when one is prevented from using it by state force.

This means that normally one has to take one's case alleging a state violation all the way to that state's highest court before filing a complaint* in the international forum. Failure to exhaust domestic remedies is a ground for inadmissibility of the complaint*.

EX OFFICIO
[Latin, lit.: from official duty]

A Latin phrase that means to do something on the basis of it being part of the functions/duties of one's office. It may also refer to a person assuming a certain position or membership in an organ on the basis of his being from a certain office. Example: The heads of European states are ex officio members of the Council of Europe's Committee of Ministers. The United States's president is ex officio commander in chief of the U.S. military.

EXPEL/EXPULSION (OF ALIEN FROM STATE)

The forcible removable or causing to flee of an alien from a country back to the country from which he came, to the nearest contiguous state, or to one of similar racial, ethnic, or religious composition; similar to deportation, which usually follows legal procedures.

Ex Post Facto Law (Retroactive Application)

Any law that creates and punishes as a crime an act that, when it was committed, was not a criminal offense. A law made after the fact of an event so as to make that prior happening illegal. Ex post facto criminal laws are prohibited under international law based on the legal principle referred to as "nonretroactivity of criminal/penal law." This principle is also expressed by the Latin phrase *Nullum Crimen, Nulla Poena sine Lege* (*see* infra), meaning, "there can be no crime, no punishment without (preexisting) law."

Expression (Freedom of)

See Freedom of Expression, infra.

Expressis Verbis
[Latin, lit.: in express words]

An adverbial expression used in treaty* interpretation to mean expressly, explicitly, in express words; it is expressly stated in the text. This is compared to what might be implicit or by way of judicial interpretation. Example: The right to conscientious objection is not set forth *expressis verbis* in the ICCPR.

Expropriation (of Property)

A government taking away or confiscating the property of persons and companies who are from other countries against their will, and sometimes without paying any money or even allowing the victims to go to court to contest the taking or the fairness of any compensation paid.

Companies operating in foreign countries may sometimes have their assets taken over by the government of the country and converted to use by that state. This happens especially where the government dislikes the state of the owner or is a socialist/communist state. An expropriation can constitute a human rights violation but is more a matter of private international law than classical human rights law, which protects human beings not companies. It is often treated in the field of human rights

The main sources of human rights norms applicable to expropriation are the UDHR (article 17) as it relates to the right to own property and the ICCPR (article 14 on procedural due process of law, article 2.1 on nondiscrimination, and article 26 on equality before the law).

Extermination

The creation of conditions of life calculated to bring about the destruction of a numerically significant part of a particular victim population. Normally, this act requires that the conduct be committed as part of a mass killing of members of the civilian population. It requires that a particular population be targeted, and its members killed or otherwise subjected to such conditions. The targeted population does not necessarily have to have any common national, ethnical, racial, or religious characteristic. Extermination covers situations even when some members of a group are spared while others are killed.

Extraconvention(al) Mechanism/Procedure (aka Charter-Based/Non-Treaty-Based Mechanism/ Procedure)

A human rights mechanism/procedure that is not established within and by a human rights treaty*, e.g., the "1503 procedure" of the UN Commission on Human Rights is an extraconvention(al) procedure.

EXTRADITION (OF CRIMINAL SUSPECT)

The surrender by one state of an individual accused or convicted of an offense committed outside its own territory and within the territorial jurisdiction of another (demanding) state to that state or other lawful authority, which, being competent to prosecute and to punish the accused, demands his surrender. Extradition of a fugitive, whether a convicted criminal or a criminal suspect, is usually grounded on the provisions of a bilateral treaty or statute between the demanding state or other authority and the other (surrendering) state or authority having jurisdiction to prosecute the person.

EXTRAJUDICIAL EXECUTION (OF PERSON) (AKA EXTRALEGAL EXECUTION)

An unlawful and deliberate killing carried out by the state by order of the government or with its complicity and without prior capital criminal conviction and sentencing or without proper judicial safeguards. Also called "extralegal execution." *See also* Summary Execution.

EXTRALEGAL (VS. LEGAL)

That which is outside of what is permitted by law and therefore not legal. That which is done without legislative, executive, or judicial authorization, e.g., extralegal execution.

EXTRATERRITORIAL APPLICATION (OF NORM)

The state's attempt to apply its legal jurisdiction over anything outside of the territorial or other legal boundary of that state. Example: Attempting to interdict a boat full of intending refugees on the high seas as an extension of a state's immigration laws. Also, in the sense of how a state exercises its jurisdiction outside of its territory.

EXTRATERRITORIAL EFFECT (OF A LAW)

An effect occurring outside the territorial boundaries of a given state or the application of a law beyond the physical and jurisdictional boundaries of the state that enacted it.

EXTRATERRITORIAL JURISDICTION (OF STATE)

The legal extent of a state's exercise or attempt to exercise its jurisdiction in the territory of another state or in a nonstate area, such as in space or on the high seas.

FACT-FINDING

1. Process: Generally, the fact-finding process is any activity designed to obtain detailed first-hand knowledge of the relevant facts of any dispute or situation.

The UN Training Manual on Human Rights Monitoring states that fact-finding describes a process of drawing conclusion of fact from monitoring activities.

2. Mission / Trip: The human rights investigation mechanism of a fact-finding mission or trip involves an individual or team of persons going in person to a place, usually in another state, to investigate,

gather first-hand information, and seek to discover the most accurate information. They then verify the facts and prepare a report about the true facts concerning a human rights violation, situation, condition or issue, and submit the report back to where the fact-finders came from, such as from an IGO. This is done by talking to victims, witnesses, government officials, and any others, such as NGOs, union leaders, or church officials, who can provide factual information about a general or specific human rights matter.

In the human rights context, the term most often refers to a process whereby members of an IGO organ, such as a human rights commission, a special rapporteur, or their staff, go to places where an event, such as a massacre or disappearances happened, to gather evidence to help determine the true facts. This is often done at places such as government offices, hospitals, prisons, police stations, mass grave sites, or military bases. Fact-finding can be about a thematic report or general country conditions, or it can concern the factual basis of a specific case based on a formal complaint*.

FAILURE TO ACT (LOAC)

Failure of military commanders to prevent or repress breaches of the LOAC when in a position and with authority to do so. Under humanitarian law commanders have a duty to take affirmative acts to prevent or stop breaches. They must take all feasible measures within their powers to prevent or repress such violations. *See* P I, article 86.

Also used generally to describe a government's failure to fulfill an affirmative obligation/duty under law with respect to human rights.

FAIR BALANCE

A phrase that refers to the legal standard for balancing the human rights of individuals with the legitimate and reasonable interests of society. In the Council of Europe human rights system, the legal doctrine has developed that human rights norms should be not interpreted in a way that gives total and unquestioning deference to state sovereignty nor to unrestrained and complete individual freedom. It involves human rights organs weighing both the community's interests, such as public safety, against human autonomy and civil liberties. The proper or "fair balance" is the one that considers both such values and best accommodates and protects the interests of both sides, individual and community.

FAIR TRIAL (RIGHT TO)

A judicial or quasi-judicial legal proceeding, whether civil or criminal, that meets all international human rights standards of fairness. A substantive and procedural human right to have a civil or criminal judicial proceeding comply with all human rights legal standards of procedural due process. This includes the right to fair notice, to a public hearing, to be heard and present evidence, to obtain evidence, to compel witness attendance, to necessary translation, to an independent and impartial court (judges), so that the decision/judgment of the court is the product of and meets accepted international standards of justice.

International Human Rights Law imposes an obligation on states to provide a society based on rule of law. This requires that there be a legal system with judicial remedies to enforce human rights and that judicial issues be resolved through resort to legal proceedings, which are both fair to all parties and appear in reality to be fair.

The primary international human rights standards on fair trial are set forth in article 14 of the ICCPR. This article sets forth many of the specific rights included in the international legal norm. Every state that has ratified the ICCPR has an obligation to provide fair trials to everyone within their territory and subject to their jurisdiction. The Human Rights Committee can thus monitor fair trial issues so as to assure the states parties fulfill their obligations under article 14. Other states parties can also address issues to the other states parties for denials of a fair trial. Having ratified the ICCPR, the matter of fair trials is no longer simply a national or local issue, but an international one.

Fair trial is also found in article 10 of the UDHR. This norm is probably binding as a matter of customary international law.

Fascism

A political ideology of the extreme right that advocates an authoritarian society characterized by the rule of an elite group headed by a supreme leader, e.g., Italy under Mussolini. This system is usually a reaction to a perceived leftist or other subversive threat to take over the state, and it elevates the national interest over individualism and individual rights, which are suppressed for the national good, usually in a brutal and oppressive manner.

Federal Clause (of a Treaty*)

A clause in a treaty* that sets forth the norm concerning the applicability of the treaty* to the political subunits of a state party, such as cantons or states in a federal system, as in Canada or the United States. Each treaty* sets its own federal application scope. This tells the impact/applicability of the norms on the federal subunits of a state party. *See*, e.g., the federal clause of the ICCPR, article 50, which, for example, would tell whether or to what extent the covenant applies to the State of California and not just to the U.S. federal government.

Female Circumcision (aka Female Genital Mutilation)

See Female Genital Mutilation.

Female Genital Mutilation (fgm) (aka Female Circumcision)

A practice in some states, usually done pursuant to religious or tribal custom, wherein females have their sexual organs altered, usually by cutting off the clitoris. This is sometimes done voluntarily in a ritual, though often it is involuntary. The mutilation is often done to assure the chastity of a woman by denying her sexual pleasure. It is generally and increasingly considered a human rights violation.

Field Presence (of an Organization)

The physical or administrative presence of agents (e.g., human rights monitors, election monitors, police) of an international organization, or possibly an NGO, in a place where human rights violations have occurred or are likely to occur. The agents usually are placed visibly "in the field" for the purpose of deterring further violations by letting potential violators know that they will be observed/reported/stopped/arrested; to support national/local authorities; to lessen the fear/terror of the target population; to report back to a headquarters or organizational seat for political/legal action regarding the situation.

First Generation Human Rights

The term that was formerly used to describe a class of human rights, which comprise all civil and political human rights: voting, expression, religion, movement, assembly, equality, fair trial, and life. "First Generation Human Rights" are individual and immediate rights. These are contrasted with what were called "second" and "third" generation human rights. Second generation human rights are economic, social, and cultural in nature. Third generation human rights are the "solidarity" rights.

The ICCPR is a general human rights treaty that contains predominantly first generation human rights.

Caveat: The use of the term "generations" does not imply a chronological order or hierarchy of the importance of human rights. It is more of a political-ideological conceptual categorization.

The idea and use of the term "generation" has come into disuse, and the terms first, second, and third generation human rights should no longer be used because they breed conceptual confusion.

Forced Assimilation

The process of a society forcing a group of people who are different from them to take on the characteristic attitudes of the dominant group so that the assimilating group becomes like the dominant group,

losing its differences, and the society becomes homogenous. Forced assimilation is inconsistent with international human rights law, which seeks to achieve pluralism, tolerance, diversity, equality, and broadmindedness in a society.

Forced Disappearance (of Persons) (aka Enforced Disappearance)

The same as "Enforced Disappearance" and "Disappearance." *See* Disappearance.

Foreign Sovereignty Immunity Act (fsia)

A U.S. statute found in articles 1601–1611 of Title 28 of the U.S. Code, which limits situations wherein a foreign state government can be sued in U.S. federal district courts for certain unlawful acts.

Many cases have been filed in U.S. federal district courts against foreign governments for committing human rights violations against the plaintiffs or their family members. It is a principle of law that states enjoy sovereign immunity for acts they commit within their jurisdiction. And when someone files a suit against a foreign government in U.S. courts, this can interfere with international diplomatic relations between the defendant state and the U.S. For this reason, the U.S. Congress has enacted this statute to spell out just when a foreign state can be sued in U.S. courts. Section 1604 spells out the general rule, and section 1605 spells out the exceptions.

Forum
[Latin, lit.: public meeting place]

An official public place, assembly, or institution, be it an organization, committee, court, or commission, where issues of common concern are dealt with by investigation, discussion, and legal procedures, if any are provided. An example is the United Nations Commission on Human Rights, which is a forum for discussing human rights issues. The word "fora" is the proper plural form of forum.

FORUM INTERNUM
(RELIGION/BELIEF)
[Latin, lit.: internal/interior forum]

The internal beliefs, thoughts, and opinions that inform the way a human being thinks, reasons, and perceives. This term is normally seen in relation to freedom of religion or belief. Under international human rights law, everyone has the right to freedom of thought, conscience, religion, or belief. One's internal religious or nonreligious beliefs and one's thoughts and opinions are absolutely protected under all circumstances at all times, and not subject to limitation or derogation.

The external manifestation of one's religion or belief can be limited for certain legitimate aims, such as public safety, order, health, or morals, or the rights and freedoms of others. *See* ICCPR, article 18.3; ECHR, article 9.

FORUM OF SHAME

The exposure of a state or regime to public scorn by publishing its human rights violations in public forums, such as the news media, in the hope that the violator will be embarrassed into ceasing or remedying violations. One sometimes refers similarly to the "mobilization of shame," i.e., spreading the word of a state's violations by all available public channels.

"FOUR FREEDOMS"
(ROOSEVELT SPEECH)

Refers to an historical speech given by Franklin Delano Roosevelt in January 1941, wherein he stated that the existence of world peace was linked to four essential freedoms. These freedoms include freedom of expression; freedom of worship; freedom from want (i.e., economic security); and freedom from fear (i.e., reduction of arms). This speech later became a key document in the underpinnings of the efforts to establish the United Nations and provided for the promotion of human rights. The speech was given before the United States entered World War II, but the world wars proved his assertion.

FOURTH INSTANCE (COURT OF)

A principle applied by human rights quasi-judicial and judicial bodies in determining the admissibility of a complaint*. One usually sees this phrase used such as "This commission/court will not sit as a court of fourth instance over domestic legal decisions." It means that the international forum is not to act as a sort of appellate court as to the correctness of a national court's judgment under its national law. This fourth instance formula states briefly that the international forum will not second-guess the national forum's findings of fact nor whether the national court has applied their national law properly. The international forum will not review judgments issued by national courts acting within their competence and with due judicial guarantees unless it considers that a violation of the subject international human rights treaty* is involved. This is because the international forum's only purpose is to ensure compliance with the international human rights treaty obligation, not how the national court has complied with its own domestic law or legal procedures.

FRAMEWORK CONVENTION

A treaty that is primarily a statement of principles, compared to a normal treaty, which is a detailed set of obligations.

A special type of treaty used primarily in the area of environmental law but starting to be used in human rights, such as in the Framework Convention for the Protection of National Minorities.

FREE AND FAIR ELECTIONS

A term used in and by the international community to describe elections that take place in a state under conditions in which those eligible to vote are in fact able to do so without impediment or coercion and the underlying circumstances of the election are such that the outcome reflects the fairness of the elections in every respect, thereby reflecting the will of the electorate. After an election is monitored by international election observers, a statement is issued based on an analysis of all observers' observations as to whether the election was "free and fair." If found to be "free and fair," the election will be deemed by the observers to be internationally valid and the elected government will be recognized as legitimate.

FREEDOM

The right to act in a certain way in the absence of any law limiting such act. The power or capacity of acting without any external compulsion. Absence of restraint; the power to choose one's actions, especially vis-à-vis the state.

Freedom is stronger, broader than "liberty," and is all-encompassing in scope.

Often seen in the term "fundamental freedoms," a term that denotes a freedom that is deemed absolutely necessary for the maintenance and protection of the dignity of a human being in an organized society, as a sort of minimum acceptable protection.

FREEDOM OF EXPRESSION

A specific substantive human rights norm that allows an individual to externalize information, ideas, opinions, and beliefs through any manner of speech, writing, or symbol, including artistic expression, without limitation from the state and subject only to certain limitations.

This is a civil human right that is a basic requirement of any free society. It allows for free unimpeded transmission and exchange of ideas, opinions, and beliefs, creating the so-called "marketplace of ideas." It has both positive and negative aspects. This right includes the positive right to express something and the negative right not to be compelled to express something.

Freedom of expression, as found in international human rights instruments, includes the freedom to seek, receive, and impart information and ideas of all kinds. This can be done either orally, in writing, or in print in the form of art or through any other media of one's choice. Freedom of expression is one of the "fundamental freedoms," a term that denotes a freedom that is considered absolutely necessary for the maintenance and protection of the dignity of a human being. This freedom is primarily found in article 19 of the UDHR and article 19 of the ICCPR.

The exercise of freedom of expression carries with it certain special duties and responsibilities on all members of society. It can be restricted by the state for certain narrowly defined reasons such as public order, public safety, public morals, national security, and the reputation of others. An example of a clause containing such limitation is found in ICCPR, article 19.3.

The international protection of free expression was largely influenced by the American experience of its free speech clause in the first amendment to the U.S. Constitution, which served as a model for many other states. The international human rights norms of free expression represent a balance between individual freedom on the one hand, and the needs of a society to sometimes regulate expression in the broader interest of society.

FREEDOM OF RELIGION

See Religion, infra.

FRENCH DECLARATION

The short name for the 1789 French Declaration on the Rights of Man and of Citizen. This French Declaration and the U.S. Declaration of Independence (1776) serve as the key historical documents setting forth the philosophical basis of human rights, primarily that human rights are inherent in individuals and not granted by a sovereign, and that the basis of government authority is the will of the people.

FRIENDLY SETTLEMENT

The product of a formal conciliation process or informal negotiations between a complainant/petitioner/applicant and a state alleged to have breached its normative human rights obligations wherein the complainant, etc., and respondent state come to an agreement on how to settle/resolve the case. If an agreement is reached to resolve the complaint*, the two sides are said to have reached a "Friendly Settlement." It is very often an agreement by the state government to pay money to the complainant, etc.; to annul or modify a law; or to discontinue a state practice.

This conciliation process is usually facilitated by members of the forum where the complaint* was filed, such as a commission or committee, who effect conciliation efforts seeking a friendly settlement. Usually, the forum must ensure that the settlement is in principle consistent with respect for human rights.

FRIENDSHIP, COMMERCE, AND NAVIGATION (FCN) (TREATY* OF) (AKA AMITY AND COMMERCE TREATY*)

Also known as a treaty* of "Amity and Commerce."

A bilateral treaty* establishing the relationship between the two states parties (*inter sese*) in various areas such as trade, finance, diplomacy, communication, and the rights and immunities of each others' citizens within the territory of the other. They are sometimes seen by their acronym: FCN. Some FCNs contain human rights-type provisions, such as access to and equality before courts, freedom of religion, the right of ownership of property, and the right to work. They establish, inter alia, the standard of treatment of each other's citizens on the other's territory, whether "National Treatment" or the "Minimum (International) Standard" of treatment (*see* infra).

Fulfill Human Rights (Obligations)

One of four legal obligations held by a state with regard to implementing human rights norms found in treaties and in customary international law. The other three are the obligations to respect, to protect, and to ensure.

The obligation to fulfill is an obligation of states under human rights norms to take appropriate legislative, administrative, budgetary, judicial, and other measures toward the full realization of human rights. This obligation requires that states will take all necessary steps to ensure that individuals subject to their jurisdiction can fully enjoy their human rights substantively and procedurally in reality.

Full Enjoyment

The legal, political, and social condition wherein a particular human right can be fully exercised by individual holders of the right. This requires the human right to be fully respected and protected by the state under a rule of law system, subject only to legitimate limitations and to any derogation by the state, when and to the extent permitted by law. Full enjoyment implies that the state is doing nothing to prevent an individual from fully exercising his human rights and assuring that nongovernmental parties do not restrict such full exercise.

Full Powers (aka Plenipotentiary; French: *Pleins Pouvoirs*)

The capacity of a person being officially designated by a state to represent the state for the purpose of negotiating, adopting, or authenticating the text of a treaty*, for expressing the consent of the state to be bound by the treaty*, or to do any other act regarding the treaty*. According to article 1(C) of the Vienna Convention of 1969, this term "means a document emanating from the competent authority of a state designating a person or persons to represent the state for negotiating, adopting or authenticating the text of a treaty, for expressing the consent of the state to be bound by a treaty, or for accomplishing any other act with respect to a treaty." One who holds "full powers" is also known as a "plenipotentiary." The French term is *pleins pouvoirs*.

Fundamental Freedoms (Human Rights and)

A basic liberty absolutely necessary for the protection and preservation of one's inherent human dignity. This term is almost synonymous with human rights, and in many treaties* and declarations one sees the term "human rights and fundamental freedoms." These freedoms are fundamental to the protection of human dignity.

Fundamentalism/Fundamentalist

A belief that there is only one true worldview or interpretation, whether religious, political, or philosophical, and that mine is the only true one. All others are false and worthy of contempt, or worse. One who holds such a view is a called a fundamentalist.

FUNDAMENTALLY ADEQUATE SYSTEM OF JUSTICE

A system of justice that is capable of providing to those under its jurisdiction / competence, a minimal level of justice as defined in international human rights legal norms established in both customary and treaty sources, and which norms are binding on the state and applicable to the issues involved. This is a legal system that is capable of rendering justice as a whole, even though errors may occur in a given case.

Such a system should, at a minimum, ensure full compliance with ICCPR articles 2.1, 9, 10, 13, 14, 15, 16, and 26.

FUNDAMENTAL STANDARDS OF HUMANITY

The concept that there exists in this world minimum standards of conduct between nations, groups, and people that are acceptable to the international community. They consist of a set of minimum standards that are nonderogable and applicable at all times, in all situations, including and regardless of the nature of any armed conflicts or the existence of any other treaty* provisions to the contrary.

It is most commonly applied in internal armed conflict situations where there is little applicable international law protective of humanity.

GEMEINSCHAFT (SOCIETY) (vs. GESELLSCHAFT [SOCIETY]) [German, lit.: community]

A German term used to describe a conception of societies in which the individual has no identity outside of the state society; the needs and will of the whole society are superior to any claim of individual human rights. Also called a "Communitarian" society. This is compared to a "*Gesellschaft*" society, wherein individuals have some means of individual autonomy.

GENDER

A complex and controversial term that does not have a generally accepted definition. Some have defined it as identical to the biological-anatomical description "sex," as in the male and female of the human species. Sex refers to biological differences between men and women, not the way humans act. Some have defined it as the way women and men are perceived and expected to think and act in a particular social, economic, political, and cultural context. However defined, gender can be affected by other factors such as age, race, class, or ethnicity. It is also regarded as a socially defined or constructed expectation regarding roles, attitudes, and values, which communities and societies ascribe as appropriate for one sex or the other in the public or private domain. To some, gender differences exist because of the way society is organized, not because of biological differences.

In the field of human rights this term comes into play mostly in relation to the human rights of nondiscrimination and equality before the law.

GENDER BIAS

A behavior or decision making process that is based on or reveals stereotypical attitudes about the natures and roles of men and women, perceptions of their relative worth, or myths or misconceptions about the social and economic realities encountered by both sexes.

GENDER CRIME

A crime based on the perpetrator acting against the victim on the basis of the victim's gender.

GENDER DISCRIMINATION

The act of creating a preference, restriction, limitation, or exclusion based on the gender of the victim, aimed at limiting the victims full enjoyment of all his / her rights.

GENDER FEMINISM
(vs. EQUITY FEMINISM)

A term describing the philosophy of a portion of the feminist community, namely that women are the victims of a system of male dominance in society that impedes their development as individuals from the earliest ages. Human rights theory and law calls for equality between men and women and nondiscrimination between men and women in the enjoyment of all human rights. The reality in the world is that such equality and nondiscrimination does not yet exist in many societies.

Issues for gender feminists include gender stereotyping in literature, movies, and other media, and traditional roles for women. Gender feminism is often referred to as second wave feminism.

In the field of human rights this term comes into play mostly in relation to the human rights of nondiscrimination and equality before the law.

GENDER MAINSTREAMING

A process of assessing the implications for women and men of any planned action, including legislation, policies, and programs in any area and at all levels. It is a strategy for making women's as well as men's concerns and experiences an integral dimension in the design, implementation, monitoring, and evaluation of policies and programs in all political, economic, and societal spheres so that men and women benefit equally, and inequality is not perpetuated.

GENDER RACISM

The express policy or practice of restricting or excluding women from the decision-making processes of states or international organizations, even where the decisions have a disparate impact on women. It is claimed, particularly by feminists, to be a conscious attempt to keep women from having the power to impact these decision-making processes.

GENERAL ASSEMBLY (UN) (UNGA)

One of the principal organs of the United Nations, consisting of the representatives of all member states that meet annually in the fall to act as a sort of international parliament where international issues are debated. The General Assembly decides the major activities and course of the UN and votes on various resolutions to delegate to the UN bodies.

Other IGOs such as the Organization of American States have "general assemblies," and this term generally means the administrative/political body/process/place where all members gather together to participate generally in the institution. Most often, a reference to the "General Assembly" refers to the UN General Assembly.

GENERAL COMMENTS (UN)

Written statements issued by UN treaty*-based human rights bodies such as the

Human Rights Committee (ICCPR) or the Committee on Economic, Social and Cultural Rights (ICESCR), which serve as the official collective statement of the expert members of that treaty* supervising body to all states parties, as to how to best fulfill their obligations under the treaty* instrument.

General comments will usually be issued concerning one or more specific issues, such as requirements for reports or concerning one or more articles of the treaty*. General comments sometimes contain analysis of the meaning, content, and scope of application of a particular substantive norm, or point out deficiencies in and make suggestions on how to improve reports submitted by states or how to clarify the requirements of the treaty* in any respect. General comments suggest ways to overcome obstacles to compliance, or to generally strengthen cooperation among member states in the implementation of the treaty*.

Much of the general comments are based on the body's review of the written periodic reports submitted by states in accordance with their reporting obligation under the treaty*. They may also consider any jurisprudence (case law) of that body. While general comments are not legally binding, they do have strong moral and political force because of the expertise of the members of the body, and states parties should follow them. *See* ICCPR, article 40.

GENERAL CONSULTATIVE STATUS (NGO) (VS. SPECIAL CONSULTATIVE STATUS)

The description of the status of NGOs as established by ECOSOC Resolution 1996/31, which describes an NGO that is involved in most all of the human rights matters dealt with at the UN by ECOSOC and its subsidiary organs, such as the Commission on Human Rights. This status determines the level of participation of such an NGO in the work and proceedings of the organ. These status descriptions are post-1996. *See also* Special Consultative Status.

GENERAL HUMAN RIGHTS LEGISLATION

Domestic legislation that seeks to ensure that all other states, or any state which has dealings with the legislating state, implements or increases respect for and protection of human rights. It is not aimed at any particular state. It may, for example, legislate that any state committing gross human rights violations will be cut off from receiving any future foreign aid from the legislating state.

In the U.S. context the term refers to federal congressional legislation that establishes U.S. law relative to how other countries should fulfill their international human rights obligations in a way that is conducive to beneficial relations with the U.S., such as in trade, military assistance, foreign aid, finance, and even cultural and other types of activities.

The U.S. Congress seeks to influence the way other countries respect human rights by passing laws that condition our relations to the fulfillment of their human rights obligations in a certain area or certain way. The Congress does this by either country specific legislation or general human rights legislation. The former only applies to one particular country. The latter applies equally to all countries.

An example of general human rights legislation would be the International Religious Freedom Act of 1998 (IRFA). This act conditions U.S. relations with all other countries upon the fulfillment of their obligation under international law to respect religious freedom, such as under the ICCPR, article 18. This act also establishes a committee to monitor countries in this field and report to Congress so that it can inform U.S. policy and action.

GENERAL INTERNATIONAL LAW

A confusing term with two widely held meanings. To some, this term describes the norms found in two sources of international law known as conventional, i.e., treaty* law, and customary international law, to the extent that these norms apply generally to all states of the world; whereas others say that it refers only to customary international law as it applies generally to all states. The first of these two meanings is probably the better one. Caveat: General International Law is not the same thing as "General Principles of Law."

GENERAL PARTICIPATION CLAUSE (OF TREATY*) (AKA *SI OMNES* CLAUSE)

A clause or stipulation found in many classic international law treaties*. This clause provides that the obligations of the treaty* will only be applied to a situation when all states involved in an issue are states parties to the subject treaty*. It creates a mutual, reciprocal legal relationship with all other states parties. This applies primarily to treaties* involving armed conflict. *See also Si Omnes* Clause.

GENERAL PRINCIPLES OF INTERNATIONAL CRIMINAL LAW

Legal principles that have developed since and largely out of the Nuremberg Trials, such as the principles of individual criminal responsibility, nonretroactivity, *Nullum Crimen*, *Ne Bis in Idem*, Statute of Limitations, mistake of law/fact, and command responsibility. These principles are generally accepted internationally as applying to the prosecution of those accused of committing international crimes.

GENERAL PRINCIPLES OF LAW (SOURCE OF NORMS)

A legal doctrine intermediate between international law and municipal law referring to principles common to most legal systems. This source is most known to introduce norms of procedure or evidence. It is also understood as those principles of law, both private and public, which examination of the legal experience of civilized nations leads one to believe are valid maxims of jurisprudence. It is a source of international law norms, but is a controversial and not well-defined doctrine.

GENERAL RECOMMENDATIONS (OF UN TREATY-BASED BODIES)

Recommendations made by UN treaty-based bodies after a review of the reports of states parties to the treaty*, and usually meeting with the states discussing the reports. These recommendations are the ideas of the supervising body as to how the subject state can improve its compliance with the treaty* norms, such as recommending change of a domestic law to establish a better state monitoring system. These recommendations are not legally binding, but states should follow them as a sign of their good faith attempt to comply with their treaty* obligations.

GENERAL TREATY* (VS. SECTIONAL/PARTICULAR/ TOPICALLY SPECIFIC TREATY*)

A treaty* adopted at the global or regional level that concerns all or a large portion of human rights norms applicable to all persons, an example being the ICCPR. This is distinguished from a "sectional," "particular," or "topically specific" treaty* that covers only a limited subject, such as genocide or torture, or certain persons, such as children or refugees.

GENERATING EFFECT (OF UN RESOLUTIONS)

The so-called "generating effect" is a theory that says that sometimes UN resolutions become the motivation for, and focal point of, subsequent practice by states, which can eventually ripen into a norm of customary international law. The resolution is said to generate the effects of creation of a legal norm. This requires the existence of a consistent, settled state practice (usage) and *opinio juris*. The UDHR was a nonbinding declaration of human rights adopted by a UN resolution and later ripened, at least in part, into customary international law.

GENEVA CONVENTION(S) (LOAC)

Most often refers to the four treaties of International Humanitarian Law adopted in 1949 under the International Committee of the Red Cross (ICRC) in Geneva, Switzerland. The conventions extend international legal protection to victims of armed conflict on land and at sea, to prisoners of war and to civilians. Sometimes this term is also used more generally to include the two protocols (I and II of 1977) with the four conventions. There were also earlier Geneva conventions adopted in 1864 and 1929, but when reference is now made to "the Geneva Conventions" it most often means the four conventions of 1949 (GCs I–IV).

GENEVA LAW (VS. HAGUE LAW) (LOAC)

A term used to refer to all treaty* law in the area of international humanitarian law that was adopted under the aegis of the International Committee of the Red Cross (ICRC), which has its headquarters in Geneva, Switzerland. "Geneva Law" refers to the city in Switzerland where this area of international law was created. "Geneva Law" primarily covers the legal protection of victims of armed conflicts.

It is contrasted with "Hague Law," which refers mainly to the 1899 and 1907 Hague Conventions that dealt mostly with the methods and means of attack and that are primarily in customary international law status. "Geneva Law" includes most importantly the four Geneva Conventions of 1949 and the two Protocols of 1977, but this is not all of "Geneva Law."

GENOCIDE

An international crime that consists of the commission of harmful acts committed in wartime or in peacetime with the intent to destroy, in whole or in part, a national, ethnic, racial, or religious group of human beings. It is the systematic elimination of a people based on these characteristics, and can include acts that seriously injure or subject a group to conditions calculated to partially or completely destroy the group. Genocide is a human rights violation and is prohibited under both treaty law (*see* Genocide Convention) and as a matter of customary international law. It is an international crime under the Statute of the International Criminal Court and, within the court's inherent jurisdiction, defined exactly as in the Genocide Convention.

GENOCIDE CONVENTION

The Genocide Convention of 1948 is an international treaty that prohibits genocide (*see* supra) and provides for its prosecution as an international crime.

The internationally accepted definition of genocide is taken from that convention, which states:

> Genocide means any of the following acts committed with intent to destroy, in whole or part, a national, ethnic, racial, or religious group:
> (a) Killing members of the group;
> (b) Causing serious bodily or mental harm to members of the group;
> (c) Deliberately inflicting on the group, conditions of life calculated to bring about its physical destruction in whole or in part;
> (d) Imposing measures intended to prevent births within the group;
> (e) Forcibly transferring children of the group to another group;

Acts that constitute genocide can include acts that kill or seriously injure a group, or subject that group to conditions that are calculated to partially or completely destroy them. Genocide is a human rights violation and constitutes an international crime. It is prohibited under both treaty law and as a matter of customary international law; thus, it is binding on all countries, even those that have not ratified the Genocide Convention.

The preceding definition of genocide was enunciated by the international community in the Genocide Convention. The Genocide Convention was adopted by the members of the United Nations in 1948. Its purpose was to establish a conventional, legal norm that defines and establishes punishment for the act of genocide. Its full title is the Convention on the Prevention and Punishment of the Crime of Genocide. In addition to defining genocide, it established international criminal responsibility for acts that violate the convention, and it authorized universal jurisdiction for all state parties to prosecute violators in national courts. It does not matter that the person accused acted in an official capacity for a government.

The 1948 convention also makes reference in article 6 to "such international penal tribunal as may have jurisdiction" to prosecute genocide under the convention. In July 1998, a statute (treaty) was adopted establishing such a permanent International Criminal Court. The statute (articles 5 and 6) includes genocide as one of the core international crimes within the court's inherent subject matter jurisdiction. It uses the definition of genocide set forth in the 1948 convention.

Genocide was not a crime prosecuted at the Nuremberg Trials. It was defined as a crime after Nuremberg (1945). The acts that constituted genocide were, however, prosecuted under the classification of "crimes against humanity." A person can also be guilty of committing genocide if he enters into a conspiracy with others to commit genocide; or directly and publicly incite others to commit genocide (as happened in Rwanda); or is in some way aiding and abetting genocide before or after the act. Classic historic examples of genocide are the

Holocaust of World War II, the Rwanda Massacre of 1994, and the Armenian Genocide of 1915. Genocide is a violation of the collective human rights of members of a particular group. It is not the same thing as ethnic cleansing.

GESELLSCHAFT (SOCIETY) (VS. GEMEINSCHAFT [SOCIETY])

A German term used to describe a conception of societies in which individuals have some measure of personal autonomy within a society. Also called an individualistic society. This is compared to a *"Gemeinschaft"* conception of society wherein an individual has no identity outside of the society, and the needs and will of the whole society are superior to any claims of the individuals.

GHETTO

Initially this term referred to the Jewish quarter in an Italian town or city. Used particularly in World War II, it meant the quarter of a city where Jews lived in greatest numbers, for example, the Warsaw Ghetto. Now by extension it can refer to any section of a town inhabited predominantly by members of a specific ethnic, national, or racial group. It can even refer to any group isolated by external pressures, with an implication of inferiority.

The causes of this social/demographic phenomenon usually arise from social or economic pressure.

GIRL CHILD

A term used to refer to a female minor (nonadult) child, seen in such human rights contexts as sexual abuse, slavery, exploitation, and pornography; child labor, female circumcision, marriageable age, and other issues particular to young girls. A minor is a child eighteen years old or younger, unless under national law the age of majority is younger.

GLOBAL COMPACT (UN 2000)

A United Nations program initiated in 2000 at the World Economic Forum at Davos, under UN Secretary General Kofi Annan, which had as its aim getting international business interests to help in the realization of human rights. Actually, this compact was meant to be a compact between the UN, civil society, and the international business community. This compact was to be done by an acceptance between them of "shared values and principles." The view of this compact is to seek good corporate citizenship by transnational corporations (TNCs) so as to prevent the types of human rights abuses that were being committed by such large and powerful corporations, particularly as to environmental protections and human and workers rights.

Its goal is also to try to get TNCs to use their power and influence to get states to improve their human rights records. It seeks to harmonize business economic growth with contemporary human rights standards. It is an attempt to minimize the negative impact of globalization on human rights and to "give a human face to the global market." The text of the compact states that businesses accepting the compact agree to "support and respect the protection of internationally proclaimed human rights within their sphere of influence and make sure they are not complicit in human rights abuses."

Most elements of the compact are not legally binding upon corporations because they are nonstate actors, which in most cases are not legally bound by human rights norms.

Globalization

A form of institutionalization of the twofold process involving the universalization of particularities and the particularization of universalities; a global, transnational, political, social, cultural, but especially economic process.

Good Faith (Interpretation and Application of Treaty* Norms) (aka *Bona Fides*)

See Bona Fides, supra.

Good Governance (Principle)

An evolving principle that roughly means that the inherent dignity of individuals and their collective holding of human rights entitle them to "good governance," within state societies, meaning they deserve a government characterized by rule of law, having a democratic political basis (elected by plebiscite), and responsive to the people. Good governance also includes adequately structured state institutions with efficiency and transparency of institutions and procedures and respect by all governmental authorities for the human rights of all persons within the territory of the state; with access by individuals to means of redress for violations of law; accountability of public officials for misconduct, malfeasance, and human rights violations; and a public sector with an active and free civil society.

Good Offices

In international relations/law this refers to friendly efforts made by a state, organization, or public official on the part of a third state or international organization to encourage disputing states or other parties to enter into or to resume negotiations to resolve issues. It is acting as a well-intentioned intermediary in an international dispute. Usually the act is requested by one of the disputing state/parties to initiate the contact ("good offices") on its behalf, usually because the requesting party believes the other party will respect or honor the request of the state/organ exercising good offices.

Governmental-Nongovernmental Organization (gongo)

An NGO created by a state. The same as GANGO. Its members are government agents.

Government-Appointed Nongovernmental Organization (gango)

Known as "Government-Appointed NGO," or GANGO. An organization that looks and acts like a nongovernmental organization but that is in fact run or directed by a government, usually to act as a seemingly private public relations tool to react to/combat criticism of the state for human rights violations. Its members are appointed by the government but appear to be private individuals.

Grave Breach(es) (of 1949 Geneva Conventions/of 1977 Protocol I) (loac)

The most serious violations of the Law of Armed Conflict (LOAC), the *jus in bello*, as found in Geneva Law, the four Geneva Conventions of 1949, and Protocol I, are set forth in an article in each of those instruments: GC I, article 50; GC II, article 51; GC III, article 30; GC IV, article 147; and P I, article 85. They are, by definition, war crimes constituting international crimes giving rise to universal jurisdiction, in contrast to regular "breaches."

GROSSO MODO (INTERPRETATION)
[Latin, lit.: in a large manner]

A Latin adverbial expression used to mean an approximate, loose, or broad interpretation, application, or definition of something. This is as opposed to a narrow, precise, and definite manner.

GROSS VIOLATION(S)
(OF HUMAN RIGHTS)

A term used but not well defined in human rights resolutions, declarations, and treaties* but generally meaning systematic violations of certain human rights norms of a more serious nature, such as apartheid, racial discrimination, murder, slavery, genocide, religious persecution on a massive scale, committed as a matter of official practice. Gross violations result in irreparable harm to victims. The U.S. *Restatement of Law*, 3d ed., says that "a violation is gross if it is particularly shocking because of the importance of the right or the gravity of the violations."

There is an ongoing attempt in the United Nations to define "Gross Violations." The "1503 Procedure" of the United Nations deals with consistent patterns of "Gross Violations."

GROUP (HUMAN) RIGHTS
(VS. INDIVIDUAL RIGHTS)
(AKA COLLECTIVE RIGHTS)

Identical to "Collective Rights." They are human rights that are said to be either
1. Held by the group for the individual members of the group; or

2. Held by the individual members of the group collectively for the benefit of the group; and some say they are simply held by the group for the group.

These rights are generally contrasted with individual rights that are held by each individual regardless of his appurtenance to a group. Some rights, such as minority or indigenous rights, are said to be collective or group rights. The conception of collective or group rights is controversial and is not universally accepted.

GUERRILLA WAR(FARE)/
SOLDIER (LOAC)

Describes a soldier or a type of armed conflict wherein combatants are engaged against a force occupying a territory from within or nearby and fighting in an unconventional manner, most often not wearing distinctive military uniforms or emblems that would distinguish them from the civilian population and concealing weapons until shortly before an armed attack. Guerrilla tactics are usually characterized by the use of surprise, secret attack, and ruse.

GUIDELINES (UN)

A written set of general considerations, criteria, and steps that states should take/ use and apply in national legislation and practice as applied to a particular group of governmental authorities in a society, e.g., police. Prepared under the UN, these guidelines are not legal norms in a legal instrument, but if they are accepted and implemented by a state through training and education they will cause the subject group to act in such a way that human rights of members of the society will be protected and respected. For example, there is a set of UN *Guidelines on the Role of Prosecutors*, adopted in 1990, whose purpose is to secure and promote the effectiveness, impartiality, and fairness of prosecutors in criminal proceedings. States may accept or reject the application of these guidelines within their domestic systems. They are aimed at helping national authorities to avoid violating human rights.

Habeas Corpus (Procedure)

Refers to a legal proceeding instituted by a petition for a writ whose object is to bring a person held in government custody before the court, most commonly to force the person to be released unless the government can prove the legality or constitutionality of the arrest and detention. A similar procedure, known as *Amparo* (*see* infra), exists in Spanish-speaking states.

Hague Law (of Armed Conflict) (loac)

This is a term used to identify the body of international conventional and customary law that was adopted in the Hague, a city in the Netherlands. This body of humanitarian law, which covers many aspects of the *jus in bello* but also some *jus ad bellum* is mainly comprised of the 1907 Hague Convention IV: Respecting the Laws and Customs of War on Land and the Regulations attached to that convention, which codified existing customary law on armed conflicts, and some 1899 Declarations on asphyxiating gases and dum-dum bullets. Hague Law is primarily concerned with restricting the methods and means used by belligerents in armed conflicts. This is compared to Geneva Law, which primarily covers

the protection of victims of armed conflicts, such as prisoners of war. *See also* Hague Regulations.

Hague Regulations (loac)

The rules of international humanitarian law found attached to the 1907 Hague IV Convention. These regulations set forth international norms on the methods and means of combat. They are now considered general principles of international law and/or customary international law. Violation of these norms can entail international criminal responsibility. These rules traditionally are applied only to international armed conflicts, but are now coming to be considered binding in non-international armed conflicts.

Hard Core (Human) Rights (aka *Noyau Dur*)

A term generally used to describe human rights that are nonderogable and hence absolute. These would include such things as slavery, genocide, torture, summary execution, etc. The French term *noyaux durs* is sometimes used in this context. It means "hard core" and refers to the hard core human rights.

Hard Law (vs. Soft Law)

Norms creating precise, generally accepted legal rights and obligations. The normative system of international law found in treaty* law, customary international law, and general principles of law that are usually followed by states.

Hard law is contrasted with "soft law," which is more vague and not, strictly speaking, legally binding but may have moral or political force.

Harmonizing Domestic Legislation

The process of a state scrutinizing and changing its national laws or enacting new laws, so that the national laws are in full harmony with the international legal norms binding upon the state under international law. Most human rights treaties* have a clause requiring states parties to transform treaty* norms into domestic national law. This implies that the transformation results in domestic law becoming consistent with the international norms, so that the members of a society can invoke and seek enforcement of the norms in the domestic legal system. *See* iccpr, article 2.2.

Hate Crime

A hate crime is a criminal offense against someone that is motivated by the perpetrator's dislike or hatred for certain types of persons. It is characterized by the willful use of force or threat of force to cause injury, intimidation, oppression, or damage to persons or their property. It is based on antagonism toward some characteristic of the victim, such as their actual or perceived race, color, religion, ancestry, national origin, disability, gender, or sexual orientation.

Hate crime is a term used both in the general and particular sense. In the general sense it is used to characterize any type of criminal act motivated by such antagonism against race, religion, etc. In the particular sense it can refer to a specific type of criminal statute aimed at eradicating harmful conduct against someone because of their distinguishing characteristics, such as race, color, or religion, which prevents victims from exercising their constitutional and statutory rights.

Hate crimes are acts of discrimination and abuse of the victim's human equality and dignity. They are intolerable if committed at any time against anyone, whether an individual or a group. If not prevented, they can lead to social strife, conflicts, and even war. Hate crimes can be committed by agents of the government or by private individuals or groups.

Hate crime legislation is an attempt by society to assure the equal enjoyment of all human rights by all persons by eliminating the manifestations of intolerance. It is an attempt to get people to treat the "other" humanely and respectfully without discrimination. It is a human rights obligation of government to investigate, prosecute, educate against, and eliminate hate crimes.

Hate Speech

Oral and written statements expressing hate, anger, vilification, and disdain, demeaning to a certain group of people in a way meant to be offensive or to cast a bad light on the group.

Article 1 of the udhr states that all human beings are born free and equal in dignity and rights. They are endowed with reason and conscience, and should act towards one another in a spirit of brotherhood.

Hate speech treats other persons as less equal and of less dignity. It causes others to dislike the victim group and makes violence and damage to them more possible; it can create civil strife in a whole country.

Even though, under international human rights law, everyone has freedom of expression including speech, this is not absolute. Article 19 of the ICCPR allows limitations of speech for

1) Respect for the rights and freedoms of others;
2) Protection of national security, public order, or of public health or morals.

Article 20 of the ICCPR states: Any advocacy of national, racial, or religious hatred that constitutes incitement to discrimination, hostility, or violence, shall be prohibited by law.

Hegemonic Stability Theory

A theory of international relations that states that hegemonic state powers tend to create international institutions, such as the U.S. and Russia with the United Nations, in a way as to try to stabilize international relations in a way that is to their liking and in their national self-interest.

Helsinki Accords

Another term for the Helsinki Final Act of 1975.

Helsinki Final Act (of 1975)

A political instrument not of a legally binding character, adopted in 1975 by the Conference on Security and Cooperation in Europe (CSCE), now the Organization on Security and Cooperation in Europe (OSCE). A post-World War II political organization composed of the United States, Canada, and most of the European countries. The original thirty-three-state (fifty in 1997) body adopted this act, which contains ten guiding principles. Article VII specifically addresses human rights, as do four "baskets" (chapters for various areas of cooperation concerning human rights), especially Baskets I and III. The act expressly calls for all member states to fulfill their human rights obligations under international law. It has proved to be a very significant and effective human rights instrument despite its nonbinding character. Its follow-up mechanism has led the way to the establishment of the OSCE "human dimension mechanisms" involving human rights. Also called the "Helsinki Accords."

Helsinki Process

A term used informally to describe the activities of the OSCE/CSCE in the field of human rights within the member states. These activities fall within the terms of reference of the 1975 Helsinki Final Act, as implemented in subsequent follow-up documents (Copenhagen, Vienna, Moscow).

High Commissioner for Human Rights (UNHCHR)

The title of the highest United Nations official (an Undersecretary General) who is charged with coordinating and heading human rights activity at the United Nations. The High Commissioner sits as head of the UN Office of the High Commissioner for Human Rights, operating primarily out of the UN Secretariat in Geneva, Switzerland.

The High Commissioner for Human Rights is an office established in 1995 to coordinate and make more efficient all UN human rights activities. In addition, the High Commissioner travels around the world to check on human rights conditions and makes helpful suggestions to governments for implementing human rights. The High Commissioner works on the basis of the UN human rights instruments such as the UDHR, ICCPR, ICESCR, and other UN related treaties. The High Commissioner cannot force any country to do anything.

The person selected as the High Commissioner is usually a very high-level political figure who has particular expertise in human rights.

HIGH COMMISSIONER FOR REFUGEES (UNHCR)

A high official of the United Nations, chosen by the General Assembly and delegated with the task of overseeing all United Nations activity as it relates to refugees and forced migrations. Its mandate covers both "convention(al) refugees" (covered by the 1951 Refugee Convention and its 1967 Protocol) and nonconvention(al) refugees. Acronym: UNHCR.

Caveat: Note that this is not the same person/office as the United Nations high commissioner for human rights, whose acronym is UNHCHR.

HIGH CONTRACTING PARTY (TO TREATY*)

A term used in some international human rights treaties* to designate those states that ratify*/adhere to/accede to/succeed to and thus become bound by the treaty*. *See* ECHR, article 1, for example.

HOLDER (OF RIGHTS) (AKA BEARER)

One who possesses and can assert a human right. The legal personality, whether a group or individual, who is the subject of a human right under international law is known as the "holder" or "bearer" of the right. It also usually refers to the one who has the right to defend such rights. Human beings are the holders or bearers of human rights, not states.

HOLDING (OF A COURT/ TRIBUNAL) (VS. *DICTUM*)

The precise and specific ruling of a court or tribunal in a given contentious case. In a judicial forum the parties may submit many different legal issues to the court/tribunal for adjudication and resolution. The judicial forum may chose to decide the case on any issues it deems itself legally competent to resolve. The particular ruling on the particular issues it chooses to adjudicate is called the "holding" of the case. It is what is actually decided by the forum.

In a common law system the holding becomes binding not only on the parties to that particular case, but on all subsequent parties raising the same legal issues in subsequent cases. This is called the principle of *Stare Decisis*.

The holding is contrasted with the *Dictum*, also called *Obiter Dictum* in the decision/judgment/ruling. These are statements made by the judges in the decision/judgment/ruling, which are not necessary for the decision/judgment/ruling. *Dicta* and *Obiter Dicta* are not legally binding on the parties to that case, nor upon parties to a subsequent case.

HOLOCAUST (WORLD WAR II)

The systematic annihilation of twelve million persons by Nazi Germany during World War II based on the victims' race, religion, or other characteristics. It is used most often in reference to those of Jewish background who were killed as part of the Nazi "Final Solution," although the

Holocaust was not solely a phenomenon pertaining to Jewish victims. Many others, such as Catholic priests, gypsies, and homosexuals, were also victims of the Holocaust.

Hominum Causa Omne Jus Constitutum Est (Principle of Interpretation and Application of Treaties*)
[Latin, lit.: every right is established for the sake of humans]

The principle of all law, including human rights treaties*, that says that all law is created for the benefit/sake of human beings. All law must thus be interpreted and applied in a way that best serves and protects human beings. Under this principle all human rights legal instruments and customary norms must be interpreted and applied in the manner most protective of the human dignity of human beings, not the manner that is best for the state.

It is also known as the principle of *Pro Homine*. (*See also Pro Homine*.)

Homophobia

An anti-homosexual attitude based on fear of a perceived harm to society, morals, health, or values. A morbid fear of persons with a homosexual orientation. Homophobia is an attitude that can lead to human rights abuses against homosexuals, such as hate crimes and so-called gay-bashing.

Horizontal Effect/ Horizontality (Effect of Normative Obligation) (aka *Drittwirkung*/Third-Party Effect)

The so-called third-party effect of human rights norms. Horizontal effect refers to the theory that human rights norms create legal obligations between private individuals and that the state is responsible for seeing that private individuals and groups do not violate the human rights of others. Whereas the primary human rights obligation is between the human being and the state, called the "vertical effect" of the norms, the horizontality/horizontal effect theory argues for human rights and obligations at the human being-to-human being level, (between/among individual humans), i.e., the horizontal level. The results of this theory are argued to be the following:

1. The state can be held responsible for certain private acts it fails or refuses to stop or prevent;

2. Private individuals have the right to remedy against private individuals who violate their human rights.

This theory is also known by its German name, *Drittwirkung* (*see* supra), and as the "Third-Party Effect" (*see* infra).

Hors de Combat (Combatant) (loac)
[French, lit.: outside of combat]

A legal term used to describe a combatant, a soldier, who is in the power of an adversary and expresses an intent to surrender or is unconscious or otherwise physically incapable of engaging in hostilities.

It is prohibited under international humanitarian law to harm combatants who are *hors de combat*.

Hostis Humani Generis
[Latin, lit.: enemy of the human race]

A term of public international law applied to a person who has committed an international crime. International crimes such as genocide, war crimes, and crimes against humanity are considered to be crimes against all humankind, against the whole human race, regardless of which state they occur in. They are so serious that those who perpetrate them are called an enemy of the human race: *Hostis Humani Generis*. Because such acts are deemed to have harmed the interests of every state, every state has an interest in the apprehension and prosecution of them.

House Arrest

Forcible detention by the government in one's own house rather than in a prison. Used as a method in some states to silence dissidents without creating bad publicity from criminal trials or public controversy.

Human Dignity

The innate value or worthiness of a human being, existing by the very nature of humanity and recognized as the juridical philosophical basis of all human rights. This human dignity is preserved and enhanced by the setting of international human rights standards that limit the state from committing acts or failing to act in such a way as to violate human dignity. Human rights protect human dignity. Every human being possesses this dignity, which is inherent and inalienable. The basis of human rights is often referred to as "inherent human dignity."

Human Dimension Mechanisms (osce)

The name given to the human rights mechanisms established within the framework of the Organization on Security and Cooperation in Europe.

Humane Treatment (of Persons in Armed Conflict) (vs. Inhumane Treatment) (loac)

A term often found in humanitarian law used to refer to basic humanitarian treatment. It requires inter alia protection and provision with food, water, clothing, medical attention, shelter, with no physical or mental disrespect or mistreatment of persons under one's power.

Treatment that respects the human dignity of persons. The basic minimum standard of treatment of human beings in armed conflicts. *See* GC III, article 3(1).

Humanitarian

Anything beneficial to mankind in general or to a particular group of people in a particular circumstance: to ensure respect for the human dignity of human beings.

Humanitarian Assistance

The provision of relief supplies, foodstuffs, and medicine to people who are subject to a public, natural, or man-made disaster.

Humanitarian Intervention (Doctrine)

A doctrine of international law, established in the eighteenth century, which stated that it is legally permissible under international law for one state to use military force in the territory of another country to stop that country from committing widespread and brutal mistreatment of its own citizens in a way that shocks the conscience of all mankind of all nations.

The coercive deployment of military forces by a state or states for purpose of alleviating a grave humanitarian crisis, that is, one characterized by genocide, crimes against humanity, or war crime, against the violating state. This doctrine was claimed as the basis of the NATO bombardment of the former Yugoslavia in 1999 in response to the alleged atrocities in Kosovo.

This was the first doctrine of international law that provided that states were limited as to how they treat their own citizens. It suggests that where the acts of a state against its own people are so widespread and brutal as to shock all nations, the doctrine of sovereignty becomes subjected to the right of the international community to see all human beings treated humanely everywhere. It would allow one or more states to violate the sovereignty of another state by entering and using violent force to protect the victims from further atrocities.

This doctrine became abused by states using it as an excuse to overthrow a government or change the political situation. Most scholars believe that the UN Charter article 2.4 made resorting to humanitarian intervention unlawful, thus forcing states to work collectively through the UN to prevent or remedy such human rights violations.

The requirements of humanitarian intervention are

1) Widespread and brutal atrocities committed by a state against its own people;

2) The entry into the state was not requested by the guilty state;

3) The purpose of the use of force was only to effectuate protection of victims;

4) The entry was not part of a UN action.

Every time any country acts in violation of the territorial integrity or sovereignty, it must have a legal basis for doing so. It was intended by the UN Charter that states not make such unilateral judgments about when to use force, but would use collective measures through the UN and other international organizations to stop such atrocities.

HUMANITARIAN LAW (ARMED CONFLICT) (LOAC)

The body of international law rules applicable in international and noninternational armed conflicts, which limits the permissible methods and means of warfare and protects persons not or no longer taking part in hostilities. It applies to armed conflict (usually called "war") and seeks to limit the damage, destruction, pain, unnecessary suffering, and loss caused to human beings by violence resulting from military force. It sets forth legal norms governing the actions of the parties to the conflict both as to how they treat the victims of the conflict, both combatants and noncombatants, and limiting the methods and means (tactics and weapons) by which they fight. Its legal sources are customary international law, treaty law, and some say general principles of law.

Humanitarian law mainly comprises the four Geneva Conventions of 1949 and their two Protocols, I and II of 1977, although there are various other applicable treaties. It also includes the 1899 and 1907 "Hague Rules," which codified customary norms and serve as a basis for customary law norms now, and some other treaties on particular weapons.

It is referred to in Latin as the *jus in bello*

HUMANITY (PRINCIPLE) (LOAC)

It is prohibited for belligerents to employ any kind or degree of force for the purpose of the partial or complete submission of the enemy with a minimum expenditure of time, life, and physical resources and a minimum of suffering or injury.

Humanity is a sentiment or attitude of active good will toward mankind.

Human Rights

There is no universally accepted and authoritative definition of a human right. Many define it as a legally enforceable claim or entitlement that is held by an individual human being vis-à-vis the state government, for the protection of the inherent human dignity of the human being. Others say human rights are claims, legitimate, valid, justified claims, by every human being upon his/her own society —claims to guarantees and safeguards, and to goods and benefits that are essential to personal well-being and dignity.

The UN Training Manual on Human Rights Monitoring states that human rights "are universal legal guarantees protecting individuals and groups against actions by governments that interfere with fundamental freedoms and human dignity."

These rights are held by human beings as attributes of their human personality and not as rights granted by any human authority, be it state, monarch, or other authority, secular or religious. They are rights that allow the human beings to protect their inherent human dignity from the abuse of power by the state and from nongovernmental actors from whom the individual has a right to state protection. The essential characteristics of human rights are that they are universal, meaning that everyone holds them; they are inherent, meaning that humans are born with them; they are not given by anyone; and they are inalienable, meaning that

they can not be given away or taken away, although they can be limited in certain situations.

These are also called "fundamental freedoms" or are seen in the phrase "human rights and fundamental freedoms." They are not the same as "civil rights" as utilized in the sense of civil rights as found in the United States. This is because the civil rights of the United States are granted by legislative enactment, whereas human rights are inherent and are held by humans qua humans. Some say that human rights are "individual"; that is, they are held only by separate individuals without regard to collective society. Others hold that human rights can also be held by collective groups of human beings. (*See* Collective (Human) Rights or Group (Human) Rights, supra.)

Human Rights Abuses

A term referred to in the UN Training Manual on Human Rights Monitoring as broader than human rights violations and includes norm violative conduct committed by nonstate actors.

Human Rights Approach

The factoring in of international human rights norms and concepts in a nonhuman rights policy, program, or project, such that the human right implications of such policy, program, or project are the ultimate focus, and human rights are best protected and respected. A human rights approach is aimed at protecting human dignity and full development of individual human beings and ensuring consistency and harmony of all governmental and nongovernmental actions with existing international human rights standards.

HUMAN RIGHTS COMMITTEE (UN) (HRC)

A UN treaty-based organ set up in the International Covenant on Civil and Political Rights (ICCPR). The states parties to that human rights treaty set up the HRC to supervise and monitor implementation of its human rights norms by states that have ratified and are parties to and thus bound to comply with them.

Most international human rights treaties* set up a mechanism or organ such as a commission, committee, or court to monitor and supervise the implementation of the substantive norms of the treaty. Article 28 of the ICCPR established the HRC as its "treaty-based" implementation or supervisory organ to monitor compliance with the ICCPR and its two Optional Protocols. The First Optional Protocol provides a mechanism for HRC handling complaints by individuals claiming to be victims of a violation of the treaty. The Second Optional Protocol calls for abolition of the death penalty.

The HRC is known as a "quasi-judicial" organ. Its eighteen members are not judges but are legal experts in human rights. They examine complaints and apply the law of the ICCPR to the facts. If the complaint is admissible, the HRC can handle it, and if the complaint is not resolved to the parties' satisfaction, the HRC can set up a "Conciliation Commission" to try to resolve it. If this is unsuccessful, the HRC can submit a report on its findings and "views" as to whether a violation was found (the "merits") and its recommendations. Views are not legally binding decisions but are usually followed by states. The HRC has no power to invalidate a respondent state's laws or order the state to do anything.

The HRC can make an urgent request to a respondent state for a halt to imminent state action if immediate protection is needed, such as in a deportation or execution case. In addition, the HRC will periodically issue its "General Comments" on what it thinks is the scope and content of any particular right in the covenant. This helps states parties understand how the committee views the ICCPR legal obligations.

HUMAN RIGHTS EDUCATION,

See Education (Human Rights).

HUMAN RIGHTS IMPERIALISM

A claim against the international human rights movement or at least against some actors in the human rights arena that imposing international human rights norms on certain societies constitutes an act of human right imperialism against local cultural norms. It is claimed by some states as a defense to complaints of human rights violations, but is not a legally valid defense.

HUMAN RIGHTS MONITOR

See Monitor/Monitoring, infra.

HUMAN RIGHTS MOVEMENT

This term commonly refers to the post-1945 governmental, intergovernmental, and nongovernmental (civil society) developments, in both national and international contexts, in the recognition and protection of human rights.

HUMAN RIGHTS NGO

A wide range of organizations whose purpose is to deal with human rights issues, whether thematically, such as slavery, or as to a certain country, or both. Those organizations of civil society, local, national, and international whose purpose is to promote respect for and fulfillment of human rights. Some NGOs deal exclusively with human rights, and some deal with human rights as part of a broader mandate, which includes human rights issues and nonhuman rights issues.

There are domestic human rights NGOs that operate in a local area, national human rights NGOs that deal with the whole state, regional human rights NGOs that deal with certain regions such as Europe or Asia, and international human rights NGOs. These organizations operate within the scope of their respective mandates and agendas.

HUMAN RIGHTS OFFICER (HRO) (UNHCHR)

A member of the staff of the United Nations human rights organization or field operation, who performs monitoring, reporting, technical assistance, promotion, or any other technical function.

HUMAN RIGHTS REPORTS

See Reports / Reporting, infra.

HUMAN RIGHTS VIOLATION

The failure of a state to act in a manner consistent with its legally binding human rights obligations.

Human rights are legal rights found primarily in international treaties* and in customary international law. These rights create legal norms, or standards of conduct of government, which a state must meet in order to respect human rights and fulfill its legal obligations. Where a state acts or omits to act in a way that is inconsistent with the standard of

conduct in human rights norms, it is said to be violating human rights.

The result of violations is that certain legal measures can and should be taken, usually as set forth in a human rights treaty*, to stop and to redress the violations. These measures are normally taken before courts, commissions, committees, and other permanent or ad hoc bodies set up for that purpose.

Human rights violations are acts of a state that violate the human dignity of individuals subject to its jurisdiction. They are the legitimate concern of all people of all states.

HUMAN SECURITY

Security in the international realm refers to the quality or state of being, or feeling secure from danger and harm, or from interference with desired activity or with physical freedom. Security can exist at different levels such as national, global, or community. Human security is security that places the individual human being at the center of the discussion or debate about security. This is because all law, including national and international human rights law, must be interpreted and applied in a way that most protects the dignity of, and allows for the full development of, individual human beings.

There has historically been a tendency of governments to place national security as the top priority at the expense of individual security and human rights. International human rights law requires that the individual human being be placed as the focus, immediate, and ultimate beneficiary of any system of security.

It is said that the key to enhancing human security is for all governments to pursue a comprehensive human rights program.

HUMAN SHIELD (LOAC)

The intentional use by a party to a conflict of one or more human beings, usually civilians or captured members of the adversary's forces (e.g., POW), placed between the adversary and themselves in a way meant to deter an attack against the forces using the human shields, for fear of killing or harming the unarmed shields. The shields are in effect hostages used for strategic purposes. When it occurs in an international or noninternational armed conflict, using human shields is a breach of the LOAC because it endangers the shields so long as they are unarmed noncombatants. *See* P I, article 51(7).

ICC (INTERNATIONAL CRIMINAL COURT)

The acronym for the International Criminal Court established under the UN by a statute (multilateral treaty) adopted by the international community at a diplomatic conference in Rome on July 17, 1998. The ICC Statute entered into force in July 2002, whereupon the Assembly of States Parties to that treaty proceeded to set up the court and bring it to reality.

This court is a permanent international judicial organ to prosecute and punish individuals who are accused of committing "the most serious crimes of international concern." The crimes within its inherent jurisdiction are genocide, war crimes, crimes against humanity, and aggression (which is to be subsequently defined and applied). The ICC will be a body separate and independent from the United Nations, but will have a relationship to the United Nations by a special international agreement with it.

The ICC will act under the principle of "complementarity" in relation to national criminal jurisdictions, meaning that it will only be able to exercise its jurisdiction if and when national courts that should prosecute are either genuinely unable or unwilling to fully prosecute such crimes. The goal of the court is to end the "culture of impunity" concerning the commission of international crimes, which results from the failure of national criminal jurisdictions to prosecute effectively.

Cases can be triggered by the UN Security Council under its Chapter VII authority, by a state party to the statute of the ICC, or by the independent prosecutor acting on his own motion (*proprio motu*), under his own authority (*ex officio*) granted by the statute.

Such a criminal court was contemplated at the start of the UN, especially in light of the Holocaust, and was even referred to in article VI of the Genocide Convention of 1948. The process of establishing this court began at the UN in the 1950s, but was shelved due to cold war political problems. This process was renewed in 1989 and drew much impetus from the Bosnia conflict and Rwanda genocide of the early 1990s.

ICCPR/CCPR/CPR

Acronyms for the United Nations International Covenant on Civil and Political Rights (1966).

ICESCR/CESCR/ESCR

Acronyms for the United Nations International Covenant on Economic, Social and Cultural Rights (1966).

ICJ

Acronym for either the International Court of Justice, a principal organ and the judicial arm of the United Nations, or the International Commission of Jurists, a worldwide nongovernmental organization of lawyers that advocates in the field of human rights at various international fora, especially at the UN, where it holds consultative status.

ICRC (LOAC)

Acronym for the International Committee of the Red Cross, which is the nongovernmental international organization whose headquarters are in Geneva, Switzerland, and which promotes standard-setting and the adoption of treaties* of international humanitarian law, monitors the application of humanitarian law norms, visits prisoners of war, traces missing family members, and monitors relief operations to civilians in international and noninternational armed conflict situations.

ICTR (INTERNATIONAL CRIMINAL TRIBUNAL FOR RWANDA)

Acronym for the International Criminal Tribunal for Rwanda, established by the UN Security Council in 1994 to prosecute and punish under international criminal law those persons alleged to have committed genocide and crimes against humanity in the Rwanda massacre of 1994. It is an ad hoc tribunal established by UN Security Council resolution 955 of 1994, under the Security Council's authority of Chapter VII of the UNCH.

ICTY (INTERNATIONAL CRIMINAL TRIBUNAL FOR THE FORMER YUGOSLAVIA)

Acronym for the International Criminal Tribunal for the former Yugoslavia, established by the UN Security Council in 1993 to prosecute and punish under international criminal law those persons alleged to have committed violations of international humanitarian law in the Bosnia conflict since 1991. It is an ad hoc tribunal established by UN Security Council resolution 808 of 1993, based on the Security Council's authority under Chapter VII of the UNCH.

IDEOLOGY

A system of beliefs or theories, usually political, held by an individual or a group of people. Communism and capitalism are examples of ideologies.

IFI (INTERNATIONAL FINANCIAL INSTITUTION)

An acronym for an international financial institution. The World Bank and the International Monetary Fund are examples of "IFIs."

IGO

Acronym for an intergovernmental organization. These are international organizations made up of the governments of member states. There are global IGOs and regional IGOs: the UN is a global IGO; the Council of Europe is a regional IGO. International human rights treaty* systems are usually established within the political context of IGOs.

ILLEGAL ALIEN (VS. LEGAL ALIEN)

A noncitizen (alien) who is in a state without the legal right to be present there either because he entered without permission (visa) or because he entered with permission but no longer possesses the right to remain there. Aliens have human rights that must be respected even when they are illegal.

Illegal Combatant (aka Unlawful Combatant/ Unprivileged Combatant/ Belligerent) (loac)

In classic loac, an illegal combatant is a person who did not have the legal right (*jus ad bellum*) to engage in armed conflict hostilities, and whoever does so, as a result, has no protection as a pow if captured and may be prosecuted and punished for murder and other ordinary crimes under national law simply for his participation in the conflict. Such a person does not enjoy the international legal protection of the loac as normal armed forces and other lawful combatants do. Often this designation is given to certain types of belligerents, such as spies, saboteurs, and mercenaries. It is also commonly applied to a person who engages in armed conflict but does not qualify as a combatant for failure to meet one or more of the classic criteria of a lawful combatant, such as wearing a distinctive uniform or emblem, or fighting according to the law of war

In the loac, the legal protections that arise to combatants include the right to lawfully engage in harmful, deadly, and destructive hostile activities, which would otherwise be the commission of common crimes under national law. If captured, a lawful combatant normally has all the rights of pow status under Geneva and Hague law. If the combatant is found to have lacked the legal status as having the jus ad bellum, that person is deprived of much of the protection of the loac accorded to prisoners of war and can be prosecuted for all his belligerent acts. However, even if a person is an illegal combatant, he still retains all his internationally recognized and applicable human rights plus a minimum core of rights under the loac. Actually, under the loac persons found in the context of an armed conflict can only be either civilians or combatants. Legally speaking, if one is not a combatant, one is a civilian. Therefore, a person designated as an illegal/unlawful combatant would be deemed a civilian and entitled to the loac protection of civilians, e.g., under gc IV, although they could be prosecuted for wrongful acts committed. Normally under the loac, if there is any doubt as to the legal status of a combatant, article 5 of the Third Geneva Conventions of 1949 (on pows) and customary international law would require the state to allow the person involved access to a court or tribunal to have their status determined in a court of law. International human rights law is strongly against any person being deemed stripped of any basic due process rights, legal personality, or access to courts to determine the legality of their detention.

In the present state of the loac and international human rights law, basically only spies, saboteurs, mercenaries, and those who do not meet the treaty definition of "combatant" (*see* gc III, article 4) and who engage in armed conflict can be declared and designated as unlawful combatants. Everyone else is a civilian.

Caveat: This term is very similar to, but not the same as "enemy combatant," a term used by the U.S. government. *See also* Unlawful Combatant.

Ill-Founded (Complaint*)

A term used to describe a complaint* filed against a state when it does not, on the basis of the facts alleged, set forth a prima facie case of a violation of an article of a human rights treaty*. It is a ground of inadmissibility. More often, the term *manifestly ill-founded* is used.

ILO (UN)

Acronym for the International Labor Organization, a specialized agency of the United Nations that deals principally with labor rights and related socioeconomic rights/issues.

IMMEDIATE (HUMAN) RIGHT (vs. PROGRESSIVE OR PROGRAMMATIC [HUMAN] RIGHT)

A human right that, in theory, can be enjoyed/exercised by an individual immediately upon the state becoming a party to a treaty* by ratification*. This is contrasted with a "programmatic" or "progressive" right, which, in theory, merely obligates the state to begin to take steps to allow the fulfillment of the right eventually, usually as the state's resources allow. The ICCPR and ECHR are examples of treaties* that contain immediate rights. The ICESCR is an example of one containing programmatic or progressive rights.

IMMIGRANT

An alien who has entered a state with the intent to reside there permanently or indefinitely, abandoning residence in a former state of citizenship or residence. One can be either a legal or illegal immigrant: the former holding legal status to be present in the state, the latter having no such status. *See* Illegal Alien.

IMMUNITY (FROM LEGAL RESPONSIBILITY/ARMED ATTACK)

Receiving immunity most often means that the person receiving it is marked by exception and protection from the normal applicability of the law for one's own personal wrongful actions committed. This means that one cannot be prosecuted and or held civilly liable for any criminal offenses/human rights violations, even if the requisite acts and motivation for commission of such wrongs was in fact done by that person. Usually, this term is used to apply to the government and its agents, e.g., military, police, executive, who commit unlawful acts but who are not prosecuted and punished because of such immunity. Immunity is a shield from individual criminal and civil responsibility. When the case involves human rights violations, it is almost always wrong to grant immunity. It is inconsistent with the principle of accountability and in some case the principle of individual criminal responsibility regardless of status or official position.

Immunity is usually given as a way to bring about an end to a conflict or social convulsion, and normally is granted to all sides in a conflict.

In the law of armed conflict (LOAC) context immunity is sometimes used to mean that a certain type of person(s) cannot be attacked or terrorized, particularly the civilian population, which under humanitarian law is considered "immune" from such violence.

IMMUNITY CLAIMS/RIGHTS (vs. RESOURCE CLAIMS/ RIGHTS)

A type of legal claim or right held by the individual by which the individual can limit what the government may do to the individual. It is a negative right by which the state has a duty to not act or to refrain from acting in a certain way towards the individual. Privacy is a type of immunity right. So is the right to security of person.

These are simply things the government cannot violate against individuals. These are contrasted with "resource" claims or rights by which an individual can require the government to do something for the individual.

IMMUNITY/IMPUNITY AGREEMENTS (ICC) (BIA)

Legal agreements entered into between two or more states wherein these states agree not to hand over any of the nationals of the other state for prosecution for international crimes, or to cooperate with the subject forum so as to prevent the forum from obtaining jurisdiction/competence over those individuals.

In the context of the International Criminal Court this term refers to legal agreements entered into at the initiative of the U.S. (which has not ratified and is not a party to the ICC Statute) with other states, aimed at protecting American servicemen and civilians from ever being prosecuted by the ICC for crimes under the ICC's jurisdiction. These agreements were being pushed by the U.S. near the time of the entry into force of the ICC Statute and were purportedly based on article 98 of the statute. These agreements are quite controversial, and many states argued they are not allowed under article 98 and would have the effect of undermining the effectiveness of the court.

Sometimes referred to as bilateral immunity agreements (BIAS).

IMPARTIALITY (PRINCIPLE)

A principle applied to the supervision and implementation of human rights that states that international intergovernmental organizations and their organs shall neither favor nor disfavor any

state in the monitoring, supervising, and implementing of human rights norms. They will act in a manner impartial to all states and treat all states alike. This means applying the same objective standards to all states.

IMPERFECT OBLIGATIONS (VS. PERFECT OBLIGATIONS)

A legal obligation that is not clear and accepted as to the holder of the duties involved, the particular "duty-holder," and the particular methods of fulfillment and realization in society are not established.

A right can only be legal if it is capable of being realized and the duty-holder and methods of implementation are established. Imperfect obligations do not normally give rise to valid or concrete human rights. Rights claims that are noble but incapable of being realized may be called manifesto or abstract rights.

IMPERIALISM

The taking over or subordination by one government of another government or territory and its people, creating a superior-inferior relationship between the dominant and servient peoples. It is often accomplished by force. Colonialism is a twentieth-century example of imperialism.

IMPLEMENT/IMPLEMENTATION (OF HUMAN RIGHTS NORMS)

A word used to mean the taking of steps through legislation, policy, and action to give practical effect to, and to ensure, the actual, full enjoyment of human rights by concrete measures. This word is used in the field of human rights instead of the word *enforcement*, which implies the use of force to correct violations. Human rights are "implemented," not enforced.

Implementation is a word used to describe all methods and means used to assure the realization of human rights. For example, reporting systems, courts, special rapporteurs, and mobilization of shame (bad publicity) are all "implementation" measures.

IMPLEMENTING LEGISLATION

Laws (statutes and regulations) enacted by a national legislature or authority whose purpose is to transform international legal norms into national (domestic/municipal) law so that it can be used by persons in the domestic legal context to implement human rights and fulfill the state obligation to establish domestic legislation and remedies where they did not previously exist. Implementing legislation is necessary unless the international treaty* norm is "self-executing," in which case no implementing legislation is needed.

IMPLIED RIGHTS

Human rights which are implied from looking beyond the express language of a human rights legal instrument with a view to making the express rights therein more effective. In some human rights systems, rights are implied to assure the successful attainment of the objectives of the particular human rights community states. Such rights are implied as part of the doctrine of effectiveness in order to make a treaty* more effective in protecting all substantive rights in the treaty*. For example, the right to receive legal aid can be implied from the right to access to a court to seek a fair trial.

IMPRESCRIPTABILITY (CRIMINAL OFFENSE)

A principle of criminal law that states that certain criminal norms/prescriptions are not subject to any statute of limitations. This means that criminal responsibility for the violation of such norms never ends over the passage of time, and perpetrators can always be prosecuted. Genocide is an example of an imprescriptable criminal offense.

IMPRISONMENT

The deprivation of personal liberty, usually in a prison or correctional facility, as a result of a final conviction for a criminal act.

Imprisonment of an individual depriving him of personal freedom is not a violation of human rights norms so long as the criminal conviction was made pursuant to law, following a criminal proceeding fully complying with all national and international procedural human rights protections for an accused (*see* ICCPR, article 14). Moreover, the punishment must comply with the principle of proportionality. An imprisonment that does not comply with such laws and norms is an unlawful detention and possibly an arbitrary detention that would violate the human rights of the accused.

Some imprisonments can become not only human rights violations but even constitute crimes against humanity, such as one saw in the Bosnia conflict in the 1990s. Imprisonment as a crime against humanity would be any form of arbitrary physical deprivation of liberty without due process of law, that is widespread or systematic, committed against a civilian population.

Under ICCPR, article 10, all persons

deprived of their liberty shall be treated humanely and with respect for their inherent human dignity.

IMPUNITY (FROM PROSECUTION FOR HUMAN RIGHTS VIOLATIONS)

The factual or legal exemption or freedom from any punishment, loss, or harm to those who have committed human rights violations, usually resulting from a government's refusal or failure to take legal or other enforcement action against the violators—or by an official act/grant of amnesty whereby a state officially forgives such offenses. Impunity is highly disfavored in international human rights law.

IN ABSENTIA TRIAL/PROSECUTION
[Latin, lit.: in absence]

A criminal proceeding (trial) in which the accused is prosecuted without being present at the trial, usually because the prosecuting authority will not permit the defendant's presence, the defendant's whereabouts are unknown, or the defendant is taking refuge in a place that refuses to turn him over. It is prosecution for crimes without the accused's presence or meaningful participation in the proceeding, very often because of the political nature of the trial.

IN ABSTRACTO (VS. IN CONCERTO) (COMPLAINT*)
[Latin, lit.: in the Abstract]

A Latin adverbial expression seen primarily in the case law of the ECHR regarding admissibility of a complaint* (application), usually as to standing, that is, whether the complaint* sets forth that the complainant is a "victim" of a violation. Under ECHR, article 34, the European Court of Human Rights will not deal with complaints (called "applications") presenting issues "*in abstracto,*" that is, where there has been no actual violation of a norm and there is only a hypothetical case, not an actual adversarial case and controversy wherein the complainant has been damaged and can claim to be a "victim" of a violation.

In abstracto is a term also used generally in other contexts to mean something like "hypothetically" or "in the abstract." The opposite of *in abstracto* is "*in concreto.*"

INADMISSIBLE/INADMISSIBILITY (OF COMPLAINT*) (VS. ADMISSIBLE/ADMISSIBILITY)

The criteria upon which a written complaint* alleging human rights violations by a state party is rejected from consideration/adjudication by a human rights forum, such as a court or commission. The status of a formal written complaint* being deemed not admissible, such as for reason of failure to exhaust domestic remedies or the complaint* being deemed incompatible with the treaty*. If a complaint* is inadmissible, the judicial or quasi-judicial body examining it has no competence/subject matter jurisdiction to handle (seize) the case and to determine the merits (application of law to facts). If a case is inadmissible it is rejected/stricken from the role.

INALIENABLE RIGHTS (AKA UNALIENABLE RIGHTS)

Describes rights that at least in theory cannot be voluntarily or involuntarily transferred or surrendered by the holder/bearer of the right nor taken away or annulled by another or by the state. This is so because human rights inhere in human personality based on human dignity, which can never be taken or given away. They cannot be alienated.

In Camera (Judicial Hearing)
[Latin, lit.: in the chamber]

The holding of a judicial hearing/court session in the chambers of the judge or otherwise out of the public view and hearing of the courtroom. *In camera* hearings are an exception to the usual general rule that all criminal and civil hearings should be open to the public so that there can be transparence and public awareness of what is happening in the judicial realm. Most often the judge(s) will allow *in camera* hearings for exceptional circumstances, such as protection of a national security secret or the identity of a witness, or to take testimony of an exceptional witness who requires secrecy, or for the judge(s) and attorneys to meet to deal with procedural or evidentiary matters best dealt with out of public hearing.

Incendiary Weapons (loac)

Military weapons made of substances whose purpose is to burn in flames and destroy by fire and heat. An example is napalm, i.e., a chemical compound resembling "jellied gasoline," which ignites upon impact and scatters, covering and burning all that it contacts.

Inclusion/Inclusive (aka Nonexclusion/Exclusive) (vs. Exclusion/Exclusive, Noninclusion/Inclusive)

The acceptance of everyone without exception and inclusion of them as an equal part of a society, or as covered by a law, or as beneficiaries of a program, project, or system, such as education. It is not discriminatory and reflects the principle of equality. The opposite is noninclusive. Human rights require, with certain exceptions, the inclusion of all human beings in all parts of society.

The nondiscrimination and equality provisions of international human rights instruments are legal measures aimed at promoting inclusion. *See* iccpr, articles 2.1 and 26.

Incommunicado Detention

A Spanish term meaning not being able to be communicated with. "Incommunicado" means that one is held against one's will by the government—or those acting as its agents or with its consent—in detention in such a way that it is impossible to communicate with anyone on the outside. The detainee's whereabouts are concealed or permission to communicate is not granted, so that no one can communicate with the detainee. Purposeful prevention of communication by/with a person in official detention.

Incompatible/Incompatibility (Complaint*) (vs. Compatible/ Compatibility)

The state of something being incapable of being associated or consistent with another thing. Used in human rights complaint* procedures to describe the condition of a written complaint* that is inadmissible because it is not in accordance with, or consonant with, the requirements of the norms of the treaty*, such as regards the person who filed the complaint*, when it was filed, its contents, the time when the events occurred, the place where they occurred, or whether it claims a violation of a substantive right in the treaty*.

If a complaint* is incompatible with the underlying treaty* that is grounds for finding the complaint* inadmissible and for ceasing consideration and refusing to be seized of the matter. This determination of compatibility is usually made initially by a commission or court, depending upon which system is involved.

INCOMPATIBLE RESERVATION

A treaty* reservation that is not compatible with the object and purpose of the treaty*, and thus infringes on a core aspect of the treaty* bargained for by the states that adopted the treaty*.

A state party to a treaty* may not, when ratifying* the treaty*, submit with the ratification* a reservation that would defeat the purpose and *raison d'etre* of the treaty*.

The legal effect of submitting an incompatible reservation is controversial and not universally established.

IN CONCRETO (VS. IN ABSTRACTO) (COMPLAINT*)
[Latin, lit.: in Concrete/In Substance]

A Latin adverbial expression seen primarily in the case law of the ECHR regarding the admissibility of a complaint* (application). usually as to standing— that is, whether the complaint* sets forth that the complainant is a "victim" of a violation. Under ECHR, article 34, the European Court of Human Rights will only handle complaints (called "petitions") alleging *in concreto* violations of the convention, that is, real/actual violations rather than hypothetical issues of an "*in abstracto*" nature.

The phrase *in concreto* is also used generally in other contexts to mean real, concrete, actual. The opposite is "*In Abstracto*" (*see* supra).

INCORPORATION (OF INTERNATIONAL NORMS)

A principle by which international customs and rules are considered to be part of municipal law. In some states, international norms do not automatically become binding in domestic law unless the process of incorporation exists by which such norms are "incorporated" into domestic law. Compare this to "Transformation (of Norms)," infra.

INDEMNIFICATION (REPARATION)

The provision for compensation made for a violation of human rights, usually by way of a monetary payment to cover any damages or injuries incurred, paid to the victim or the victim's family. Usually, indemnification is ordered by a judicial or quasi-judicial forum as a means of reparation for the loss suffered by victims of human rights violations.

INDEMNITY/INDEMNITIES

Compensation made for a violation of human rights, usually by way of a monetary payment to cover any damages or injuries incurred, and paid to the victim or his family.

INDEPENDENT AND IMPARTIAL JUDICIARY

A term describing the condition of a judicial organ as one wherein the judges are

1. Independent: Free and separate from any external influences such as governmental officials, persons, political parties, and anything else that could influence the decision-making of the judges, and

2. Impartial: Not favoring, being biased, or prejudiced in any way for or against anyone in the determination of his judicial decisions.

This especially requires independence from, and impartiality as regards to, the government. This condition is a prerequisite for a person being assured the human right to a fair civil or criminal trial, i.e., procedural due process wherein judges will make objective decisions based only on the law and facts, the merits, in a rule of law system.

INDEPENDENT EXPERTS

Persons with particular expertise in human rights generally or in specific subject areas, such as children or refugees, and who act not as a representative of any state interest or agency, but as individuals. These are contrasted with experts aligned with a state or other party to a human rights issue. Independent experts are supposed to seek the truth of a situation or issue objectively and neutrally.

The UN Sub-Commission on Promotion and Protection of Human Rights is composed of independent experts in human rights, not state representatives.

INDEPENDENT MONITOR

A person or group that is present and watching a particular human rights situation or place where human rights issues are arising, and who is not related in interest with any of the parties involved in the human rights issues. The ICRC sometimes monitors compliance with LOAC norms in armed conflicts as an independent monitor in places where violations may be occurring.

INDICTMENT (CRIMINAL)

A formal charging document against a person or persons accusing them of having violated one or more penal laws, and requesting their arrest and commencement of a criminal proceeding. It is the initial criminal pleading by the state or prosecuting authority.

Different criminal justice systems have different means of commencing prosecution against an individual or individuals who are accused of committing a crime. Indictment is a means used normally when the criminal acts were not witnessed by law enforcement authorities who could thereupon make an immediate arrest. In many systems a public prosecuting attorney gathers evidence of a crime, writes up the charging document, and submits it to a court/tribunal, or perhaps a grand jury, for confirmation and follow-up.

INDIGENOUS PEOPLE(S)/POPULATIONS

The word *indigenous* itself generally means having originated in and living or occurring naturally in a particular region or environment. When used with "people(s)" or "populations," it is difficult to define. There is no universally accepted authoritative definition of this term, although the UN Commission on Human Rights and Subcommission have been struggling to find an acceptable one. Some sense of definition can be gleaned from the following suggested descriptions taken from several sources: the people native to the area; the people in residence when "civilization" arrived (some define this as dating back to prehistoric times); communities or nations having an important historical continuity with societies that inhabited the same general territory and that predated colonization or invasion by other peoples.

Some say the basic elements of indigenous groups are

1. Preexistence: Those who descended from those who inhabited an area prior to the arrival of another group;

2. Nondominance: The group is usually subservient to, or marginalized from, the rest of the later-arriving inhabitants of the society/state;

3. Culturally different from the later arrivals; and

4. Self-identifying as an indigenous group: the group believes itself to be the descendents of the original inhabitants and wishes to preserve its distinct identity, culture, and control of its land and resources.

INDISCRIMINATE ATTACK/ FORCE (LOAC)

A bombardment or other attack or use of force against an enemy, either offensive or defensive, wherein the force is not directed at a specific military target, or one that employs a method or means of armed force that cannot be directed at a specific military target and thus cannot discriminate between civilian and military objects and persons. Indiscriminate attacks are prohibited by the LOAC as a violation of the "Principle of Discrimination."

Examples of indiscriminate attacks or force would be lighting forests on fire where both civilian and combatants are found; carpet bombing in mixed civilian-military areas; or the firing of guns, missiles, or other weapons generally in the direction of the enemy but not such as to consciously avoid civilians and to minimize "collateral damage."

INDIVIDUAL CAPACITY (VS. REPRESENTATIVE CAPACITY)

A term referring to the status of a person who is sitting as a member of a committee, commission, subcommission, or working group or other implementation body as an independent individual or private person, usually as an expert and not as a representative of a state's government. This person can at least in theory act and vote independently as he feels correct and not as his state dictates, unlike one who sits in a "representative capacity." Those who are chosen to be members of a body sitting in their "individual capacity" are usually experts chosen for their particular expertise and objectivity.

INDIVIDUAL COMPLAINT* (VS. STATE COMPLAINT*)

A complaint* that is filed by, or on behalf of, an individual or group of individuals alleging a state's violation of human rights. This is compared to an "Interstate (i.e., state[s] vs. state) Complaint*."

INDIVIDUAL CRIMINAL RESPONSIBILITY (PRINCIPLE)

A principle of international law that says that all individuals who participate in the planning, preparation, or execution of acts that constitute violations of international criminal norms, such as genocide or war crimes, are subject to criminal prosecution and punishment as individuals without regard to their belonging to, or acting on behalf of, a state armed force or any other entity. This principle arose primarily from the Nuremberg Principles of 1945 (*see* infra). This principle aims at deterring such criminal acts and at avoiding the public imposition of collective guilt on a whole society for the criminal acts of only a few members of that society.

INDIVIDUALISM (VS. SOCIALISM)

A concept on which most democratic systems of government are based that states that the primary purpose of government is to create conditions in society that best advance the well-being of the individual and allow each individual in society the means to realize his full human potential as individuals.

INDIVIDUAL RIGHT (VS. GROUP/COLLECTIVE RIGHT)

A human right held by an individual human being as the holder/bearer of that right without reference to being a part of any society or group.

INDIVISIBILITY (OF HUMAN RIGHTS) (PRINCIPLE)

A principle of international human rights law that says that all human rights together form a whole that cannot be divided into subsets or that a state cannot choose to respect certain human rights or certain categories of human rights and to exclude others. For example, the state cannot accept economic or social rights and not respect civil and political rights.

It is aimed at preserving the "universality" of human rights from claims that they are culturally relative and that one group of rights can be accepted and respected while another group cannot, or cannot yet, be respected because of circumstances in a state.

It is usually seen in the context of other terms, such as "interrelated," "interdependent," or "interconnected."

IN EXTENSO
[Latin, lit.: in extensive manner]

A Latin expression meaning to express something, usually a treaty* text or article, fully or completely, not just the most pertinent part or most important part.

IN FINE (END OF AN ARTICLE)
[Latin, lit.: at the end]

A Latin adverbial expression describing the location of a particular part of a text as being "at the end" of an article of a treaty*. It means located at the end of the article. An example: In the ICCPR the right against double jeopardy is found in article 14 *in fine*.

INFRA (VS. SUPRA)

An adverb used in writing to refer the reader to a later place after or below the spot where the word "infra" appears. A Latin term meaning "below this point" or "later in this written work/document/ instrument." In a case citation it usually means that the case will be subsequently referred to or that the citation will be given further on in the text of that decision or judgment.

Example: "*See* INGO, infra."

INGO

An acronym for an International Nongovernmental Organization. This refers to an NGO of international scope, such as Amnesty International or the ICRC.

INHERENT (DIGNITY/RIGHT)

That which belongs to someone by its very nature and involvement in the essential character or constitution of that person. It is used to describe a permanent characteristic of human dignity/human rights. It is part of the nature of human beings as human beings that was not created or granted from anyone outside of man.

INHERENT JURISDICTION (ICC) (AKA AUTOMATIC JURISDICTION)

See Automatic Jurisdiction, supra.

INHERENT LIMITATIONS (OF RIGHTS)

A theory/concept found in the case law of the European Convention system that argues that there are certain limitations to the exercise of human rights by certain persons by the very nature of their circumstances, such as what a prisoner experiences regarding freedom of expression or movement. The argument that these limitations are necessary, legitimate, and thus do not violate such person's human rights has not generally been accepted.

INHUMANE TREATMENT (OF PERSONS IN ARMED CONFLICT) (VS. HUMANE TREATMENT) (LOAC)

Very similar to "Inhuman Treatment" (*see* infra), but is a term used in the LOAC to describe brutal, barbarous, or cruel acts or treatment. These are acts or treatments committed against other persons by a party to an armed conflict that do not meet basic minimum humanitarian standards. Such treatment would be destitute of compassion for suffering.

"Inhumane Treatment" is bad because it fails to respect the human dignity of persons in armed conflicts. *See* GC III, article 3(1).

INHUMAN TREATMENT/PUNISHMENT

State treatment or punishment of human beings under its jurisdiction in a way that suggests the victim is in a subclass of humanity. It is such treatment as deliberately causes intense physical and mental suffering, although not rising to the level of torture. This type of treatment is usually prohibited in a human rights norm, which also prohibits torture and cruel or degrading treatment or punishment.

These all represent different levels of severity of treatment/punishment of a human being, inconsistent with human dignity. Inhuman treatment and punishment are different:

1. Inhuman "treatment": If the inhuman acts are not being done for purposes of punishment of the victim for a prior act, such as for a criminal or other violation, the term "inhuman treatment" is used;

2. Inhuman "punishment": If the inhuman acts were done for purposes of punishing the victim for his prior conduct, such as for a criminal conviction, the term "inhuman punishment" is used.

In either case, such treatment/punishment is inconsistent with a victim's inherent human dignity and violates human rights. *See* ICCPR, article 7. (Compare "Inhumane Treatment," supra).

In the *Tadic* case the ICTY held that inhuman treatment was, as defined in its statute in the context of international criminal law, an intentional act or omission, which, judged objectively, is deliberate and not accidental, causing serious mental or physical suffering or injury, or constituting a serious attack on human dignity.

In the *Soering* case the European Court of Human Rights, in deciding that the U.S. "death row syndrome" constituted inhuman treatment, said that to so conclude, the court must consider the following factors:

1. The nature and context of the treatment;

2. The manner and method of execution;

3. The duration;

4. The age, sex, and state of health of the victim.

IN LIMINE LITIS (AKA PRELIMINARY)
OBJECTIONS (TO COMPLAINT*)
*[Latin, lit.: in the threshold of the
litigation]*

Refers to the phase of a formal complaint* process, such as one before a human rights commission or court, that takes place before the consideration of the merits (application of the law to the facts) of the case. Usually used in connection with the term "Objection," which is a formal challenge to the court as to its competence or to the admission of evidence.

Objections *in limine litis* are the same as "Preliminary Objections." They are usually made and resolved in the admissibility phase of a complaint* procedure. Such objections are raised by a state to have the forum rule the complaint* inadmissible.

IN LOCO (INVESTIGATIONS/
FACT-FINDING/VISIT)
[Latin, lit.: in the place]

An investigation that takes place at the place or the scene where or near where a human rights violation occurred. It is often done by a supervising/implementing body that sends a delegation of its members/agents to visit a place (country) to gather immediate, credible, firsthand evidence/information to report back to the body. *See also* In Situ and On-Site Investigation/Fact-Finding, which mean the same thing.

IN SITU (INVESTIGATIONS/
FACT-FINDING/VISIT)

Same as *In Loco* (*see* supra) or "On-Site Investigation" (*see* infra).

INSTITUTIONAL HUMAN RIGHTS LAW

Human rights norms and limitations imposed on an intergovernmental body created by states. Normally, human rights norms are legal obligations of states imposed by treaty* and customary law norms, and theoretically not binding on individuals or institutions/organizations. However, in recent years there has been a call, primarily from the NGO community for international intergovernmental organizations to themselves conduct their business according to human rights norms.

INSTRUMENT (GLOBAL/REGIONAL/
NATIONAL/SUBSIDIARY/LEGAL/
NONLEGAL/POLITICAL, ETC.)

A formal, official, written act of a state or states set forth in a document, such as a treaty*, in which a state expresses its intention with regards to certain human rights principles or norms. Some instruments set forth human rights principles in a nonbinding document, whereas some instruments set forth human rights legal norms binding upon the states parties who ratify* it. In the context of an IGO, the most common human rights instruments are treaties* that set forth substantive human rights norms and mechanisms and procedures for their implementation. Instruments can be, inter alia, of a global or regional scope; legal or nonlegal, i.e., political or moral. The ICCIPR and the ECHR are international human rights instruments. Such instruments can serve as the terms of reference of an organization and the standard for judging the effectiveness of such organs. Examples of different types of instruments are as follows:

A global instrument: Involving all states of the world, such as a Geneva Convention;

A regional instrument: Involving only states in a certain region or political organization, such as the Council of Europe;

A national instrument: Involving only one state;

A subsidiary instrument: Covering secondary areas or themes, such as the Refugee Convention;

A legal instrument: One that is legally binding;

A nonlegal instrument: One that is not legally binding;

A political instrument: One that is not legally binding but is politically coercive;

A sectional instrument: Covering only a specific human right or a certain group of people;

A slice instrument: Covering a specific human right in a separate treaty* that was taken from a general human rights treaty*. This instrument amplifies the right and its implementation mechanisms to make it better defined and respected.

INSURGENCE/INSURGENT (LOAC)

An act or instance of a person revolting against civil government, authority, or an established political system, usually by the use of armed force.

INTEGRITY OF THE CONVENTION (TREATY*)

The traditional international legal proposition that no reservation to a particular treaty* is valid unless it is accepted by all the contracting parties without exception.

INTEGRITY RIGHTS

A description of a certain type of human right that has as its purpose the protection of the mental, moral, or physical integrity of human beings. Integrity has the sense of wholeness, well-being, soundness, and safety.

Examples of integrity rights are the right to life, freedom from torture, freedom of religion, right to privacy, right to found a family.

INTER ALIA (ABBREV.: i.a.)
[Latin, lit.: among other things]

A Latin expression meaning that a certain, specified, enumerated thing is among other unspecified, unenumerated things in a given context. For example: "The ECHR, article 4, prohibits, inter alia, slavery"; or "The first-generation of human rights protects, inter alia, the right to vote."

INTER-AMERICAN COMMISSION (ON HUMAN RIGHTS)

The Inter-American Commission on Human Rights is commonly referred to as the Inter-American Commission. It is the quasi-judicial regional human rights body of the Organization of American States and handles petition cases under the IACHR, and against non-IACHR states. The commission sits in Washington DC

INTER-AMERICAN COURT (OF HUMAN RIGHTS)

The Inter-American Court of Human Rights is commonly referred to as simply the Inter-American Court. This court is the judicial body created by the Inter-

American Convention on Human Rights to judicially monitor state party compliance with the norms of the IACHR within the human rights system of the Organization of American States. This court, which sits in San Jose, Costa Rica, has the competence to handle both contentious cases (individual and interstate cases) and advisory opinions.

INTERDEPENDENCE (OF HUMAN RIGHTS) (PRINCIPLE)

A principle applicable to all human rights that states that whatever type of human rights is involved, each individual human right is dependent upon every other human right, so that every human right is potentially at risk if even one is. It is somewhat like saying human rights are like a house of cards; taking one away will cause all the others to topple.

Usually seen with its fellow principles of "Indivisibility" and "Interrelatedness." This principle is used to combat arguments of cultural relativism and attempts at hierarchical separation and differentiation between norms and generations of norms.

INTERFERENCE (WITH DOMESTIC/ INTERNAL AFFAIRS)

Any form of governmental involvement in the affairs of another state. It is a principle of international law that states may not interfere in matters that are essentially within the domestic jurisdiction of another state. *See* UNCH, article 2.7. This is known as the "principle of noninterference." *See also* Intervention.

Generally speaking, this principle does not apply to human rights violations by a state.

INTERFERENCE WITH ENJOYMENT/ EXERCISE (OF HUMAN RIGHTS)

The action of a state that prevents a human being from fully and freely exercising a particular human right. In cases of human rights complaints* under consideration by a judicial or quasi-judicial human rights forum, the first issue to be decided as to the merits of the case is whether there has been an "interference" by the state with the victim's exercise of a human right norm within the jurisdiction of the forum. This issue involves the question of whether the state in fact did something that prevented the victim from being able to exercise or enjoy a human right or rights fully.

INTERGOVERNMENTAL ORGANIZATION (IGO) (VS. NGO)

A separate governmental (made up of member state government agencies or officials) organization that is either global or regional in scope and whose activity involves, inter alia, standard setting and compliance with the international law of human rights among states. The United Nations and the Council of Europe are intergovernmental organizations. These are abbreviated as IGOs.

There are international IGOs open to all states in the world, and regional IGOs open only to states in a certain geographical-political region, such as the Organization of African Unity.

INTERIM MEASURES (AKA PREVENTATIVE/ PROVISIONAL MEASURES)

Urgent measures that a judicial or quasi-judicial body requests that a state take, in a case brought against that state in that forum. The purpose of the request is to get the alleged violator state to take immediate steps to protect the alleged victim from some imminent harm, such as a capital punishment or deportation to another state. The request is usually made at the time or soon after a complaint* alleging human rights violations is filed with the forum, and usually the complaining party specifically makes a request for such precautionary interim measures. Such measures preserve the status quo and allow the forum to decide whether a violation has occurred or will occur while not allowing the state to undermine the case or render a decision meaningless, such as if a person who is innocent or wrongly convicted is executed.

See also Preventative Measures, infra.

INTERNAL ARMED CONFLICT (LOAC)

An armed conflict that takes place within the territory of only one state. International Humanitarian Law applies to certain internal armed conflicts, particularly common article 3 of the four GCs, and the 1977 Protocol II to the GCs, for states that have ratified that Protocol. Human rights instruments and customary international law binding on the state involved will also apply during such conflict, except as to any rights properly derogated by the state.

INTERNAL DISTURBANCE (LOAC)

Situations in which, although there is not, strictly speaking, an armed conflict, there is a serious or lasting internal confrontation, which includes acts of violence ranging from spontaneous isolated acts of revolt to a struggle by groups in various stages of organization against the authorities in power. These situations do not necessarily escalate into an open struggle, but the authorities use large police forces, and even the armed forces, to restore order within a country.

INTERNALLY DISPLACED PERSONS (IDP)

Human beings who are forced by circumstances to leave their home areas and move to other places within the state, and are temporarily or permanently prevented from returning home. Defined in the London Declaration of International Law Principles on Internally Displaced Persons (2000) as:

> Persons or groups of persons who have been forced to flee or leave their homes or places of habitual residence as a result of armed conflict, internal strife, or systematic violations of human rights, and who have not crossed an internationally recognized State border.

These are not refugees, who are people who flee into another country to flee past or feared persecution based on race, religion, nationality, political opinion, or membership in a particular social group. This term is often seen abbreviated as IDPS.

INTERNATIONAL ARMED CONFLICT (vs. NONINTERNATIONAL ARMED CONFLICT) (LOAC)

An armed conflict between two or more states. Such a conflict is governed by the Law of Armed Conflict, which includes International Humanitarian Law.

INTERNATIONAL BILL OF RIGHTS

A term used in the field of human rights to refer to the human rights and fundamental freedoms and implementation mechanisms contained in four of the

key foundational international instruments of human rights. The International Bill of Rights consists of the following instruments:

1. The Universal Declaration of Human Rights (1948);

2. The United Nations International Covenant on Civil and Political Rights (1966);

3. The Optional Protocol (First) to the UN Covenant on Civil and Political Rights (1966);

4. United Nations Covenant on Economic, Social, and Cultural Rights (1966).

Some sectors of the international human rights community would add the Second Optional Protocol to the ICCPR, on abolition of the death penalty; however, this is not yet generally accepted as of the time of this writing.

These instruments together set forth all of the human rights and remedies deemed by the international community as necessary to protect human dignity. The texts of these four instruments are set forth in full in Appendix B at the end of this work.

INTERNATIONAL CIVIL PRESENCE

The placing of a nongovernmental person from other states in a place where conflict has occurred or may occur, or for a critical event such as an election, in order to observe and monitor the actions of all persons so that law and order prevails and no human rights violations occur.

In certain conflict situations, it is helpful to defuse or stabilize volatile situations by injecting the presence of foreign observers. This is done with the intention that a presumably objective, neutral, and vigilant presence is in place so that the members of society, both govern-

mental and nongovernmental, are deterred from acting inappropriately. If any members of the target state do not act appropriately, the persons representing the international civil presence can report and bring to light any misdeeds to the suitable authority to correct the situation.

INTERNATIONAL COMMITTEE OF THE RED CROSS (ABBREV. ICRC) (LOAC)

See ICRC.

INTERNATIONAL COMMUNITY

The sum total of all states, international intergovernmental organizations, and all of civil society acting collectively. Often in talking about human rights norms one refers to what is the attitude or position of the international community, that is, a sense of what the whole world or its state representatives accepts as valid and legitimate. Sometimes also referred to as the "community of nations."

INTERNATIONAL COURT OF JUSTICE (ICJ) (UN)

A principal judicial organ of the UN, granted jurisdiction over certain contentious (adversarial) cases between states and is authorized to issue advisory opinions to the various organs and agencies of that body.

INTERNATIONAL COVENANT ON CIVIL AND POLITICAL RIGHTS (ICCPR/CCPR/CPR) (UN 1966)

A general human rights treaty adopted by the United Nations in 1966 and entered into force in 1976, which established legally binding human rights norms as to the civil and political rights of individual members of states that ratify it. It is the key human rights legal instrument forming part of what has come to be known as the International Bill of Rights. *See* Appendix B.

Modern human rights instruments started in 1948 with the adoption of the Universal Declaration of Human Rights in the UN. This instrument set forth the first list of specific internationally recognized human rights. But the UDHR was not a legal document that created binding obligations on states. The ICCPR was intended to put into a legal instrument those civil and political rights found in the UDHR, in more expansive form.

The UDHR contained civil, political, economic, social, and cultural rights. Because of the philosophical differences between East and West after World War II, there could be no agreement on one legal instrument containing all those types of rights. Therefore, the states of the UN decided to make two separate treaties (called covenants), one setting forth civil and political rights, and the other setting forth economic, social, and cultural rights (the ICESCR).

The ICCPR implementation is supervised by the Human Rights Committee. This organ can hear complaints by one or more states parties against another state if the complaining states submitted a declaration accepting the power of the committee to do so under article 41. The HRC can also receive individual complaints of violations by victims against a state that has ratified the [First] Optional Protocol to the ICCPR.

As of the date of this book, no state has ever filed a complaint against another state for a violation. Approximately 138 countries have ratified this treaty.

There is a Second Optional Protocol for abolishing the use of the death penalty in states that ratify* it.

The text of this covenant is set forth in Appendix B.

INTERNATIONAL COVENANT ON ECONOMIC, SOCIAL, AND CULTURAL RIGHTS (ICESCR) (UN 1966)

A general human rights treaty adopted by the United Nations in 1966 and entered into force in 1976, which established legally binding human rights standards as to the economic, social, and cultural human rights of individual members of states that ratify* it. Some of these rights were also seen in the UDHR, which was the historical source of the ICESCR.

The text of this covenant is set forth in Appendix B.

INTERNATIONAL CRIME (VS. DOMESTIC/NATIONAL CRIME)

A penal offense created by international law both from treaties*, e.g., the Genocide Convention, and from customary international law sources, e.g., war crime violations of the *Laws and Customs of War*. It is a criminal offense against the Law of Nations, i.e., public international law, as opposed to national criminal law systems.

International crimes are crimes against the whole of mankind. In Latin it is known as *delicti juris gentium*. Piracy, slavery, torture, and crimes against humanity are examples of other international crimes.

INTERNATIONAL CRIMINAL COURT (ICC)

See ICC, supra.

INTERNATIONAL CRIMINAL LAW

A body of principles and rules in international law that involves defining crimes that are considered as harming all of humankind, and arresting, prosecuting, and punishing persons accused of such crimes.

In the seventeenth century the international community began to consider some acts as violating the peace, order, and stability of the whole world, with its condemnation of piracy at sea as an international crime, which any state could prosecute. International criminal law developed slowly from then until World War II, wherein the international community experienced the horrors of the Holocaust and decided to do what it could to punish and prevent such things from happening again. Since the Nuremberg Trials held against Nazi war criminals in the late 1940s (based largely on the 1907 Hague IV Convention and Rules), the international community has been continuing to develop a system of international criminal law, which makes it an international crime to commit certain types of human rights violations, such as torture, genocide, war crimes, and crimes against humanity.

This effort includes the development of international criminal standards and sanctions by multilateral treaties such as in the Convention on the Prevention and Punishment of the Crime of Genocide and the Geneva Conventions of 1949 and 1977 Protocols. It also involved the continued development and articulation of customary international law, such as in the Draft Code of Crimes against the Peace and Security of Mankind prepared by the UN International Law Commission. It culminates in the attempt of the international community in the late 1990s to create a permanent international criminal court by the 1998 adoption of the Rome Statute of the International Criminal Court. The Rome Statute en-

tered into force in July 2002. Put into place by the Assembly of States Parties in 2003, that court is to prosecute the worst international criminal law violations: genocide, war crimes, crimes against humanity, and waging an aggressive war (aggression). This evolution also included the creation of procedures, such as extradition of suspects or fugitives, the investigation and prevention of crimes, and state cooperation in the international criminal process; and the establishment of specific enforcement mechanisms such as the UN ad hoc International Criminal Tribunal for the former Yugoslavia (ICTY) and the International Criminal Tribunal for Rwanda, which apply such law.

Basic principles of this body of international law (Nuremberg Principles) include the principle of individual criminal responsibility, which states that every human being shall be individually responsible for any acts committed against international law regardless of whether he did such acts in an official capacity (such as a soldier or government official) on behalf of a state, and that there is no official immunity for anyone, even a sitting president, for committing them.

INTERNATIONAL DECADE (UN)

See Decade.

INTERNATIONAL HUMAN RIGHTS LAW (AKA INTERNATIONAL LAW OF HUMAN RIGHTS)

That part of the body of public international law that sets forth the international legal norms, rules, principles for the protection of the human rights and fundamental freedoms of every individual human being. Buergenthal, Shelton, and Stewart define it in their book simply as "the law that deals with the protection of individuals and groups against violations of their internationally guaranteed rights, and with the promotion of these rights." These norms, rules and principles establish the legally acceptable and, in theory, legally enforceable minimum standards of conduct of government to protect the inherent human dignity of human beings.

This body of international law comes from two major sources; international treaties such as the ICCCPR, and customary international law, which is formed by the consistent practice of states over the course of time (Usage), accompanied by the subjective element that it is considered binding as a matter of law (*opinio juris*). Other sources are general principles of law, and the writings of experts and international case decisions.

Some human rights norms are legally binding and are part of what is called hard law, while some norms contained in some resolutions, declarations, guidelines and sets of principles form what is known as soft law. Though not legally binding upon states this soft law serves as a more specific guide to states as to how they can comply with their hard law human rights obligations.

To some scholars International Human Rights Law includes that body of law called International Humanitarian Law, which applies only in times of armed conflict.

INTERNATIONAL HUMAN RIGHTS MOVEMENT

A general term referring to the whole of the activity of governmental, intergovernmental, and nongovernmental/civil society actors, both groups and individuals, aimed at theorizing, articulating, standard setting, supervision, implementation, monitoring, and criminal enforcement of all human rights at the national, regional, and global level. It most particularly concerns all those who are actively engaged in the promotion and protection of human rights as understood in the international human rights sense.

INTERNATIONAL INTER-GOVERNMENTAL ORGANIZATION (IIGO) (VS. REGIONAL IGO)

An IGO of global/international character, open to all states in the world. Such organizations are abbreviated as IIGOs. The United Nations is an IIGO. This is contrasted with a regional IGO, such as the Council of Europe, which is open only to states in a certain region.

INTERNATIONALIZATION OF HUMAN RIGHTS

The historical concept that human rights have evolved from an idea found in the domestic laws of countries, such as certain constitutional law protection of civil liberties, and have become accepted as international norms generally applicable to all states. It also refers to the development of international human rights law and legal and political systems in international organizations for the promotion and protection of human rights in all countries. It grew out of an international idea that how human beings are treated anywhere is the concern of everyone everywhere, including internationally.

INTERNATIONALIZED ARMED CONFLICT (LOAC)

An armed conflict occurring within only one state but when either the state or an armed opposition group has brought in an outside state for help or an outside state has voluntarily/unilaterally intervened militarily on one party's behalf.

Also said of an armed conflict governed by the 1977 Protocol I of the Geneva Conventions, as to noninternational armed conflicts wherein a people is fighting alien occupation, colonial domination, or apartheid in a struggle to achieve self-determination. These are considered "internationalized" armed conflicts, which would otherwise only be noninternational. International humanitarian law applies to internationalized armed conflicts.

INTERNATIONAL LEGAL PERSONALITY

A legal term signifying that an entity has standing as a member of the community of nations and possesses certain rights and has certain obligations as a subject of international law. International legal personalities are primarily states; however, international intergovernmental organizations, belligerent groups, corporate bodies such as NGOs, and even individuals can also possess some aspects of an international legal personality for certain purposes. This is particularly and increasingly so in the field of international human rights.

INTERNATIONAL MILITARY TRIBUNAL (IMT)

The international criminal court established by the U.S., U.S.S.R., France, and Great Britain in 1945 for prosecution of the leading Nazi war criminals at the end of World War II. The court was to sit in Nuremberg, Germany, and to prosecute the major Nazis, both military and civilian, who caused the worse international crimes, such as war crimes, crimes against humanity, and crimes against peace (planning or waging an aggressive war ("aggression"). The IMT prosecuted such persons as Goebbels and Hess.

There were other international criminal prosecutions at other places in Germany and other states against other Nazis under Control Council Law No. 10.

INTERNATIONAL MINIMUM STANDARD (OF STATE TREATMENT) (VS. NATIONAL TREATMENT STANDARD)

See Minimum (International) Standard

INTERNATIONAL NONGOVERNMENTAL ORGANIZATION (INGO)

A nongovernmental organization (NGO) that is international in scope and activity, maintains offices in different countries, and is involved in various international matters.

INTERNATIONAL SOLIDARITY

The concept of all states in the world cooperating and working together with each other in a positive, friendly, sharing, and mutually beneficial manner to solve problems of concern to all, and with a sense that, while respecting the existence of different states, nations, and peoples, this is one planet with one people, and all peoples in all states should work together as one.

INTERPRETATION (OF TREATY* NORM)

1. General: The search for the meaning of the language of a treaty* norm in order to discover its true meaning in the abstract or as applicable to certain situations. Interpretation of a treaty* is a process that normally requires examination of the treaty* text in good faith, in accordance with the ordinary meaning

given to the treaty* terms in their context, and in light of the object and purpose of the treaty*. One may also look to subsequent state practice or instruments and to the preparatory works (*travaux préparatoires*) for further help. *See* Vienna Convention of 1969, articles 31 and 32.

2. Instrument of Interpretation: A legal instrument filed by a state upon treaty* ratification*, wherein the state party expresses its written understanding of the meaning of a particular article or words of the treaty*. This sometimes happens when a state feels the article/word is vague or ambiguous or when it needs to be understood in light of the state's constitution or high court decisions. It is also called an "instrument of understanding." *See* Understanding.

Often an instrument of interpretation is also submitted along with the state's reservations and declarations.

Interrelatedness (of Human Rights) (Principle)

The concept of a mutual or reciprocal relation among all human rights. A principle of human rights that says that all human rights are closely related to each other, e.g., the rights to food, expression, movement, association, and the right to vote. There is a logical and conceptual legal relationship between all human rights, and this relationship must be factored into any application or interpretation of human rights.

Inter Se/Inter Sese (Treaty* Obligation/Agreement)
[Latin, lit.: between each other/themselves]

Refers to treaty* obligations existing between two states, as opposed to obliga-tions to other states in general or multi-laterally or to other types of legal obligations, such as obligations *erge omnes*. Sometimes the obligations of states *inter se/inter sese* conflict with these other types of obligations. *Inter se* and *inter sese* mean the same thing.

Interstate Complaint* (vs. Individual Complaint*)

A complaint* filed in an international judicial or quasi-judicial forum by a state (or states) party to a treaty* against another state party, usually when both complainant(s) and respondent states have accepted the competence (jurisdiction) of the body handling the complaint*. In such a complaint* a state or states allege that another state has breached its obligations under a human rights treaty* and that the forum should seize the matter and resolve it according to the treaty* regime.

Interstate Cooperation in Penal/Criminal Matters

The official cooperation of one state in the criminal investigation, arrest, and prosecution of crimes by another state upon that state's request. Such cooperation often involves the arrest of fugitives, extradition, rendition, legal assistance, transfer of legal proceedings, transfer of prisoners recognition, and enforcement of foreign penal judgments, seizures, and forfeitures.

Intervene (Right to)

A claimed or emerging international legal norm that would say that a state, a group of states, or certain international organizations may have the legal right to intervene in what would otherwise be the domestic affairs of a state where there are systematic and massive violations of human rights that pose a threat to world or regional peace.

INTERVENTION

1. Political: International or state involvement in which various forms of coercion are employed against a state. It is a principle of international law found in article 2.7 of the UNCH that a state or international organization may not intervene in the domestic affairs of another state. This generally does not apply to human rights violations by the state.

2. NGO: A written or oral statement submitted by an NGO to an open meeting of an international forum such as the ECOSOC or its subsidiary organs. It is the injection of an NGO's facts and opinions as to a matter under consideration by the body so as to inform and influence the body's deliberations on an issue.

INTOLERANCE (VS. TOLERANCE)

The attitude of a person or group of persons who do not accept, or wish to tolerate, the differences of other persons or groups, usually based on the race, religion, language, political opinion, or ethnicity of the group. Intolerance is not accepting other people as they are. It is condemned as a threat to human rights and for its disrespect for inherent human dignity and the full legal equality of all human beings.

IN TOTO

A Latin adverbial phrase that means wholly, fully, every part, as opposed to only in parts or partially. Example: "State

X adopted the four Geneva Conventions *in toto.*"

INVALID RESERVATION

A reservation submitted with a state's instrument of ratification*, which reservation is legally invalid because it is inconsistent with the object and purpose of the treaty*. A state may, if it chooses, ratify a treaty* subject to certain reservations, which are express written modifications of an underlying obligation in the treaty*. Under international law, a state may not submit a reservation to a treaty* if that reservation is inconsistent with the object and purpose of the treaty, meaning that it would be contrary to the *raison d'etre* of the treaty and undermine its effectiveness in achieving the goals set by those states which drafted and adopted it.

An example would be a reservation to the Torture Convention, which said that a state could torture someone if it were necessary to find out where a bomb that was about to explode was located. Such a reservation would be an invalid reservation because the prohibition against torture is a *jus cogens* norm and cannot be limited, derogated, or excepted under the Torture Convention. Allowing torture in such a situation would be inconsistent with the object and purpose of the Torture Convention.

Some human rights treaties state that no reservations to them will be allowed. If a state submitted a reservation to such treaty, that would also be an invalid reservation.

The legal effect of a state submitting an invalid reservation is controversial and not firmly established. Different human rights systems have decided this issue differently, and there is an attempt to formulate a universal standard.

INVESTIGATIVE MANDATE

A resolution issued by an organ of an intergovernmental organization, such as the UN Commission on Human Rights, which gives authority and sets terms of reference to someone to engage in a fact-finding investigation concerning a particular state or human rights situation.

INVOLUNTARY SERVITUDE

The forcing of individuals to engage in work against their will as a punishment or to exploit them economically. The state of being involuntarily subject to a master, lacking liberty, and not being able to determine one's way of life. Certain forms of forced work, such as military service or penal sentence labor, are usually excepted. It is different from slavery, which is any exercise of property ownership rights in a person.

IPSO FACTO (VS. IPSO JURE)

A Latin term meaning by virtue of the very fact itself. As a necessary consequence of an act or fact. Example: A human being of five years old is *ipso facto* a child.

IPSO JURE (VS. IPSO FACTO)
[Latin, lit.: by the very law itself]

By that same law itself. By the mere operation of the law. Example: Under the Refugee Convention, refugees are entitled *ipso jure* to protection of the principle of non-*refoulement*.

IRREDENTISM

A policy or program by a state or political group to seek recovery and reunification to one country of a region or regions, which, for the time, are being subjected to the sovereignty or control of another state. The situation of the Kosovo region of former Yugoslavia is an example of such policy or program. The population of Kosovo prior to the 1999 NATO bombing was about 90 percent ethnic Albanians and 10 percent ethnic Serbians. Those ethnic Albanian "Kosovars" were citizens of and under the sovereignty of former Yugoslavia because Kosovo is within the territory of former Yugoslavia. Albania and the Kosovo Liberation Movement (KLM) (of ethnic Albanian Kosovars) believed that Kosovo had been and should be again made part of Albania. The KLM began a secessionist conflict that resulted in Yugoslavian countermeasures, which caused the NATO intervention. The policy of the KLM and attitude of Albania were characterized by irredentism. Though not a human rights term per se, one sees this term used in historical situations that were characterized by irredentism, e.g., Sudetenland in World War II and Saddam Hussein seeking the return of Kuwait as the twenty-ninth province of historical Iraq.

The principal human rights issues involved with irredentism are the right to self determination, to equality before the law, to nondiscrimination, and so-called minority rights.

IRRELEVANCE OF OFFICIAL POSITION (PRINCIPLE)

A principle of international criminal law, which states that it is no defense to a charge of an international crime, such as a war crime, that the accused person held an official position in a government and acted pursuant to the duties of that position or office in the commission of the alleged crimes. This principle comes from the famous Nuremberg Principles, arising out of the Nuremberg Trials after World War II. This principle applies to both military and civilian officials. An example of this principle was the indictment of Slobodan Milosevic in the late 1990s for war crimes and crimes against humanity he or his subordinates allegedly committed while he was president of Yugoslavia. The fact that he held an official position in the Yugoslav government at the time he allegedly became responsible for the acts of his government agents was no defense to his criminal prosecution. One's status in a government is irrelevant to a charge of commission of an international crime.

This principle can be found in article 27 of the ICC Statute.

JACKSON-VANIK AMENDMENT (19 U.S. CODE SECTION 2432)

An amendment to the Trade Act of 1974, which authorizes the granting of U.S. trade benefits (most favored nation trading status, now known as "normal trading status") to other countries, and conditions those trade benefits on a country allowing its people to leave (emigrate from) that country.

The Jackson-Vanik Amendment was a congressional amendment made primarily to get the former Soviet Union to allow Soviet Jews to leave and go to other countries such as Israel or the U.S. It involved the granting of most favored nation trading status to countries with nonmarket economies. It allows a country to trade with the U.S. on as favorable a basis as with any other country. This creates an economic advantage for a state to entice it to allow dissidents or certain persecuted ethnic or religious groups to

leave a country or face losing their MFN status. Though it was originally enacted for the benefit of Soviet Jews, it is a piece of general human rights legislation and can be applied to any country that denies its people the right to leave the country to avoid human rights violations.

The amendment states that the president must determine if a country is denying or obstructing emigration, and he must certify that fact to Congress and refuse to grant MFN status to that country during any period such actions are occurring.

JOHANNESBURG PRINCIPLES

A set of soft law principles articulated by international human rights legal experts at a conference held in Johannesburg, South Africa, in 1994, regarding limitation of the exercise of freedom of expression and access to information in relation to government claims of protection of national security.

These principles relate largely to the scope of permissible government restrictions or limitations on the exercise of ICCPR article 19 to protect national security. The purpose of these principles is to establish a set of guidelines to apply to national security claims so as to prevent states from misusing claims of national security as a pretext for limiting freedom of expression or access to government information beyond that which is allowed by binding international legal norms to which the state has voluntarily undertaken to be legally obligated.

JOINT CRIMINAL ENTERPRISE (INTERNATIONAL CRIMINAL LAW)

A criminal act engaged in by more than one person in concert with each other and creating vicarious criminal legal responsibility of all participants for the criminal acts of the others engaged in the perpetration and furtherance of the criminal enterprise.

A joint criminal enterprise can involve persons who

1) are the actual perpetrators of the acts, those who participate directly in the commission of the crimes; or

2) are present at the time the crime is committed or about to be committed and with knowledge that it is being committed:

a. intentionally assist or encourage another participant in the enterprise to commit that crime; or

b. act in furtherance of a particular system in which the crime is committed by reason of the accused's position of authority or function. The accused must have knowledge of the nature of that system and intent to further that system. It has elements of common law conspiracy and vicarious liability, such as for those who aid and abet a crime, and accomplices before and after the fact, who share the same criminal intent.

This is a term most commonly used in international criminal tribunals.

Judgment (Court / Tribunal)

A final or interlocutory judicial decision by a court or tribunal that determines the main questions between parties.

Judicial (Forum / Body) (vs. Quasi-Judicial)

Of or relating to the administration of justice or belonging to a branch of an organization charged with resolving legal disputes by formal application of law to facts (i.e., merits), interpretation, and construction of law. It is a forum / body whose officials are called judges. Courts and tribunals are judicial fora / bodies. The International Court of Justice is a judicial forum.

In contrast, "Quasi-Judicial" refers to an organ that is not judicial and is not presided over by judges who render judgment, but is a forum / body that is presided over by members with other titles, such as commissioner or committee member, who examine cases of alleged human rights violations and apply the international legal norms as standards with which to judge a state's action.

The UN Human Rights Committee and the Inter-American Commission on Human Rights are two examples of "Quasi-Judicial" bodies. They examine cases and render decisions and reports on cases that can, under certain circumstances, then be referred to courts for full judicial scrutiny by judges who will then render a judgment. Quasi-judicial decisions are usually not legally binding.

Judicial Review (of Court decisions)

The power of a judge / court / tribunal to review the decisions / actions of government for the purpose of determining whether those decisions / actions were legal. The power to review judicial decisions by appeal to affirm or reverse / quash such decisions. Judicial examination of the law / merits by a higher court on appeal by a party to the action.

Juncto
[Latin, lit.: joined with]

An interpretive term meaning "taken / considered together with something else." Used to describe a reference to treaty* provisions when a particular article/norm of a treaty* is looked at along with another article as to its applicability to an issue. A manner of interpreting and applying treaty* provisions by looking at two or more treaty* provisions together. Sometimes in a case being decided by a forum the facts will be found not to constitute a violation of a specific article but may constitute a violation when the facts are applied to one article looked at together with another article. For example, see the ECHR system, where one cannot apply article 14 (on discrimination) alone but must apply it in conjunction with (*juncto*) another article, e.g., "The court finds a violation of article 14 *juncto* article 8 of the convention." This is because article 14 has no "autonomous existence/application."

JURIDICAL

Of or relating to the administration of justice or the office of a judge; of or relating to law or jurisprudence.

JURISDICTION

The power, right, or authority to interpret and apply the law; the power of a court to hear and decide a particular case (subject matter jurisdiction) or a case against a particular person (personal jurisdiction); the authority of a sovereign power to govern or legislate; the power or right to exercise authority; the limits or territory within which authority may be exercised. The subject matter jurisdiction of a human rights forum is usually referred to as its "competence." *See* Competence/Competence-Competence.

JURISDICTION TO ADJUDICATE

A type of legal power/authority/competence of the state to judicially determine certain cases. Every state has the jurisdiction to subject persons or things to the process of its courts or administrative tribunal, whether in civil or in criminal proceedings, whether or not the state is a party to the proceedings.

This power exists primarily in regard to matters that arise within the territory of the state. Such jurisdiction may go beyond that territorial scope in certain instances. An example would be an exercise of universal jurisdiction for a war crime committed outside a state's territory.

JURISDICTION TO ENFORCE

A type of legal power/authority/competence of the state which gives it jurisdiction to induce or compel compliance or to punish noncompliance with its laws or regulations, whether through the courts or by use of executive, administrative, police, or other nonjudicial action.

This jurisdiction exists primarily in regard to matters that arise within the territory of the state. Such jurisdiction may go beyond that territorial scope in certain instances. An example would be a state exercising military action to enforce a UN Charter chapter VII resolution outside its territory.

JURISDICTION TO PRESCRIBE

A type of legal power/authority/competence of the state which gives it the right to make its laws applicable to the activities, relations, or status of persons, or the interests of persons in things, whether by legislation, by executive act or order, by administrative rule or regulation, or by determination of a court.

This jurisdiction exists primarily in regard to persons, things, and matters that are found within the territory of the state. Such jurisdiction may go beyond that territorial scope in certain instances. An example would be a state passing legislation prohibiting a conspiracy in a foreign state to import illegal drugs into the legislating state.

JURISPRUDENCE

1. Case Law: Often used in the sense of what the case law of a given human rights judicial or quasi-judicial system, such as the European Court of Human Rights or the UNHuman Rights Committee, is saying about a certain principle/norm/interpretation.

It means what the case law (decisions/judgments/views, etc.) is saying about how the forum should rule on a particular issue based on how it has previously ruled. *See also* Constant Jurisprudence.

2. Science of Law: The study of the history, philosophy, and evolution of law in general. The science of law as a subject.

JUS AD BELLUM
(VS. JUS IN BELLO) (LOAC)
[Latin, lit.: right to war]

A Latin phrase used to describe the principle of international law that recognizes a legal right permitting a state and its agents (military, etc.), separately or collectively with other allied states, to legally engage in armed hostilities under international law against another state or states. It is part of the "Law of War" or the "Law of Armed Conflict" (LOAC). For example, a state has a *jus ad bellum*, an international legal right to engage in self-defense, if it is attacked.

The doctrine of *jus ad bellum* sets forth the grounds of justification for a state to lawfully engage in a hostile use of force and for individual combatants to engage in combat without risk of criminal sanction for fighting, so long as they do not breach humanitarian law, the *jus in bello*.

JUS COGENS (VS. JUS
DISPOSITIVUM) (NORM)
[Latin, lit.: compelling right]

The body of those general rules of law whose nonobservance may affect the very essence of the legal system to which they belong to such an extent that the subjects of the law may not, under pain of absolute nullity, depart from them in virtue of particular interstate agreements. Thus, the *jus cogens* restricts the freedom of the states parties to any treaty*; its rules are absolutely binding on all states in the world, at all times. In English this is known as a "peremptory norm." One result of the application of this doctrine is that *inter se* agreements (between states) derogating from peremptory norms are prohibited and are null and void.

The rationale of the *jus cogens* rule is to protect some common international concerns of the subjects of law. In an organized international legal order the function of the *jus cogens* norm is to protect the global society and its institutions from harmful consequences of individual state agreements that vitiate the common international order. Genocide, slavery, and torture would be examples of *jus cogens* norms. The obligation is owed to the international community as a whole, which is expressed by the Latin term *erge omnes*. *See also* Peremptory Norm.

JUS DISPOSITIVUM
(VS. JUS COGENS) (NORM)
[Latin, lit.: a right which can be displaced]

A law/rule/norm capable of being modified by contrary, consensual, legal agreements of states, such as by treaty*. This is contrasted with a *jus cogens* norm, which cannot be modified by contrary, consensual, legal agreements, as it is a "peremptory norm."

JUS IN BELLO (vs. JUS AD BELLUM) (LOAC)
[Latin, lit.: right in war]

A Latin term denoting the rules and principles of international law applicable to international and noninternational armed conflicts, including rules on the protection of victims and concerning the methods and means of conducting hostilities. It is mainly comprised of the four GCs of 1949 and its two PS, I and II of 1977, but it also includes the 1899 and 1907 Hague Conventions, especially Hague IV with annexed Regulations, and some other treaties* covering such areas as chemical, gas, and other particular weapons. Same as "Humanitarian Law."

JUS NATURALE
[Latin, lit.: natural right]

This is the Latin term meaning "natural law." It is the dictate of right reason involving moral necessity independent of any institution—human or divine.

A body of law found in the nature of the way the world and mankind must necessarily act. A body of law or a specific principle held to be derived from nature and binding upon human society in the absence of or in addition to positive law.

JUS SANGUINIS (vs. JUS SOLI) (PRINCIPLE OF CITIZENSHIP)

A principle that serves as a legal basis for citizenship by virtue/right of a person's legal/biological relationship to a citizen, usually as a child. At birth, children usu-

ally automatically obtain the citizenship of their parents. The other basis of citizenship is jus soli, when citizenship is based on what state a person is born in. Most people automatically obtain citizenship based on the state in which they were born.

JUS SOLI (vs. JUS SANGUINIS) (PRINCIPLE OF CITIZENSHIP)

A principle that serves as the legal basis for citizenship by virtue/right of being born within the territory of a state. At birth, children usually automatically obtain the citizenship of the state in which they are born. The other basis of citizenship is jus sanguinis, when citizenship is based on a person's biological relationship to a citizen, i.e., the son or daughter of a citizen.

JUSTICIABLE/JUSTICIABILITY (ISSUE)

A word describing the character of an issue as legally capable of being resolved by resorting to a judicial process. One asks whether an issue is justiciable, i.e., whether a court/tribunal has the power to handle/resolve the issue. Certain issues cannot be resolved by courts but must be resolved by executive/administrative or diplomatic procedures. It is a question both of the competence of the court/tribunal and the nature of the issue. In some jurisdictions, e.g., political questions are considered to not be justiciable by courts. Such issues are called nonjusticiable. They are to be resolved in a nonjudicial forum.

JUST SATISFACTION

A term used to describe a remedy for a human rights violation under the ECHR. Found in the ECHR complaint system, it means that the European Court of Human Rights may make an award in the form of reparation, such as payment of monetary compensation, to adequately redress a violation of a human right established in an application against a responding state, where the law of that state is deemed to not offer adequate redress. *See* ECHR, article 41. It is most often, but not always, a monetary award.

Just War (Theory) (loac)

A moral historical theory that sets forth criteria for determining if and when it is morally permissible for a society, such as a state, to use military force and engage in armed conflict (war) against another society. This theory was originally articulated in the Roman Catholic Church as far back as St. Augustine. It is based on the presumption against the use of force, based on the Biblical command to love and do no harm to one's neighbor. If a society can prove that a use of force meets all of the criteria of the just war theory, then and only then is a society morally right in using military force against another society and killing human beings.

Although originally a religion-based theory, it has been widely employed in secular contexts in the international community, including the so-called "War on Terrorism." It includes both elements of the *jus ad bellum* and *jus in bello*. The *jus ad bellum* establishes when a state has the international legal right to engage in armed conflict; the *jus in bello* deals with how the conflict is fought, namely the methods and means of conflict.

This theory has evolved over the years. The modern criteria for a just war are as follows:

1. A just cause. The reason for the use of force must be to prevent damage by the aggressor that is lasting, grave, and certain (also called a "real and certain danger"), to protect innocent human life, to preserve conditions necessary for decent human existence, and to secure human rights;

2. The armed conflict must be declared only by the competent legal authority with the legal power and authority to protect the public order;

3. The party must be sufficiently right in the dispute with the other such that the values at stake override the presumption against war (this is called a comparative justice analysis);

4. Armed conflict can be waged only for the right reasons set forth above, with the right intention, and not for some subsidiary or ulterior motive, such as overthrowing a disliked regime in another state;

5. Every possible peaceful alternative to avoiding armed conflict must be fully exhausted, impracticable, or ineffectual, and there is no other recourse available to prevent the real and present danger;

6. There must be a serious prospect of winning the armed conflict and thus preventing the real and certain danger;

7. The use of arms must not produce evils and disorders greater than the evils to be eliminated. The damage and the cost incurred in the actual conflict and the damage and cost anticipated in its aftermath, such as in occupying and rebuilding the conquered state, must be proportionate to the good expected. The principle of discrimination between combatants and civilians must be followed, and only the unjust aggressors may be targeted. In secular parlance this would mean following the Laws of Armed Con-

flict, including both the *jus in bello* and *jus ad bellum* and applicable human rights law.

Labor Rights

A description of a type of human rights that has as its purpose the protection of the right to work and to organize collectively for the common good. It would include the right to collective bargaining and to strike, equal pay for equal work, rest and leisure, and safe working conditions.

Most labor rights are found in the treaty* law under the ILO, but the UDHR and ICESCR also contain labor rights.

Lacuna
[Latin, lit.: hole, gap]

An area or subject not covered by any law, a gap in the law. Sometimes when searching for legal norms covering a certain subject one finds that there is no law covering it. This constitutes a *lacuna* in the law, where something is missing or is not covered by a law or procedure. This term is used most often in referring to a gap in the coverage of human rights norms, where there is some act that is arguably not covered by any human rights norms.

Example: For many years international humanitarian law did not cover nor prohibit certain sexual crimes by soldiers against civilian women as war crimes. This lacuna has now been filled in the new Rome Statute of the ICC, largely based on case law from international criminal tribunals.

This term is also used generally to apply to any subject in which there has been a failure to deal with a certain part of that subject.

Latu Sensu (vs. *Strictu Sensu*)
[Latin, lit.: in the wide/broad sense]

A Latin adverbial expression that means "given a broad or liberal interpretation." When reading a text *latu sensu*, one gives the wording of the text the broadest, most generous interpretation, as opposed to a strict or narrow interpretation, which is called *strictu sensu*.

Law

A binding custom or practice of a community; a rule of conduct or action prescribed or formally recognized as binding or enforced by a controlling authority; having been promulgated by an authorized legislative source.

Lawful Interference

The interference by the state in the exercises of human rights, which is legally permissible under international human right instruments.

A state may not seek to limit or restrict the exercise of human rights unless such action is done pursuant to law and is necessary for accomplishing certain specific, legitimate aim. Such aims may include public health, public order, public safety, and the rights and freedoms of others. Only if such action is consistent with such a legitimate aim and the measure taken is proportionate to this aim will the restriction be deemed a lawful interference with the exercise of a human right. If not, it constitutes an unlawful interference by the state and is a human rights violation.

Law-Making Treaty*

An international legal agreement (treaty*) concluded between and ratified* by states for the purpose of establishing general rules of conduct (norms) among a considerable number of states. They establish, recognize, or codify norms of conduct and become binding legal obligations on all states parties to the agreement. They can also modify or abolish existing rules.

A law-making treaty* is a "standard-setting instrument." The ICCPR is a law-making treaty*.

LAW OF ARMED CONFLICT (LOAC)

The body of rules and principles found in international law, which constitute legal norms that apply to situations of armed conflict either between two or more states, or within a state, such as a civil war or a war against alien occupation, colonial domination, or a racist regime. This body of international law limits when states can use force, how they use it, and how they treat victims.

The Law of Armed Conflict is a body of law that has two parts: the law that regulates when a state can legally use armed force against another state or states; and the law regulating how, by what method and means, a state uses such force, and how it treats those who are victims of the conflict, such as the wounded or shipwrecked, prisoners of war, or civilians in occupied territory. The second part is known as international humanitarian law. Properly speaking, only the second part directly involves human rights norms. Some scholars consider this body of law to be part of the larger body of law known as international human rights law. It is the part of human rights law that applies when an armed conflict is going on. It applies in both international and internal armed conflicts.

This body of law is based on many rules and principles, which have been officially accepted by the member states of the international community. This body of law is a sort of minimum common denominator of conduct of nations during the worst of times the times of armed conflict between human beings that beget death and destruction and that seem irrational and hardly subject to any law.

The truth is that there are many international legal limitations on how military forces can do battle and how victims of the conflict must be treated. These limitations have the force of law because they have been established in treaty* law, such as in the Geneva Conventions, or are norms that have ripened under the doctrine of customary international law, such as the Nuremberg Principles, or the inherent right of self-defense. The bulk of norms as to when a state can use armed force is contained within the UN Charter, sometimes referred to as the "UN Charter paradigm" on the use of force. The principle source of the norms of the second part, humanitarian law, are contained in the Geneva Conventions of 1949 and its two amendments, the 1977 Protocols I and II to the Geneva Conventions of 1949.

The most important function of the Law of Armed Conflict is to make the warring parties, whether states or revolutionary forces, know that regardless of their military power and ability they cannot do whatever they want, and that the whole international community has an interest in seeing that they play by clearly defined rules with consequences for violations. As a matter of international humanitarian law, it is simply not true that "all is fair in love and war." This is legally false. War is hell, but it is usually hell be-

cause the parties to a conflict do not follow the rules of this body of law. The goal
of this law is to minimize human pain,
loss, and suffering, in a world that still
has not been able to prohibit armed conflict all together.

The violation of many norms of this
law can result in individual criminal responsibility of those responsible, and often their commanders, for war crimes,
crimes against humanity, and the crime
of aggression.

Unfortunately, the greatest fault or
weakness of this body of law is that it is
virtually unknown by most people. It is
known mostly by military lawyers who
give legal advice to military commanders
as to what the Law of Armed Conflict
allows or prohibits in a given military
action. There is little civilian oversight
to this process on behalf of the civilians
who will make up about 80 percent of
the victims (dead or wounded) of a given
conflict.

It is primarily up to all the states to enforce the Law of Armed Conflict. States
must prohibit violations of this law in
their own domestic law. They must act to
prevent, suppress and repress, and prosecute violations. However, there have
also been some collective international
measures taken to punish and deter violations. The international community
established international tribunals that
have prosecuted violators, such as the Nuremberg Trials after World War II. There
are now two international tribunals that
are prosecuting alleged violators of this
law, one regarding the Bosnia Conflict of
the early 1990s and the other regarding
those responsible for the Rwanda massacre of 1994. There is also an International Criminal Court that was established in 2003 by certain member states

of the international community. This international court will prosecute the worst
violations of the law of armed conflict,
where states fail or are unwilling to prosecute persons who commit such violations. *See* Appendix C, Rome Statute of
the International Criminal Court, articles 1, 5, and 8.

LAW OF NATIONS (AKA INTERNATIONAL LAW)

International law is also known as the
"Law of Nations," although international
law is classically about the law governing
the relationship between states, not nations as such, in the international context
and is known as "public international
law." "Law of Nations" is an older generic
term taken from the Latin term *Lex Gentium.* "International law" is the more appropriate term now used.

LEAGUE OF NATIONS

The first international intergovernmental organization, established in 1920 at
the close of World War I. It was established through the Treaty of Versailles
and only included fifty-eight member
states, which never included the United
States. Although the League of Nations
dissolved before World War II, it served
as the predecessor to and became a model
for the United Nations in 1945.

Some of the league's organs and activities, such as the ILO, Mandate, and Minorities Systems, served as antecedents to
modern international human rights laws
and institutions.

LEGAL INTEGRITY (RIGHT TO)

A classification of human rights based on
that aspect of a whole human being that

is being protected by such rights. This classification is not officially accepted but is an academic theory tool for understanding different human rights. Human rights protect human dignity by protecting certain aspects of human existence, such as physical integrity, standard of living, family, and moral integrity. Legal integrity protects the intangible aspect of personhood by assuring that every individual has rights and the means and capacity to call upon society to protect one's human rights in equality and nondiscrimination.

Examples of legal integrity right are the right to a nationality, to recognition as a person before the law; equality before the law, fair trial/due process of law, no retroactive penal laws, rights of the accused, and remedy for miscarriage of justice.

LEGALITY (PRINCIPLE OF) (AKA *NULLUM CRIMEN, NULLA POENA SINE LEGE*)

A principle of international criminal law that states that no one can be punished for any conduct unless that conduct is prohibited by a law that is specific and detailed and is duly promulgated and accessible to persons so that they can know how to regulate their conduct and that the law was in effect when the acts are committed. This principle applies to domestic and international law. Sometimes seen in the context of civil law applied to limitation clauses and meaning that limitations by states are only valid if they are prescribed by specific and accessible laws issued by an authoritative source. It is primarily applied to penal law and is expressed by the Latin term *Nullum Crimen, Nulla Poena sine Lege* (*see infra*).

LEGAL POSITIVISM

A theory that says that law is only that which is actually issued from an authorized legislative source and promulgated by it. It denies the existence of any "higher law," such as natural law. In international law, it means that only the expressed will of states alone can constitute a valid source of international law.

LEGAL RIGHTS (VS. MORAL RIGHTS)

Rights that are granted or recognized by an authority empowered to grant and promulgate them and that can be asserted and defended before a court of law that can enforce them.

LEGISLATIVE HISTORY (OF A TREATY*/NORM) (AKA *TRAVAUX PRÉPARATOIRES*/ PREPARATORY WORKS)

The combined written record of the negotiations and drafting history of a treaty*/norm, setting the proposed draft texts and the oral and written submission of the drafters. This is referred to as a subsidiary source to aid in determining the correct interpretation of a text.

LEGITIMACY (PRINCIPLE)

A principle applied in judicial or quasi-judicial contexts when a court or other legal forum is determining whether a limitation or restriction clause is being properly applied by a state. It refers to a restriction that is justifiable because it is based on one of the aims specifically set forth in a human rights treaty*. In principle, limitations/restrictions can only be valid if they pursue a legitimate public aim, such as protection of public health or safety. Limitations clauses set forth the specific legitimate aims of restrictions within a given treaty*.

LEGITIMATE AIM (LIMITATION/ RESTRICTION CLAUSE)

A particular aim, goal, purpose, or interest of a state that serves as a legal justification for a state to restrict or limit the individual's exercise of a human right. Human rights treaties* contain many norms that are not absolute and are subject to limitation or restriction clauses that permit a state to achieve particular goals such as public safety. *See* ICCPR, article 18.3.

Each limitation/restriction clause spells out exactly what are the legally permitted aims, goals, purposes, or interests of the state that allow the state to limit exercise of a particular human rights norm. Examples of typical legitimate aims are public health, public order, public safety, national security, and the rights and freedoms of others. Legitimate means that a particular aim is one of the specified aims justified in principle and applied proportionately, and are otherwise fully consistent with the state's treaty* obligation.

Example: Restricting the sale of alcohol at a sporting event might be considered a legitimate aim in protecting public safety and order.

LÈSE HUMANITÉ
[French, lit.: harm/injury to humanity]

A term of international law and relations, referring to certain acts of states and some nonstate actors that do serious harm and injury to all humankind, not just to a state or some people. Examples of such acts include war crimes, geno-

cide, and international terrorism. The Rwanda genocide of 1994 was an act of *lèse humanité*.

LEX FERENDA/DE LEGE FERENDA (VS. LEX LATA/DE LEGE LATA)
[Latin, lit.: law being produced/brought forth/proposed]

A Latin expression to describe an idea that some are proposing or contending should be a binding legal norm, when as a matter of existing law it is not accepted yet as a legally binding. It is a law in the process of being formulated, advocated, and accepted but not yet having ripened into generally accepted hard law. Examples would be the "right to democratic governance" and, to some extent, the "right to development." Sometimes this phrase is used to denote something one proposes be accepted and established as a norm but which is not yet so, for example, the right to individual standing before all international human rights courts.

It is used as *lex ferenda* in the nominative case and *de lege ferenda* in the ablative case. Both *lex ferenda* and *de lega ferenda* mean the same thing. They are contrasted with *lex lata/de lege lata*, which are norms that are clearly and generally accepted as already legally binding. Law that is in force. A treaty* that has not entered into force may be considered *lex ferenda*.

De lege ferenda usually has the sense of "on the basis of a norm that is not yet legally binding."

LEX GENTIUM (AKA JUS GENTIUM)
[Latin, lit.: law of nations]

A Latin term meaning the "law of nations." Ancient Roman law for governing non-Roman citizens, i.e., citizens of other nations subject to Rome, or between Romans and aliens. It was the international law of the Roman Empire.

In medieval times it was used to denote public international law.

LEX LATA/DE LEGE LATA (VS. LEX FERENDA/DE LEGE FERENDA)
[Latin, lit.: produced/completed law]

A Latin expression to describe an idea that some are contending is a binding, in force legal norm generally accepted as such by the legal community. Example: The freedom of expression is *lex lata*, whereas the right to democratic self-governance is *lex ferenda*. *Lex lata* is used in the nominative case and *de lege lata* is used in the ablative case. Both "*lex lata*" and "*de lege lata*" mean the same thing.

They are contrasted with *lex ferenda/de lege ferenda* (*see* supra), which mean proposed norms or norms in the process of being accepted as binding but which are not yet binding.

LEX SPECIALIS
(INTERPRETATION OF NORM)
[Latin, lit.: a special law]

A specific rule that overrules a general principle or rule of law. It also refers to a specific law within a more general field of law. For example, freedom of religious expression ("manifestation of religion") can be considered a *lex specialis* of the norm of freedom of expression. It carves out a particular area of a more general subject for special normative treatment. It is usually used in the interpretation of treaty* norms as a rule that states that a specific rule will always overrule a general rule covering the same subject.

LIBERALISM

A twentieth-century ideology that calls for free political institutions, individual freedoms such as free expression and religious tolerance, and support for the idea that government should have a strong role in regulating capitalism for the general good and for constructing a welfare state in which the needs of the poor are met as best as possible.

LIBERTY

The idea of a person being free from not only physical constraints to one's person, but free in the enjoyment of all one's faculties, free to use them in all lawful ways; to live and work where one will; to earn one's livelihood by any lawful calling; to pursue any livelihood or avocation; and to enter into contracts to achieve any lawful ends by any lawful means. Liberty includes the freedom to go where one may choose and to act in such a manner as one's judgment may dictate (not inconsistent with the equal rights of others) for the promotion of happiness; that is, to pursue such callings and avocations as may be most suitable to develop one's capacities and give to them one's own highest enjoyment. Human rights are legal tools to assure the maximum liberty of human beings in relation to society.

LIBERTY AND SECURITY OF PERSON

The human right of individuals to be free from unwarranted and otherwise unlawful government searches and seizures and similar restrictions on personal freedom. Human beings have a right to be free from any government intrusion unless there is a valid legal basis for government intervention. It is the right to feel free, safe, sound, and secure from unjustified government activity, such as police stops for identification, detention, arrest, wiretaps, surveillance, searches of one's home, person, or belongings, or monitoring of a person's activities. This right assures everyone a peaceful existence with no fear of the state or its agents causing physical or emotional harm.

It relates primarily to arrest and detention by law enforcement authorities. Every human being has the human right to liberty and security of person. Human rights are really limitations on the power of government in relation to individuals. They are legal measures aimed at keeping government out of certain areas of the lives of human beings. They are things government cannot do to human beings, consistent with human dignity. They are means of protecting the mental and physical integrity of human beings.

The right to liberty and security of person is a specific human right found in many general human rights instruments. Article 3 of the UDHR states:

Everyone has the right to life, liberty and security of person.

Article 9 of the ICCPR states:

1. Everyone has the right to liberty and security of person. No one shall be subjected to arbitrary arrest or detention. No one shall be deprived of his liberty except on such grounds and in accordance with such procedures as are established by law.

2. Anyone who is arrested shall be informed, at the time of arrest, of the reasons for his arrest and shall be promptly informed of any charges against him.

3. Anyone arrested or detained on a criminal charge shall be brought promptly before a judge or other officer authorized by law to exercise judicial power and shall be entitled to trial within a reasonable time or to release. It shall not be the general rule that persons awaiting trial shall be detained in custody, but release may be subject to guarantees to appear for trial, at any other stage of the judicial proceedings, and should occasion arise, for execution of the judgment

4. Anyone who is deprived of his liberty by arrest or detention shall be entitled to take proceedings before a court in order that the court may decide without delay on the lawfulness of his detention and order his release if the detention is not lawful.

5. Anyone who has been the victim of unlawful arrest or detention shall have an enforceable right to compensation.

LIEBER CODE (LOAC)

The first formal military manual setting forth the law of armed conflicts applicable during the U.S. Civil War for Union soldiers. It was drafted for the purpose of preventing unnecessary suffering, death, and destruction, and preserving discipline during the Civil War.

In 1863, Francis Lieber, a Columbia law professor, wrote the Lieber Code for the Union forces, which set a code of how soldiers could fight. This code was a codification of existing international law on armed conflicts. This code served as the basis for later laws on armed conflicts. The present Code of Military Justice is an evolved version of the Lieber Code.

It recognized that even war was subject to law and that those who are not involved as combatants should not be victimized by armed conflicts. To the extent to which it seeks to protect human beings from the effect of the Civil War, it was in effect a human rights related code.

Its formal name was the Instructions for the Government of Armies of the United States in the Field. One of its major components of this code was the concept of military necessity, which holds that force may only be used where there exists a military necessity for doing so.

LIFE PLAN (AKA PLAN OF LIFE / *PROYECTO DE VIDA*) (REPARATIONS)

A concept or factor in formulating a type or amount of reparations for violations of human rights. It deals with the injury to full individual self-actualization of a victim, such as to life plans, ambitions, potential and calling in life, and particular circumstances that would permit the victim to set specific life goals and work freely to attain these goals. It concerns the impact of human rights violations on personal fulfillment. This is contrasted with pure economic losses, such as medical bills or funeral expenses. This concept was articulated in several contentious cases within the OAS human rights system.

LIMBURG PRINCIPLES (ECONOMIC, SOCIAL, AND CULTURAL RIGHTS)

Refers to the Limburg Principles on Implementation of the International Covenant on Economic, Social, and Cultural Rights, agreed upon at a conference of experts on such rights convened in Limburg, Holland, in 1986. These set forth principles regarding how the obligations to economic, social, and cultural rights—the so-called programmatic or progressive rights—were to be implemented.

LIMITATION (CLAUSE)

A clause in a human rights treaty* article that has as its purpose the setting forth of permissible state restrictions on the exercise of the substantive rights. Normally, these limitations must be prescribed by law and deemed necessary (in a democratic society) to achieve a legitimate aim such as the protection of public health, safety, order, welfare, morals, or the rights and freedoms of other persons.

This term means the same as the term "Restriction" (clause) or "Clawback Clause." They are a form of recognition that not all rights are absolute and that most rights are actually prima facie rights that can be limited. Limitation clauses are strictly construed against the state. *See* ECHR article 10.2 for an example of a limitation clause. Limitation clauses lare a balance of the government's need to operate and the need for individual freedom.

LINGUISTIC MINORITY/GROUP

A "linguistic group" is a term used to refer to a group of people who speak the same common language. If the group's language is not that spoken by the majority of the state's population, then the group is considered a linguistic minority.

LINKAGE / LINK (TO HUMAN RIGHTS)

The action, law, or policy of establishing a mandatory connection between compliance with human rights norms and some other goal, such as trade, recognition as a state, or grant of foreign aid.

Linkages create a quid pro quo so as to promote state compliance with human rights standards. "De-linking" would be the opposite.

LOCUS CLASSICUS
[Latin, lit.: the classic place]

A Latin expression meaning the place where one finds the central key instance, reference point, or definitive text of something. The locus classicus could refer to a case decision, a certain treatise, story, or report, or even an event. An example of a locus classicus is the *Caroline* case concerning the legality of the British seizure and destruction of the American ship the *Caroline* for its participation in the Canadian rebellion of 1837. The *Caroline* case is now considered the locus classicus of international law doctrine of the right of states to use force in self-defense against armed attack. It establishes the basic criteria for, and limits of, that right.

LOCUS STANDI (AKA STANDING)
[Latin, lit.: place of standing]

The right to file a complaint* and appear before a court/tribunal, committee, or commission empowered to receive and resolve cases of alleged human rights violations or to request an advisory opinion. It is a condition of admissibility of a written complaint* that the complaining party must have *locus standi*, also called "Standing," usually by being the actual victim of the violation. If the complaining party does not have *locus standi/* standing, then the case will be deemed inadmissible *ratione standi*, or sometimes it is stated as *ratione personae*.

The full expression for standing is *locus standi in judicio*.

LODGE (COMPLAINT*/ MEMORIAL/DOCUMENT)

To physically submit a complaint*, legal brief (memorial), or other document with a forum as part of a human rights case being handled by such forum. These are usually formally registered with the registrar's office.

LONDON CHARTER (1945) (LOAC)

Same as Nuremberg Charter (*see* infra).

LUSTRATION LAWS

Laws usually enacted after a violent transition of government that prevent certain persons from running for, or being appointed to, government positions because those persons were part of a prior government, which was removed as a result of systematic human rights violations. The goal of lustration laws is to prevent a return of certain persons to power and to remove their ideas, movements, and parties so as to prevent a return to the prior situation and the possibility of further human rights violations or the return of a political/ideological system incompatible with respect for human rights.

MAASTRICHT GUIDELINES (ON VIOLATIONS OF ECONOMIC, SOCIAL, AND CULTURAL RIGHTS) (AKA MAASTRICHT GUIDELINES)

A set of 32 separate guidelines established for elaborating principles as regards the nature and scope of violations of economic, social, and cultural human rights, and appropriate responses and remedies for those violations. These guidelines are not legally binding but are considered by some scholars to be part of "soft law" obligations that serve as a guide for how to comply with the actual hard law norms of the ICESCR. These guidelines were created by a group of human rights experts on economic, social, and cultural rights meeting in Maastricht, Netherlands in 1997. Usually referred to as the Maastricht Guidelines.

Caveat: Do not confuse the Maastricht Guidelines with the Maastricht Principles/Rules. The latter involve monetary and financial norms in the European Union.

MAINSTREAMING

A process of assessing the implications for a particular group, of any planned action, including legislation, policies, and programs, in any area and at all levels, and implementing them in a way that best results in full and equal enjoyment of human rights. When used in the context of human rights, it is a strategy for making the target group's concerns and experiences an integral dimension in the design, implementation, monitoring, and evaluation of policies and programs in all political, economic, and societal spheres so that all persons and groups benefit equally, and inequality is not perpetuated. Gender mainstreaming is one example of a human rights mainstreaming process.

MALTA DECLARATION (2002)

A human rights declaration on social human rights issued at a Conference of the Council of Europe held in Malta in 2002, concerning increasing access to and realization of social human rights. The conference was attended by experts from the Council of Europe states and some foreign observer states. It called on governments to make greater efforts in the realm of social rights.

MANDATE (ADMINISTRATIVE/ POLITICAL/LEGAL)

The content of a resolution of a body of people expressing the desire of the group to grant and describe/circumscribe certain limited power to a person (such as a special rapporteur) or a body (such as a human rights commission) to carry out certain activities as part of its program or project. It is an authorization or an order to act or to do something. A person or body granted a mandate to do something can only act within the scope (terms of reference) of that mandate. To act outside of one's mandate is to act *ultra vires*. The scope of what a person, group, or body is legally permitted by an organization to do within that organization. For example, the mandate of the United Nations is found in the UNCH.

In some political systems, such as the United States, it has acquired the connotation of an overwhelming and clear election victory, which gives the successfully elected official a clear and unequivocal communication of what he is supposed to do as the express will of the majority of the people.

MANDATE SYSTEM (LEAGUE OF NATIONS)

A political system created by article 22 of the 1920 Covenant of the League of Nations and applicable to former colonies of states that had lost in World War I. It established certain victorious powers, e.g., France and the United Kingdom, as "mandatory powers" to rule over specific colonies in a way consistent with the "well-being and development of [these native] peoples." The mandate system ended with the demise of the League of Nations and was succeeded to some extent by the UN trusteeship system.

This system is considered an historical antecedent to modern human rights systems as it set an international standard of how a state may treat people under its control and established an international mechanism, a reporting procedure, to monitor how the mandatories were discharging their duty.

MANDATORY COERCIVE MEASURES

The use of measures against a state involving the use of force so as to coerce a state into changing its conduct. Such measures are ordered to be taken by all states members of an organization, such as the UN. An example is the attack on Iraq in the Persian Gulf War of 1990, by which the UN Security Council passed a resolution under Chapter VII of the UNCH ordering all states to take such measures against Iraq, leading to the Desert Storm invasion.

Normally states cannot be physically coerced to stop, prevent, or remedy human rights violations. The term most often refers to measures taken by the UN Security Council under Chapter VII of the UNCH. These would only be done if human rights violations gave rise to a breach of the peace, a threat to the peace, or an act of military aggression. Human rights violations are normally remedied by noncoercive and peaceful political and legal measures.

MANIFESTLY ILL-FOUNDED (COMPLAINT*)

A term describing a complaint* that is inadmissible in that it does not appear to present a situation falling within the purview of the forum, commission, or court. It is a ground of inadmissibility of a complaint*. If the complaint* is found to be manifestly ill-founded, it will not be found admissible, and the merits of the complaint* will not be examined and decided. A finding of "manifestly ill-founded" is made at the admissibility stage. The basis of such finding would be, for example, where the forum determines that it is impossible to envisage a violation of the convention based on the facts presented by the complaint*, that the complainant has not presented a *prima facie* case of a violation of any article of the treaty*, or that the facts alleged in the complaint* are proven to be false according to the evidence before the forum.

This criterion of admissibility is mostly seen in the ECHR application system (*see* ECHR, article 35.3). There has been much confusion as to the precise meaning and applicability of this term. It is basically a finding that the complaint* is without substance. The Inter-American system uses the term "manifestly groundless." *See* IACHR, article 47 (C).

MANIFESTO RIGHTS

This philosophical concept conveys the sense that a certain claim can be made as a moral entitlement or a need requiring the active protection of society. These claims have been called by some human rights philosophers the natural seeds from which rights grow, but which are not yet actual hard, justiciable legal rights. This lack of hard law status comes from the fact that international community has not determined and identified who are the duty-holders of the legal obligation vis-à-vis the person[s] claiming such right, nor the sources or methods of realization of the right yet determined.

An example of one human right being argued as a manifesto right is the right to development, whose status as a right is still much debated.

Marginalize(d) (Person/Group)

The status of persons or groups being relegated to a relatively powerless and unimportant position in a society, sometimes by being forced to the distant, undeveloped, politically unimportant border areas, or by being denied the right to meaningfully participate in politics, even in matters that affect their well-being. Sometimes this term is used generally to mean that someone has been rendered politically/socially/economically unimportant, excluded, or powerless within and as compared to the rest of society.

Margin of Appreciation (Limitation/Restriction Doctrine)

A term found principally in the jurisprudence of the ECHR system in applying and interpreting the phrase "necessary in a democratic society," a phrase found in the limitation/restriction clauses of the ECHR. It is a factor in determining the scope of judicial review of state action and the degree of deference afforded to states parties in deciding on the application and implementation of rights guaranteed by the ECHR. In determining whether a limitation/restriction measure taken by a state meets a "pressing social need," the European Court of Human Rights accords a certain degree of discretion, deference, some leeway, and some benefit of the doubt to the state in

evaluating the compatibility of a course of state conduct with the requirements of the ECHR. This discretion is known as the "margin of appreciation." It is a reflection and encapsulation of the principle of subsidiarity, which makes international legal norms subsidiary to national laws and systems.

As the European Court stated, the reason for this doctrine is that by reason of their direct and continuous contact with the vital forces of their countries, state authorities are, in principle, in a better position than the international judge to give an opinion on the "necessity" of a "restriction" or penalty, and that it is for the national authorities to make the initial assessment of the reality of the pressing social need implied by the notion of necessity in this context.

The states's margin of appreciation is always subject to supervisory monitoring by the European Convention organs to assure that it is not exceeded or misused.

The term is also used generally in other legal and political contexts to mean giving a state some leeway, some discretion in determining what measures to take that limit the exercise of human rights, because the state is deemed to be in a better position to know the facts/the problem and often must act expeditiously.

This term is similar to and sometimes used in place of the term "margin of discretion."

Margin of Discretion

Substantially the same as the concept of margin of appreciation, but often applied in situations outside of the ECHR system, including to any governmental, intergovernmental executive, or administrative body. It is a concept that recognizes that the body needs some leeway in making decisions as to how to best act to fulfill its mandate and is assumed to be in the best position to ascertain and deal with the facts involved in any issue. This margin of discretion must be subject to supervision by an organ capable of ensuring compliance with human rights obligations.

This term is similar to and sometimes used in place of the term "Margin of Appreciation," supra.

Martens Clause (aka de Martens Clause) (loac)

A "Martens Clause" is found in most international humanitarian law (loac) treaties* adopted under the icrc, principally the four 1949 Geneva Conventions and their 1977 Protocols (*see* gc IV, article 142; p I, article 1). This type of clause was originally found in the preamble of the Hague Convention II of 1899. In essence, it says that "until a more complete written code of humanitarian law is issued, the high contracting parties deem it expedient to declare that, in cases not included in the regulations adopted by them, the inhabitants and belligerents remain under the protection and the rule of the principles of the law of nations, as they result from the usages established among civilized peoples, from the laws of humanity, and the dictates of the public conscience."

This clause, also sometimes referred to as a "de Martens Clause," is a legal safety net to normatively cover areas not covered by positive, conventional humanitarian law. It obligates state parties/belligerents to seek a solution to particular issues based on basic humanitarian principles when there is no specific treaty*

norm so as to minimize/mitigate the harmful consequences of armed conflicts on combatants and noncombatants alike.

Martial Law

The use of military forces to temporarily govern the civilian population as a public necessity requires. This often is accompanied by the suspension of certain civil liberties or a period of derogation wherein certain human rights are derogated or suspended during the period. Often heard in the context of the derogation of human rights. Under martial law the military and not the civil society govern the state and its people. It is an exceptional situation.

Massacre

An indiscriminate and wanton killing of a number of human beings in a cruel manner.

Mass Exodus/Migration

The mass movement of peoples out of a state caused by external and internal conflicts or systematic human rights violations, forcing people to leave their habitual place of residence.

Material Application/ Scope (of Treaty*)

The substance of what human acts and needs are included within the parameters of a particular norm; all of what a human right protects. It is the issue of whether or not an attempt to apply a norm to a particular human act or need is permissible. For example, whether abortion is a right within the material scope of the right to privacy. Expressed in Latin as *Ratio Materiae*.

MATERIAL BREACH (OF TREATY*)

The failure of a state party to a treaty* to act according to its obligation thereunder, in a way not permitted by international law, and in a way that indicates the state's repudiation of the treaty* itself; or, a state party's serious violation of a provision of the treaty* that is absolutely essential to the accomplishment of the object and purpose of the treaty*. *See* Vienna Convention (1969), article 60.

As to human rights and humanitarian law treaties*, the effect of a material breach by any state party does not relieve any other state party from complying with their obligations under the treaty*.

MATERIAL DAMAGE (REPARATIONS)

The real and concrete damage, injury, and cost incurred thereby, caused by a human rights violation. In bringing a case before a quasi-judicial or judicial forum such as the European Court of Human Rights, the court may, if it finds the responding state has violated a victim's human rights, order reparations to be awarded to the victim. These reparations can include monetary payments for the actual damages and injuries incurred, such as medical bills, repair of one's damaged house, or loss of income. This type of damage is compared to moral damages, which are for the intangible harm done, such as pain and suffering.

MEANS OF IMPLEMENTATION (OF A TREATY*)

The specific bodies, measures, and procedures that are set forth in a human rights treaty* by which the treaty* is to be implemented and supervised. The ICCPR, for example, established a body named the Human Rights Committee and established a reporting system and complaint* system. These are some of the means of implementation for this treaty. *See*, for example, Appendix B, ICCPR article 28 and First Optional Protocol to the ICCPR.

MECHANISM

A body, organ, procedure, or office that can be used to bring about compliance with human rights norms. Used principally in international, intergovernmental organizations, such as the UN, such as in references to "special mechanisms." An example of a mechanism would be the UN Working Group on Disappearances.

MEDIATION (OF DISPUTES)

A process for solving a dispute concerning alleged violations whereby a third party not involved in the dispute helps the disputing parties (state versus state or individual/group versus state) to settle their disagreement by discussing the issues and alternative solutions until both sides of the dispute come to an agreement and are satisfied.

MEGACRIMES

Major crimes of international stature and magnitude such as to constitute international criminal law violations. Genocide, aggression, war crimes, and crimes against humanity would constitute "megacrimes." They are the most serious crimes and are violations of the interests of the whole human race. These are the types of crimes for which the ICC was established, for defining, deterring, and prosecuting such violations of international law. *See* Appendix C, Rome Statute, articles 1 and 5.

MEMBER STATE (IGO)

A state that is a member of an intergovernmental organization (global/regional/other). State membership is gained by the state ratifying* the charter or other constituent treaty* instrument that set up the organization. Usually only member states can be involved in the activity and vote on the resolutions of the organization as they share mutual interests in a legal relationship. Example: By ratifying* the UNCH, a state becomes a member state of the UN.

MEMORANDUM OF UNDERSTANDING (MOU)

A less formal international instrument, often setting out operational arrangements under a framework of international agreement or otherwise dealing with technical or detailed matters. An "MOU" has political or moral force but is not legally binding.

MEMORIAL (FRENCH: *MEMOIRE*) (LEGAL BRIEF)

The written legal brief of a party to a contentious international case. In it, the party sets out its version of relevant facts and law, contentions as to the merits, and other pertinent submissions in relation to its claims.

MENS REA (CRIMINAL LAW)

The mental state that a person must have at the time of committing an act or omission so as to be held responsible for the commission of a crime. The mental state (mens rea) usually must accompany the act or omission that constitutes the physical element (*actus reus*) of the crime in order for the perpetrator to be guilty of the crime. Knowledge and intent are common "mens rea" states of mind.

MERCENARY (LOAC)

A soldier for hire who is hired by a state or an armed group engaged in an armed conflict to help with waging the armed conflict. A national of a third state who is recruited to fight and actually fights as a soldier in an armed conflict and whose motivation is not the cause of his military force, but private gain, especially money.

Although under the command of the hiring force, a mercenary has no allegiance to the state or other force. Mercenarism is prohibited in the LOAC. It is commonly perceived that mercenaries tend to be too brutal and little concerned about whom they kill and how, because they are fighting for money, not for a cause. There is a trend toward making all mercenarism illegal under international law.

A mercenary is not generally entitled to protection of the LOAC as a regular combatant and not entitled to POW status and treatment if captured. If captured, a mercenary can be treated as a common criminal and prosecuted for his military acts, but retains some minimum protections under the Geneva Conventions.

MERITS (OF A CASE/COMPLAINT*)

In a case involving a complaint* of alleged human rights violations by a state, and when the complaint* is being decided by a judicial or quasi-judicial body, the analysis of the application of the law to the facts is called the "merits" of the case. A complaint* must first be examined and deemed "admissible" before the body can examine the merits of the case. Analyzing the merits is aimed at determining whether upon examination of the evidence presented the complainant has proved a valid human rights violation or a breach of the treaty* that the offending respondent state must redress.

An examination of the merits results, after deliberation of the forum, in a finding (decision/judgment/views, etc.) as to whether or not a violation has been found.

METARIGHT

A philosophical concept of rights that describes a right that may not be immediately achievable, but can be achieved and realized if appropriate and effective policies and action are adopted by the society to make them real. The right to development and the right to a clean environment are examples of such rights.

METHODS AND MEANS OF COMBAT (LIMITATION) (LOAC)

The legal limitations in humanitarian law concerning the kinds of weapons and tactics used by military combatants in armed conflict. How and with what arms and other devices an armed conflict may be fought consistent with respect for human rights.

It is not true that all is fair in war. Some say that war is hell (which it is), but it is also true that there is a well-established body of international law regarding how wars and other armed conflicts are fought.

This is a basic principle of humanitarian law, which is a branch of human rights law applicable in armed conflicts, that the two sides to an armed conflict (war) cannot use any types of weapons they want and attack the enemy any way they want. Legally, they can only use weapons and tactics that will accomplish their military goal with the least amount of physical damage, human death, and suffering. This principle must be obeyed by all combatants, even guerrilla warriors. "All-out war" is no longer legally permitted because it hurts innocent people and even harms combatants more than necessary to achieve military goals. Weapons and tactics can only be employed where there is a real military necessity for using them, where the damage they cause to noncombatants is proportional to the military advantage gained by the attack, and where the methods or means do not cause unnecessary suffering or damage.

Prohibition of the use of napalm, chemical or gas weapons is an example of a regulation of the methods and means of combat. So would be the setting of a fire in a field near a town where enemy soldiers and civilians are located so as to kill everyone in the town. So would be the dropping of cluster bombs in an area full of civilians.

Many argue that the use of nuclear weapons and other weapons of mass destruction per se violates this principle, but certain nuclear powers officially oppose this position. Nuclear weapons and other weapons of mass destruction have for the most part been politically forced into the realm of "disarmament" talks and under the "law of disarmament," and out of the realm of human rights and humanitarian law where they belong and would likely be very restricted or prohibited.

MILITARY COMMISSION

A judicial body established by a state, normally by a field commander or commander in chief for use in time of armed conflict, normally to try enemy combatants for offenses against the international law of armed conflict (LOAC), such as for committing grave breaches of the Geneva Conventions of 1949, which constitute war crimes.

Military commissions are subject to compliance with international humanitarian law (such as GC III, article 5, PI article 75) and human rights norms, (such as ICCPR, articles 2.1, 7, 9, 10, 14, 15, 26), as well as national constitutions and laws, with some exceptions.

MILITARY NECESSITY (LOAC) (PRINCIPLE)

A legal principle of the LOAC used to determine whether there exists a legal justification for military attacks on legitimate military targets that may have adverse, even deadly consequences for civilians or civilian objects. This principle states that an armed force may legitimately and legally attack and neutralize enemy military objects and combatants if and only if there is a military necessity for the attack. The attack meets the requirement of military necessity where the neutralization of the targeted enemy military combatant or objects offers the attacking force a concrete and substantial military advantage in the armed conflict. Because military attacks are destructive of human life and valuable objects, they can only be carried out if necessary to advance achievement of a military objective. Armed force cannot be used solely to destroy things or people, military or civilian, just to hurt or scare the enemy. All-out war is not legally permitted under the LOAC.

The relation to human rights is that if there is a military attack against an enemy where there is no military necessity for launching the attack, the damages resulting from the attack constitute human rights violations. Attacks made without military necessity also constitute a violation of the *jus ad bellum* and *jus in bello* under the LOAC. Under the LOAC an armed force does not have the *jus ad bellum*, the right to use armed force, even against a military object or combatant, unless there exists under the circumstances at that time a military necessity to do so. Even if military necessity is found to exist, the attack is still subject to all other LOAC rules, such as proportionality.

This concept was first established in the Lieber Code, the field manual used by Union troops in the U.S. Civil War.

MINIMUM HUMANITARIAN STANDARDS

A set of humanitarian norms articulated and intended to apply in situations where there is little binding and applicable human rights or humanitarian law norms to cover what is going on in an internal conflict. It is an attempt to cover the gray areas where so many human rights violations occur, especially in noninternational armed conflicts, where international law is still not very well developed. It is an attempt to ensure that a minimum level of humanitarian civility and respect for human rights exist in every conflict.

The Turku Abo Principles are an instrument that attempts to set forth such minimum humanitarian standards.

MINIMUM (INTERNATIONAL) STANDARD (OF STATE TREATMENT) (AKA INTERNATIONAL MINIMUM STANDARD) (VS. NATIONAL TREATMENT)

The internationally accepted minimum normative level of treatment by a state of all individuals within the state, including foreigners. A state may treat all or some of the individuals within its jurisdiction better than this minimum standard, but it cannot go below this standard as to anyone, even, e.g., an illegal alien criminal convict. This ever-increasing minimum standard represents the international community's norm as to what the standard of civilized conduct states must live up to as members of the global community so as to assure global peace, harmony, and development. Most would say that the minimum standard roughly corresponds to the level of conduct set by the standards of international human rights law.

The term is usually applied to how a state treats foreigners (aliens), especially illegal aliens, within its territory. It is sometimes found in treaties* of "Friendship, Commerce, and Navigation" to set the bilateral standard of care by one state as to the treatment of citizens of the other state. This standard is one of the two classic standards of the state treatment of foreigners. The other is the "National Treatment" standard (*see* infra).

Minorities Treaties System (League of Nations)

A set of treaties fashioned by the League of Nations after World War I. These treaties were between the league and the newly emerging states, such as Poland, Hungary, and Yugoslavia, and were aimed at protecting ethnic, linguistic, or religious minority groups within these new states. The first was with Poland in 1919, which set the model for the others. Under that treaty, the new state undertook to refrain from discriminating against members of protected minorities and promised special rights for minori-

ties to preserve their integrity, including the rights to official use of their language, to maintain their own schools, and to practice their own religion.

Minority (Group of People)

Minority is a term used to describe a group of human beings classified, among other things, by their race, language, religion, ethnicity, or nationality, within the context of a larger society in which they are nondominant. It also refers to an individual member of such a group. There is no one commonly or officially accepted definition of a "minority" in international human rights law as yet, even though the international community primarily under the aegis of the UN is already in the process of human rights standard setting as to the protection of minorities.

One definition of "minority" in use today is by Capotorti: a minority group is a "group numerically inferior to the rest of the population of a state, in a nondominant position, whose members —being nationals of the state—possess ethnic, religious, or linguistic characteristics differing from those of the rest of the population and show, if only implicitly, a sense of solidarity, directed towards preserving their culture, traditions, religion, or language."

As for the term "national minority," here, too, there is no single officially accepted definition. There are two definitions currently in use, one in the UN and one in the Council of Europe System.

The first definition refers to members of a group in a subject state who are nationals (citizens) of that state, as opposed to nonnationals (noncitizens). Under this definition, a state would only be responsible for respecting minority rights for groups whose members are nationals of that state.

Second, the term is used in the sense similar to a classification such as "religious minority," when it refers to a group of persons who are not nationals of the state in which they reside. Example: A group of citizens of state A residing in state B would be a "national minority" of state B.

Minority Rights

Minority rights is a term generally designating those human rights that offer specific protection to members of racial, ethnic, national, religious, or linguistic minority groups, or to the group as such. One of the most important areas of human rights that have developed since World War II is the protection of various types of minorities, known as minority groups. This is because the Holocaust and other atrocities have taught the world that sometimes a society can demonize and dominate another group of people based on differences such as color, religion, or ethnicity, which can result in attempts to destroy, remove, or marginalize such a group from that society. Much of the work of defining minorities and their human rights has gone on at the United Nations.

The main work of the UN has been done in standard setting and studies. This includes specific provisions in general human rights instruments, such as ICCPR, article 27, and even nontreaty instruments such as the Declaration on the Rights of Persons Belonging to National or Ethnic, Religious or Linguistic Minorities, (UN 1992) and to the activity of the UN Human Rights Commission and its Sub-Commission on the Promotion and Protection of Human Rights (formerly the Sub-Commission on Prevention of Discrimination and Protection of Minorities) as they deal with minority issues.

Mistreatment (Persons/Groups)

Any kind of treatment of an individual or group that is inconsistent with human dignity, as set forth in international human rights norms. An example of such a norm is ICCPR, article 7. *See* Appendix B.

Mitigation (of Criminal Sentence)

A lessening or reduction of a punishment or sentence for a valid reason. Example: The defense of "following orders" to a charge of committing a war crime does not excuse such a crime, but it will be considered as a factor in mitigation and will result in a lessening of the punishment.

Mixed Armed Conflict (loac)

An armed conflict between a government and an opposition group that takes place within a country and is assisted by another country entering into the conflict to fight for one of the parties (e.g., Vietnam, Afghanistan). It is also known as an "internationalized" armed conflict.

Mobilization of Shame (against Violators)

A term used to signify the action of NGOs/groups/individuals, and possibly other states, to focus broad public attention on a certain state for its human rights violations, especially through the media. It is an attempt to publicly shame a state in the world's eyes so that the offending state will hopefully remedy its violations and/or deter from any other violations when it realizes that its actions are being watched. Example: NGO action as to China regarding Tibet.

MOBILIZING PRINCIPLES

The principles around which an organization, institution, or program's operations are focused and energized, and which drive its activity. These are the principles that all members and participants share and agree upon, and they believe will lead them to accomplish their goals. Human rights very often serve as mobilizing principles for organizations, institutions, and programs. There can be any number of mobilizing principles used. The principles of equality and nondiscrimination are examples of common mobilizing principles.

MODEL TREATY

A treaty* prepared to serve as a model to be used in a certain subject matter. These are usually prepared by experts from international, intergovernmental organizations to help states and organizations wanting to have legal expertise to help in drafting a treaty*. They can be bilateral or multilateral. The model treaty is usually used as a starting point, and each provision is negotiated and accepted as is, modified, or removed, and other new provisions are added until the treaty* is in the form and content desired by the forum.

Model treaties in principle are drafted consistent with all other pertinent legal norms, including international human rights norms. An example would be a model treaty on extradition.

MONISM/MONIST LEGAL SYSTEM (VS. DUALIST)

A "Monist Legal System" is one in which there is no difference between international and domestic law; they both form part of a single (mono) legal system. This system is contrasted with a "dualist" legal system, which distinguishes between domestic and international law as two separate legal systems. In this system, international law and municipal law are equal and on the same level, and both apply to municipal (national/domestic) matters.

MONITOR/MONITORING (COMPLIANCE)

1. A human rights monitor: A human rights monitor is a person, group, or body that is engaged in the function of watching, observing, or checking the status of a state's compliance or noncompliance with human rights norms. Usually, an international body charged with implementation of the norm will monitor states parties' compliance, but NGOs also perform monitoring functions, usually followed by reports of their observations and other legal, administrative, or diplomatic follow-up. Monitoring is a way to assure that states comply with their human rights legal obligations.

2. Monitoring human rights: In the UN Training Manual on Human Rights Monitoring it states that to monitor human rights compliance "describes the active collection, verification, and immediate use of information to address human rights problems," and that it "includes gathering information about incidents, observing events (elections, trials, demonstrations, etc.), visiting sites such as places of detention and refugee camps,

discussions with government authorities to obtain information and to pursue remedies and other follow-up." It includes firsthand fact-finding. It usually takes place over a protracted period of time.

Much monitoring is done in the field — that is, where the human rights related events are taking place.

MORAL AUTHORITY (VS. LEGAL AUTHORITY)

Authority grounded on the basis of a value of what is morally right. It is sometimes said that human rights have moral authority, or that a particular document such as the UDHR has moral authority whether or not it has legal authority. Moral authority is based on what is the right thing to do, and human rights are the right things for government to do or not do vis-à-vis individual human beings. Moral authority by itself does not give rise to legal obligations.

MORAL DAMAGES (REPARATIONS)

A court award to a petitioner in a contentious case as reparation against the responsible state, beyond the actual monetary losses incurred. Compensation awarded by a court for the intangible losses suffered by a victim of a human rights violation for nonpecuniary losses. Such damages may include, for example, monetary compensation for pain and suffering, loss of reputation, loss of physical liberty, humiliation, loss of enjoyment of life, mental distress, and loss of dignity.

One human rights court has said that moral damages should be based on the principles of equity and consider the special circumstances of the particular case.

MORAL INTEGRITY (RIGHT TO)

A classification of human rights based on that aspect of a whole human being that is being protected by such rights. Human rights protect human dignity by protecting certain aspects of human existence, such as physical integrity, standard of living, family, and legal integrity. Moral integrity protects the intangible sense of who one is, what one believe and thinks, and how one orients oneself to the world, the interior person.

Examples of moral integrity rights are freedom of thought, conscience religion, privacy, reputation, honor, opinion, and culture.

MORAL RIGHTS (VS. LEGAL RIGHTS)

Claims or entitlements made by individuals or groups based on principles of fairness, ethics, justice, or religious tenets. Moral rights are not legally binding.

MORALS (LIMITATION/RESTRICTION)

There is no officially accepted definition of morals in international human rights law, even though some general human rights instruments, such as the ECHR, contain references to morals.

The concept of morals means something like the accepted values of a society as manifested in customs, habits, or conduct, based on what a society feels is ethically right. An example is a prohibition against marriage between siblings, divorce, and sexual relations of adults with children. Morals may refer to those acts that are deemed acceptable and thus legally permitted.

Protection of morals is a legitimate aim of limitation clauses; that is, a state may limit the exercise of certain human rights when necessary to protect generally accepted public morals. *See* ICCPR, article 19.3(b), and ECHR, article 9.2. In the ECHR system some scholars say there are two notions of morals: one refers to the protection or safeguarding of the moral ethos or moral standards of a society as a whole, the common or established morality. The other is more of the constitutional meaning, which reflects that one element of morals is the protection of the rights and freedoms of others, especially those individuals and groups who require special attention and protection, such as the sick or disabled, the immature, or the dependent.

MOST-FAVORABLE-TO-THE-INDIVIDUAL (CLAUSE)

A clause in a human rights treaty* that provides that no provision of the treaty* shall be interpreted as restricting the enforcement or exercise of any right or freedom recognized by virtue of the laws of any state party or another treaty* to which one of the said states is a party. *See* ACHR, article 29(b). The purpose of such a clause is to prevent states parties from relying on a provision of the treaty* as grounds for limiting more favorable or less restrictive rights to which an individual is otherwise entitled under either national or international law. Such a clause seeks to achieve the maximum protection of the individual under both national and international law.

MOST FAVORED NATION TRADING STATUS (MFN) (AKA NORMAL TRADING STATUS)

A very favorable trading status between two states whereby a state grants another state the best possible tariffs as are granted to any other state. The official granting by the government of the lowest level of tariffs to other countries with whom it is trading.

To some degree a state may set the terms of international trade between itself and other states. This includes the amount of tariff imposed on the import of another state's goods. Conceptually, a state voluntarily chooses, within limits, to grant or not to grant to another state, trade conditions at least as favorable as all other trading partners are granted. This originates in the General Agreements on Trade and Tariffs (GATT) Treaty system.

The grant of MFN status brings about the most favorable and profitable commercial relations to the state that gets it. This concept has had greatest application in foreign trade with the U.S. In recent years the granting of this status by the U.S. has often been linked to a state's human rights record. This adds some "leverage" to the U.S. attempt to make another state more attentive to that state's poor human rights practices and hopefully to improve them so as to obtain such status. It is an economic incentive to improve its human rights situation.

Since 1974 U.S. law has required that in order to grant MFN status to a totalitarian state, the president must grant a waiver each year to that country on the basis that such waiver is in the U.S. national interest. If the president makes a decision to grant MFN status, both Houses of Congress must vote in order to overturn the waiver, or it enters into effect.

This term has come to be replaced by the term "normal trading status," although both terms are still heard. Normal trading status is now the correct term to use in the U.S. context.

Multilateral Forum

An international forum where more than two and usually many states in the world or in a region are engaged in matters of mutual interest and can discuss them, make decisions, and take collective action on them, including in relation to human rights.

Most states have historically been involved in legal and political affairs in the international arena of states. With the founding of the United Nations in 1945 in San Francisco, states have been able to become members of that major multilateral forum on human rights. As well as being a multilateral forum, the UN is also known as an international, intergovernmental organization. The Council of Europe, the Organization of African Unity and the Organization of American States are also multilateral fora (the plural of forum) that deal with human rights.

Multilateral means "many sided." The purpose of a multilateral forum is to create an official place where matters of mutual interests between states, such as human rights violations, can be discussed and acted upon collectively and peacefully in relation to the legal norms applicable to that system, such as human rights treaties*.

Multilateral Intervention (vs. Unilateral Intervention)

The act of an organized group of states without prior UN authorization but with arguable tacit approval of the UN Security Council to forcibly intervene in the internal affairs or on the territory of another state to stop breaches of the peace, threats to the peace, or acts of military aggression. This is compared with a collective intervention, which is one expressly authorized by the Security Council under Chapter VII; and contrasted with unilateral intervention, the forceful interference by more than one state into the internal affairs or on the territory of another state without prior authorization or legal justification.

Multilateralism (vs. Unilateralism)

A political term referring to the action of two or more states acting in concert together in a particular matter in the international arena. The implication is that the states work together for the common good and not unilaterally out of national self-interest. Multilateralism is contrasted with unilateralism where a state acts on its own and mostly out of its own sense of national self-interest. This term is often used in the context of situations of intervention by one state in the affairs of another state, particularly regarding instances of humanitarian intervention. The UNCH intended to limit unilateralism in many ways by providing for collective, that is, multilateral, action aimed at achieving the best interest of the whole international community.

Multinational Corporation (MNC)

A corporation or company of whatever legal status that operates in more than one state, most often in numerous states. These are often abbreviated or referred to as MNCs. Often large corporations/companies have a substantial impact upon the economy and even politics of states in which they operate. They may even commit acts, which, if committed by states, would constitute human rights violations, such as gender discrimination.

Some MNCs act in complicity or collusion with the state in the latter's violation of human rights to secure their economic benefit. MNCs have been the target of much human rights activity because of the role they have played in the occurrence of violations or because of their potential positive power to cause states not to violate human rights. One phenomenon of the late 1990s and early 2000s has been the emergence of corporate "codes of conduct," which are sets of guidelines written up for a company to apply in its business and administration so as to allow MNCs to act consistently with international human rights standards, even though they are not states. MNCs are also sometimes referred to as nonstate actors in the field of international law and relations.

This denomination of multinational corporation, MNC, is being replaced by the denomination of transnational corporation, abbreviated and referred to as TNC.

Municipal Law (vs. International Law) (aka Domestic Law)

Generally refers to the national law of a state that is applicable within the boundaries of its territory. "Municipal Law" or "Domestic Law" are terms used to distinguish such law from "international law," which applies to states in the international arena.

Caveat: International human rights norms found in treaties* can be incorporated or transformed into municipal or domestic law via constitutional law, thereby becoming binding within a state's national legal system as municipal/domestic law.

Mutatis Mutandis
[Latin, lit.: having changed the things which must be changed]

A Latin expression used in judicial interpretation when applying a principle or a case holding/jurisprudence to a different case or situation. It means something like "by analogy." It means that if one changes the factual details (names, dates, places) of a different case, the same principle/holding/jurisprudence will apply to a present case under the present facts.

Mutuality of Consent/ Obligation (International Law)

The classical principle of international law that says that each state's consent to be bound by the legal obligation of a treaty* is mutually dependent and reciprocal on every other state's consent and fulfillment of their respective obligations. Thus, if one state breaches its treaty* obligation, for example, by violating an essential treaty* norm, the other state or states might be relieved from their legal obligations to comply, or are at least relieved vis-à-vis the violating state. Under modern human rights and humanitarian law, legal obligations are no longer subject to this principle. They are nonmutual and nonreciprocal. *See* Vienna Convention (1969), article 60.5.

Nation

A people or aggregate of persons existing in a form of an organized jural society, usually inhabiting a distinct portion of the earth, speaking the same language or having an accepted common dominant language, using the same customs, possessing historic continuity, distinguishing themselves from other like groups by their racial origin and characteristics, and generally, but not necessarily, living under the same government and sovereignty.

NATIONAL

1. Political/legal status (noun): A citizen of a state.

2. International (descriptive): A characteristic of a person/institution/or thing belonging to a state, as opposed to belonging to an international organization or body.

NATIONAL INSTITUTIONS (ON HUMAN RIGHTS)

Institutions and organizations performing general or specific activity in the promotion and protection of human rights domestically within their own state. National institutions are not a part of the government. Such institutions promote human rights at the national level and are basically assuring the domestic implementation of international human rights norms within the state.

NATIONALISM

The attitude of a people who identify themselves as a nation, that their nation is the highest good and highest authority and that everything should be done for the benefit of that nation regardless of how that affects any other nations or peoples. It is not the same as patriotism, which is a love, respect for, and allegiance to one's own state.

Under human rights law all people are born equal to all other people in status and rights. There is no state, nation,

people, or race superior to any other. There is nothing inherently wrong with nationalism where it exists in the sense of patriotism, that is, a pride in one's people and its culture. The problem arises for human rights where nationalism elevates the status and needs of one group of people over another, resulting in demonizing, domination, discrimination, or violence against the "other," those who do not belong to the nation. This is often the cause of many human rights violations. It is often seen in the people of one nation trying to remove from their territory all those who are not members of that nation. This is also known as "ethnic cleansing."

At its extreme, nationalism can lead to the ultimate human rights violation, which is genocide. Genocide is the destruction of another group of people because of their nationality, ethnicity, race, or religion. This is the lesson of the Holocaust.

NATIONALITY (AKA CITIZENSHIP)

The citizenship of a person; the state or states to which an individual owes allegiance and from which he is entitled to protection from other states. Usually determined by where one is born ("Jus Soli") or the nationality of one's parents ("Jus Sanguinis"), or by an administrative process called "naturalization."

NATIONAL LIBERATION MOVEMENT

A military/political movement arising most commonly in developing nations to expel colonial powers or alien occupation so as to most fully realize independence and the right to self-determination as a people/nation. Usually accomplished through guerrilla warfare.

NATIONAL MINORITY

See Minority.

NATIONAL NONGOVERNMENTAL ORGANIZATION

A nongovernmental organization which is present and operating in and dealing with human rights in only one state.

NATIONAL SECURITY (LIMITATION/RESTRICTION)

The protection of the very existence of the state from any internal or external threats or dangers. Protection of national security is one of the legitimate aims in certain limitation/restriction clauses in certain international human rights treaties*. By such clauses a state is allowed to limit or restrict the exercise of certain human rights, such as freedom of expression, if it is necessary, proportional, and prescribed by law for protection of national security. *See* ICCPR, article 19.3(b).

National security can be wrongfully used as a cloak by government to cover up human rights violations or lack of accountability or transparency of a society's compliance with human rights obligations. Human rights law recognizes the need to balance the freedom of the individual and the right of the state to protect its existence for the good of the whole society.

NATIONAL SELF-INTEREST

That which seems to a state to be in the best interest of that state. When the gov-

ernment of a state acts in a certain way because it believes that this is what most benefits that state itself, regardless of how it affects another state or anyone else, it is acting in the national self-interest.

Even though all states belong to an international community that has established certain principles for the peace, harmony, and prosperity of all, very often states act in whatever way they believe will most benefit their individual state. Sometimes this involves economic benefit, sometimes political, and sometimes military.

Many times when people wonder why a government seems to fail to protect human rights within its own boundaries or elsewhere, the answer is that it is acting in its own perceived national self-interest. National self-interest is judged to be more important than protection of human rights or fulfillment of international legal obligations and advancement of the whole human community.

NATIONAL TREATMENT (STANDARD) (VS. INTERNATIONAL MINIMUM TREATMENT)

One of the two classic levels of state conduct as to the treatment of individuals who are not citizens of a state, i.e., foreigners (aliens). The "National Treatment" standard means that a state's justice system is obligated to treat foreigners (aliens) within its territory at a standard that is no less favorable than that enjoyed by its citizens (nationals). This standard cannot, in any case, fall below the other classic standard, the "International Minimum Standard," which roughly corresponds to international human rights norms, both treaty* and customary.

NATION-STATE

"Nation-State" refers more to a defined group of people who perceive themselves as a separate group of people, as a nation, and politically as a state, whether or not legally recognized as such, and living within the bound areas of one state and ruled by a single government.

NATURAL LAW (AKA JUS NATURALE)

The dictate of right reason involving moral necessity independent of any institution, human or divine. A body of law found in the nature of the way the world and humanity must act. A body of law or a specific principle held to be derived from nature and binding upon human society in the absence of or in addition to positive law.

NE (OR NON) BIS IN IDEM (PRINCIPLE OF DOUBLE JEOPARDY) *[Latin, lit.: not twice in the same thing]*

A general principle of international law applicable in criminal proceedings that says that a person may not be prosecuted for the same crime twice. It is the principle of double jeopardy in international law; it now most commonly refers to double prosecution at the international and domestic level.

Ne bis in idem and *non bis in idem* have the same meaning.

NECESSARY IN A DEMOCRATIC SOCIETY (LIMITATION)

A term found in some human rights treaty* norms containing limitations clauses. It specifies that in order for a limitation to be valid, it must first be determined to be "necessary in a democratic

society" so as to achieve an enumerated, legitimate aim, such as protection of national security, public health, safety, welfare, morals, order, etc. *See* ECHR, article 9.2 and IACHR, article 15.

"Necessary in a democratic society" means, in other words, that this limitation is necessary for the state because the viability of the democratic society is at stake and the measure taken represents a balance between the competing interests of the individual and the collective society. It meets a "pressing social need," the term used in the ECHR system. Stated as a principle, it is sometimes seen as the "principle of democratic necessity."

Some treaties* do not contain the word *democratic* and merely say "necessary to protect." *See* ICCPR, article 12.3.

NECESSITY (MILITARY)

See Military Necessity, supra.

NEGATIVE OBLIGATION (VS. POSITIVE OBLIGATION)

A state's obligation to refrain from doing something vis-à-vis the individual, for example, the obligation not to torture anybody. It is the forbearance of action by the state.

A state can have both a negative and a positive obligation regarding a human right. An example of a positive obligation would be a state's obligation to take affirmative steps to stop acts of torture from being committed by nonstate actors.

NEGATIVE RIGHT (VS. POSITIVE RIGHT)

A human right that permits its holder not to do something, that is, not to be forced by the state to do something one does not want to and cannot be legally forced to do. A negative right obligates a state to refrain from doing something to force, or allow others to force, an individual to do something that he has a right not to do. Example: A right not to believe any religion, not to express an idea, or not to join a trade union.

Also sometimes understood as a human right to prevent the state from doing something to a person. This type of right also requires the forbearance of action by the state. It is the right to not be subjected to state, and sometimes third-party, action violative of human dignity. The right to privacy is a negative right in that it permits the holder not to have something done to him by the state, such as surveillance or a wiretap; or an individual has the negative right not to be tortured, i.e., to be free from torture.

Negotiation

1. The process whereby people, states, NGOs, and IGOs involved in a dispute talk to each other about the issues that have arisen in order to arrive at a resolution to the problem.

2. The formal part of a treaty*-making process whereby states get together through their authorized representatives to propose and draft treaty* norms. It is the actual process of discussing a proposed norm and crafting an acceptable provision on a certain subject so as to have a proposed text be voted on, adopted, and ratified*.

Negotiation involves consideration of draft provisions, suggestions for changes, compromises, and statements of understanding, interpretation, and application

of a norm, all of which will later form part of the "legislative history" or *travaux préparatoires* of a text.

Nemo Tenetur Edere Contra Se (Principle against Self-Incrimination)
[Latin, lit.: no one may be held to disclose against one's own self]

The Latin expression of the principle (right) against self-incrimination. This principle says that the government (police, courts, etc.) cannot force a person to testify or say anything or provide evidence against oneself that would lead to incrimination of oneself. It is akin to the right to remain silent in the face of criminal charges. Also seen as the Latin expression *non accusare se debet*.

Neutrality/Neutral (vs. Belligerency/ Belligerent) (loac)

The international legal status of a state that completely and expressly abstains from participating in an international armed conflict. During a war, a neutral state adopts an official policy and attitude of impartiality towards all the states at war, which it recognizes as belligerents. If it does so, then the belligerent states cannot attack it in any way because it is neutral.

A separate set of international legal norms applies to neutral states as to their rights and obligations between themselves and the states that are in a state of belligerence (war). There is a body of law called the "Law of Neutrality" within international law that sets forth the norms on neutrality.

Nexus

A link, a connection, or a direct relationship to something. For example, a common issue of international humanitarian law is whether there needs to be a nexus between armed conflict and acts claimed to be crimes against humanity. In some historical contexts, such as the Nuremberg Trials, crimes against humanity required that there be a nexus between the criminal acts and an armed conflict in order for it to constitute a crime against humanity. Such nexus is no longer required.

Non Accusare se Debet (Principle against Self-Incrimination)
[Latin, lit.: one may not accuse oneself]

An occasionally seen alternate form of the Latin term *Nemo Tenetur Edere contra Se*, supra. *See also* Self-Incrimination.

Nonbinding (Treaty*/ Declaration/Resolution/ Norm/Obligation) (vs. Binding)

Having no legal force; not constituting a mandatory, legally enforceable duty or obligation on a state. Opposite of "Binding," supra.

Non Bis in Idem (aka Ne Bis in Idem) (Principle of Double Jeopardy)
[Latin, lit.: not twice in the same thing]

A general principle of international law applicable in criminal proceedings that says that a person may not be prosecuted for the same crime twice. It is the principle of double jeopardy in international law; it now most commonly refers to double prosecution at the international and domestic level.

Non bis in idem and *ne bis in idem* mean the same thing.

Noncombatant (vs. Combatant) (loac)

A term used in humanitarian law to describe an inhabitant of a belligerent state who is not taking part in the hostilities. Also known as a "Civilian." A noncombatant has no legal right (*jus ad bellum*) to engage in hostilities and cannot be attacked.

Nonconvention(al) Mechanism/Procedure

Same as "Non-Treaty-Based" mechanism/procedure, infra.

Nonconvention(al) Refugee (vs. Convention[al] Refugee)

A person who is fleeing from his country but does not meet the criteria to qualify as a "convention(al) refugee," which means a refugee as defined under the 1951 un Refugee Convention or its 1967 Protocol.

Nonderogable (Rights) (vs. Derogable Rights)

Nonderogable rights are those rights specified in a human rights treaty* as not capable of being suspended by the state during periods of public emergency, such as a civil war or invasion. An example of a nonderogable right is freedom from torture. Most nonderogable human rights are also known as "hard core" human rights. Nonderogable rights are always in force and must be respected by states parties under all circumstances. *See* ICCPR, article 4.2 and ECHR, article 15.2, which set forth the nonderogable rights of those two treaties.

NONDISCRIMINATION (PRINCIPLE)

Nondiscrimination is a principle of human rights that states that no one can be denied the right to the exercise and enjoyment of human rights on the basis of possessing specified characteristics, such as race, religion, nationality, language, sex, birth, or social or other status.

This principle means that a state may not condition or limit the enjoyment of human rights based on any of these characteristics. A state may not treat people differently as to who enjoys human rights and who does not unless there is a reasonable and objective justification for such distinction and a reasonable alternative measure cannot be found.

A "nondiscrimination clause" is a clause found in a human rights document that sets forth the principle and grounds of nondiscrimination. The nondiscrimination clause is often used to reinforce the specific substantive rights listed in the body of an instrument. An example of a nondiscrimination clause would be article 2.1 of the ICCPR, which reads:

> Each State Party to the present Covenant undertakes to respect and to ensure to all individuals within its territory and subject to its jurisdiction the rights recognized in the present Covenant, without distinction of any kind, such as race, colour, sex, language, religion, political or other opinion, na-

tional or social origin, property, birth or other status.

NONEXCLUSION/EXCLUSIVE (AKA INCLUSION/INCLUSIVE) (VS. EXCLUSION/EXCLUSIVE, NONINCLUSION/INCLUSIVE)

That which accepts everyone without exception and includes them as an equal part of a society, or as covered by a law, or as beneficiaries of a program, project, or system, such as education. It is not discriminatory and reflects the principle of equality. The opposite is noninclusive. Human rights requires, with certain exceptions, the inclusion of all human beings in all parts of society.

The nondiscrimination and equality provisions of international human rights instruments are legal measures aimed at promoting inclusion. *See* ICCPR, articles 2.1 and 26.

NONEXECUTED TREATY* (VS. EXECUTED TREATY)

A treaty that is not self-executing and requires implementing legislation, and for which no implementing legislation has yet been enacted.

In order for international human rights treaty norms to be transformed from international law to domestic law, either the treaty must be self-executing or it must be implemented (executed) by national legislation into domestic law. If a treaty is nonexecuted, it has not been transformed into national legislation, and therefore such treaty norms are not legally binding internally within a state that has signed and ratified it. It must be executed by domestic legislation to become binding within the state's national legal system.

Nongovernmental Entity (nge)

A political body, such as an armed opposition group, that is not a party to international treaties* and so is not technically bound by them. Some argue, *a contrario*, that some international legal norms do apply to NGEs. For example, some argue that Common Article 3 of the 1949 GCs concerning noninternational armed conflicts can be legally binding on such groups. An example of an NGE is the so-called Republika Srpska in Bosnia, which was recognized as an "entity" but not as a state in the Dayton Agreement (1995). NGEs are a type of nonstate actor in international law and relations.

Nongovernmental Organization (ngo) (vs. Intergovernmental Organization (igo))

A non-governmental organization is an organization of private individuals working for the promotion and protection of human rights in either a general (all human rights) or a special (specific, focused on certain human rights issues) focus and which can be local, national, regional, or international in structure, presence, and activity. Nongovernmental organizations are part of civil society. Such an organization is abbreviated and commonly known as an NGO.

NGOs may be permanent or *ad hoc* organizations; thematic or country-focused; and they may have open or closed membership and constitutions. NGOs monitor and compile information and draft reports on human rights viola-

tions, circulate information on violations and norms procedures, and occasionally provide legal and financial support to victims, even to the filing of complaints* in international and national human rights fora. They also lobby governments and IGOs, provide input in standard-setting processes, influence public opinion, assist in human rights education and join together in coalitions with other NGOs on certain issues.

The Encyclopedia of International Law (1986) defines them as private organizations not established by a government or by intergovernmental agreement that are capable of playing a role in international affairs by virtue of their activities. The International Law Dictionary (1987) defines an NGO as a private international organization that serves as a mechanism for cooperation among private national groups in international affairs. Generally speaking, the term NGO refers not only to organizations that deal with human rights but those that deal with any subject, issue, or state.

None of the existing definitions of NGOs describes them fully, and an effort is being made to redefine them. In relation to human rights they are the most important and active part of civil society.

Examples of human rights NGOs are Amnesty International, Human Rights Watch, and the International Committee of the Red Cross (ICRC).

Nonimmunity (Principle)

A principle of international law that holds that states and their agents are not immune from scrutiny, criticism, and accountability from other states for their human rights violations. It means that criticism and legal consequences may follow from a state's violation.

Historically, when accused of human rights violations, states have often claimed that they were immune from any outside scrutiny, criticism, and accountability for violations. They claimed immunity and defended that any criticism or action towards accountability would violate the related principle of noninterference in domestic affairs.

Generally speaking, under article 2(7) of the UNCH, states are immune from any outside interference by other states with matters that are essentially within their domestic jurisdiction and affairs. This is a sovereignty-based principle. But under international human rights law no state can claim immunity for committing human rights violations, because human rights violations are considered not properly within a state's domestic affairs. No state can tell any other state or any international or nongovernmental organization to stay out of its internal human rights affairs, because such acts are not protected under the noninterference principle. Thus no state can any longer claim that it or its agents are immune from international accountability for what they do internally as it relates to human rights

This principle is part of customary international law.

Noninclusion/Inclusive (aka Exclusion/Exclusive) (vs. Inclusion/Inclusive, Nonexclusion/Exclusive)

That which does not accept everyone without exception and does not include them as an equal part of a society, or as covered by a law, or as beneficiaries of a program, project, or system, such as education. It is a discriminatory act and violates the principles of equality and nondiscrimination. The opposite is inclusive. Human rights requires, with certain exceptions, the inclusion of all human beings in all parts of society.

The nondiscrimination and equality provisions of international human rights instruments are legal measures aimed at promoting inclusion. *See* ICCPR, articles 2.1 and 26.

Non Ingérence (in Domestic/ Internal Affairs) (Principle) *[French, lit.: Noninterference]*

Roughly the same as the principle of "noninterference." This is a French term sometimes used in the English-language literature on international law/relations, especially as it relates to the claimed right to humanitarian intervention. The principle is that a state may not engage in any unwarranted interference in the domestic affairs of another state. *See also* Noninterference.

Noninquiry (Rule of Extradition)

A rule involved in extradition proceedings, which says that the judge of the court of the state that is asked to extradite a person to another state will not inquire into the legal quality of the judicial proceedings in the courts of the state where the person will be tried, or whether punishment upon conviction would violate the human rights of the accused if returned to the requesting state.

This rule says that the highest official

of foreign affairs, such as a secretary of state, shall be the only one to consider such issues in determining whether to issue a decree of extradition. This means that traditionally the court in the requested state would not consider any potential human rights violation of the requesting state as to defendants due process rights or possible mistreatment, such as torture. This rule predated modern human rights law and is changing due to the emergence of international human rights norms.

NONINTERFERENCE (IN DOMESTIC / INTERNAL AFFAIRS) (PRINCIPLE)

A fundamental principle of international law now enshrined in article 2.7 of the UNCH, stating that states shall refrain in their international relations from interfering, intervening, or meddling in matters that are essentially within the domestic jurisdiction of another state. This principle is often raised as a defense by states that are accused of human rights violations. Such states will claim that the criticism or scrutiny violates the state's right to noninterference in matters within its domestic jurisdiction. This is now held to be an invalid, outdated defense because violations of human rights are not considered to be matters that are essentially within the domestic jurisdiction of states. No state has the right to violate human rights as part of its domestic jurisdiction.

NONINTERVENTION (IN DOMESTIC AFFAIRS) (PRINCIPLE)

Roughly synonymous with "Noninterference" (*see* supra).

NONJUSTICIABLE

The opposite of "Justiciable" (*see* Justiciability/Justiciable, supra).

NON-REFOULEMENT (PRINCIPLE)
[French, lit.: not expel back]

A principle of customary international law usually seen in the field of refugee law that says that a state may not return or expel a person to the frontiers of any state in which his life or freedom would be threatened on account of race, religion, nationality, political opinion, or membership in a particular social group. This principle is codified in conventional law in article 33 of the 1951 Refugee Convention.

NONRETROACTIVITY OF CRIMINAL / PENAL LAW (PRINCIPLE) (AKA EX POST FACTO LAW)

The legal principle of criminal law that says that lawmakers cannot pass penal legislation that purports to have the retroactive effect of criminalizing conduct that was not prohibited by law at the time the conduct was committed. Criminal laws cannot have a retroactive effect. Only the promulgation and existence of a duly enacted penal law, and not the arbitrary will of a leader, can criminalize an act. A governmental authority may not prosecute and punish anyone for a crime unless the conduct was prohibited by law in force that was clear and accessible to all at the time of the subject acts. This also brings into play the principle of *Nullum Crimen, Nulla Poena sine Lege* (*see* infra), which says that there can be no crime and no punishment without a law existing at the time of the alleged criminal offense.

Nonselectivity (vs. Selectivity) (Principle of Scrutiny of State Action)

The quality or state of not being selective and not being characterized by choosing to focus only on certain objects. It means not tending to use human rights practices as a tool to single out and pick on one or a few chosen states as a political / ideological vendetta. This term is used to describe the practice of states and IGO bodies of consistently scrutinizing the human rights practice of some states while refraining from doing so to others that are equally worthy of scrutiny. The principle of "Nonselectivity" in consideration of human rights issues means that the state/forum will not pick only certain states to criticize, e.g., communist states, dictatorships, or Islamic states, but will look at all states equally.

Non-Self-Executing (Treaty*) (vs. Self-Executing Treaty*)

Describes a treaty* whose provisions are not, in whole or in part, automatically the law of the land and enforceable before municipal courts but that require the state authorities to perform a formal or specific act in order to incorporate them into domestic law. A non-self-executing treaty* requires implementing legislation in order to implement its norms into domestic law.

Nonstate Actor (nsa) (vs. State)

Traditionally, human rights law, as part of public international law, distinguishes between, and concerns, public actors known as "states," not private actors. States are legal-political entities that are recognized as states by the international community of states. Nonstate actor is a term referring to any actor in society who or which is not a recognized state, such as an NGO, national liberation movement, political party, transnational corporation, and even a private individual. Some have defined it as any organization lacking formal or legal status as a state or agent of a state, or any constituent subunit such as a province, autonomous region or municipality, or agent of such entity.

Although not strictly private, sometimes IGOs are also referred to as nonstate actors because IGOs are not states, but they have international legal personality. In its classical theory, human rights law prevented *states* from violating human rights found in either treaties* or customary international law norms binding upon them. These norms were not addressed to nor considered binding upon anyone that is not a state. This distinction has become blurred as human rights theory has evolved and seeks to expand responsibility for the protection of human rights to all sectors of society, with accountability for all.

This term is most often seen in the context of the issue of the "third-party effect" or *Drittwirkung*" theory of human rights legal obligations, that is, whether the state is responsible for the actions of such private personalities (nonstate actors) or whether nonstate actors can be legally bound by international human rights obligations. Examples of these issues would be whether a national liberation army, which is not a state, is bound to follow the Geneva Conventions in combat against the government; or whether the state would be responsible for murders committed by a private paramilitary death squad.

The major issue concerning nonstate actors is usually determining the nature of the state government's duty to protect individual rights from violation by third parties not linked to the state, by taking affirmative steps to prevent such third-party acts.

Individual agents of nonstate actors can be prosecuted for violating certain international crimes, such as genocide and crimes against humanity, under international criminal law and the principle of individual criminal responsibility.

Nonstate Entity (nse)

An international actor that is not generally recognized as a state under international law, but is involved in activity bringing it within the attention of the international community. The Republica Srpska and the Palestinian Authority are early twenty-first century examples considered by many to be nonstate entities. These are groups of people that have created a state-like organ or polity that has not been recognized as a state by the international community.

Normally, public international law deals only with states, but this has been changing. The issue of responsibility of nonstate entities for human rights violations under international law is an important developing human rights issue. It is very similar to and sometimes used interchangeably with the concept of "Nonstate Actor," supra, which is a broader category.

Nonstate Party

A state that is not legally bound to a particular treaty* because it has not ratified* it. When a state ratifies* a treaty*, it becomes a state party to that treaty*. Every other state is known as a "nonstate party." A state which has signed but not ratified* a treaty* is called a signatory or signatory state.

Non-Treaty-Based (aka Charter-Based) (Organ/ Body/ Mechanism/ Procedure)

A term meaning that the source of authority for a body, organ, etc., of an intergovernmental organization is not from a law-making treaty but from a constitution or charter or by resolution of the general assembly or a representative body.

This is contrasted with "treaty-based" body and is synonymous with "charter-based" organ, body, etc.

Norm

A defined, authoritative standard of conduct that is legally binding on the state as a matter of international or domestic law. A principle of right action binding upon the member states parties to a treaty* or by customary international law serving to guide, control, or regulate proper and acceptable state and human behavior. Human rights treaties* contain human rights "norms," both substantive, i.e., what is allowed or not allowed to the individual, and procedural, i.e., the mechanisms and procedures for implementing substantive rights.

Normal Trading Relations/ Status (aka Most Favored Nation Trading Status)

Same as "Most Favored Nation Trading Status." This term started being used instead of the term "most favored nation" trading status in the U.S. in the late

1990s. *See* Most Favored Nation Trading Status.

NORMATIVE

Relating to norms or standards. Usually means that which prescribes binding norms or rules of conduct. When it has entered into force, a treaty* becomes a "normative" instrument.

NORM ENTREPRENEURS

Persons or organization that are actively engaged in attempting to get international, intergovernmental organizations to articulate, establish by standard setting, and disseminate hard human rights norms, creating legal obligations on states to act according to the human rights norms. Often this is a slow process from proposals to adoption of a nonbinding declaration and eventually to a legally binding hard law instrument, such as the ICCPR.

Many, and some say, most internationally recognized human rights norms were first articulated, argued, and pushed for acceptance into international law by individuals, by groups, and by national and international organizations. An example would be the Torture Convention, which was initially proposed and pushed by groups such as Amnesty International.

Norm entrepreneurs seek standard setting with a goal to creating both substantive and procedural human rights norms and effective supervisory mechanisms.

NORTH-SOUTH (WORLD POLITICAL/ ECONOMIC DIVISION)

In the post-Cold War era there has come to be a view of the world as being no longer divided in terms of spheres of influence into a bipolar East-versus-West division but now into a North-versus-South or North-South division. The North is seen as the developed and more politically powerful states, and the South is considered to be the underdeveloped and less powerful states that are competing for a fair and equitable share of the earth's resources.

NOYAU DUR (AKA HARD CORE HUMAN RIGHTS)
[French, lit.: hard core/pit]

A French term meaning a hard core or pit, but used with human rights to mean "Hard Core Human Rights," which include the right to life and to freedom from torture and slavery. Roughly synonymous with "nonderogable human rights."

NULLUM CRIMEN, NULLA POENA SINE LEGE (PRINCIPLE) (AKA PRINCIPLE OF LEGALITY)
[Latin, lit.: no crime, no punishment without a law]

This is a Latin expression for the principle of legality, which says that a person cannot be prosecuted criminally for an act unless that act was criminal at the time it was committed. This principle also means that any criminal law must be precisely formulated and accessible so that one can know what is prohibited. Otherwise stated, a punishment cannot be inflicted by a state upon a person unless a preexisting law sets forth the nature of the prohibited conduct and the punishment and matches that punishment to the crime. *See also* "Ex Post Facto" laws, which are rendered illegal by this doctrine.

Nuremberg Charter/ Rules/Law (1945) (LOAC)

Refers to the legal basis of the War Crimes Tribunals at Nuremberg, Germany, in 1945, under which Nazi war criminals were prosecuted for the commission of crimes under international law at the Nuremberg Trials by the victorious allied powers. The Nuremberg Charter, also known as the London Charter, set forth the legal basis for international crimes resulting in individual criminal responsibility. They are composed of three categories of international crimes:

1. Crimes against peace.
2. War crimes.
3. Crimes against humanity.

These criminal norms, sometimes also referred to as the "Nuremberg Rules," or even "Nuremberg Law," were largely based on the Hague Conventions of 1899/1907 as customary international law. Later, the United Nations reaffirmed these rules as being declaratory of customary international law, and they are still legally binding as customary law.

Nuremberg Principles (1945) (LOAC)

A set of four principles taken from the 1945 Nuremberg Charter, supra, regarding individual criminal responsibility of Nazi war criminals, which were applied during the Nuremberg Trials after the end of World War II.

These principles provided, first, that anyone who committed an international crime is individually responsible and liable for punishment; that the national law of states where international criminal acts were committed does not prevent international criminal responsibility; that heads of state and government officials who commit such acts are not immune from prosecution; and that even complicity in the commission of any of the Nuremberg crimes is a crime under international law.

OAS (Organization of American States)

An acronym for the Organization of American States, a regional IGO covering North, Central, and South America. It has a human rights system with a human rights commission based on the American Declaration of the Rights and Duties of Man, and for those states that are state parties to the American Convention on Human Rights the commission and a court supervise compliance.

OAU (Organization of African Unity)

An acronym for the Organization of African Unity, a regional IGO for states in Africa. It has a human rights system based on the African Charter on Human and Peoples' Rights, supervised by the African Commission on Human and Peoples' Rights.

Obiter Dictum (vs. Holding) (aka Dictum)

See Dictum, supra.

Object (vs. Subject) (of International Law)

In international law theory this term is used to describe the person/group/state for whom an international legal right is ultimately meant to benefit. It is the ultimate object of the law as contrasted with the "subject" of international law, which is the person/group/state that is the holder or bearer of the right itself. In human rights theory, the human being and not the state is the "subject" of such rights.

OBJECT AND PURPOSE (OF TREATY*) (INTERPRETATION)

The term used to describe the two factors that must be examined regarding a treaty* in order to enable one to properly interpret the treaty*. To interpret a treaty*, one must look at the language in good faith according to its ordinary meaning within the context of the treaty's* "object and purpose."

The object of a human rights treaty* is to establish human rights norms and procedures; the purpose may be, for example, to protect the human rights of children or refugees or to eliminate torture.

This term is found in article 31 of the Vienna Convention (1969) and is a general principle of international law regarding the interpretation of human rights treaties*.

OBJECTION (TO RESERVATION TO TREATY*)

The express statement of a state that is a signatory or contracting party to a treaty*, usually by written instrument, that, in its opinion, a reservation to the treaty* being submitted by another ratifying* state is invalid because incompatible with the object and purpose of the treaty*.

OBJECTIVITY (PRINCIPLE OF SCRUTINY OF STATE PRACTICE)

The state or quality or relationship of being objective, i.e., only focusing on the external elements of reality to the neglect of the subjective. This term is sometimes used to describe the attitude or conduct of a state or human rights body in looking at the human rights practices of a state. It means that, as a matter or principle, states and IGOs should scrutinize the human rights practices of a state without any biases, preconceived notions, or prejudgments as to compliance or lack thereof.

Objectivity answers the complaint* that all states are not being treated alike in the international scrutiny of their human rights practices. This term is often seen with the related terms (principles) of "Impartiality" and "Nonselectivity."

OBLIGATIO ERGE OMNES

See Erge Omnes, supra.

OBLIGATION (INTERNATIONAL LAW)

Something a person or a state or an international organization is legally bound to do or refrains from doing as a prescribed conduct or course of action. A requirement imposed on a state by international law or previous agreement enforceable under international law.

A human rights norm creates an "obligation" or a "duty" on the state to respect that right. Violation or breach of the obligation entails recourse to implementation measures, depending upon the institutional context, such as individual or interstate complaints* seeking reparations or other redress, or possibly criminal prosecution, or the imposition of economic sanctions.

OBLIGATION OF CONDUCT (AKA OBLIGATION OF MEANS) (VS. OBLIGATION OF RESULT/EFFECT)

A term describing the nature of a state's legal obligation as requiring the state merely to act or not act in a certain way. The state fulfills its duty by acting or refraining from acting in a certain way regardless of the results. It is not focused on the result but on the state's manner of acting. For example, not torturing people is an obligation of conduct. Obligation of conduct requires action reasonably calculated to realize the enjoyment of a right.

Some human rights norms impose obligations of conduct or means, whereas others impose obligations of result/effect. Eliminating illiteracy would be an example of an obligation of result/effect. Obligation of conduct is also known as obligation of means.

OBLIGATION OF EFFECT (AKA OBLIGATION OF RESULT) (vs. OBLIGATION OF CONDUCT/MEANS)

A term describing the nature of a state's legal obligation as requiring the state to achieve a particular result or effect in order to fulfill its duty under a treaty*. It is not focused on conduct so much as on the result, the goal to be met, such as elimination of hunger. Some human rights norms impose obligations of effect/result, whereas others impose obligations of conduct/means. Eradicating illiteracy would be an obligation of effect.

Obligation of result obligates a state to achieve specific targets to satisfy a detailed substantive standard.

Sometimes obligation of effect is called "obligation of result."

OBLIGATION OF MEANS (AKA OBLIGATION OF CONDUCT)

Same as Obligation of Conduct, supra.

OBLIGATION OF RESULT (AKA OBLIGATION OF EFFECT)

Same as Obligation of Effect, supra.

OBLIGATION TO ENSURE

See Ensure Human Rights (Obligations), supra.

OBLIGATION TO FULFILL

See Fulfill Human Rights (Obligations), supra.

OBLIGATION TO PROTECT

See Protect Human Rights (Obligations), infra.

OBLIGATION TO RESPECT

See Respect Human Rights (Obligations), infra.

OBSERVATION (HUMAN RIGHTS SUPERVISION/ IMPLEMENTATION PROCESS)

The UN Training Manual on Human Rights Monitoring states that observation refers to "the more passive process of watching events such as assemblies, trials, elections, and demonstration." It is an aspect of human rights monitoring that requires on-site presence.

OBSERVATIONS (UN TREATY-BASED BODY)

A statement by a treaty* supervising body on review of a state report as to the completeness, accuracy, timeliness, or other aspect of the report that the body wishes to bring to the attention of the reporting state. This is done with a view toward improving the quality and effectiveness of the reporting process by the state, thus improving the effectiveness of the supervising body and ensuring better compliance with human rights norms.

Observers

Observers are persons who are placed in a location to be able to observe what is going on as to human rights violations, the freeness and fairness of government elections, or the fairness of trials. These are persons who can identify any wrongdoing and report to an institution or government as to their observations, so that action can be taken to remedy any wrongdoing.

Occupied Territory (loac)

A term of the Law of Armed Conflict referring to the status of territory that is militarily occupied by the armed forces of an enemy state or by a state not having legal sovereignty over that particular territory. It requires the actual exercising of authority over the territory and is only intended to be temporary. It is also known as "belligerent occupation." There is a whole section of the Law of Armed Conflict (Humanitarian Law) that sets forth norms regarding limitations on the occupying force. *See* GC IV (1949), articles 47–73, and the Hague Conventions of 1899 and 1907, which set forth norms protecting inhabitants of occupied territories.

Official Languages (of Treaty* Text)

The language or languages into which a human rights treaty* is translated and which are deemed to be official text translations. Only an official language text of a human rights treaty* instrument can be referred to and cited as an official legal text. Human rights treaties* are adopted by and meant to apply to many states with different languages. It is legally, politically, and administratively impractical to allow the treaty* to be referred to in all or even many different languages.

Most human rights treaties have a clause that states which particular language translations of a treaty* are to be designated as "official" text translations. *See* ICCPR, article 53.1. The official languages are chosen by the states that take part in the negotiation and drafting of a treaty* text.

In most quasi-judicial and judicial fora, the parties to the case and the forum must make use of only the "official" language texts.

Ombudsman

A government official appointed to receive and investigate complaints* made by individuals against abuses or capricious acts of public officials. They may issue reports, findings, and help mediate equitable settlements.

On-Site Investigation / Fact-Finding (aka *In Loco* or In Situ Investigation / Fact-Finding)

A term used to describe going to the actual site where human rights issues arise so as to obtain firsthand information and evidence of the matter being examined. The investigators travel to the region, country, or municipality at issue to interview witnesses and government officials and any other individuals / organizations, such as NGOs, to find out exactly what happened or what is presently happening. It does not imply that an actual case is pending or has been filed. Such investigations may be made in the course of preparing a country report or a thematic report, but usually they refer to an actual case of an alleged human rights violation. Its purpose is to obtain the best possible information because information supplied by governments may be suspect.

It is also called *in loco* or in situ investigation.

OPINIO JURIS (CUSTOMARY INTERNATIONAL LAW)
[Latin, lit.: opinion or belief about law]

One of two elements of the doctrine of customary international law (the other is consistent state practice). *Opinio juris* refers to the psychological element accompanying state action in the international arena as being done in the belief that the action is required as an obligation of international law and not merely as a matter of courtesy, comity, necessity, or expedience.

It is the subjective, qualitative component of customary international law, a source of human rights law norms.

The full Latin expression is *opinio juris sive necessitatis* ("opinion or belief about law or necessity").

OPINION (FREEDOM OF)

The result of the internal mental processes of a human being by which one forms conclusions about values and reality, and develops a conscience and makes decisions about how to see the world and how to act in it. It is the activity of a person's internal forum, the *forum internum*. It is close to the ideas of thought and belief, but more apt to be applied to political convictions and secular and civil matters. Opinion is more the result of thought process. It is also close to conscience, which is the internal value system and outward application of one's opinions, and the personal policies and values one holds from those opinions. It is also related to freedom of thought.

Under international human rights law everyone has the human right to have whatever opinion one wants, about anything. This right is sometimes found as an implication of the freedom of expression but most often stands by itself. *See* UDHR, article 19; ICCPR article 19; ECHR, article 10; ACHR, article 13. This means that everyone has the legal right to think what they want, how they want, and if they want. One cannot be forced by the state or anyone else to think a certain way.

This freedom does not allow a person to act in any way he wishes. Actions based on one's opinions may be limited in certain ways in certain situations.

OPPRESSION

The unjust and excessive exercise of governmental authority or power; unreasonably burdensome or severe government action. Such acts are called "oppressive."

OPTIONAL CLAUSE (OF TREATY*)

A clause in a treaty* that a state party may of its own will choose to accept or not accept. It is not compulsory for the state to accept to be bound by it. The state must usually submit an instrument containing a declaration stating that it expressly consents to be bound by the provisions of the clause. Such clauses could, for example, provide for the treaty* to cover certain matters, such as the use of certain weapons, or cover certain crimes or specific economic rights. Often such a clause is used to set forth the option for the state to accept the jurisdiction/competence of a commission/court/committee to handle (seize) cases presented to it alleging violation of the rights contained in the treaty* by the state accepting the optional clause.

The difference between an optional clause and an optional protocol is that an optional clause sets forth optional norms contained within or appended to a general treaty* text. When the state ratifies* the treaty*, it contemporaneously also consents or declines to consent to the particular optional clause norms. In comparison, an optional protocol sets forth optional norms in a separate legal (treaty*) instrument called a protocol, which must be separately ratified* by each state in addition to the treaty* it is amending. The protocol usually, but not always, is ratified* after the treaty's* ratification*.

Optional Protocol (to Treaty*)

A treaty instrument that amends an existing treaty* and provides for the state parties to exercise their sovereign will to accept to be bound by its provisions. It is not compulsory for a state to become bound by it, even though the state is bound by the underlying treaty.* Usually, such an instrument sets forth a new procedural or substantive norm. It may set up an implementation mechanism, such as providing for individual complaints* against violating states, or it may call for certain state acts/legislation, such as abolishing the death penalty.

Most often this term is seen to refer to the Optional Protocol to the International Covenant on Civil and Political Rights (ICCPR-OP, UN 1966), which is one of the four instruments of the International Bill of Rights and which provides for states parties to declare their consent to the jurisdiction/competence of the UN Human Rights Committee to receive complaints against them filed by individuals who claim to be victims of violations.

Oral Intervention

An oral statement presented to a forum such as an IGO body stating the facts and opinions of the presenting party (intervenor) on an issue before the body or one that the presenting party wishes to bring to the body's attention. Oral interventions are commonly presented by NGOs at public sessions of IGOs such as the UN and their subsidiary bodies, such as the UN Commission on Human Rights. Oral interventions are generally the verbal input from outside parties to assist the body in doing its job.

Ordinary Crime (aka Common Crime) (vs. International Crime)

An act or failure to act in a manner that constitutes a crime under the domestic (national or local) law of a state. This is contrasted with an international crime, which is prohibited by the international community, such as genocide. Some acts can constitute both an ordinary crime and an international crime at the same time. For example, if someone kills another person, the killer has committed an ordinary crime, which would constitute an act of murder under national law. That same murder could also constitute the international crime of genocide or a war crime if that act were committed as part of a larger genocidal act or military attack with the requisite mental state. Sometimes the same act is prosecuted before an international criminal tribunal and a national criminal tribunal. International crimes are those that have an element that brings them within the interest of the whole international community, whereas ordinary crimes are deemed of interest only or primarily to the national or local community.

ORDINARY MEANING OF TERMS (OF A TREATY*)

A phrase referring to how the words of a treaty* instrument are to be read so as to arrive at the proper interpretation of the instrument. According to article 32 of the Vienna Convention on the Law of Treaties (UN 1968), all treaties* governed by international law must be interpreted in good faith in accordance with the "ordinary meaning" to be given to its terms in their context and in light of the object and purpose of the treaty*. It is the primary method used for interpretation. Where such primary method does not work, such as where a text is unclear or ambiguous, recourse can be had to "Supplementary Means of Interpretation" (*see* infra), such as the preparatory works.

ORDRE PUBLIC (LIMITATION)
[French, lit.: public order]

A French legal term found in some limitation clauses; it denotes a vast conception of the totality of life in a society on the administrative and political level and the public policy that seeks to protect a given society's public order. It is more like public policy than public order. It is a basis of permissible limitation found in the limitation clauses of the ECHR. Most often it is seen in texts as "public order," which is the English translation of the term. *See* ECHR, Protocol 4, articles 2.3 and 9.2, and ICCPR, article 14.1.

ORGANIZATION OF AMERICAN STATES (OAS)

An international political organization made up of almost all governments of the states in North, Central, and South America to discuss and take political and legal action on matters of mutual concern to them, including human rights issues.

This regional intergovernmental organization contains a regional international human rights system known as the Inter-American Human Rights system. This system is based on the American Declaration* on Human Rights and the American Convention on Human Rights and its two Protocols; it is monitored by the Inter-American Commission on Human Rights (which sits in Washington DC) and Inter-American Court of Human Rights (which sits in San Jose, Costa Rica).

ORGANIZATION ON SECURITY AND COOPERATION IN EUROPE (CSCE)

The new title for the former Conference on Security and Cooperation in Europe (*see* supra).

OSCE (FORMERLY CSCE)

Abbreviation for the Organization on Security and Cooperation in Europe, supra.

OTHER (THE)

An expression referring to someone other than the speaker and whom the speaker sees as different and who should be regarded and treated differently from the speaker. This concept is most used in discussions of bigotry, racism, intolerance, discrimination, and nationalism. It refers to the perceptions of an individual toward another individual or group and about the perceptions of a group toward anyone from another group based on some distinguishing characteristic, such as religion, race, nationality, or color. With the sense of difference often comes a sense of the other's inferiority, or that they pose some danger to the society or culture of the speaker. There are often implications of hostility, rejection, non-inclusion, and separation. These are inconsistent with the principles of equality and human dignity. This attitude can result in discrimination, mistreatment, hate crimes, crimes against humanity, and even genocide, as was seen in the Bosnia conflict.

Example: Many Americans see and treat illegal aliens as the "other." The alien is not one "one of us."

Outrages upon the Personality (loac)

A violation of humanitarian law found in common article 3 of the four Geneva Conventions of 1949, under the terms "outrages upon the human personality." It is a general term, but often applied to harmful injurious acts such as rape or other types of sexual assault, and is applicable in noninternational armed conflict. Commission of such acts is a crime under international criminal law.

Pact (Treaty Instrument)

Synonymous with "Treaty." It is one of many terms used to title or describe an international legal instrument. A formal pact is usually a treaty between two or more states, governed by international law.

Pacta Sunt Servanda (Principle)
[Latin, lit.: agreements must be kept]

A general principle of international law that means that states must obey the treaties* they have ratified*. It means that treaties* are legally binding obligations on states, and if a state fails to comply with a treaty* (i.e., breaches the treaty*), then the state is in violation of this principle. This may entail legal responsibility and/or sanctions for redress of violations, regardless of whether the state's action is legal or constitutional under its own national (domestic/municipal) law.

Pact of San Jose (aka American Convention on Human Rights)

An alternate term referring to the American Convention on Human Rights (achr). This general human rights treaty was adopted by the Organization of American States in 1969 in San Jose, Costa Rica. Human rights instruments are sometime referred to by the name of the place where they were adopted. *See* Appendix C, American Convention on Human Rights.

Pari Materia (also, In Pari Materia)
[Latin, lit.: in like matter]

A rule that is sometimes followed in interpreting laws. This Latin term means roughly "in the same/similar matter" or "on the same subject." It states that laws that deal with the same subject matter should be construed together, such as in relation to one another, so as to arrive at consistent meanings. This rule is to ensure harmonization of different laws covering the same subject matter.

PARI PASSU (ALSO, *IN PARI PASSU*)
[Latin, lit.: in equal step; equally]

A Latin adverbial legal expression: "without preference"; "equally"; "in equal measure/steps."

PARIS MINIMUM STANDARDS
OF HUMAN RIGHTS NORMS
IN A STATE OF EMERGENCY

A set of soft law human rights standards created by a group of human rights experts in 1984 to more fully define how and what human rights norms apply in times of a state of emergency. It is a set of standards concerning the derogation of human rights made to help states parties to human rights treaties* fulfill their legal obligations under the treaties* during periods of derogation. One of the purposes of these standards is to prevent states from misusing states of emergency as an excuse or cover for committing human rights violations.

These standards are not legally binding upon states but should be applied and followed as guidelines on how to fulfill their hard law obligations under human rights treaties*.

PARTICIPATORY (HUMAN) RIGHTS

The human rights of individuals to participate in the direction and development of a society by being engaged in public affairs so as to assure that their human rights, such as to food, education, and religious exercise, are realized. ICCPR, article 25, for example, says that every citizen has the right to "take part in the conduct of public affairs." This looks to the increase in democracy and its advantages, especially in economic development resulting from the active, free, and meaningful participation of individuals in public society.

The right to vote and to run for public office are examples of participatory human rights.

PARTICULARITIES (CULTURAL,
ETC.) (AKA SPECIFICITIES)

The characteristics or qualities of being that are peculiar to particular individuals or groups. Usually used in discussing differences or diversities in cultures. Cultural particularities are those characteristics of a group that make that group different from others, such as religion, tribal structure, legal system, or customs. One may also speak of "religious," "linguistic," or "ethnic" particularities. Any type of difference that distinguishes the person or group can be spoken of as a "particularity."

Some argue that human rights are universal, i.e., to be applied the same to everyone, everywhere alike, which is known as the theory of "universality of human rights." Others argue that human rights are to be applied differently according to different cultural and other particularities under the doctrine of "Cultural Relativism." The universalist argument is currently the predominantly accepted one.

The term "Particularities" is roughly the same as and interchangeable with the term "Specificities" (*see* infra), i.e., cultural specificities.

PARTICULAR SITUATIONS
(1503 PROCEDURE)

In the context of the UN Commission on Human Rights, this refers to the status and content of a communication alleging human rights violations under the 1503 Procedure, along with the reply of the accused government. Under the 1503 Procedure, the Commission can only handle "particular situations that appear to reveal a consistent pattern of gross and reliably attested violations of human rights and fundamental freedoms." The Commission's Working Group on Situations examines the communications and government replies, which together form the particular situation. Finding a particular situation does not mean that the government is found to have actually violated human rights as alleged in the communication.

If the particular situation does reveal the possible existence of a consistent pattern of gross and reliably attested violations, it can proceed with the confidential 1503 process and can make a decision to find the state responsible for such violations, if the merits warrant such finding.

PARTY (TO TREATY*)

Usually refers to a state that has signed and become bound by an international human rights treaty*. In order to determine whether a state is in violation of a treaty* or whether it even is under an obligation to comply with the treaty*, one must know whether a state is a "party" or a "state party." In some treaties*, the terms "contracting party" or "high contracting party" are used. They are synonymous with each other. To say that a state is a party, state party, or a high contracting party to a treaty* means that the state has voluntarily consented to become bound by the treaty*. This is done by the state giving its approval to the treaty* by formal written instrument ex-

pressly stating the state's agreement to comply with the treaty*. When this instrument has been duly deposited with the designated depository institution, the state becomes a party. Sometimes this goes into effect a certain period of time after deposit, e.g., six months. *See* State Party, High Contracting Party.

PASSIM
[Latin, lit.: here and there; all over]

A Latin adverb used in reference to where something can be found in a text to which a writer makes reference, usually in a footnote. It means that the subject or other reference can be found all over, or here and there in the text to which reference is made. Example: "The rights of refugees fleeing persecution for political reason can be found in the 1951 Refugee Convention, *passim*."

PASSIVE PERSONALITY PRINCIPLE (BASIS OF CRIMINAL JURISDICTION)

A legal basis for the exercise of criminal jurisdiction over certain acts that take place outside the territory of a state. This is a form of extraterritorial jurisdiction. Under this principle a state may exercise criminal law jurisdiction over acts taking place outside its territory if the victim of the crime is a citizen of the prosecuting state. Thus, if someone in his own state kills a person from another state, the state of the victim could exercise criminal jurisdiction over the perpetrator even if the act was not committed in the prosecuting state and the perpetrator was not a citizen of that state. Some human rights violations could constitute crimes, which could be prosecuted under this principle.

Peacekeeping (International)

The United Nations glossary defines peacekeeping as a hybrid political-military activity aimed at conflict control, which involves UN presence in the field (usually involving military and civilian personnel) with the consent of the parties to the conflict, to implement or monitor the implementation of arrangements relating to the control of conflict (cease fires, separation of forces, etc.) and their resolution (particular or comprehensive settlement) and/or to protect the delivery of humanitarian relief. In UN parlance peace-keeping is called a Chapter VI operation. Peace-keeping measures serve to prevent or limit the violation of human rights and humanitarian law.

Peacemaking (International)

A diplomatic process of brokering an end to an existing conflict principally through mediation and negotiation, as, for example, under article VI of the UN Charter. The diplomatic efforts are often accompanied by military activity. Military activities that contribute to peacemaking include military to military contacts, security assistance, shows of force, and preventative deployments.

Because many human rights violations arise during, or are the cause of, armed conflicts, peacemaking is very important as a means to ending such violations and restoring respect for human rights and rule of law.

People/Peoples

In the singular, this word refers to persons who form part of the aggregate of all human beings, as distinguished from lower animals. In the plural form it has a rather unique and specific meaning with important legal consequences, but the process of trying to define "Peoples" is still ongoing. It refers, in a sense, to a body of persons who are united by a common culture, tradition, ethnic background, and sense of common kinship that often also constitutes a distinct, politically organized group. The UNCH preamble begins with "We the Peoples of the United Nations . . ."

The legal significance of being recognized as, or achieving the status of, a "Peoples," is that the right of self-determination, such as found in ICCPR, article 1, can be asserted only by "Peoples." "Peoples" have the collective human right of self-determination whereby they can freely determine their political status and pursue their economic, social, and cultural development together. *See also* ICESCR, article 1.

Peoples' Rights

A term used in the title of the AFR to refer to collective rights in the African context that deals with many tribal groups. Peoples' rights are intended to protect the rights of collective societies/groups in Africa, especially tribes. This term is sometimes used outside of the AFR.

Peremptory Norm (*Jus Cogens*)

A peremptory norm of general international law is a norm accepted and recognized by the international community of states as a whole with no derogation permitted. The norm can be modified only by a subsequent norm of general international law having the same character. Also known as a "*Jus Cogens*" norm. The obligation is owed to the international community as a whole, which is expressed by the Latin term *erge omnes*.

According to article 53 of the Vienna Convention of 1969, a peremptory norm is as follows:

1. A norm of general international law
2. Accepted by the whole international community of states, which
3. Permits no derogation and
4. Can be modified only by new peremptory norms.

The function of a peremptory norm is primarily to protect overriding international values and concerns by limiting the rights of subjects of law to conclude agreements *inter se*, between two states, which could injure those interests. *Inter se* agreements derogating from peremptory norms are invalid.

Perfect Obligation (vs. Imperfect Obligation)

A legal obligation that is clear and accepted as to the holder of the duties involved, the "duty-holder," and the particular methods of fulfillment and realization in society are clearly established.

Perfidy (loac)

Perfidy is the commission of acts by armed forces intending to invite the confidence of the enemy by leading them to believe that they are entitled to, or are obliged to accord protection, such as by not attacking, under international humanitarian law. It is prohibited conduct because it feigns legal protection under humanitarian law and leads to disrespect for humanitarian law. An example of "perfidy" is displaying a white flag of surrender when not intending to surrender but doing so as to induce the adversary to relax its guard so it can be attacked.

Permanent Normal Trade Relations/Status (pntr)

See Most Favored Nation Trading Status.

Permissive Jurisdiction (vs. Mandatory Jurisdiction) (of Court/Tribunal)

The power and authority of a court/tribunal to exercise jurisdiction over a case and over a state or other party, but for which the state or other party has the right and power to choose to object to such exercise of jurisdiction and not to submit to this jurisdiction.

In some judicial systems, the states have set up the court systems so that the states subject to that judicial body have previously agreed to allow states to voluntarily submit to the court's jurisdiction any time a case is filed against it. The state has the power to object to the exercise of jurisdiction in a given case where the court has been endowed only with permissive jurisdiction.

This is compared with mandatory jurisdiction where states cannot choose whether they want to submit to a judicial body but are legally obligated to do so. This is because they have previously accepted binding treaty* obligations by which they expressly accepted such mandatory jurisdiction.

Perpetrator (of Violations)

A person/state that commits a human rights violation and sometimes used to describe one that causes such violation to occur. It can be an individual, group, or state but usually refers to individuals.

Per Se
[Latin, lit.: through itself]

A Latin phrase that means "by itself," "in and of itself," "all by itself," "through itself," "in its own nature."

It is most often seen in law as meaning "in and of itself," such as if one were to say "shooting a prisoner of war without justification would be, per se, a violation of the GCs of 1949."

Persecution

There is no universally accepted definition of this word in the field of human rights. Its meaning depends on the legal context in which it is used. Some definitions in current use are

- Harassment, affliction, injury, grief, or serious deprivation intentionally caused to a person or group by the state or its agents.
- Sustained or systematic violation of basic human rights, which demonstrates the failure of a state to protect a person. (Hathaway)
- The infliction of suffering or harm upon those who differ, in a way regarded as offensive. (US asylum law)
- The threat to life or freedom, or other serious violations of human rights on account of race, religion, nationality, membership in a particular social group, or political opinion. (UNHCR Handbook)
- Intentional and severe deprivation of fundamental rights contrary to international law by reason of the identity of the group or collectivity on political, racial, national, ethnic, cultural, religious, or gender, or other grounds universally recognized as impermissible under international law. (ICC Statute and Elements of Crimes)

Persistent Objector Rule (Customary International Law)

A theory of customary international law that says, roughly, that a state will not be bound by a norm of customary international law if it persistently and from the very start dissents from the general view that a certain procedure has ripened into a binding norm. Some say that the existence of a persistent objector will block the ripening of general custom; some say it will not. This argument is based on the concept of international law being based on the consent of the sovereign state.

Personal Jurisdiction

The judicial authority to make judicial decisions binding upon an individual. Jurisdiction of a court/tribunal over a person is defined in the statute or treaty* creating the forum, or in national law. If a court does not have personal jurisdiction over an accused individual, that court cannot allow a criminal prosecution in such case. Personal jurisdiction answers the question: What persons are legally subject to this court? This is compared with subject matter jurisdiction (competence), which is about whether a court has the legal power to decide a case about a certain subject matter or under a certain law.

Persons in the Power of the Enemy (loac)

Any individuals captured by or who are in the physical custody of a warring party to a noninternational armed conflict or

"Civil War." Used especially as a reference to captured rebel insurgent soldiers or guerrillas in place of the term "Prisoner of War," a term not employed in most civil wars.

PETITION (AKA COMPLAINT)

A formal written application to an official body requesting that the body exercise its authority to prevent, remedy, or at least find a violation of human rights norms. A petition is a complaint filed by an individual, group, state, or states claiming that another state has breached its obligation regarding human rights and is seeking redress. In addition to the word "petition," the words "application," "complaint," and "communication" all represent nearly the same concept, i.e., written complaints filed with a body authorized to exercise jurisdiction over it. Different human rights systems may use a different term.

PETITION-INFORMATION SYSTEM

A formal complaint system under a human rights treaty* and under certain non-treaty-based mechanisms whereby victims of human rights violations and sometimes others related to them, and other states parties, can submit to a forum a formal written complaint against a state or state party. The objective of this type of complaint system is aimed at obtaining information that will help that body determine what issues require their attention and what type of attention. The 1503 Procedure under the UN Commission on Human Rights and its Sub-Commission is an example of a petition-information system because even if the Commission finds a consistent pattern or gross and reliably attested human rights violations, it does not provide any redress to victims.

PETITION-REDRESS SYSTEM

A formal complaint system under a human rights treaty* whereby victims of human rights violations and sometimes others related to them, and other states parties, can submit a formal written complaint*to a judicial or quasi-judicial forum against a state party. Such a complaint* will be handled by the forum, and if a violation is found, there will be certain redress ordered or recommended in order to provide reparation and measures to ensure that such violations will not occur again. The European Court of Human Rights is an example of a petition-redress system.

PETITION SYSTEM
(AKA COMPLAINT SYSTEM)

A judicial or quasi-judicial system for receiving and deciding written complaints* in contentious cases against a state party to a treaty*, claiming that the state has violated its legal obligations under the treaty*. There are petition systems which handle both state versus state complaints* and individual complaints*. These are also known as complaint systems.

As an example, the ICCPR established the UN Human Rights Committee to supervise implementation of that treaty and established a petition system to receive complaints by states parties against other states parties (interstate complaints) and by individuals against states that ratified the first Optional Protocol to the ICCPR.

PHYSICAL INTEGRITY (RIGHT TO)

A classification of human rights based on that aspect of a whole human being that is being protected by such rights. Human rights protect human dignity by protecting certain aspects of human existence, such as moral integrity, standard of living, family, and legal integrity. Human beings have a right to physical integrity, which protects the physical well-being and sense of security and safety and wholeness of the individual.

Physical integrity is that part of the human personality that deals with the physical needs and wants of humans, which protects and advances their human physical wholeness. The human rights to life; to freedom from torture, cruel, inhuman treatment, or punishment; to freedom from arbitrary arrest and detention; and to freedom of movement are examples of rights to physical integrity.

PILLAGE (AKA PLUNDER) (LOAC)

The unjustified taking of personal property of an enemy combatant or noncombatant. Under the LOAC it is prohibited to take the personal property of an enemy away from him, other than for security reasons, such as taking a POW's rifle upon capture. This includes any organized seizure of property carried out within the framework of the systematic exploitation of occupied territory as well as individual acts of looting for private gain. It may be of public or private property.

The ICRC defines it as the systematic and violent appropriation by the armed forces of moveable public or private property belonging to the enemy state; to

wounded, sick, or shipwrecked persons; or to prisoners of war.

It is also known as plunder. *See* GC III, article 18.

PLAUSIBLE DENIABILITY (OF VIOLATIONS BY GOVERNMENT)

The action of a government or government official accused of the human rights violation of disseminating information and images through any kind of media, usually radio, television, or newspapers, which serves to counter, rebut, or cast doubt on the veracity of claims of the violation by creating a believable argument that the violations did not occur.

PLENIPOTENTIARY (FRENCH: *PLEINS POUVOIRS*)

A person holding full powers from a state to act as its agent to enter into international agreements by signing a treaty*.

PLUNDER (AKA PILLAGE) (LOAC)

The unjustified taking of personal property of an enemy combatant or noncombatant. Under the LOAC it is prohibited to take the personal property of an enemy away from him, other than for security reasons, such as taking a POW's rifle upon capture. This includes any organized seizure of property carried out within the framework of the systematic exploitation of occupied territory as well as individual acts of looting for private gain. It may be of public or private property.

The ICRC defines it as the systematic and violent appropriation by the armed forces of moveable public or private property belonging to the enemy state; to wounded, sick, or shipwrecked persons; or to prisoners of war. It is also known as pillage. *See* GC III, article 18.

PLURALISM

A state of a society in which members of diverse ethnic, racial, religious, or social groups maintain an autonomous participation in and development of their traditional culture or special interest within the confines of a common civilization. Often seen in the phrase "pluralism, tolerance, and broad-mindedness"—those characteristics necessary for a democratic society respectful of human rights.

POGROM

A massacre or persecution instigated by a government or by the ruling class that is directed against a helpless minority group. Most commonly used to refer to such acts against the Jews. Its purpose is usually to exterminate the group or to cause it to flee to another state or area.

POLICE BRUTALITY

The use of excessive physical force by law enforcement agents in the exercise of their duties, causing injury or harm to the victim, and constituting a violation of the victim's human rights.

Law enforcement agents, particularly the police, are persons whom society trains, hires, and places in the local public sector and on whom it relies for the protection and security of everyone by enforcing the existing law. Police are given legal authority by society to use force to do their job. However, they are only given the legal authority to use a type and amount of force, such as night-sticks, firearms, or battering rams, that is reasonable according to law, constitution, and human rights norms. Brutality is the use of force beyond that which is reasonable and legally defensible under the circumstances.

Sometimes law enforcement agents use more force than they are allowed by law and human rights norms under the circumstances. When a person is impacted by this force, it can constitute police brutality. Many believe that police intentionally use excessive force because they either believe it is necessary to deal with a particular situation, or because they are angry with the victim of their abuse.

Police brutality is a violation of human rights. It can constitute a violation of the ICCPR, article 7 (torture, cruel, inhuman treatment, or punishment); article 10 on humane treatment in custody; and article 6, if the victim dies. Police brutality is a particularly dangerous evil in society especially when it reflects racist attitudes or an attitude that the police are above the law and a law unto themselves, not accountable to society. Acts of police brutality can also very well constitute human rights violations under the Convention against Torture.

As has been said: "Power tends to corrupt, and absolute power corrupts absolutely." (Lord Acton) Sometimes the power given by society corrupts those very persons who are sworn to uphold and enforce the law. This is why a rule of law system with effective civilian supervision of law enforcement personnel is absolutely necessary for respect for human rights and to preserve society from the abuse of power by the police. Police brutality violates the inherent human dignity of its victims and violates the trust society places on law enforcement. Every state has the affirmative obligation to prevent or remedy acts of police brutality.

POLICE POWER

A U.S. Constitutional concept of all powers of government, whether traditional, municipal, or state powers, or those specially delegated by the Constitution, such as regulating commerce, establishing zoning laws, providing police to enforce the law, and establishing armed military forces to protect national security. It is used beyond the U.S. context to generally describe certain powers of state government.

Powers of government inherent in every sovereignty to the extent of its dominions; the power of sovereignty to govern men and women within the powers of its dominion. Such power is given and exercised to maintain the national existence and to maintain right and justice, the public welfare, and the primary social interests such as safety, morals, and order.

All police power must be exercised by the state in a manner consistent with its national and international legal obligations to respect, protect, ensure, and fulfill all human rights for all persons subject to its jurisdiction.

POLICE STATE

A state whose ruling government/regime maintains social order and obedience by the threat and use of force by the police, military, or other security forces, usually in a brutal and arbitrary manner and with disregard for human rights. Usually characterized by an extensive domestic intelligence network to monitor people's activities.

POLITICAL ASYLUM

An asylum claim or status that is based on a person having been persecuted or having a well-founded fear of persecution in his state of nationality or last residence on account of his political opinions.

POLITICAL CORRECTNESS / POLITICALLY CORRECT

The quality of an act or statement or any kind of message (e.g., advertisement, television program, Internet message) being consistent with a certain usually unspoken code of conduct or speech, which is meant to avoid causing offense to any individual or group of people who would otherwise be offended. The quality of a message of any kind (newspaper article, television ad, speech) or action being consistent with a code of speech or action considered sensitive and proper by politically liberal standards because it would not cause offense to anyone.

For the most part, political correctness is an attempt to force everyone in a given social context to follow certain rules of speech and conduct such that no one will give offense against anyone else for what or who they are. Such attempts at protecting people's sensitivities and preserving group harmony and peace run up against and most always violate the human right to freedom of expression, as found in UDHR, article 19 and ICCPR, article 19.

Education of people in tolerance, diversity, pluralism, and broadmindedness, by teaching about the human dignity and human rights of everyone, is the key to changing the speech and conduct of people who would otherwise hurt or harm another group of people bearing a certain characteristic. Enforcing political correctness by set limits on conduct or speech is usually in violation of the human rights to freely express and manifest opinions and ideas.

Political (Human) Rights

Human rights that relate to an individual vis-à-vis the public society, the conduct of government, and how that individual can participate in and effect change in a society to his benefit. These are rights that assure to a member of society the opportunity for making/changing/proposing/administering governmental public policy, especially in matters affecting such members.

Political human rights are a type of what were called "First Generation (Human) Rights" that protect a person's right to participate in the direction and development of a society, such as the right to vote and to run for government office. "Civil" and "political" human rights together made up the so-called "first generation" of human rights.

Politically Motivated Prosecution

The institution of criminal proceedings against a person, not because that person deserves to face criminal justice and that justice must be served, but because those instituting or promoting the prosecution are seeking to accomplish a political objective such as embarrassing a state or its military, or causing an official to be removed from office or to lose an election.

This issue arose in relation to the ratification of the Statute of the International Criminal Court. The United States stated that one of the reasons it refused to sign and ratify the ICC Statute

was that it feared politically motivated prosecution of its soldiers in such situations as peacekeeping forces or in collective defense of other states. The U.S. feared that certain states and groups would seek to start prosecutions against U.S. military or governmental agents for reasons other than justice, such as embarrassing the U.S. before the world community.

Political Offense (Extradition Rule)

A criminally implemented act committed for a political purpose or from a political motive. Political offenses are usually an exception to extradition treaties*, i.e., if a person committed what is determined to be a "political offense," he will not be extradited under most extradition treaties*. Assassination of political opponents is typical of the type of acts claimed as political offenses. The modern tendency is toward limiting this rule by narrowing the definition and scope of this doctrine in light of terrorism and the need to deny safe havens for terrorists.

Political Will

The collective national will, held and expressed by the government of a state to accomplish a certain human rights goal or to conduct its own affairs in a way consistent with its human rights obligations; or the attitude of a state manifested through its government to desire and intend to act in a way that promotes the fullest implementation of human rights obligations of a state and which seeks to foster similar action by other states. The will of a state to fulfill its human rights legal obligations and take all necessary steps to do so.

States of the world are sovereign and independent. They can decide to do something or not. Their decision to do something as a state is called the political will of a state. States will only comply with their international obligations to respect and protect human rights if they have the political will to do so. States should have the political will to fulfill all their human rights obligations, not only within their own boundaries, but should also do what they can to see that other states do so. Human rights are the rightful concern of all states of the world, because, as the preamble to the UDHR and ICCPR state, respect for human rights is *the* foundation of freedom, justice, and peace in the world.

It often seems that human rights are mere ideas or rhetoric, and respect for human rights is just a sound bite that states like to voice to improve their image. This is because states often lack the political will to act consistently with their legal obligations or even with what they proclaim as the state's policy and practice as to human rights. Political will usually reflects the perception of the government as to what is in a state's best interest, not what is right as a matter of law or principle.

Popular Pluralism

A belief that one cannot know that any one worldview is true; so therefore, all worldviews are equally true.

Popular Sovereignty

The political concept that the source of sovereignty of a state is from the collective authority of the individuals in the state exercising their social contract by expressing their collective will through some type of voting process. In such a society, individual persons have the right to join in the social contract and in the institutions and practices of the government that represents them The source of authority that undergirds sovereignty is the will of the people. This would be compared, for example, with a monarchy where the king/queen is deemed to be the sovereign and alone entitled to exercise sovereignty.

The phrase "We the people of the United States, in order to form a more perfect union. . ." at the beginning of the U.S. Constitution is an implicit expression of popular sovereignty. It implies that individual members of society have the right to join in the social contract and to institute and participate in forming and directing the government that shall represent them.

Positive International Law

Refers to international law as found in international treaties* or customs that have been authoritatively established by intergovernmental authority, such as through the United Nations or Council of Europe, in their respective human rights standard-setting processes. Contrast "Positive International Law" to "Natural Law" (supra), or any other conception of a higher law.

Positive Obligation (vs. Negative Obligation)

The legal obligation of a state to take certain action, such as preventing murders or providing medical care, as required by the state to fulfill its legal obligations under human rights norms. A duty to protect someone from harm would be a positive state obligation. Sometimes this concept is also called "Affirmative Obligation" (supra).

Positive Right (vs. Negative Right)

Positive rights allow the bearer/holder of the right to do something without government interference and can also obligate the state to do something for the bearer/holder.

The right of an individual to do something or to have something done or provided to him by the state. This positive type of right requires the state to refrain from committing certain actions against the individual, such as preventing free movement or expression or requiring the state to actually provide goods or services to the individual. A right to education would be a positive right. Such rights, i.e., positive rights, are very often thought of as rights to goods and services, but they also include most civil and political rights, such as voting, running for political office, and practicing religion.

Positivism (Legal)

A theory of international law. *See* Legal Positivism.

Postmodern/Postmodernity

The description of the predominant philosophical characteristic of the late twentieth and early twenty-first century. By this philosophy is meant that there are no universally accepted absolutes, that all is relative to its particular historical context, and that all values, philosophies, religions, moral and ethical systems are equally valid and must be tolerated.

The implications for human rights concerns the foundation, the philosophical basis of human rights. It raises the question of what can serve as the foundation for a claim to universal human rights if there are no absolute values.

Preamble (International Instrument)

The first part of an international human rights declaration or treaty* instrument, which states the reason why the declaration or treaty* is being made and what the instrument is trying to accomplish. It is not a legally binding part of the instrument but is used in helping to understand, interpret, and apply it in actual practice.

The preamble sets the "tone" of an instrument, and in that way gives parameters for its interpretation. It states the motives (the ideology, philosophy, object, and purpose) for the creation of the document. In the field of human rights law, as in many law-related fields, there is a danger of using and interpreting human rights norms incorrectly and out of context in order to serve one's own purpose or to create "loopholes." The preamble of an international human rights instrument is a safeguard against that kind of action; it helps preserve the correct understanding and application of the substantive and procedural norms in the instrument. Though the preamble is not legally binding, it does present the aspirations of the people, organizations, and states that are presenting it to the international community for acceptance and compliance of states and individuals with its norms.

Preambles in treaties and declarations have a series of phrases called "*consideranda*" that constitute the statements of purpose. These phrases begin with words such as "considering that," "whereas," "convinced that," "conscious of," "recalling," and "recognizing that."

Precautionary Measures (loac)

Measures taken by military forces in an armed conflict for purposes of avoiding the infliction of injuries to civilians and civilian property of the adversary. The LOAC requires combatants to distinguish between civilians, combatants, and non-military property and to only direct attacks against military targets. In order to minimize the risk of civilian casualties p I, article 57 states that in the conduct of military operations, constant care shall be taken to spare the civilian population, civilians, and civilian objects. And where it is unclear whether a target is used for military purposes, it shall be presumed not to be so used. (article 52(3)). Protocol I specifies measures required to be taken by those who plan or decide on an attack. These include doing everything possible to determine that the target is a military target, taking precaution in the choice of methods and means of attack, such as choice of munitions, advance warning to civilians unless circumstances do not permit, and refraining from launching the attack if it can be expected to cause incidental loss of civilian life, injury to civilians, and damage to civilian objects, or a combination thereof, which would be excessive in relation to the concrete and direct military advantage anticipated. (p I, article 57(2)).

Preemptive Self-Defense (loac)

A proposed doctrine espousing an international legal justification to the use of armed force in international relations to prevent future attacks by an adversary state or nonstate actor. This doctrine was proposed by George W. Bush in the context of the 2003 Iraq invasion, and more generally concerning the "war on terrorism." There is no such legal justification

under international law. It is primarily an ideological statement.

Self-defense is an inherent right of all states under international law, and protected under article 51 of the UN Charter. Under the UNCH the right to self-defense only comes into play when there is an armed attack against the state. The doctrine of preemptive self-defense would seek to defend a state against attacks that were based on purely speculative concerns about the offending state or another adversary's possible future action, and not on clear and convincing evidence of an actual attack. This doctrine had been consistently opposed by the U.S. prior to the war on terrorism. It has not been accepted by the international community as a valid and legal form of self-defense.

This doctrine is also called "Preventative Self-Defense" and is a variation of the proposed doctrine of "Anticipatory Self-Defense" (*see* supra).

Prejudice

An attitude of negative feelings or perceptions against an individual, group, or state based on assumptions of fact without knowledge of the truth or falsity of those facts. Prejudging anyone without knowing the truth. In judicial context it refers to a negative impact against a party, which could result in an unfair or partial decision.

Preliminary (*in Limine Litis*) Objections
[Latin, lit.: in the threshold of a case]

"Preliminary" is any objection by a respondent state to the jurisdiction (competence) of a commission or court or to the admissibility of a written complaint* or any other objection the decision of which is requested before further proceedings on the merits are undertaken. Examples of very common preliminary objections are the state's claim that a complainant has failed to exhaust domestic remedies or lacks standing as a victim. The forum must resolve these objections before continuing to examine the complaint* on its merits. If the objections are found to be valid, the complaint* will usually be declared inadmissible by the forum.

Preparatory Commission (icc)

A group of individuals chosen and mandated by an organization to engage in certain activity preliminary to a coming event or process. Most often heard in the context of the preliminary work on the establishment of the International Criminal Court. This Commission was established after the adoption of the icc Statute and composed of representatives of the states who had signed the statute. This Commission was established to start work on creation of the legal framework of the court, such as preparing elements of the crimes, rules of procedure and evidence, financing, and relations with the un.

It is somewhat confusing that there has been both a Preparatory Committee and a Preparatory Commission regarding the icc.

Preparatory Committee (Prep. Com.) (icc)

A group of individuals chosen and mandated by an organization to engage in certain activity preliminary to a coming event or process. Most often heard in the context of the preliminary work on the drafting of the Statute of the International Criminal Court. The member states of the un in the mid 1990s established a Preparatory Committee to work on a draft statute for the establishment of the icc. This group and process was referred to as the Prep. Com. The mostly legal expert members gathered together periodically in meetings and worked on a draft text of the icc Statute, working from an earlier draft prepared by the International Law Commission. That draft was submitted to a diplomatic conference in Rome, wherein the states hammered out and adopted the final icc Statute in July 1998.

Preparatory Works (aka Legislative History or *Travaux Préparatoires*, abbrev. tps)

The written record of the diplomatic work (negotiating and drafting a treaty* text) that went into the establishment of a treaty* instrument and that is sometimes used as an aid in the interpretation of the treaty*. It contains the legislative history, deliberations, and discussions about the wording, scope, and content of norms from which one can determine the intent of the drafters. *See also* Legislative History.

Prep. Com.

An abbreviation for a preparatory committee. Most often seen in relation to the process of establishment of the International Criminal Court. *See* Preparatory Committee, supra.

Prescribed by Law (Limitations)

A term found in many human rights norms containing limitation clauses. It is spelled out as a necessary condition in limitation clauses that the limitation must be "Prescribed by Law." This means that the limitation must be legal, issued by a lawful authoritative source, adequately accessible to all, and formulated with sufficient precision to enable a person to know how to regulate his conduct accordingly. Most often, the limitation also indicates the scope of discretion conferred upon competent authorities. This concept can also be identified in some instruments that express the words, "in accordance with law."

Pressing Social Need (echr Limitation / Restriction Standard)

The legal standard for the state to prove the necessity of a state taking certain measures pursuant to a limitation/restriction clause in the echr. This concept is mostly found in contentious cases heard by the European Court of Human Rights. In order for the state to take measures restricting or limiting the full enjoyment of a *prima facie* human right, the state must show that the measure was prescribed by law, adequately accessible, has a legitimate aim, and that it is "necessary in a democratic society." Whether it is "necessary" in a democratic society requires the state to show that there is a pressing social need for the state to take such measures, not merely that such measure would be helpful or beneficial in some way.

Pressing social need is a stronger test than "reasonable" or "desirable," and carries with it the condition that the measure is proportional and the least restrictive measure that can be taken to achieve the legitimate aim. This effectuates the

principle that freedom is the rule, and any restrictions on freedom must be proven by the state to be necessary for compelling reasons.

Presumption of Innocence (Principle)

A basic principle of criminal law, which holds that every human being is presumed to be innocent as regards any criminal accusations made against him until a court of law with proper jurisdiction has found the person guilty. It is the principle that everyone is innocent until proven guilty

As a matter of international human rights law, the rights of those accused of engaging in criminal conduct includes the most basic right, which is that before a society (local, national, international) can find someone guilty of a crime and deprive him of his liberty, he must be deemed and treated as though he were innocent. Only when a competent court has determined criminal guilt does that presumption of innocence give way to the consequences of having committed a crime against a society's acceptable standards of conduct.

Even when an accused person was actually seen and caught in the act of committing the crime the presumption of innocence applies. And even if the accused is under arrest and detained in a jail facility pending criminal proceedings, he is still presumed innocent and must be treated as an innocent person. Even captured terrorists or enemy soldiers accused of crimes hold this right to be presumed innocent. The burden is on the government to prove the criminal conduct by the appropriate standard of proof before it can punish an individual for committing a crime. This principle of presumption of innocence is transformed into an express, binding human rights norm in article 14 of the ICCPR. It is arguably a binding norm of customary international law.

PRETRIAL DETENTION

The state's holding an accused criminal suspect in custody (in jail/detention facility) before and until the start of the trial to determine culpability.

PREVENTATIVE DETENTION (AKA ADMINISTRATIVE DETENTION)

The compulsory incarceration of a person following a perceived threat adjudicated by a public executive official without the appearance of the detainee before an ordinary court of law pursuant to a formal criminal charge and without any objective finding as to the guilt of the detainee or the correctness of the executive perception. Usually the basis for such detention is the government's fear that the person detained may be part of some organization, movement, or criminal conspiracy that may engage in unlawful violent acts. The justification often given for such detention is the protection of public safety, or even national security, by preventing such persons from committing any of the feared acts, e.g., terroristic bombing. It is substantially the same as "Administrative Detention."

PREVENTATIVE MEASURES (AKA INTERIM/PROVISIONAL MEASURES)

Urgent measures that a judicial or quasi-judicial body requests that a state take in a case brought against that state in that forum. The purpose of the request is to get the alleged violator state to take immediate steps to protect the alleged victim from some imminent harm, such as a capital punishment or deportation to another state. The request is usually made at the same time or soon after a complaint* alleging human rights violations is filed with the forum, and usually the complaining party specifically makes a request for such precautionary measures. Such measures preserve the status quo and allow the forum to decide whether a violation has occurred or will occur while not allowing the state to undermine the case or render a decision meaningless, such as if a person who is innocent or wrongly convicted is executed.

In a general sense it refers to the taking of measures aimed at preventing human rights violations from occurring or continuing to occur. An example would be an increase in a visible police presence in an area known for racial tension or ethnic conflict to deter lawless conduct, or halting an imminent execution. *See also* Interim Measures, supra.

PREVENTATIVE SELF-DEFENSE (LOAC)

See Anticipatory Self-Defense and Preemptive Self-Defense, supra.

PREVENTION (OF VIOLATIONS)

The concept of creating conditions in a society so that human rights violations are prevented from occurring. Human rights norms are not simply legal standards used to determine whether a state has violated someone's rights after the fact. They are norms also aimed at providing a policy tool for transforming, reforming and reorganizing, and policing a society so that human rights violations will not occur in the first place. It is preferable that states take action for the prevention of violations so that less resource and attention needs be given to remedial measures such as more police or courts. Human rights violations should be prevented.

Prima Facie (Case/Complaint*/ Human Right)
[Latin, lit.: at first sight/appearance; on its face]

1. Prima Facie Case/Complaint*: "Prima facie" is a Latin phrase that conceptually means "so far as can be judged from the first appearance/disclosure/reading," "presumably," or "a fact presumed to be true unless disproved by something"— something that at first sight appears to be evidence to the contrary. A prima facie case or complaint* is one that at first look, before examining the actual evidence, appears to show a violation of human rights or at least to have adequately stated facts alleging a violation.

2. Prima Facie (Human) Right (vs. Absolute [Human] Right): A prima facie human right is a substantive human rights norm that appears to be absolute in its first clause (at first appearance) but then is followed by a "limitation clause" permitting limitation/restriction of the norm, such as to protect public health, safety, or welfare. It may also be a derogable right, meaning that it can be suspended in a time of public emergency that affects the life of the nation. An example of such a norm may be found in ICCPR, article 19.1: Freedom of expression is a prima facie human right because it is not absolute but is subject to limitations, which are found in article 19.2.

The opposite of a prima facie right is an "absolute" human right, such as the right to freedom from torture. Absolute rights are not subject to any limitations or derogations.

Primary Rules (vs. Secondary Rules)

The broad and basic norms established by a standard setting process, which sets forth the basic substantive rules aimed at accomplishing the object and purpose of the instrument. A primary rule, for example, would say that a state may not commit torture. A secondary rule would state how the primary rules are to be implemented, and how, or by whom, or in what forum, violations can be remedied. Rules are either primary or secondary. This is similar to but not exactly the same as the difference between the concepts of substantive and procedural norms.

Principle (of Law)

A comprehensive and fundamental law, doctrine, or assumption; a general rule or code of conduct/behavior.

Principles are general statements extracted from specific legal rules to provide a common denominating reason for those rules. Principles tell us the "why" of the rules. For example, under the LOAC, the "principle of discrimination" between civilians and combatants during armed attacks is to assure that only combatants will be the target of armed forces in an armed conflict, and thus civilians will not be harmed.

Principled Pluralism

An insistence that a deep commitment to the truth of one worldview can produce a generous respect for the differing worldviews of others, despite profound disagreement.

Prisoner of Conscience (poc)

Persons who are imprisoned, detained, or otherwise physically restricted "by reason of their beliefs or because of their ethnic origin, sex, sexual orientation, color, language, religion, national or social origin."

This is the definition found in the statute of the international NGO, Amnesty International. Amnesty's definition also includes the qualification that the person "has not used or advocated violence." Also seen under the abbreviation poc.

Prisoner of War (pow) (loac)

A member of the armed forces of an opposing party who has fallen into the hands or power of his adversary by capture, surrender, wounds, or unconsciousness. A prisoner of war is a protected class of person under GC III of 1949 and P I of 1977 and is thus entitled to legal protection and humane treatment and a host of other rights by virtue of this status. Most commonly, prisoners of war are referred to by the abbreviation pows.

Prisoners' Rights

The human rights of persons deprived of their liberty and in a physical detention at the hands of the state, particularly in jail or prison. These include the human right to be treated humanely, administrative or judicial due process for offenses in custody, and conditions of confinement consistent with the inherent human dignity of the prisoner. Some of these rights are found in the ICCPR. In the context of the LOAC the rules are found primarily in the Third Geneva Convention of 1949 on prisoners of war, and P I.

Privileges and Immunities

Certain legal benefits and exemptions from legal obligations and personal inviolability, which flow from a person's official status as an agent of a state or of an international organization or body. It may include not being subject to criminal laws, not being subject to civil lawsuits, and not having to pay taxes. The purpose of these privileges and immunities is to facilitate the work and function of the person holding such privileges and immunities. As an example, diplomats hold certain privileges and immunities when acting on behalf of their state in another state. Although this is most often used in reference to diplomats, it also applies to certain officials and functionaries of international organizations, such as judges of international criminal tribunals. They may enjoy privileges and immunities in the state in which they work so that they can fulfill their international judicial function as efficiently as possible.

In the U.S. context it refers to two provisions of the Constitution, article IV sec. 2 and the 14th amendment. These provisions protect certain benefits of federal citizenship to U.S. citizens so as to be able to exercise these privileges and immunities in every state, such as the right to travel from state to state.

Procedural Right (vs. Substantive Right)

Those rights/norms found in a human rights treaty* that provide procedures for the implementation of the substantive rights.

These are rights set forth in a treaty*

giving a person, group, or state the right to take some procedural action to seek state compliance with, or redress violations of, the treaty's* substantive norms. The right to file a written complaint* against a state, the criteria for admissibility, and the time limit for filing would be such procedural rights. This type of procedural right deals with how to remedy violations and determine the manner of implementing substantive human rights norms.

Sometimes one also speaks of certain substantive rights, such as procedural due process-type rights, as also being "procedural rights." Examples include the right to a public trial, to a fair hearing before an impartial judge, or to compel attendance of a witness in a criminal case.

Procès-Verbal
[French, lit.: verbal trial]

An instrument containing the written record of a meeting or proceeding; the "minutes" of a meeting. Concerning treaties*, it refers to a record of certain understandings agreed upon by the contracting parties.

Programmatic (Human) Right (vs. Immediate Right)

An adjective describing the nature of economic, social, and cultural human rights that require government programs (e.g., health, housing, or education) according to the availability of state resources in order to fulfill the state's obligation. These are also called "Progressive (Human) Rights," and they are contrasted with "Immediate (Human) Rights" obligations, which can be enjoyed immediately upon ratification* and usually require no implementing measures.

Progressive (Human) Right (vs. Immediate [Human] Right)

An adjective describing the nature of economic, social, and cultural human rights that require progressive government action (such as building schools or creating jobs) in order to fulfill a state's obligations. These are also called "Programmatic (Human) Rights" and are compared to "Immediate (Human) Rights," which can be enjoyed immediately upon ratification* by the state.

Progressive Realization (Principle)

An emerging principle concerning economic, social, and cultural human rights under the ICESCR, requiring that there must be a continuous, gradual improvement in the realization of these rights by virtue of states taking concrete steps to the maximum of their available resources to implement these rights. This principle is taken from article 2 of the ICESCR and supported by the 1986 "Limburg Principles" (*see* supra) on the implementation of the ICESCR.

Pro Homine (Principle of Application and Interpretation)
[Latin, lit.: For the sake of/in favor of man]

A principle of the international law of human rights that requires that international human rights norms must always be interpreted and applied in a way that most fully and adequately protects human beings. And where more than one human rights norm or instrument applies to a particular situation, the one that gives the most protection or freedom to the individual should prevail over those offering less. Whatever application and interpretation of such norms is most favorable to the individual human being and protective of human dignity should prevail.

For example, if a person were convicted and sentenced to a certain punishment and the law was thereafter changed to lessen the punishment for such crimes then, applying the Pro Homine principle to this situation, the convicted person should be allowed to benefit from this change and have his sentence reduced.

Project of Life
(*Proyecto de Vida*)

See Life Plan, supra.

Prolonged Arbitrary Detention

The holding of a person in custody by the authorities, who continue to hold the person for an excessively lengthy period of time without any formal criminal charges being filed or pursued. Usually applied in situations of social unrest, guerrilla, or civil war against persons the state believes to be a threat to society or to the particular government/regime in power. Usually, detention is in a jail or prison, but this would also apply to someone detained (institutionalized) for medical/psychological reasons or in a refugee-type camp.

Promotion (of Human Rights)

The act of fostering the growth or development of human rights, primarily through the furtherance of the awareness and acceptance of human rights by states, groups, and individuals. This can be accomplished through public information, education, standard-setting, technical assistance, advisory services, or any way that convinces someone without coercion to believe in and help implement international human rights standards. It does not imply any coercive action.

Propaganda

The use of any of different forms of mass media for mass communication in order to create, reinforce, or change either domestic or international public opinion.

Propaganda is often a tool used to stir up public sentiment against individuals, groups, or states in a way that gives rise to human rights violations and leads to armed conflicts. Under article 20 of the ICCPR, any propaganda for war and any advocacy of national, racial, or religious hatred that constitutes incitement to discrimination, hostility, or violence shall be prohibited by law.

Proportionality (Principle)

A principle running all throughout international law, including human rights law, which states that a state and its agents (armed forces, police, secret service, judges, legislators, etc.) are only permitted to take measures, e.g., enactment of a penal prohibition of certain conduct, imposition of a criminal sentence, an act of armed self-defense, wherein the measure taken bears a reasonable relationship to the aim of the measure. For example, sentencing a criminal to death for shoplifting would violate the principle of proportionality because the measure to be taken is not proportional to the seriousness of the crime. Dropping a nuclear bomb on a lightly defended enemy city with little military value would not be proportional to the military objective/advantage sought and would likely violate this principle. This principle seeks to regulate the use of state power exercised through criminal laws, military force, police action, and judicial action to only that which is reasonably necessary to protect society. Even if a state has a legitimate aim for an action it takes, such actions are always subject to scrutiny as to compliance with the principle of proportionality.

If a state acts in a manner in which the results are disproportional to the goal of the measure, the state's action can be deemed a violation of human rights. Every action of state can be examined as to the proportionality of the measure taken or any harmful result.

In the law of armed conflict, a rule on proportionality in the use of armed force can be found in P I, article 51, 5b.

PROPRIO MOTU
[Latin, lit.: having been moved by itself/ on its own motion]

On its own initiative or own motion and not at the request of another. When an official such as a prosecutor or a body such as a commission or court takes an action *proprio motu*, that means that he/it is acting from his/its own motivation and initiative and not because he/it was requested/moved to do so by some other party such as a state, individual, or NGO to a pending or contemplated case. For example, a court will sometimes request a state in a case just filed against it to refrain from a certain action, such as a deportation or execution, as a provisional remedy and may sometimes do so *proprio motu*, on its own motion, by its own power, if its terms of reference implicitly or expressly permit it to do so. Another example would be the prosecutor for the International Criminal Court (ICC) who may initiate a criminal investigation if he has discovered information indicating

the commission of a crime, rather than having been requested/moved to do so by a third party such as a state party to the ICC Statute or the UN Security Council. The prosecutor may act *proprio motu* because he has been given this authority under the Statute as part of the duties of his office (ex officio) to do.

The issue in such *propio motu* situations is most often whether or not the official/body had the legal authority to act on his/its own under the terms of reference of that office/body.

PROSELYTISM

The act of communicating to another person through any medium, a religious, social, political message or point of view, and trying to get the other person to accept those views and live and act according to them.

This term is primarily used in the context of religious proselytism, which is the sharing of one's religious beliefs with the intention of getting the listener to believe the message and converting to the proselytizer's religion, religious organization, or religious worldview. Proselytism has a negative connotation, but legally it is not in and of itself wrong. Proselytism is permitted as an exercise of the human right to freedom to manifest religion by teaching, as found, for example in article 18.2 of the ICCPR and article 9 of the ECHR.

Where not involving communications relating to religion, proselytism is considered a form of expression and would be covered by human rights norms such as ICCPR article 19 and ECHR article 10.

PROTECTED PERSON(S) (LOAC)

A term used in the four GCs of 1949 and its P I and P II to refer to classes of persons who are specifically granted specific protection and humane treatment in that conventional body of law, during and as victims of armed conflict.

These include the sick, shipwrecked, and wounded members of armed forces who have ceased to take part in the hostilities; prisoners of war; civilian persons who, because of a conflict or occupation, are in the power of a party whose nationality they do not possess, medical and religious personnel; parliamentarians; civil defense personnel; and persons assigned to the protection of cultural property. *See* GCs I–IV, articles 15.

PROTECT HUMAN RIGHTS (OBLIGATIONS)

One of four legal obligations held by a state with regard to implementing human rights norms found in treaties* and in customary international law. The other three are the obligations to respect, to fulfill, and to ensure such norms. The obligation to protect human rights means that states have an affirmative legal obligation to take steps necessary to prevent violations of human dignity by acts of third parties, such as private individuals or groups. Failure of the state to take such steps and to protect the individual in relation to other members of society constitutes a violation of human rights by the state.

PROTECTING POWER (LOAC)

In humanitarian law, particularly the four GCs of 1949 and the P I of 1977, a "protecting power" is a neutral state that is not a party to an armed conflict, but has been designated by a state party to the armed conflict to act as its representative, and such designation is accepted by the

adverse party. The protecting power accepts to carry out functions assigned to it by the protected state under the Geneva Conventions and Protocols, such as visiting prisoners of war of the protected state. A protecting power acts to safeguard interests of the parties and helps to assure compliance with international legal obligations, particularly under international humanitarian law. If no protecting power can be agreed on, the states in conflict can designate an international organization, such as the International Committee of the Red Cross, to act as a protecting power.

PROTECTION (OF HUMAN RIGHTS)

To cover or shield someone's rights from violation. To actively intervene between a state and a human being or between human beings so as to shield or cover the potential victims from human rights abuses. In the context of human rights it implies an affirmative obligation and state activity to ensure that no human rights violations occur. It is a term usually, though not exclusively, applied to the obligation of the state. The state has the primary obligation to protect the human rights of all persons subject to its jurisdiction. The international norms and implementation systems are secondary ("subsidiary") protections when states fail to do so.

PROTECTIVE PRINCIPLE (BASIS OF CRIMINAL JURISDICTION)

A legal basis for the exercise of criminal jurisdiction over certain acts that take place outside the territory of a state. A form of extraterritorial jurisdiction. Under this principle a state may exercise criminal law jurisdiction over acts taking place outside its territory if that state has a significant national interest, such as protection of its national security, political independence, or territorial integrity.

An example would be if a person committed an assassination of a government official in a state other than that of the government official, which could adversely impact the victim's state security, then the victim's state could argue it had the right to prosecute the assassin under the protective principle. This principle could be applied to certain perpetrators of human rights violations.

Protocol (to Treaty*)

Most often this term is used to describe an international legal instrument that is established to amend or modify an existing treaty*. Protocols are used to either add new substantive rights or to modify an existing substantive norm, or to set up or modify implementation mechanisms, such as by establishing a supervisory body or a reporting procedure. It is most often established after the treaty* it amends but may be contemporaneous, e.g., the ICCPR-OP.

This word has other meanings in other contexts but, as seen in the field of human rights, it almost always refers to this treaty*-amending/modifying instrument.

A protocol is itself actually an international treaty and must go through all the procedural formalities (negotiation, adoption, ratification*, deposit, etc.) in a fashion similar to all other treaties before it can become binding.

Provisional Measures (aka Interim/Preventative Measures)

See Interim Measures, supra.

Proyecto de Vida
[Spanish, lit.: project/plan of life]

See Life Plan, supra.

Public Denunciation (of State Violations)

A statement, written or oral, made to the general public by private individuals, groups, nongovernmental organizations, or agents of an international, intergovernmental human rights forum, such as a special rapporteur, claiming that a certain named state is violating human rights. It is similar to and part of the process of the "mobilization of shame," which is meant to tell the world about the violations in order that the target violator state feels publicly shamed and embarrassed by this disclosure and, as a result, is induced or persuaded to stop the violations and make reparations or prosecute violators.

Public Emergency (Derogation)

A legal term that designates a major emergency situation, problem, or catastrophe in a state, whether political (e.g., revolution), military (e.g., armed attack/invasion), or physical/natural (e.g., volcanic eruption, hurricane, etc.) that affects all of society and threatens the very viability and existence ("life") of the state. This term is found in "derogation clauses" in human rights treaties.* Such clauses set forth the circumstances as to when a "Public Emergency" affecting the life of the nation may justify the suspension (derogation) of certain human rights. Public emergencies are usually associated with a government declaration of a "state of emergency," "state of siege," or "state of exception," of which it notifies the pertinent IGO. The existence of a public emergency justifies the governmental suspension of certain human rights necessary for the government to deal with the public emergency but only so long as the emergency lasts.

Some human rights known as "non-derogable rights" cannot be suspended, even during public emergencies, e.g., torture, the right to life.

Public Health (Limitation)

A matter that affects the general health of the public, such as the spread of a disease. Public health is one of the enumerated "legitimate aims" of state limitation of the exercise of substantive human rights and is found in most human rights treaties* in the limitation clauses. *See* ECHR, article 9.2, and ICCPR, article 21.

Public International Law

A system of rules and customary practices that regulates relations between states and, in some areas, between states and individuals or groups of individuals or between states and international organizations, such as the UN. International human rights law is one part of the corpus of public international law.

Public Order (Limitation)

A vast conception of the totality of life in a society on the administrative and political level. It is found in the limitation clause of most human rights treaties* as a legitimate aim of state limitation. It is something like "public policy" and the preservation of a harmonious, orderly society. Sometimes seen in a treaty* text next to *ordre public*, as though they are synonyms. *See Ordre Public*; ICCPR, article 21.

Public Policy

The interpretation and application of the law consistent with the values expressed by the legislature, and administered by the executive branch of the government.

Public Safety (Limitation)

A state's protection of the public well-being. Measures taken to protect the safety of a state's inhabitants. Protection of public safety is a legitimate aim, enumerated in most limitation clauses found in human rights treaties*. It does not mean the same thing as "Public Order," though it may be an element of a public order measure taken by a state. It includes safety from certain natural acts (force majeure) and from harmful acts of individuals or groups. *See* ICCPR, articles 12.3 and 18.3.

Qua
[Latin, lit.: by which]

A Latin relative pronoun used in juridical writing to mean "as," "insofar as," or "in the capacity or character of (something)." This means that something is the way it is by virtue of it having a certain status/character/capacity. Example: "Human rights are legal rights that are held by a human being qua human being." That is, human beings hold human rights because they are human, in the capacity or status of being a human being.

Quarter (No Quarter) (loac)

Usually seen in the term *no quarter*, which is a military term describing an order, policy, or practice during an armed attack of intentionally not taking any prisoners, even if enemy soldiers try to surrender. It means to kill all enemy soldiers with no survivors, even if there is no military necessity to do so or no resistance offered. Such an order or policy is not valid under present humanitarian law, and so a "No Quarter" ("take no prisoners") order by a commander would be a breach of humanitarian law. *See* P I, article 40.

QUASI-JUDICIAL (BODY/FORUM/ORGAN)

A term describing a body/forum/organ that handles complaints* but that is not a formal judicial body with judges who issue judgments. Rather, one that determines admissibility, gathers evidence, takes testimony at hearings, applies law to facts, and makes decisions/reports on admissibility and the merits of whether violations of human rights norms have been committed. For example, the Inter-American Commission on Human Rights is a "Quasi-Judicial" body.

QUATER (DRAFT ARTICLES: BIS, TER, QUATER)

1. Draft Treaty* Articles: A Latin numerical adverb used to identify a certain proposed draft article of a proposed treaty*. In the drafting of an international instrument, often different parties will submit various draft articles or alternative wordings for consideration. Each of these drafts is accorded a sequential Latin designation. The second proposed draft is given the designation "bis," meaning the second proposed draft, e.g., "article 5 bis." The next proposed article 5 is designated "ter" (third), and the next is "quater" (fourth), e.g., "article 5 ter." The drafting states will negotiate and deliberate over which proposal to adopt as the

authentic treaty* text. This helps identify the various proposals for correctness and ease of comprehension, understanding, and negotiation.

2. Generally: "Quater" can also be used generally to refer to a fourth item, version, or section of something.

QUID PRO QUO
[Latin, lit.: something for something]

Something that is given or agreed upon in exchange for/as the price for getting something else. It is sometimes used in the sense of something someone is willing to trade/compromise to obtain something ultimately desired. Example: If a government were to offer a complainant some money in exchange for dropping his complaint*, then the money is the quid pro quo for what the government wants, dismissal of the complaint.

QUIET DIPLOMACY

A method of behind-the-scenes discussion used by international human rights fora, such as the UN Commission on Human Rights, its Sub-Commission, the Human Rights Committee, and even the General Assembly to induce states to respect human rights. For example, when a state is under scrutiny of the Commission on Human Rights under the 1503 Procedure, the Commission members, in a confidential setting not open to the public, can interface with a state under its scrutiny to suggest and urge particular changes by the state to cease or remedy its human rights violations.

QUOTIDIENNES VIOLATIONS (VS. GROSS VIOLATIONS)

Those human rights violations that happen every day but are never reported, often not noticed, seldom acted against, and are often accepted by the society as almost normal and acceptable, although regrettable. They are not the serious or gross violations that usually give rise to action to prevent or remedy them. Examples would be a policeman prohibiting a person from engaging in political speech in a park or a judge not allowing a defendant to put on a full defense in a minor criminal matter.

Race / Racial

Race is a division of mankind insofar as it possesses traits that are transmissible by descent and sufficient to characterize a person or group as a distinct human type. It is also used more loosely to designate national, ethnic, and cultural groups. For some, race is used to refer to one's color of skin. "Racial" means of, relating to, pertaining to, or based on race.

In the human rights context, race is most often defined broadly. Article 1 of the UN Convention on Elimination of All Forms of Racial Discrimination (1965) defines its prohibition against racial discrimination to include discrimination based on "race, color, descent, or national or ethnic origin." *See* Racial Discrimination.

Racial Discrimination

In article 1 of the UN Convention on Elimination of All Forms of Racial Discrimination (1965), racial discrimination is defined as "any distinction, exclusion, restriction, or preference based on race, color, descent, or national, or ethnic origin that has the purpose or effect of nullifying or impairing the recognition, enjoyment or exercise, on an equal footing, of human rights and fundamental free-

doms in the political, economic, social, cultural, or any other field of public life."

Racism

A belief resulting in an attitude that race is the primary determinant of human traits and capacities and that racial differences produce an inherent superiority of a particular race. Such belief leads to intolerance, discrimination, and persecution based on race.

Radical Cultural Relativism

A concept of political philosophy, which holds that culture is the sole source of the validity of a moral right or rule.

Radical Universalism

A concept of political philosophy, which holds that culture is irrelevant to the validity of moral rights and rules that are universally valid.

Rape (International Crime)

An criminal act involving sexual penetration of the body of another, violating the physical and mental integrity and human dignity of the victim. Rape is a subject dealt with in the international law of human rights and humanitarian law and international criminal law. Most particularly, in the ICTR and ICTY and establishment of the core crimes of the ICC, there has evolved an international jurisprudence and consensus on a legal definition of rape in the international context. At the international law level it has been defined by the ICTY as having the following elements:

- The sexual penetration, however slight, of the vagina or anus of the victim by the penis of the perpetrator or any other object used by the perpetrator; or of the mouth of the victim by the penis of the perpetrator;

- By coercion or force or threat of force against the victim or a third person.

Rape has been found to be an act serving as the basis of a crime against humanity, war crimes, and an element of sexual enslavement.

RAPPORTEUR
[French, lit.: one who brings something back]

A French word denoting the title given to a person appointed by a body, for example, the UN Commission on Human Rights, from among its members to prepare an official record/report on the work of the forum. The rapporteur is the person who keeps the notes of what goes on and what was said at meetings so as to create a written record. This is somewhat different from a "Special Rapporteur," usually a nonmember, who prepares a report on a human rights situation in a particular country or on a particular human rights issue/theme, for example, religious intolerance. *See* Special Rapporteur.

RATIFICATION* (TREATY*, INSTRUMENT OF)

The process whereby a state becomes legally bound by a treaty* it has signed.

In the national context it denotes the process whereby a state legally indicates its acceptance/approval of the obligations contained in a treaty*. This is ratification in the constitutional sense, when the legislature or other designated national (domestic) authority decides whether to ratify the action of the government in signing a treaty*. It is ratifying the signature of its agent. A state does not have

to ratify; it may refuse to do so, or it may do so subject to reservations, declarations, and understandings/interpretations, which it may submit along with its ratification* instrument.

In the international context it means the final confirmation given by states parties to a treaty* concluded by their representatives and usually includes the exchange of "instruments of ratification*" or their deposit with a "depository." "Ratification*" is a word used to refer to the approval by a state that was one of the states initially negotiating and adopting the document's text. Procedurally, states involved in a typical multilateral human rights treaty's* creation go through the following process:

1. Negotiation of the articles of the treaty* instrument's text.

2. Adoption of the official authentic text by vote on a resolution.

3. Opening the treaty* for signature by states or by a state agent holding "full powers."

4. The signing state(s) takes the treaty* instrument back to its government for it to "ratify*" and thus approve the signature.

5. Whereupon the ratifying* state executes and deposits its "instrument of ratification*" with the depository, usually designated in the text of the treaty*.

This word is sometimes used to refer generally to all types of state official approval/acceptance of a treaty*, such as accession, adhesion, or succession, all of which are acts by which a state expresses its consent to be bound by the instrument.

RATIFICATION STATUS (OF TREATY*)

The status of a treaty* instrument as to how many states have signed and/or ratified* the treaty* at a given time. It may apply to how many ratifications* have occurred or may refer to the status of a particular state.

Ratification* status may determine whether a treaty* has entered into force or not.

Ratio Decidendi
[Latin, lit.: reason for deciding]

A Latin juridical term meaning the reasoning behind a quasi-judicial or judicial decision/judgment in a case. It means the reasons or general principles upon which an issue/case was decided. Most often, this term is used in the court/tribunal context to explain why the court/tribunal decided the way it did.

Ratio Legis
[Latin, lit.: reason for the law]

The reason for enacting a law. Somewhat similar to the object and purpose of a treaty*. The principle upon which a law is based.

Rationalization (of Human Rights Systems)

The process of examining the actual workings, structure, process, and results of a human rights system so as to assess its effectiveness and to determine whether to change the system to make it more efficient, more productive, less costly, and thus more rational and hopefully more effective. This term was applied to the process of member states examining the UN human rights systems as part of the 1993 Vienna World Conference on Human Rights. The goal of this conference process, especially through its follow-up work, was to result in the "Rationaliza-

tion" of UN human rights activity in all its organs and treaty* regimes. This process would, for example, seek to discover and avoid overlap and duplication of activity between treaty*-based or charter-based mechanisms and discover and eliminate inefficiency or wastefulness.

This term can be used generally to apply to such a process in any human rights system in order to achieve maximum effectiveness at minimum cost.

Ratione Conditionis (loac) (Principle)
[Latin, lit.: by reason of the circumstances]

The principle of humanitarian law that states that weapons and methods of warfare likely to cause excessive and unnecessary suffering are prohibited. This relates to the use of weapons causing unnecessary harm and suffering as well as to indiscriminate weapons that cannot distinguish or be aimed only at military targets rather than civilian persons and objects. This principle prohibits "blind" weapons, certain uses of "carpet bombing," and the use of incendiary weapons, such as napalm.

Ratione Loci (Territorial Jurisdiction) (Competence/Admissibility/Applicability)
[Latin, lit.: by reason of the place/location]

A basis of the competence (subject matter jurisdiction) of a judicial or quasi-judicial forum such as a commission, court/tribunal, or committee that handles individual or interstate complaints*. It is a ground of a complaint's* admissibility. This has to do with the place at which the alleged human rights violation of a treaty* norm is alleged to have taken place (the locus or situs). The question is whether the violation took place within a geographical location within the jurisdiction of the respondent state or whether that place was otherwise subject to treaty* application, such as an overseas territory of a state or by extraterritorial application. If an alleged violation occurs at a place that is not subject to a treaty* norm, then a complaint* alleging a violation of those acts will be deemed "inadmissible *ratione loci*," i.e., based on the location where the alleged violation occurred. This means that the norm was not binding in that place or to that state party.

This term is usually seen in decisions/judgments on the admissibility of human rights complaints.*

When this term is used in Humanitarian Law, it refers to the place where humanitarian treaty* norms are applicable, i.e., the territorial application of a treaty*. It is also used as a general expression to mean "by reason of where something happens, or is applied."

Ratione Materiae
(Subject Matter Jurisdiction)
(Competence/Admissibility/
Application)
[Latin, lit.: by reason of material substance]

A basis of the competence (subject matter jurisdiction) of a judicial or quasi-judicial forum such as a human rights court, commission, or committee that handles individual or interstate complaints*. This basis has to do with whether the facts alleged to have happened can be related to a substantive human rights norm found in a treaty*, and

whether the acts are within the "material scope" or purview of the treaty* norm. A complaint* will be deemed "admissible *ratione materiae*" only if the facts disclose a violation of a substantive norm of the applicable treaty*. If the complaint does not allege facts constituting a violation within the material scope of the treaty*, the complaint* will be deemed "inadmissible *ratione materiae*." Example: Alleging that under the ECHR one has a substantive right to fly to the moon at government expense. There exists no such human right within the material scope of any norm in the ECHR. Claims of such a right would thus be inadmissible *ratione materiae*.

Also used generally in other contexts to mean "by reason of, or within, the material scope/application of something." Usually seen in decisions/judgments on the admissibility of human rights complaints*.

Ratione Personae (Personal
Jurisdiction) (Competence/
Admissibility/Applicability)
[Latin, lit.: by reason of the person]

A basis of the competence jurisdiction of a judicial or quasi-judicial forum, such as a human rights court, commission, or committee, that handles individual or interstate complaints*. Usually seen in decisions on the admissibility of human rights complaints*. This involves the person or state that has lodged a complaint* and specifically (1) whether that complaining party has "standing" (*locus standi*) to submit the complaint*, (2) as to the respondent state, whether that state was bound by the subject treaty* at the time of violation, or (3) whether the respondent state was the one that in fact committed an act alleged to violate the subject treaty* norm. It is a ground of the admissibility of a complaint*. If the complainant does not have standing or the respondent state is not the proper respondent, then the complaint* will be deemed "inadmissible *ratione personae.*" One looks to the underlying treaty*, statute, or regulations of a forum to see the basis of competence *ratione personae*.

It is also used in application of humanitarian law (e.g., GCs) conventions to refer to certain types of protected persons. It is also used generally to mean "by reason of/in reference to/with regards to, the persons or parties involved."

Ratione Standi (Standing) (Competence/Admissibility)
[Latin, lit.: by reason of standing]

A basis of the competence (subject matter jurisdiction) of a judicial or quasi-judicial forum, such as a human rights court, commission, or committee. This has to do with whether the person, group, or state submitting a complaint* has the right under a human rights treaty* or a forum's regulations to submit a case, to be the complainant. It is a ground of admissibility of a complaint*. This usually has to do with whether one is a "Victim" of a violation directly or indirectly (i.e., torture victim or spouse of an executed person), or whether nonvictims may also file. This is a term usually seen in relation to the analysis of issues of "Standing" or *locus standi*. If the party that filed a human rights complaint* is not the proper party to do so, the party lacks *locus standi*. The forum will then deem the complaint* to be "inadmissible *ratione standi*" and will not hear the merits of the matter. Sometimes this basis is

also expressed as "inadmissibility *ratione personae.*" Each human rights treaty* system has different norms regarding who is entitled to file a complaint* alleging human rights violations.

Ratione Temporis (Temporal Jurisdiction) (Competence/ Admissibility/Applicability)
[Latin, lit.: by reason of time]

A basis for the competence (subject matter jurisdiction) of a judicial or quasi-judicial forum, such as a human rights court, commission, or committee, that handles individual or interstate complaints*. This has to do with whether the alleged human rights violation took place at a time when a particular human rights treaty* norm was binding upon the alleged violating state. It is a ground of admissibility of a complaint*. This basis usually has to do with violations that are argued to have occurred before the state ratified* the subject treaty*. Acts occurring before a state party ratified* the treaty* will normally not give rise to a violation of the treaty* norms. Note: Sometimes facts occurring before the date of such a binding obligation will be considered a "continuing violation" of the norm and will be cognizable by the forum, e.g., preratification* nationalization/confiscation of real property still not returned to its rightful owner.

If the violation did in fact occur at a time when the responding state was not bound by a treaty*, then the forum may deem the complaint* to be "inadmissible *rationae temporis*," and it will not hear the merits of the matter.

It is also used in the general sense to mean the temporal application of a treaty*, i.e., the time during which a treaty* norm is binding. Usually seen in decisions on the admissibility of human rights complaints. *

RDU/RUD (AKA RESERVATIONS, DECLARATIONS, UNDERSTANDINGS) (TREATY* INSTRUMENT)

An abbreviation for Reservations, Declarations, and Understandings, or Reservations, Understandings, and Declarations. RDU and RUD mean the same and are simply alternative acronyms. An RDU or RUD is a legal instrument setting forth written statements submitted by states at the time they ratify* a treaty*, regarding the what, how, and under what interpretation of terms a state agrees to be bound by the treaty*. Otherwise stated, RDU/RUDs are instruments that serve to limit, modify, clarify, or qualify a state's legal acceptance of obligations under the treaty*.

See Reservation, infra; Declaration, supra; and Understanding, infra, for the meanings of each. "Understandings" are also known as "interpretations," which are expressed in "Instruments of Interpretation."

Caveat: One must look to the function of the state's expression of its RDU/RUDs and not just the name given to it by the state. Sometimes, for example, states will submit what they call a "declaration," which is in reality and effect a "reservation" or vice versa. In interpreting a state's legal obligation, supervisory organs and judicial/quasi-judicial fora will look beyond the title used by the state, to the actual substance and apply it as it truly is.

REALIZATION OF HUMAN RIGHTS

The idea and process of human rights becoming subject to full and free exercise by every member of a society; making human rights real for human beings. Full realization of human rights can, in theory, only be actualized in a rule of law society with effective domestic remedies and a democratic government, characterized by transparency and accountability for compliance with international human rights norms. Full realization requires the full and complete transformation of all binding international legal norms into the domestic law of a society, except as already consistent with such international norms, and a government respecting and ensuring protection of human rights.

REALPOLITIK
[German, lit.: practical politics]

A political science theory that stresses international anarchy, human and national egoism and self-interest, the priority and superiority of power and security, and the need to exclude considerations of morality and ethical principles from foreign policy. A sort of international political Darwinism. In practice it means every state can do whatever it wants or thinks it can get away with based on its own power or its alliances. The theory is based on practical and material factors, usually motivated mostly by national self-interest, and not on theoretical legal or ethical principles.

REASONABLE AND OBJECTIVE JUSTIFICATION (DISCRIMINATION)

The legal criteria for justifying any discrimination against human beings based on race, color, nationality, creed, religion, belief, sex, political opinion, birth, or any of other distinguishing characteristic.

Under international human rights law

it is a basic principle that there can be no discrimination between persons with differing characteristics unless the state can prove a "reasonable and objective justification." This means that the state must prove that there is a good reason in objective fact for making a distinction or for different treatment; and the measure taken is reasonable, the least restrictive of anyone's rights, and the most likely to accomplish the results sought and most conducive to the full enjoyment of all human rights.

One sees this formula used, for example, in the views of the UN Human Rights Committee in individual complaint cases alleging violations of article 2.1 of the ICCPR.

REASONABLE FORCE (VS. EXCESSIVE FORCE)

The use of physical force by government agents in a measure that is permitted by law, and no more than is reasonable under the circumstances.

It is the use of force to a level that does not violate human rights. It is force that can be justified by law, giving the victim no right to make a claim against the government for damages or injuries suffered. It is force that does not cross the line from reasonable and lawful use to unlawful use of force.

The term could theoretically also be used in reference to government acts against the property of a person. Reasonable force is usually committed by law enforcement agents, especially the police, but could be applied to other government agencies. It most often becomes an issue during the attempt to apprehend and search for a person sought for by law enforcement or search their property.

Human rights violations are the use of power by government in a manner exceeding its lawful powers. It is an abuse of power. When excessive force is used against a human being, it violates his dignity and hence his human rights, engaging the responsibility of state under both national and likely international law. Use of reasonable force is permitted under international human rights law. The use of unreasonable or excessive force could, depending upon the circumstances, motives, and degree of force used, violate, for example, ICCPR, article 7 as to torture, cruel and inhuman treatment or punishment; or if the person dies, article 6, the right to life. It may, if torture occurs, constitute a violation of articles 1, 2, and 4 of the Convention against Torture.

The beating of Rodney King in the mid 1990s in Los Angeles was considered a classic example of the use of excessive force. Whether a particular use of force is excessive or not is often a hotly debated issue, with government usually defending its reasonableness.

Reasonableness in such situations also brings into play the overarching international law principle of proportionality. All use of force must be proportional to the ends sought in a way that most minimizes damage and injury to humans and their property.

REBELLION (LOAC)

An open armed uprising against a government in an attempt to change the government or resist its authority.

REBUS SIC STANTIBUS (PRINCIPLE) *[Latin, lit.: with matters standing as they are]*

A principle of international law regarding changes in the legal obligations of a state party under a treaty* based on the Latin expression meaning "with matters standing as they are."

This principle says that treaties* may be rescinded and legal obligations under them no longer considered binding if the fundamental facts or circumstances on which the treaty* was originally based have so changed that they are no longer relevant to the instrument. It requires a very material change of facts/circumstances affecting the object and purpose of the treaty*.

Usually this is an argument raised by a state as a defense to a claim that it has breached a treaty*. It is basically the state saying that the facts or circumstances for creating the treaty* are no longer the same and so the treaty's* legal obligations should no longer apply, and thus it has not violated the treaty*.

RECEIVABILITY (OF A COMPLAINT*)

The status of a written complaint submitted to a judicial or quasi-judicial forum being in such form as appropriate to be accepted by the forum for a determination of admissibility, and if admissible, for examination of the merits to determine if a violation has occurred. To be deemed receivable, the complaint* must be complete and signed and comply with any clerical requirements and meet admissibility criteria.

RECIPROCAL/RECIPROCITY OF (STATE) OBLIGATION (PRINCIPLE)

The classical principle of international law that means that each state must act in the interest of other states as a way to further its own interests. Otherwise stated, state A should fulfill its obligations to state B because in doing so state A will aid in the advancement of its own in-

terest. Under this "principle of reciprocity," international law was considered to be made up of reciprocal obligations between states, *inter se*.

RECOGNITION (OF STATE/GOVERNMENT)

In international law it means the act of a state accepting or acknowledging the existence of a newly emerged state or of a new government emerging irregularly within an existing state. It is an acknowledgment of international legal personality and the rights and duties that flow from international law, e.g., self-defense/sovereignty/diplomatic acts. It is usually accomplished by the exchange of diplomats. Withholding recognition manifests the withholding state's disapproval of the other state or of its government.

RED CROSS LAW (LOAC) (AKA GENEVA LAW)

The same as "Geneva Law," supra. A term used to describe international humanitarian law instruments adopted under the aegis of the International Committee of the Red Cross, hence "Red Cross Law." It covers protection of victims of armed conflicts and, to some degree, regulates methods and means of combat. Often used in distinction with "Hague Law," supra.

REDRESS (OF VIOLATIONS)

The means or possibility of seeking a remedy, the removal of the cause of a problem, or the payment or compensation for damages or injuries.

REFUGEE

A person who has fled from his country to avoid persecution. Defined in the 1951

Refugee Convention as a person who "owing to a well-founded fear of being persecuted for reasons of race, religion, nationality, membership in a particular social group, or political opinion, is outside of the country of his nationality and is unable, or owing to such fear, is unwilling to avail himself of the protection of that country; or who, not having a nationality and being outside the country of his former habitual residence, is unable or, owing to such fear, unwilling to return to it." Note that this is the treaty* (convention) definition. It can be defined more broadly than the convention context. Some contexts/instruments/laws define refugees more broadly, such as the UN High Commissioner for Refugees (UNHCR), which deals with both "convention refugees" and "nonconvention refugees," the latter meaning persons who do not meet the 1951 convention definition but are included, protected, and assisted by the UNCHR because they are within its mandate/terms of reference.

REFUGEE *SUR PLACE*
[French, lit.: on the place]

A person who, while in a country other than his own, becomes a refugee because of changes that occurred in his native state, thus making it impossible for him to return due to a fear of persecution based on race, religion, nationality, political opinion, or membership in a particular social group. An example would be a diplomat from state A who, while in state B, becomes a refugee in that state because the government of state A changed and he would thus be subject to persecution in the event that he returns to state A. A refugee *sur place* is not a person who flees his country, but one who becomes a refugee in the place he finds himself in owing to circumstances occurring back in his native country.

REGIME

Principle, norms, rules, and decision-making procedures around which states and other international actors' expectations converge in a given issue. The Council of Europe human rights system, based on the ECHR and implemented by the European Court of Human Rights, constitutes a "human rights regime."

REGIONAL CUSTOM/CUSTOMARY LAW (VS. GENERAL CUSTOM/CUSTOMARY LAW)

A material source of international legal norms applicable only in a given geographical region, such as Africa or the Western hemisphere. It is customary international law norms that arise in a particular way in a given region. These norms develop as a result of the consistent practice of states in the region, along with *opinio juris* of those states. It is a subset of the principle of Customary International Law, whose norms bind every state in the world, arguably excepting persistent objector states. Regional Customary Law would only be legally binding on all states in that particular region.

REGIONAL (HUMAN RIGHTS) TREATY*/SYSTEM/MECHANISM (VS. GLOBAL/UNIVERSAL TREATY*)

A human rights treaty*, political-legal system, or implementation mechanism pertaining and applicable only to a specific geographical region of the world under different regional IGOs. There are human rights treaty* systems at both the global/universal (i.e., worldwide) level and at the regional level, each operating separately but theoretically harmoniously and consistently. There are three regional human rights treaty* systems operative in the world: the Council of Europe system covering most of Europe, based on the ECHR; the Organization of American States (OAS) system covering North, Central, and South America, based on the ACHR and the American Declaration on Human Rights; and the Organization of African Unity (OAU), covering most of Africa and based on the ACHPR.

REGIONAL PROTECTION (OF HUMAN RIGHTS)

The concept and the international, intergovernmental systems/regimes that seek to establish and implement human rights norms applicable to a particular geographical region of the world. There exists not only a global or universal human rights regime, found primarily in the United Nations human rights system, but also several regional human rights systems/regimes. This concept of regional protection and the regional systems/regimes have been created because of a feeling of the members of the international community that a more geographically localized human rights system could be more sensitive and aware of the unique characteristics and particularities of a particular region, such as Europe, Africa, or the Western hemisphere, than the global/universal system. There are, therefore, both global/universal human rights systems and several regional human rights systems in existence. Each system/regime attempts to act in harmony with the other so that human

rights norms are interpreted and applied harmoniously and consistently by each.

REGISTRAR (OF A COURT/TRIBUNAL)

The official person who serves as a court's/tribunal's clerk with responsibilities for receiving and processing documents for consideration by the forum, keeping official records, and making translations of all proceedings.

REGULATION

Specific authoritative rules or orders made pursuant to law by an executive authority that are meant to carry the law into effect, especially at the executive and administrative levels. Regulations often reflect law as seen through the eyes of public policy, e.g., welfare regulations.

Regulations usually mean authoritative rules dealing with details or procedures. Example: *See* the 1907 Hague IV Regulations on Laws and Customs of War.

REJECT/DROP A COMMUNICATION

The procedure of an international judicial or quasi-judicial forum whereby it refuses to handle a complaint* alleging human rights violations filed/lodged with that forum for resolution. Communication is the same as complaint*. If the communication does not meet the legal criteria for admissibility to be handled by the forum, the forum may reject the communication and refuse to be "seized" of it. Sometimes complaints* are rejected even before determinations of admissibility due to defects in the complaint* such as an anonymous filing, one where the author does not reveal his real name and identity.

In the context of the UN Commission

on Human Rights, it refers to the option of the Working Group on Communications to decide whether to take no further action on a communication presented under the 1503 Procedure.

RELATIVISM (VS. UNIVERSALITY)

See Cultural Relativism, Universality.

RELIEF OPERATION

The provision by a state/IGO/NGO of materials, such as food, clothing, medicine, bedding, and other things necessary to survive, to people who need these items to survive but are unable to obtain them due to a public emergency, such as an armed conflict or natural disaster, threatening them.

RELIGION (FREEDOM OF)

Freedom of religion is an international human rights norm. However, there is no universally accepted definition of religion in the field of human rights. It is one facet of human nature and activity that is extremely important and a key element or cause of human rights violations. It can be said that the concept of religion in the field of human rights is much broader and more inclusive than the typical God/supreme being concept in the formal sense of mainstream religions such as Catholicism, Judaism, or Islam.

A closer definition of religion would be the orientation of the individual to what a person believes are the ultimate truths of reality and the words and acts by which that person externalizes those truths. It includes both the internal beliefs, known as the *forum internum*, and the external forum, where one manifests religion.

Freedom of religion is usually seen in human rights treaties* along with freedom of thought, conscience, opinion, and belief, all of which are close to, but not the same as, religion. As a human rights norm it is found protected principally in the following human rights instruments: UDHR, article 18, ICCPR, article 18, ECHR, article 9, IACHR, article 12, ACHPR, article 8, and the 1981 UN Declaration on the Elimination of All Forms of Intolerance and Discrimination Based on Religion or Belief.

RELIGIOUS DISCRIMINATION AND INTOLERANCE

In the 1981 UN Declaration on the Elimination of All Forms of Intolerance and Discrimination Based on Religion or Belief, the term religious intolerance and discrimination is defined as follows:

> any distinction, exclusion, restriction, or preference based on religion or belief and having as its purpose or its effect nullification or impairment of the recognition, enjoyment, or exercise of human rights and fundamental freedoms on an equal basis.

Note that this definition would also prohibit intolerance and discrimination based on any nonreligious type belief system, such as atheism or agnosticism. Religious intolerance and discrimination is a violation of human rights, such as freedom of religion, freedom of expression, equality before the law, nondiscrimination, and freedom of association and assembly. (*See* ICCPR, articles 2.1, 18, 19, 26, 27).

REPARATIONS

In international law, this most commonly refers to the payment made to a victor state or states by a defeated state to cover the costs incurred by the victor in prosecuting the war. Reparations are meant to wipe out, as far as possible, all the consequences of an illegal act and reestablish the situation that would in all probability have existed had the act not been committed. For example, by order of the UN Security Council, which had found the 1990 Iraq invasion to have been unlawful under international law, Iraq has been paying millions of dollars in monetary reparations to victims of the invasion of Kuwait, paid out of oil revenues seized by the UN and distributed as determined by the UN Compensation Commission pursuant to individual claims filed and substantiated.

The term is also used generally to refer to state payments made to someone who has suffered human rights violations and been damaged. It can also refer to nonmonetary measures, such as rehabilitation, public apologies, and restitution of property, that are proportionate to the gravity of the offense and act and reestablish the situation that would in all probability have existed had the act not been committed.

The types of reparations available as remedies to victims are three: restitution of the property taken or replacement in kind; indemnity, an award of money damages for moral and material losses; and satisfaction, which includes nonmonetary measures such as rehabilitation, public apologies, punishment of the wrongdoers, and taking preventative measures, all of which must be proportionate to the gravity of the harm done and aimed at making victims whole.

REPORTS/REPORTING

An implementation procedure set forth in many human rights treaties* that obligates a state to periodically submit written reports describing its level of compliance with the treaty* norms and possibly setting forth the obstacles the state experiences in implementing the norms. It may also provide an exposition of domestic legislation, case law, and factual data to allow the supervising body to review the state reports and respond, comment, and make general or specific recommendations. "Reporting" refers to the state fulfilling its obligation to submit a report.

In other contexts, the word "Report" may simply refer to any written or even oral exposition about a human rights issue, norm violation, or country situation. It refers to reports prepared by an NGO or IGO, for example, by a special rapporteur, on a thematic or country-specific topic to help the forum understand and establish compliance with human rights norms.

REPRESENTATIVE CAPACITY
(vs. INDIVIDUAL CAPACITY)

The status of a person who sits as a member of a commission, committee, or other body as a representative of his own country and its interests, as compared to someone who sits in his "individual capacity." Example: Members of the UN Commission on Human Rights sit in their representative capacity, whereas members of the UN Human Rights Committee sit in their individual capacity. Bodies made up of representative members tend to be more political and usually seek to advance the national self-interest of their state above all. Those sitting in their individual capacity are mostly chosen for their expertise and political independence and for their ability to promote human rights over their own state's national self-interest.

Repression

1. (LOAC) (Repression of Breaches): A state's penalization of certain unlawful conduct committed by a state's own agents in order to stop such conduct. An example of such conduct would be the torture of civilians during an armed conflict. International humanitarian law requires states parties to take steps to stop ("repress") breaches of humanitarian law by commencing criminal prosecution or administrative sanctions against violators. *See* P I, article 85. In this sense, the term "Repression" has a favorable meaning and connotes a state obligation. *See also* Suppression.

2. Generally: This term often refers to the attitude, action, and process of a state government, dictator, or tyrant to forcibly put down any opposition or to prevent or stifle the normal activity and expression of the people, usually in a manner not consistent with respect for human rights and fundamental freedoms.

Reprisal (LOAC)

A term of international relations law especially utilized in the law of armed conflict to refer to an unlawful harmful act committed by a state against another state as a direct response to a prior unlawful act of the other state. A reprisal is done to deter the prior offending state from committing any further violations. Reprisals are exceptionally permitted in international law for the purpose of compelling the initial offender to consent to a satisfactory settlement of a difference created by its own delinquency. In classic doctrine, the exercise of a reprisal must be preceded by a clear and timely warning and with the offer of a chance to change the offending conduct. The act of reprisal must be proportional to the prior unlawful act, i.e., not in violation of the "principle of proportionality."

If an act is committed as a reprisal, it renders the second state's otherwise unlawful act to be lawful under international law as a deterrent to further violations. If one military force unlawfully murdered some POW camp prisoners of its enemy, the state of the dead prisoners of war could kill some of the offending state's POWs, and the latter act would be considered legal under international law as a reprisal if it were done to deter that offender from further such acts and if proportionate in scope. Most types of reprisals are now prohibited under international humanitarian law.

Reservation (to Treaty*)

A legal instrument that contains a unilateral statement by the state, however phrased or named, whereby the state purports to exclude, vary, or modify the legal effect of certain provisions of a treaty* in its application to that state. A reservation is submitted by a state to the designated depository in an instrument of reservation when it submits its instrument of ratification* to a treaty*. The obligations of the state under a treaty* must be regarded in light of any reservations the state party has submitted with its ratification*.

There is a limit to a state's reservations. Any article of a treaty* to which a reservation is made is applied according to the state's reservation so long as the reservation is not inconsistent/incompatible with the object and purpose of the treaty*, nor violative of peremptory (*jus cogens*) norms. States are otherwise not obligated to comply with a norm to which they have made a reservation. *See* articles 2(1)(d) and 19 of the Vienna Convention on Treaties.

Occasionally reservations are submitted by a state along with "Declarations" (*see* supra) and "Understandings" (*see* infra). Together these are abbreviated as RDUS or RUDS: Reservations, Declarations, and Understandings or alternatively Reservations, Understandings, and Declarations.

RES JUDICATA
[Latin, lit.: a thing has been judged]

A legal doctrine by which a final judgment by a court/tribunal of competent jurisdiction is considered to be conclusive on all parties in any subsequent cases involving the same legal issue.

RESOLUTION (OF AN ORGANIZATION/FORUM)

A formal expression of opinion, will, or intent voted by an official body or assembled group. Most of the human rights activity of IGOs, such as the UN, is done by proposal of, and upon the vote for, a resolution. Resolutions are voted upon by member states. If a resolution is adopted, it authorizes a body or certain persons to take specific action, such as the writing of a report.

A resolution of the United Nations or other international intergovernmental organization is normally not legally bind-ing. It is not a treaty* and not a norm. However, resolutions of certain bodies can become accepted as part of "soft law" over time, which accords them some political/moral authority. Some resolutions may create binding legal obligations, such as UN Security Council resolutions under chapter 7 of the UNCH.

RESOLUTION 728 (UN-ECOSOC) (SO-CALLED "NO POWER" RESOLUTION)

A resolution of ECOSOC dealing, *inter alia*, with what power the United Nations would have to receive and deal with written complaints (communications) submitted to the UN and concerning alleged human rights violations. In this 1959 resolution ECOSOC decided that the Commission on Human Rights would have no power to handle such human rights complaints; thus, it was referred to as the "no power" resolution. Such complaints could only be used to identify general trends in human rights compliance. This was later followed by ECOSOC Resolution 1235 in 1967, which allowed the commission to study situations and take some action, and by the 1503 resolution in 1970, which did allow it to consider communications that revealed a consistent pattern or gross and reliably attested violations of human rights and fundamental freedoms.

RESOLUTION 1235 (UN-ECOSOC) (AKA 1235 PROCEDURE)

See 1235 Procedure.

RESOURCE CLAIMS/RIGHTS (VS. IMMUNITY CLAIMS/RIGHTS)

A type of legal claim or legal right held by an individual by which the individual can require the government to do something for the individual.

These claims include taking steps to protect the exercise of liberties such as freedom *from* torture or unlawful detention; and freedoms *to do* things, such as freedom of expression or peaceful assembly; and include the right to food and housing.

These are contrasted with "immunity" claims or rights, by which an individual can merely limit how government acts toward the individual.

RESPECT HUMAN RIGHTS (OBLIGATIONS)

One of four legal obligations held by a state with regard to implementing human rights norms found in treaties and in customary international law. The other three are the obligations to ensure, to fulfill, and to protect. The obligation to respect human rights means that states refrain from in any way interfering with individuals in the enjoyment of human rights. It is the conscious recognition of the human rights in individuals or groups, and conduct and treatment consistent with recognition of such rights. Usually this is an obligation of the state, that is, for the state to respect human rights and to refrain from interfering with these rights of those within its jurisdiction.

In international humanitarian law the term "respect" is found most importantly in the first article of all four GCs of 1949, where it calls on states to "respect and ensure respect" for those conventions. This term means that the states parties and others obligated thereby, must not violate the convention norms, and they must actively and affirmatively do what they can to cause other states

parties, and even nonstate actors, to conduct themselves consistent with these obligations as well. Ensuring respect means causing others to respect the convention norms.

RESTITUTION

A judicial remedy whereby a court can order a party to return property to another person from whom it was unlawfully taken or damaged. It can also involve ordering the party at fault to otherwise restore the injured party to its previous condition by providing something equivalent to what was lost or damaged.

RESTRICTION (CLAUSE) (AKA LIMITATION/CLAWBACK CLAUSE)

A limitation of a substantive human right, usually found in a clause in a human rights treaty* article. Such clause sets forth permissible state limitations to the exercise of a substantive human right. Normally, these limitations must be prescribed by law and must be necessary (in a democratic society) to achieve a legitimate aim, such as the protection of public health, safety, welfare, morals, public order, or the rights and freedoms of other persons. Restriction measures taken by states must be proportional to the legitimate aim pursued by them; otherwise they are invalid restrictions.

"Restriction" clause means the same as the terms "Limitation" clause and "Clawback Clause." It is a recognition that not all rights are absolute and that most rights are prima facie rights that can be limited in certain narrow circumstances. Restriction clauses are narrowly construed against the state. *See* ICCPR, article 19.3, for an example of a restriction clause.

Restrictive Sovereign Immunity (vs. Absolute Sovereignty)

Immunity of a sovereign state and its agents, where such immunity is not absolute and is subject to statutory exceptions. The Foreign Sovereign Immunity Act of the U.S. is an example of a law restricting the full immunity of foreign states and their agents. This restriction is meant to achieve some justice, equity, and accountability in the face of certain sovereign immunity claims by states.

Retaliation

In international law/relations retaliation signifies a state's act done as a direct response to another state's acts, which were perceived as injurious to the retaliating state whether or not these initial acts were actually in breach of international law. Examples of acts of retaliation are embargoes, military intervention, "Reprisal" (*see* supra), and "Retorsion" (*see* infra).

Retorsion

In international law this refers to a lawful act committed by one state against another state for unfair, unkind, or inequitable acts of the latter state, usually by doing similar acts back against it.

The initial act that offends the other state is not an illegal act nor can the act of retorsion be so. An example of a retorsion would be the dismissing of another state's diplomatic personnel in response to that state having previously done so with real justification.

Reverse Discrimination (aka Affirmative Action)

Discrimination in favor of a certain person or group done for purposes of correcting past adverse discrimination against that person or group. It is discrimination against a person or group that formerly was benefited by discrimination against someone else. The law, policy, or practice of treating a person more favorably than someone else because of a particular characteristic or status for purposes of correcting past discrimination. It is substantially the same as affirmative action.

Human rights principles require a society to consider all human beings as possessing equality and to treat everyone equally. Society cannot discriminate against persons for reasons such as race, color, religion, gender, political opinion, or nationality. Equality is the norm. In a society where a lot of discrimination has occurred, sometimes it is decided to take certain action that will correct the problem and result in a society becoming the way it would have been if the discrimination had not occurred. Reverse discrimination means that a society makes a law, policy, or practice that treats someone more favorably than someone else.

For example, if there has been discrimination against women in admission to a certain medical school, a reverse discrimination would occur if the school gave preference to women candidates over equally qualified males, so as to raise the number of women to what it would have been had there been no discrimination against women in admissions.

Revised 1503 Procedure

The UN special mechanism known as the "1503 Procedure" was revised procedurally in 2000. Thus, it is sometimes referred to as the revised 1503 Procedure. Some of the procedural revisions included the holding of the Working Group on Communications meetings immediately following the annual Sub-Commission session, allowing that Working Group to transmit to the Working Group on Situations particular situations revealing a consistent pattern of gross and reliably attested violations, informing the subject governments of the decision of the Working Group on Communications to refer a situation to the Working Group on Situations and of any decision to keep such communications pending.

Revised European Social Charter (Council of Europe 1996)

A human rights treaty on economic, social, and cultural rights adopted within the Council of Europe in 1996, which updated and consolidated the 1961 European Social Charter and added new rights.

Revision (of Court Judgment)

The process of a court after it has rendered a judgment, decree, or order that reviews the case again in light of new facts or legal considerations to determine if it should change the judgment, etc.

Right(s)

A legally recognized and enforceable claim or entitlement held by an individual (or, some argue, a group or collective) to do or not do something, or to prevent others from doing or not doing something. As used in relation to human rights, a right is a preexisting claim to do or not do something. A human right is thus a preexisting claim of a human being to obligate the state to legally do or refrain from doing something vis-à-vis the individual.

There are a multitude of different defi-

nitions of this term, so the preceding definitions are not universally accepted.

Right of Initiative

A claimed right of certain official persons, for example, special rapporteurs and high commissioners, to act on their own initiative to engage in activity that they believe to be within their terms of reference for the purpose of fulfilling their mandate. This means they can act on their own initiative even if no formal request has been made to do so, e.g., by a state or complainant. This is also known as action *proprio motu*.

An example would be a special rapporteur initiating an on-site investigation without being requested by anyone to do so.

Right of/to (Humanitarian) Intervention

A claimed legal right of states to intervene in the internal affairs of another state when in the target state there are occurring gross and systematic violations of human rights, which shock the conscience of mankind. This right would exist outside of the UN Charter, and would supercede the UN Charter provisions 2.4 and 2.7 by allowing one or more states to forcibly intervene in the affairs of another state to stop such atrocities.

In legal theory the UN Charter provision on nonintervention only covers matters that are "essentially within the domestic jurisdiction" of another state. Human rights violations are never deemed to be matters essentially within the domestic jurisdiction of any state, and hence they are proper subjects of scrutiny and certain actions by other states, consistent with other UN Charter provisions. *See also* Humanitarian Intervention and *Droit d'Ingerence*, supra.

RIGHT OF/TO RETURN
(TO HOMELAND)

An individual human right held by refugees and exiles to return to their homeland. The right to return has a solid foundation in international law. Article 13(2) of the UDHR states, "Everyone has the right to leave any country, including his own, and to *return to his country*." Speaking through the United Nations General Assembly, the international community, addressing the Palestinian refugee/exile situation, stated in Resolution 194 (III) in December 1948 that the UNGA "Resolves that the refugees wishing to return to their homes and live at peace with their neighbours should be permitted to do so at the earliest practicable date."

The principle treaty legal source for the right to return is found in article 12 of the ICCPR, under its provisions on the right to freedom of movement. Article 12 reads

1. Everyone lawfully within the territory of a state shall, within that territory, have the right to liberty of movement and freedom to choose his residence.
2. Everyone shall be free to leave any country including his own.
. . .
4. No one shall be arbitrarily deprived of the right to enter his own country.

The Human Rights Committee charged with the implementation of the ICCPR concluded in its 1999 General Comment on article 12 that such a right of return does exist under that treaty norm binding on all states parties to the ICCPR. No state party can violate it.

Further reinforcement for the existence of this right is inferred from the 1951 Convention Relating to the Status of Refugees.

Concerning the scope and obligation of this right, Human Rights Watch has reported that this right is legally held

not only by those who fled a territory initially but also by their descendants, so long as they have maintained appropriate links with the relevant territory. The right persists even when sovereignty over the territory is contested or has changed hands. If a former home no longer exists or is occupied by an innocent third party, return should be permitted to the vicinity of the former home. . . . As in the case of all displaced people, those unable to return to a former home because it is occupied or has been destroyed, or those who have lost property, are entitled to compensation. However, compensation is not a substitute for the right to return to the vicinity of a former home should that be one's choice. . . . No government can violate this right. Only individuals may elect not to exercise [this right].

Because human rights are by definition inalienable, no state, group of states, nonstate entity, or intergovernmental organization has the right to limit, waive, compromise, or bargain away, this individual right as part of a political settlement of a disputed land or refugee-return issue. The whole international community has the duty to ensure that all claims of a right to return are resolved fairly, and that individual holders of the right to return are permitted freely and in an informed manner to choose whether or not to exercise it, and that the actual process of return proceeds in a gradual, safe, and orderly manner. The legitimate security concerns of governments must be met in a manner consistent with these legal principles and other recognized human rights norms.

Rights and Freedoms of Others (Limitations)

A phrase found in the limitation clauses of most human rights treaties* to refer to a legitimate aim of a state limitation. The protection of the rights and freedoms of others is a legitimate aim for state limitation or interference with a person's substantive human rights. It is a balancing of a subject person's rights with those of other persons so as to assure the broadest, fullest, and most concrete enjoyment of rights by all persons. An example is one's right to freedom of expression, which can be limited as to the speaking of defamatory speech because the limitation of such speech is necessary to protect the rights and freedoms of others, i.e., the right to one's good reputation.

Rights-Based Approach

An approach to a program, project, or activity that factors in applicable international human rights norms as its key points of reference. It makes maximum compliance with human rights norms the key goal. It is based on specific human rights, for example, civil human rights or economic human rights, but not the general concept of human rights.

Rights of the Accused

The human rights of persons who have been accused of committing an offense against criminal law, as a perpetrator or accomplice.

Many human rights violations occur in the context of persons who have been charged by the state with criminal conduct. Once a person is formally accused of a crime by the government, the accused person has specific human rights as to how he should be treated and how the criminal process must proceed. This is particularly important if the accused has been detained and deprived of liberty pending the proceedings, or has been deprived of his liberty and is in physical detention at the hands of the state, particularly in jail or prison.

The human rights of the accused are found principally in the UDHR, articles 10 and 11, and ICCPR, articles 9, 10, 14, and 15. The Geneva Conventions of 1949 and Protocols I and II, and the Statutes of the ICTY, ICTR, and ICC are other places where rights of the accused are found. *See*, e.g., GC IV, article 3.1, and P I, article 75.

Right to Know the Truth (aka Right to Truth)

Every society has the inalienable right to know the truth about past events, as well as the motives and circumstances in which aberrant crimes came to be committed, in order to prevent repetitions of such crimes in the future. Every victim's family also has rights to know the truth about what happened to its family member. In fact, it is the right of every member of a society to know the circumstances and participants in human rights violations. This right is a necessary implication and aspect of the principles of transparency and accountability for proper democratic governance and respect for rule of law.

The state has the duty to ensure the

right of the families of victims of human rights violations and of society as a whole, to know the truth of the facts connected with the serious violations of human rights that occur in their society. Such a right has been acknowledged in certain human rights systems such as the Inter-American System (OAS). This is most appropriate in such cases as enforced disappearances where people are disappearing and the victim's families and society are not informed of what has happened so that they can take appropriate action.

The right of society is a collective right, which allows society as a whole to have access to essential information on the development of the democratic system and is an individual right that allows the families of the victims to have access to some kind of reparation, especially in those cases in which amnesty laws are in force. Access to the truth allows the victims' families to seek domestic remedies allowing for judicial protection of fundamental rights. This right is important as a factor in the fact-finding, decision-making process of human rights complaint systems and truth commissions. It is an important factor in determining reparations owed in satisfaction to victims and their families.

RIGHT TO REPLY

The procedural right of a state to verbally or in writing respond to a specific report or charge of its commission of human rights violations. In the UN Commission on Human Rights there is a right of states that have been charged with violations by an NGO to reply to the report or charges. This is their procedural right of reply to the NGO, usually denying or explaining away the allegations or denouncing the accusing party.

RIGHT TO TRUTH

See Right to Know the Truth, supra

RIPEN (INTO CUSTOMARY NORM) (AKA CRYSTALIZE)

A term describing the process and point at which a certain international practice has evolved into a binding legal norm under customary international law. Customary international law requires a consistent state practice over the course of time (usage) and the subjective element of legality known as "*opinio juris.*" When a practice has becomes consistent and a matter of international usage, and the *opinio juris* of the international community is evidenced, a practice is said to have "ripened" into a new customary legal norm, creating binding obligations upon states. Sometimes one also hears the similar term "crystalize" to describe such legal phenomenon; that is, a practice "crystalizes" into a binding legal norm.

RIYADH GUIDELINES (UN)

The name given to a set of human rights soft law guidelines formally entitled United Nations Guidelines for the Prevention of Juvenile Delinquency, which were adopted by the UNGA in Riyadh in 1990.

ROMA (AKA SINTI/GYPSY)

A term that refers to that group of people who are known as Gypsies. Gypsies can be found in many countries of the world and have different languages and customs in different states. Roma are also known by the term "Sinti."

ROME STATUTE (ICC-UN 1998)
(AKA ROME ICC STATUTE, ROME
STATUTE OF THE INTERNATIONAL
CRIMINAL COURT/ ICC STATUTE)

The popular name of the UN treaty that established the International Criminal Court. Its official name is the Rome Statute of the International Criminal Court. This treaty was adopted in Rome, Italy, in 1998. The treaty entered into force in 2002, and the Court was established in 2003.

ROSTER (NGO CATEGORY/STATUS)

A category or status of NGOs that are allowed to participate in UN human rights activities of the ECOSOC and its subordinate organs, classified under ECOSOC Resolution 1296. The roster itself refers to a list of NGOs that are not concerned with most of the activities of the ECOSOC or that do not have special competence in certain ECOSOC activities so as to be entitled to full consultative status; thus they are assigned to the "Roster" by the ECOSOC. This is the lowest level of NGO participation. Such NGOs may have representatives present at ECOSOC meetings, but they have only limited rights to submit oral or written statements.

RULE

A prescribed guide for conduct or action. A regulation or bylaw governing procedure or controlling conduct.

A norm of conduct that is precise, certain, and binding upon subjects of international law. Obedience to/compliance with rules (norms) of human rights treaties* results in the realization or implementation of those rights. A rule is

drafted so as to be consistent with a general principle.

RULE OF LAW

A principle of international law that says that every society in the world must have a system of laws applicable to all persons, that that law is the highest authority in the state, and that no one is above the law. All disputes must be decided pursuant to law and not by the arbitrary or discretionary acts of the government.

Human rights violations are abuses of power by the state and those acting under or in concert with it. Power of state can only be exercised properly where it is done pursuant to an existing law. Law must rule every action and every person. No one may be immune from responsibility and accountability for actions that violate human rights.

A rule-of-law system has an orderly, express, written, accessible, and understandable set of laws equally applicable to everyone. All members of society are legally equal. The famous sayings that "no one is above the law" and "we are a nation of laws and not of men" are statements that a society is a rule-of-law society, and that even the president or king is not above the law. In most states it is the constitution that is the basis for all law. None of those laws may violate human rights because no government, federal or state, has any legal right to violate human rights.

Rule of law is an accepted principle of international law as applied to the international community, where the nations of the world continue to establish norms for human rights and humanitarian law, so that everyone is responsible internationally for their acts. A rule of law society is considered by the international community to be a prerequisite to the effective protection of human rights.

Rules of Engagement (roes)

The military instructions given by a military command to its officers, and ultimately down to its soldiers, regarding under what condition and with what weapons and tactics an armed force is permitted to engage an opposing armed force or whether to use force against nonmilitary parties, such as civilians. Also seen as an abbreviation: roes.

Rules of Procedure

The written rules by which a body, such as a court, commission, or committee, operates on a daily basis. These are specific rules on how the members are chosen and the body functions, such as how complaints* are filed and decided, what time limits apply, and what types of motions can be filed and heard. All rules of procedure are aimed at efficient and just operation of the body within its terms of reference so as to fulfill its mandate.

Ruse (loac)

Intentional tactical acts of deception used by combatants as part of a military operation to gain an advantage over an adversary. Ruses are legal.

Acts of soldiers that are intended to mislead an adversary or to induce him to act recklessly but that do not violate the rule or principles of international humanitarian law. Examples include the use of decoys, camouflage, mock operations. These differ from "perfidy," which means

deceptive acts that falsely create a semblance of a legally protected status.

Safeguards (un)

A written set of precautionary measures drafted by experts within the context of the un, set forth within a nonlegally binding instrument, and issued to help states apply specific measures at the national level by a certain sector of the state government to prompt government action that will be consistent with international human rights legal standards. For example, the un has drafted a document entitled *Safeguards Guaranteeing Protection of the Rights of Those Facing the Death Penalty*. These are meant to assist governments, especially prison officials and executioners, to impose capital punishment in a way that is consistent with the human dignity/human rights of the person executed so as to ensure the preservation of that person's inherent dignity despite whatever crime he has committed. These are not legally binding as a matter of international law, but the un expresses its desire that these safeguards be put into practice and made legally binding and implemented under national law, if at all possible.

Sanctions

Actions taken by one state, a group of states, or an organization against another, as a punishment for committing wrongful acts violating human rights, or as a deterrent against commission of such future wrongful acts against the sanctioning party or a third party.

The U.S. sometimes imposes sanctions on countries that have violated human rights. The long running sanctions

236 • *Definitions of Terms*

against Cuba and those against Yugoslavia and formerly against Iraq, all have as a major part of their goal punishing a state for its human rights practices and trying to force the target state to change. This punitive action is used outside of the field of human rights and is used in many areas of international relations to change a state's conduct.

Savings Clause (Treaty*)

In a human rights treaty*, a "Savings Clause" is one that provides that nothing in that treaty* can be interpreted as allowing a state party to restrict or derogate from any existing human rights protections in national law or in any way to change any other state obligations protecting human rights under any international law to which the state is bound. The purpose of a savings clause is to preserve as many existing legal obligations of states as possible and to not allow states to use the treaty* obligation as an excuse to get out of respecting other existing legal obligations that are protective of human rights. *See* ICCPR, article 5.2.

Secondary Rules (vs. Primary Rules)

See Primary Rules, supra.

Second Generation (Human) Rights

A term formerly used to describe a class of human rights that comprise all economic, social, and cultural rights.

Second Generation human rights are said by some to be a more "collective" type of rights, and by their nature to be "progressive" or "programmatic" rights,

meaning they take progressive measures or programs by states, within their economic resources, to fulfill the rights, such as work, health, food, shelter, and education.

Second Generation rights are distinguished from First Generation rights, which are the civil and political rights, and are classified as "immediate" rights; and Third Generation human rights, which are also called the "solidarity" rights. The ICESCR is a general human rights treaty containing Second Generation human rights.

Caveat: The term "generation" does not imply any chronological difference or hierarchy of human rights. It was simply a political, legal, conceptual categorization. The idea and use of the term "generation" has come into disuse, and the terms first, second, and third generation should no longer be used because they breed conceptual confusion.

Sectional (Human Rights) Instrument (vs. General Instrument)

A human rights instrument, such as a treaty* or declaration, whose material scope only covers a certain narrow subject area or one specific human right (such as torture, religion, education) or a specific group of people, such as children, women, refugees. Its whose purpose is to amplify the scope of protection of such rights or of such persons. General human rights instruments, such as the ICCPR, cover a broad group of rights, e.g., civil and political rights, whereas a sectional instrument would be much narrower and focused, e.g., on the political rights of women.

SECTORIAL (HUMAN) RIGHTS

Human rights held by certain persons or pertaining to certain situations, such as children, refugees, torture. Similar to "Sectional (Human Rights) Instrument," supra.

SECURE (HUMAN RIGHTS OBLIGATIONS)

To *secure* means to put something beyond hazard of being lost or of not being received. To secure human rights means to make them certain, to ensure them, to give certitude to them, to give an adequate pledge of an obligation to respect them.

A word used to describe the nature of the state obligation in a human rights treaty*. See ECHR, article 1, for an example. The statement of "Secure (Human Rights Obligations)" is usually found right after the preamble.

SECURITY

The quality or state of being or feeling secure from danger and harm, or from interference with desired activity or with physical freedom. One goal of international human rights law is to ensure that every human being can fully experience human security, particularly in relation to the government.

SECURITY COUNCIL (UN)

The principal United Nations organ charged with the maintenance of world peace and security and made up of fifteen members: five permanent members (the United States, Russia, France, United Kingdom, China) and ten revolving members. The Security Council has power to deal with situations that constitute a breach of peace, a threat to peace, or an act of aggression. The Security Council often deals with situations involving human rights abuses, e.g., Rwanda in 1994 and the former Yugoslavia (Bosnia) in the 1990s.

SEGREGATION (VS. INTEGRATION)

The forced separation, isolation, and keeping apart of different groups of persons based on characteristics such as race, religion, color, nationality, or ethnic identity, as to places where they live, work, play, receipt of education, or participation in any other human activity usually open to members of society.

As a matter of human rights law, segregation violates the human rights of equality and nondiscrimination, and can interfere with freedom of association, movement, and assembly. Segregation can also violate the collective rights of a segregated group such as a religious, racial, or ethnic minority. (*See* ICCPR, articles 2.1, 12.1, 26, 27). Segregation of people based on such characteristics as race or religion would be a violation of human rights law unless there is a reasonable and objective justification consistent with the protection of human rights and with no other alternative. This would be quite exceptional. The prime example of segregation was South Africa up until 1994, with a system known as apartheid. The process of taking steps to reverse segregation and reintegrate a society is called desegregation.

SEIZE/SEIZED (OF A COMPLAINT*)

The status of a judicial or quasi-judicial forum having assumed jurisdiction/having determined competence over a case of an alleged human rights violation submitted to it by a formal complaint* filed by an individual, group, or state. This term is used by a judicial (court/tribunal) or quasi-judicial body (commission or committee) that is mandated to resolve formal complaints*. It means that the body has determined admissibility and finds the complaint* to be admissible. It means that the particular forum has agreed to take a case and is exercising subject matter jurisdiction/competence over it and will proceed to examine and resolve it. Sometimes this term is spelled "seise[d]."

SELECTIVITY (VS. NONSELECTIVITY)

The quality or action of a state or organization being selective in its direction of human rights criticism and being characterized by that state's choice to focus scrutiny only on certain states. It is the conduct of tending to use human rights practices to pick on only on one or a few chosen states as a means of political/ideological vendetta. This term is used to describe the practice by states and IGO bodies of consistently scrutinizing and focusing criticism on the human rights practices of some states while not doing so on other states equally deserving of criticism. The opposite term, the "principle of nonselectivity," precludes state/IGO selectivity in the consideration of human rights issues, which means that the state/IGO will not be allowed to choose only certain states to criticize, e.g., communist states, dictatorships, Islamic states. Rather it will have to look at all states equally. Usually seen with the related principles of "Objectivity" and "Impartiality," supra.

SELF-DEFENSE (PRINCIPLE) (LOAC)

An international law principle that holds that, based on customary international law, states possess an inherent legal right to use force, most often military force, to protect their independence and territorial integrity from outside aggression. Self-defense may be individual or collective, as when the defending state invites another state or states to help it defend itself. *See* UNCH, article 51, though this right is limited, e.g., by the principle of proportionality.

SELF-DETERMINATION (RIGHT TO)

A principle of international law found as a norm in certain general human rights treaties* and stating that all states or "peoples" have the right to establish their own political system and own internal order; to freely pursue their own economic, social, and cultural development; and to use their natural resources as they deem fit. It is the right of a collective society of like peoples to determine its own political and economic future, subject to international law obligations. *See* ICCPR, article 1.1, and ICESCR, article 1.1. In the international legal texts it is not clearly defined what constitutes a "peoples" for the purposes of claiming this right. There is much controversy and confusion as to the scope and application of this human right.

SELF-EXECUTING

The legal nature/status of a treaty* whose provisions are automatically, and without any formal or specific act of incorporation/transformation by state authorities, made part of the law of the land (municipal/domestic law) and enforceable in national/municipal courts.

Self-executing treaties* are binding in domestic law upon ratification* by the state and require no implementing legislation in national law. If a treaty* is self-executing, its substantive norms are directly justiciable and can be immediately applied by courts.

SELF-HELP (VS. COLLECTIVE/ MULTILATERAL ACTION)

The political concept of a state taking action alone and on its own initiative in response to some international issue, and not acting through the collective mechanisms offered by international and regional intergovernmental organizations. Self-help is not the accepted norm for resolving issues because it can be abused and stir up international political controversy if the motive and means of self-help are questionable. The norm is to not use self-help, except in self-defense, but to seek solutions in a multilateral context with states working together.

SELF-INCRIMINATION (PRINCIPLE OF CRIMINAL PROCEDURE)

The human right not to be forced by the government to say anything that could tend to prove one's criminal guilt or to provide any evidence against oneself. This right includes the right not to testify against oneself in criminal proceedings and the right against forced confessions. The Latin expression for this principle is *nemo tenetur edere contra se* or *non accusare se debet*. Violation of this principle normally results in the testimony/evidence being ruled as inadmissible for determining guilt.

SERVITUDE (INVOLUNTARY)

A status/condition of a person being involuntarily subject to a master, having no liberty, and not being able to determine his own course of action or way of life. Forcing individuals to engage in work against their will, either as a punishment or to exploit them economically. Such servitude, most often called "Involuntary Servitude," is a violation of human rights. Certain forms of forced work, such as military service or penal sentence labor, are usually excepted. It is different from "Slavery," which means any exercise of private property ownership rights to a human being.

Caveat: "Servitudes" generally has a different meaning in international law.

SIGN/SIGNATURE (TO A TREATY*)

The legal act of signing a treaty* by a state or other legal personality by its authorized, fully empowered representative ("plenipotentiary"), whereby it expresses its intent to be legally bound to the obligations of the treaty* by subsequent ratification*, unless by its terms the treaty* provides otherwise, in which case signature alone binds it, subject to any reservations, declarations, and understandings submitted.

A treaty* is "open for signature" after it is adopted by vote of the negotiating parties, which sets/authenticates the exact text of the treaty* instrument to be signed.

SIGNATORY (TO TREATY*)

A designation given to a state or other legal personality that has signed its signature to a treaty* instrument through its authorized, fully empowered diplomatic representative ("plenipotentiary"), and has thus expressed its intent to be legally bound to the obligations of the treaty* by subsequent ratification*. By the express terms of some treaties*, it may be provided that the authorized signature alone is sufficient to bind, in which case the very act of signing binds it and makes it a signatory. This is subject, in any case, to any reservations, declarations, or understandings submitted by the signatory.

SIGNATURE/SIGNATORY AD REFERENDUM (TO TREATY*)
[Latin, lit.: to refer back for approval]

Signature *ad referendum* means that the signature made by a state's, or other legal personality's, representative to a treaty* is made subject to referral back to that party for further consideration by its governing structures through constitutional or legislative processes in order to determine if it will ratify* the signature, which then would bind that party to the obligations of the treaty*. A signatory *ad referendum* is a state or other legal personality that has signed a treaty*, subject to such referral back.

SINE QUA NON
[Latin, lit.: without which not]

A Latin expression that means an absolutely necessary fact or condition or element in order for something else to exist or happen. A sine qua non is that thing that is indispensable for something else. It is of the essence or conditionally necessary. Example: For humans, breathing is a sine qua non of living; or voting is a sine qua non of democracy.

Also, a term in international law treaties* for a preliminary condition agreed to by both/all states parties, e.g., a cease-fire as a precondition of a surrender in an armed conflict. This is also called a *conditio sine qua non.*

SINTI (AKA ROMA/GYPSY)

A term that refers to that group of people who are known as Gypsies. Gypsies can be found in many countries of the world and have different languages and customs in different states. Sinti are also known by the term "Roma."

SI OMNES CLAUSE (AKA GENERAL PARTICIPATION CLAUSE)
[Latin, lit.: if all]

A clause or stipulation found in many classic international law treaties*. This clause provides that the obligations of the treaty* should only be applied to a situation when all the states involved in an issue are states parties to the subject treaty*. It creates a mutual, reciprocal, legal relationship with all other states parties. This applies primarily to treaties* involving armed conflict. It is also known as a "General Participation Clause."

SIRACUSA PRINCIPLES (ON LIMITATIONS, DEROGATIONS)

Refers to a set of principles adopted at a conference of experts in Siracusa, Italy, in 1984, regarding the interpretation, scope, and application of limitation and derogation clauses in the ICCPR.

SLAVERY

The status of a person belonging to another person as a chattel (personal property) and thus having to do whatever the owner commands. Slavery is a violation of human rights. *See also* Involuntary Servitude. *See* ICCPR article 8.1.

SLICE INSTRUMENT (VS. GENERAL INSTRUMENT)

A separate treaty* instrument that takes a specific human right from a general human rights treaty* and amplifies the right and its implementation mechanisms to make the right more clearly and broadly defined and implemented, and thus better respected. The UN Torture Convention of 1984 is a slice instrument of article 7 of the ICCPR.

SOCIAL CLAUSE

A human rights related clause normally inserted in international trade and cooperation agreements in the context of the World Trade Organization (WTO) and European Union since around 1995. A social clause provides that a contracting party cannot get the benefit of a trade or cooperation agreement if it engages in such activities as child labor, slave labor, or holds a nonunion state. This clause is reciprocal for both parties to an agreement.

The wording of such a clause is "Respect for democratic principles and fundamental human rights proclaimed by the Universal Declaration of Human Rights underpins the domestic and external policies of both parties and constitutes an essential element of this agreement."

SOCIAL CONTRACT (THEORY OF SOCIETY)

A political theory espoused by writers such as Locke and Rousseau, that says that humans are born free, equal, and independent and can choose to enter into a "Social Contract" with each other to create systems and institutions to meet their mutual needs, such as the formation of police, fire control, and armed forces, etc. It is thus considered the philosophical basis for the establishment and authority of government and ultimately of the state. Individuals exercise their social contract primarily by voting in public elections and choosing leaders.

SOCIAL (HUMAN) RIGHTS

Human rights that relate to human society, the interpersonal interaction of the individual and the group, or the welfare of human beings as members of a family/society.

1. Social (Human) Rights versus Economic and Cultural Rights: Most particularly and most commonly, "Social (Human) Rights" describes one of the three categories (economic, social, and cultural) of human rights, which together used to be called "Second-Generation (Human) Rights." These latter refer mainly to rights of individuals with regard to relationships in society in the narrow sense. Social human rights, narrowly speaking, include, inter alia, the right to marry, to found a family, to have special protection for children, or to form labor unions.

2. Social (Human) Rights versus Classical (Human) Rights: Sometimes "Social (Human) Rights" is used to refer to economic, social, and cultural human rights as one type of human right that is distinguished from "Classical (Human) Rights," which are the "civil and political" human rights. In this broader sense, "Classical (Human) Rights" refer to all formerly called "First Generation (Human) Rights," while "Social (Human) Rights" refer to all "Second Generation (Human) Rights."

SOCIALISM

A political ideology for the ordering of a society; the opposite of individualism. It is characterized by commitment to the welfare of the collective, to the interests of the society; to economic planning; to public ownership of the means of production; to a central concern for the laborer, the producer of goods; to limitation on the free market, on individual capital, on private economic enterprise, and on accumulation of private property.

SOCIAL JUSTICE

The right ordering of a society according to human rights principles in a manner that guarantees equality, justice, and fairness in reality to every person, with respect for the rule of law and for the inherent dignity and human rights of the individual, and a decent, safe, secure, and healthy standard of living and living environment. There can be no social justice without respect for human rights, and human rights norms serve as the measuring criteria for whether and how much social justice exists in a society.

SOFT LAW (VS. HARD LAW)

A term describing a doctrine of international law that describes the legal status of certain human rights related declarations, resolutions, guidelines, and basic principles. They are created by international, intergovernmental organizations, such as the UN, as nonbinding norms, setting forth nonobligatory but highly recommended standards of state conduct that should be followed. It is "soft" law because it is not legally binding, as is "Hard Law" (*see* supra). States are not legally obligated to follow soft law standards.

This term is sometimes used to refer to norms in legal instruments that are so vague or imprecise as to be not legally enforceable, and that are mostly hortatory or programmatic.

In human rights literature, it is most often in the first sense that this term is used. The main purpose of soft law is to serve as a guideline or road map to how to comply with "hard law" human rights norms, such as those found in the ICCPR. An example of soft law is the UN Standard Minimum Rules for the Treatment of Prisoners (1957).

SOFT POWER

A political concept describing a type of intangible powers that a state may develop, possess, and use, by virtue of its taking certain domestic or international positions and engaging in activities that promote the rule-of-law and human rights. It is a power that comes from accepting, saying, and doing what is morally and legally right consistent with internationally accepted human rights norms. It is the opposite of hard power, such as is represented by missiles and guns. This soft power can be asserted against another state to get that state to change or adopt policies, positions, or laws consistent with and protective of human rights.

SOLIDARITY (RIGHTS/RIGHT TO)

A term having two different uses:

1. Solidarity Rights. Describes a class of human rights norms once collectively known as "Third Generation (Human) Rights" (*see* infra). Some have called

these rights "solidarity rights" because by their nature and application these rights require international cooperation and joint activity to give them effect, such as the right to peace, to a clean environment, to development, and to humanitarian assistance, all of which have a very collective, cooperative character.

2. Right to Solidarity. This is a separate human right in the list of "Third Generation (Human) Rights." It is very difficult to define. It means something like the right to work together with other states, groups, and organizations—and the duty of all states, etc., to all work together—to accomplish human rights goals. It implies an interdependence among states.

Sovereign Equality (of States)

A general principle of international law that holds that all states are juridically (legally) equal within the community of nations and under international law and that every state has the same legal right as all others to act within the realm of international law and relations, regardless of size, population, wealth, power, or military might.

Sovereign Immunity

A legal doctrine of domestic/municipal/ national law that provides that a sovereign (such as a state) cannot be sued by another sovereign in a court of law without its express or implied consent and that a state cannot be sued by a private party for its public acts without its consent to be sued. It also means that a sovereign state cannot be made the respondent in the courts of another state without the respondent's consent. Nor-

mally, such immunity is recognized only as to public acts (*juri imperii*) and not private acts (*juri gestionis*).

Sovereignty (Principle)

The general international legal principle that provides that a state has lawful control over its own territory to the exclusion of all other states, possesses authority to govern in its own territory, and has the exclusive right to establish and apply the law internally.

Sovereignty Proviso (U.S.)

A provision inserted by the U.S. Senate into a senate resolution that ratifies an international human rights treaty*, which says that the president is required to notify all present and prospective states parties to the treaty* and that nothing in the treaty* authorizes legislation that would be prohibited by the U.S. Constitution.

The significance of this is that in the ratification* of international human rights instruments, the United States seeks to interpret them according to the laws and principles set forth in the U.S. Constitution. Some in the international community, however, criticize use of such provisos, and the lack of political will of the U.S. to fully submit itself to the international human rights systems because of the way it uses reservations, declarations, and understandings in the ratification* process to water down certain human rights norms.

Special Consultative Status (NGO)

Consultative status granted by the ECOSOC to an NGO that deals with only some types of matters that are dealt with by the human rights bodies of ECOSOC. Such status allows an NGO to participate in the work of the body, such as by attending sessions or submitting written or oral reports/interventions on an issue. This is an NGO category designation established in 1996 (*see* ECOSOC Resolution 1996/31). It was formerly called "Category II" NGO status.

SPECIAL PROCEDURES/ MECHANISMS (UN COMMISSION ON HUMAN RIGHTS)

The term used to refer to all of the thematic and country specific activities of working groups and special rapporteurs under the UN Commission on Human Rights. Examples are the Working Group on Disappearances and the Special Rapporteur on Religious Intolerance.

SPECIAL RAPPORTEUR

The official title and function given to a person appointed and given a mandate by a body, for example the UN Commission on Human Rights or its subcommission, to gather information and prepare an official report on a human rights situation in a particular country, such as Iran, or on a particular human rights issue/theme, for example, religious intolerance or human rights education. The special rapporteur reports back to the body with the report so that the body can use it to most effectively conduct its business. The special rapporteur function in the UN is considered part of the "special mechanisms" within the UN human rights. The person selected can be from among the body's members, or someone outside, usually an expert in the issue/theme or state concerned.

SPECIALTY (EXTRADITION, RULE OF)

A rule relating to extradition procedure that says that a state requesting the extradition of someone for committing a certain crime can only prosecute that person for that particular crime and no other.

SPECIFICITIES (CULTURAL, ETC.) (AKA PARTICULARITIES)

The characteristics or qualities of being that are peculiar to particular individuals or groups. Usually used in discussing diversity in cultures. Cultural specificities are those characteristics of a group of people that make that group different from other groups, such as their religion, tribal structure, legal system, or customs. Often seen in discussion/debate of the idea of whether human rights are "universal" or "culturally relative" (i.e., "Universality" versus "Cultural Relativism"). Some argue that human rights are universal, to be applied to all peoples of all states alike, while others maintain that human rights are to be applied differently according to different cultural, etc., specificities. The term "Particularities" is also used interchangeably with specificities — such as in "cultural particularities — and in the same culturally relativistic manner. The universalist argument is now the most widely accepted one: human rights are universal.

One also may speak of "religious specificities," "linguistic specificities," and occasionally other types of specificities.

STANDARD (OF CONDUCT)

A standard is roughly synonymous with a norm. A standard is a precise normative legal measure that prescribes and is used to judge state conduct with respect to human rights. It is a level of conduct that a state is required to meet to fulfill its legal obligations with respect to human rights.

STANDARD MINIMUM RULES (UN)

A written set of specific rules drafted by the UN to be used by states to help them conform their laws and practices in specific areas, such as in correctional institutions, to international human rights norms. They are an international common denominator considered by the community of nations to be the lowest acceptable standard consistent with human dignity. They are not legally binding, but states are encouraged to follow/implement them and even to transform them into domestic law. An example is the Standard Minimum Rules for the Treatment of Prisoners, adopted by the UN in 1957.

STANDARD-SETTING (PROCESS)

The process whereby an international forum, such as the United Nations, establishes legal norms/standards by its treaty*-making processes through law-making treaties*, such as the ICCPR. It is the process of negotiating and adopting specific norms of conduct on specific subjects, e.g., torture, refugees, women's rights. Usually the standard-setting process starts with a proposal made by one or more states (and/or possibly NGOs) to an IGO, such as the UN, for adoption of a "Resolution" calling for the establishment of human rights standards in a given area. After the resolution is adopted it is followed by negotiation and adoption of a "Declaration" setting forth the human rights principles agreed upon in a non-binding international instrument, e.g., the UDHR. Finally, this process is supposed to lead to the negotiation, adoption, and ratification* of a binding international legal instrument, such as a convention or covenant, that sets forth the standards in positive legal norms, e.g., the ICCPR.

STANDARD-SETTING MANDATE

A resolution issued by an organ of an intergovernmental organization, such as the UN Commission on Human Rights, which gives authority and sets terms of reference to working groups to draft proposed human rights normative standards about certain thematic issues, for example, the Draft Declaration on the Rights of Racial, Ethnic, Religious, and Linguistic Minorities.

STANDING (TO FILE/SUBMIT/ LODGE/OBJECT/APPEAL) (AKA *LOCUS STANDI*)

The right of a person, persons, group (e.g., NGO) or state, to file/submit/lodge a complaint* of human rights violations, to make preliminary objections to the admissibility of complaints*, to appeal a decision, to engage other procedures, or to request an advisory opinion and to generally appear as a party properly authorized to act before a court/tribunal, committee, or commission empowered to receive and resolve cases of alleged human rights violations. In Latin, this right is called *locus standi*.

Generally speaking, "Standing" concerns the issue of whether a person/group/state has the legal right to act within a given human rights system.

The statute or rules of the forum, or

6 7

the treaty* that establishes a treaty*-based forum, usually specifies the types of parties that have "standing" to file complaints* and otherwise act before the forum. It is a condition of admissibility of a written complaint* or other procedure in which the complaining party must have standing, usually by being the actual victim of the violation, or someone directly affected by a violation, or by the decision of the forum. Example: The Optional Protocol to the ICCPR grants standing to "individuals . . . who claim to be victims of a violation by [a] State Party of any of the rights set forth in the [ICCPR]."

If the complaining/acting party does not have standing (*locus standi*), then the case will be deemed "inadmissible *ratione standi*" and will not be considered further. Or, the objection, motion, or appeal will be disallowed *ratione standi*, which stated in English as "for lack of standing."

STARE DECISIS
[Latin, lit.: to stand or decide things]

A common law (United States, United Kingdom, etc.) legal term that refers to a foundational doctrine of common law jurisprudence, namely, that a court is bound to decide a case the same way as the courts have previously decided similar cases. It means that the "holding" of a case, which means the particular applied rule of law on which a case was decided, is a precedent that is to be resorted to as legally binding in all subsequent similar cases until the holding is overruled or reversed.

Though it is not a human rights term, it is sometimes seen in human rights literature when discussing the precedental value of commission/committee decisions or court judgments. Compare "Constant Jurisprudence," supra.

STATE

An international legal-political entity that possesses the following characteristics:
1. a defined, permanent body of people/population;
2. a more or less defined territory that it occupies;
3. an organized government capable of maintaining effective control of its territory;
4. the capacity to carry on international relations.

Increasingly, it is also being said that a state must fulfill its obligations under international law as to respect for human rights.

A state must be independent and exercise sovereignty over its territory. It possesses an international legal personality and enjoys "Sovereign Equality," i.e., it is legally equal to all other states in the world. *See also* Nation-State.

STATE CONSENT (PRINCIPLE)

A basic principle of international law that holds that states can only be obligated to comply with legal norms to which the state has given its express or implied consent.

All international law is based on the consent of sovereign and equal states. In treaty law that consent is expressly stated in the instrument of ratification* deposited with the appropriate authority. Under customary international law, the state consent is implied from the consistent practice (usage) of states, coupled with the *opinio juris*, the subjective belief that the norm is legally binding.

STATELESS PERSON (VS. CITIZEN/NATIONAL)

A person who is not recognized as a national/citizen of any state. Statelessness arises because of war related dislocations or a problem in changes of laws on nationality, which deny or strip a citizen of citizenship.

Statelessness is a problem because the stateless person has no state that can offer him the protection of a government or any government benefits available to nationals/citizens, such as a passport or social security. Article 15 of the UDHR states that every person has a human right to a nationality, citizenship in a state. The principle of sovereignty, however, grants full rights to states to determine who is and is not a national/citizen of that state.

STATE OF EMERGENCY (PUBLIC EMERGENCY) (AKA STATE OF EXCEPTION)

A legal characterization of a situation in a state wherein there exists a public emergency affecting the life of the nation. The existence and declaration of a state of emergency may permit a state to declare its "derogation" from, or suspension of, certain human rights to the extent and scope of the emergency. Periods of derogation are often, but not always, declared during states of emergency. It is a period of exception from the normal applicability of civil and criminal law and of human rights norms.

Such a state of emergency is often triggered, e.g., by an internal revolution,

widespread lawlessness, foreign invasion, or even a large-scale natural disaster.

STATE OF EXCEPTION (PUBLIC EMERGENCY) (AKA STATE OF EMERGENCY)

See State of Emergency, supra

STATE OF NATIONALITY (ICC COMPETENCE/JURISDICTION)

A legal basis for exercise of personal jurisdiction of the International Criminal Court. This court has jurisdiction over crimes committed by citizens of a state that has ratified the ICC Statute. In the 1998 Rome ICC Statute, jurisdiction of the International Criminal Court was established over crimes that are committed by a citizen of a state party to the ICC Statute. This is found in article 12.2 of the statute.

Every state has, with few exceptions, the right to exercise criminal jurisdiction over acts committed by its own citizens. The ICC can exercise complementary jurisdiction over nationals of ICC states parties.

STATE OF SIEGE (PUBLIC EMERGENCY)

A legal characterization of a situation in a state wherein there exists a public emergency affecting the life of the nation caused by an armed attack or threat upon the government to cause it to surrender. The existence and declaration of a state of siege may permit a state to declare its derogation from, or suspension of, certain human rights to the extent and scope of the emergency. Periods of derogation are often, but not always, declared in a state of siege. It is a period of exception from the normal applicability of human rights norms. Similar to "State of Emergency" and "State of Exception," supra.

STATE PARTY (TO A TREATY*)

A state that has signed, ratified*, and thus become legally bound to obey a treaty* is called a "state party" to that treaty*. A state cannot be accused of violating a human rights treaty* unless it is first established that it is a state party to that treaty*. The terms "Party" and "High Contracting Party" to a treaty* are also used. Different treaty* systems will use different terms, e.g., ICCPR and ACHR use "states parties" whereas ECHR uses "high contracting parties."

STATE PRACTICE (INTERNATIONAL LAW SOURCE/INTERPRETATION)

A source for determining what is a norm for an international law or how a norm should be interpreted. State practice can consist of the actual actions of states, their internal laws, official pronouncements, and even how they vote in international organizations.

STATE RESPONSIBILITY FOR THE TREATMENT OF ALIENS (PRINCIPLE)

A classical international law principle that served as a historic antecedent to modern human rights law. This principle provided that a state had a legal obligation to treat nationals of another state in a manner that conformed to certain minimum standards of civilization. When a foreign national was injured by the state, that state owed a legal obligation to the state of the injured person's nationality to pay compensation or otherwise remedy the injury, and the latter state could col-

lect compensation from the offending state for such damages.

STATUTE

A law enacted by the legislative branch of a government or an international legal instrument ("treaty"*) adopted by an IGO for establishing and setting up a court/tribunal or quasi-legal body and/or for regulating its scope and authority and sometimes its internal rules of procedure and operation. Examples are the Statute of the International Court of Justice and Statute of the Inter-American Court of Human Rights and the Statute of the International Criminal Court.

STEREOTYPE

A standard perception that is held in common as to all members of a particular group. This is an oversimplified and not necessarily true opinion about the group and its members' character. Stereotyping can lead to antilocution, prejudice, hate, discrimination, and human rights violations.

Example: A perception that someone who is a Gypsy is a thief and dishonest because Gypsies are commonly perceived as thieves and liars would be a stereotyping of that person.

STOCKTAKING

A term describing the periodic self-examination of an organization, such as the UN, to analyze and assess its workload, the matters it has dealt with, and its effectiveness so as to determine whether and how it should change to become more capable of fulfilling its mandate. It is a comprehensive assessment of a human rights system. It looks at and analyzes all the facts, figures, and issues, such as the number of complaints* received, number of cases completed, costs, duplication of standards, and overlap of responsibilities. The 1993 UN Vienna Conference on Human Rights was part of a major "Stocktaking" process by the UN in regards to its human rights standards, bodies, procedures, and mechanisms.

STRASBOURG PROOF(ING LEGISLATION)

A term used predominantly in the UK to refer to the process of reviewing existing and proposed laws, regulations, and administrative practices to assure that they will withstand judicial scrutiny if brought before the European Court of Human Rights, which is located in Strasbourg, France. This means that such laws and practices must be examined in reference to, and harmonized and rendered compatible with, the human rights legal norms found in the ECHR and its Protocols.

This prevents the cost and potential embarrassment to the state of having a case brought before the court in which the state law or practice is found to be in violation of the ECHR. Strasbourg proofing legislation to the point where it is Strasbourg proofed will hopefully lead to not being found in violation of the ECHR in the event any cases are brought against it concerning the compatibility of that law with the ECHR.

STRICT INTERPRETATION/ CONSTRUCTION (OF LAW)

A legal doctrine of statutory interpretation that says that certain laws must be interpreted narrowly and strictly according to the express language of the law, offering as little room for alternative interpretation or application as possible, e.g., limitation clauses are normally strictly interpreted/construed against the state to allow as few and as narrow limitations as possible.

STRICTO SENSU (VS. LATU SENSU)
[Latin, lit.: in a strict/narrow sense]

A Latin adverbial expression that means to give a strict or narrow interpretation to a text. When reading a text *strictu sensu*, one gives the wording of the text the strictest, narrowest interpretation, as opposed to giving it a broad, liberal interpretation, known as *latu sensu*.

STRIKE/STRICKEN FROM THE LIST/ROLL (COMPLAINT*)

When a complaint* is determined to be inadmissible, the complainant ceases to pursue it, or for some other reason it can no longer be handled (seized) by a judicial or quasi-judicial forum, it can be "stricken from the list" of cases then presently under consideration by that forum. This same process is also stated as "stricken from the rolls." When such an event occurs, the clerk/registrar will "strike from the list/roll" that complaint*. The list/roll is the list of all cases of which the body is seized (i.e., has under its active jurisdiction) at any given time. It is similar to the dismissal of a case in a common law system.

STRONG CULTURAL RELATIVISM

A view that culture is the principle source of the validity of a moral right or rule. Human rights serve as a check on the potential excesses of relativism. This would allow for only a few human rights that have almost universal acceptance.

STRUCTURAL ADJUSTMENT PROGRAM (SAP)

A program of policies dictated usually by an international financial institution (IFI) to a debtor state as a condition for the restructuring of overdue international debt. Such a program often has significant consequences for human rights, especially as to its adverse economic consequences on the people, particularly on women in the home due to lower wages or public assistance.

STRUCTURAL VIOLENCE

A concept initially applied to health research on racial discrimination but now used to apply to gross, structural, or large-scale human rights violations. The "violence" in this term does not refer to physical force by individuals to cause injury but to pervasive individual and institutional actions and policies, which by intent or omission result in predictable harm to the human rights of large populations. It is violence found in social fabrics, political economy, and government structure. The "structural" element is its continued, repeated, large-scale and systematic character. The violations are gross because of the extent of the harm they do to individuals. Violence committed on behalf of or with the support of a social structure. An example would be apartheid.

SUB-COMMISSION ON PREVENTION OF DISCRIMINATION AND PROTECTION OF MINORITIES (UN)

See Sub-Commission on Promotion and Protection of Human Rights, infra.

SUB-COMMISSION ON PROMOTION AND PROTECTION OF HUMAN RIGHTS (FORMERLY KNOWN AS THE SUB-COMMISSION ON PREVENTION OF DISCRIMINATION AND PROTECTION OF MINORITIES) (UN)

The UN Charter-based body that is under ("subsidiary" to) the Commission on Human Rights. The function of this body is for it to prepare studies and make recommendations to the Commission "concerning the prevention of discrimination of any kind relating to human rights and fundamental freedoms, and the protection of racial, national, religious, and linguistic minorities."

The Commission elects the "Sub-Commission's" 26 members, who sit in their "personal" capacity, that is, as independent experts, and not in a "representative" capacity, as politically oriented representatives of their respective states. This has made the Sub-Commission the UN forum most favorable and positive in promoting respect for human rights. It prepares many reports on a broad range of human rights themes, such as religious intolerance, and country-specific reports, usually with the help of special rapporteurs, and helps in human rights standard-setting, with preparation of proposed drafts of human rights declarations, such as on indigenous peoples and minority groups. It is spending an increasing amount of time studying specific human rights violations, especially under the 1503 Procedure for gross and systematic violations. It is most commonly referred to as the "Sub-Commission."

SUBJECT (VS. OBJECT) (OF INTERNATIONAL LAW)

The party for whom international law is made. Under classic international law, only states were considered the "subjects" of such law, and human beings were considered the "objects" of such law. This was because international law was, in its original theory, a set of rules governing the relation between and among states, not individuals, because only states could hold rights. Now, under the theory of international human rights law, human beings are considered the "subjects" of such law as well.

The subjects of international law are the "holders" or "bearers" of the rights and duties thereunder, and they are entitled to and capable of maintaining their international rights by bringing international or domestic human rights claims based on such law so as to ensure its full implementation.

SUBJECTIVE (HUMAN) RIGHTS

A right belonging to a subject, i.e., as a power that is part of a legal relationship. *See* Subject.

SUBSIDIARITY (PRINCIPLE)

A principle of international law that international law norms and rules and their implementation mechanisms and procedures, whether global or regional, are secondary, a backup, a fallback to domestic (national) laws, rules, mechanisms, and procedures. The national system is primary over the international. This means that where there is an issue of a human rights violation one must resort first to the subject state's domestic remedies provided in national institutions, before having resort to the international level.

SUBSIDIARY (ORGAN/ TREATY*/SOURCE)

The condition of something being secondary, auxiliary, assisting, or a back up to something primary.

1. Subsidiary Organ: A "subsidiary organ" is one emanating from a primary or principle organ, e.g., the UN Sub-Commission on the Promotion and Protection of Human Rights is a subsidiary organ of the UN Commission on Human Rights.

2. Subsidiary Treaty*: When applied to a treaty*, it means a treaty* covering a subgroup or topic, such as the Refugee Convention or ILO treaties.

3. Subsidiary Source (of law): A "subsidiary source" of international law interpretation comprises the decisions of international courts and the writings of the major legal scholars ("publicists"). This source is "subsidiary" to Treaty* Law, Customary Law, and General Principles of Law. It is also referred to as supplementary means of interpretation.

SUBSISTENCE (HUMAN) RIGHTS

A term used to describe human rights for the most basic, minimum human needs, such as food, clothing, shelter, medical treatment. These are rights considered to be absolutely necessary for preserving basic human dignity.

SUBSTANTIVE RIGHTS/NORMS (VS. PROCEDURAL RIGHTS/NORMS)

Those rights in a human rights instrument/treaty* that set forth the actual, individual human rights, such as the right to expression, movement, association, religious freedom—the things that a human can do or not be forced to do—

or the right to get something from the state, such as food.

Substantive rights/norms are usually found in a treaty* after the preamble and before the procedural rights, which are the implementation mechanisms to remedy violations and ensure compliance. Substantive rights constitute a part of the normal legal order of a society.

SUCCESSION (TO TREATY* OBLIGATIONS)

The process/instrument whereby a newly formed state or government expresses its intent to be bound by succession to the treaty* obligations of the former state/government. This is done by depositing an "instrument of succession" with the designated treaty* depository, whereupon the new state/government becomes bound in international law to respect its predecessor's treaty* obligations.

SUI GENERIS
[Latin, lit.: of its own kind/type]

A Latin expression meaning that something is unique and of its own kind or type. It is treated differently than other things, such as legal norms. Applied to law it refers to norms that are of a distinct character and must be interpreted and applied in a certain manner and not as another general set of legal norms.

SULLIVAN PRINCIPLES (CODE OF CONDUCT)

A set of ethical principles formulated by the late Reverend Leon Sullivan in the 1970s, to be applied by multinational companies doing business in South Africa. The purpose of these principles was to fight against apartheid by getting companies doing business there to act in a way consistent with and promoting the human rights of the black African people. These served as the first model of a sort of business code of conduct consistent with human rights. The principles included provisions such as equal pay for men and women, and no discrimination in job promotions.

SUMMARY EXECUTION (AKA EXTRAJUDICIAL / EXTRALEGAL EXECUTION)

An unlawful and deliberate killing carried out by government order or with a government's complicity, by its agents or others without prior judicial sentence from a court after a criminal trial that was capable of imposing capital punishment had been held.

SUPERFLUOUS INJURY (PRINCIPLE) (LOAC)

A term found in humanitarian law to describe any injury inflicted by a belligerent beyond that necessary to neutralize an enemy and caused by the weapons used or tactics employed by the belligerent. Most commonly used to describe injury caused by weapons that inflict injury beyond that minimally necessary to achieve a military objective.

It is prohibited as a principle of international humanitarian law to employ methods or means of combat that cause superfluous injury to an adversary. Examples would be the carpet bombing or cluster fire bombing of a whole city or the use of poison-tipped projectiles or asphyxiating gas. It is a principle of humanity under humanitarian law to minimize unnecessary human suffering. *See also* Unnecessary Suffering.

SUPERIOR ORDERS
(CRIMINAL DEFENSE) (LOAC)

A term describing a legal defense, originally asserted at the Nuremberg Tribunal by Nazi war crime defendants of lower rank who sought to defend their actions by claiming that as soldiers they acted out of obligation and were merely "following orders" from their military superiors. This criminal defense is not valid for avoiding criminal culpability/responsibility but can be considered as a factor in mitigating a sentence if the defendant is found guilty of committing a war crime.

SUPERVISION (OF
TREATY* COMPLIANCE)

The action, process, or occupation of supervising; especially a critical watching and directing (of activities or a course of action) of states in their implementation of international human rights norms. All human rights implementation procedures and mechanisms are instituted with the aim of establishing whether human rights standards are in fact being respected and complied with by states. Supervision is the process of a body or forum overseeing the actions of states parties in fulfilling their normative obligations.

This is most commonly done by way of the supervisory body (commission/committee) reviewing reports submitted by states parties pursuant to a treaty* obligation, and critically commenting on a state's law and practice, and making recommendations for changes in the state so as to effect increased compliance with the norms and enjoyment of the substantive rights. It would also include processing and deciding complaints* of violations filed against states.

SUPERVISORY MECHANISMS

Organs and procedures established in treaties* or in intergovernmental institutions whose purpose is to supervise the human rights performance of states involved and to seek to get them to comply with applicable human rights norms. The UN Human Rights Committee with its state reporting system and complaint system is an example of a supervisory mechanism created in the ICCPR.

SUPERVISORY ROLE

The subsidiary, secondary, and supportive role of international human rights institutions in relation to states. International human rights is meant to be implemented primarily by states at a national and local level with the international institutions, such as the European Court of Human Rights, to act only in a secondary, supervisory role. This means that the international organs will act to see if the state is allowing and following a fair balance between the conflicting interest of individuals and groups with the state, will give the states a lot of discretion (margin of appreciation) in taking specific measures, and will only act where these measures violated the applicable human rights norms. This is largely the product of the principle of subsidiarity, by which the international system is subsidiary, a backup, to the national. It reflects a belief of states that there are areas where the state must exercise genuine discretionary powers, such as a policy for the protection of a minority group or dealing with a national emergency, which powers the international system shall respect. The international human rights organs are not meant to direct and control or limit a state, but only to supervise its conduct to best assure its full compliance with human rights norms, which fairly balances the needs of state with the freedom of individuals and groups.

Supplementary Means of Interpretation (of Treaties*)

A phrase referring to a secondary or subsidiary method of interpretation of international law treaties*. By this method, where the interpretation of a treaty remains unclear or ambiguous, recourse can be had to supplemental means such as in case decisions of certain courts applying or interpreting international law, in the writings of major legal scholars, in the legislative history (*Travaux Préparatoires*), or in subsequent agreements between the states parties or subsequent state practice.

This norm comes from the Vienna Convention on the Law of Treaties and has ripened into customary international law.

Suppression (of Violations/ Breaches of Humanitarian Law) (loac)

The act of a state pursuant to its legal obligation under international humanitarian law to take measures to put a stop to breaches of such norms by its own armed forces, or of other's forces under the state's jurisdiction and control. Suppression of violations of humanitarian law is mandated on states parties under the gcs

of 1949. *See* gc IV, article 146. *See also* Repression.

Supra (vs. Infra)
[Latin, lit.: above]

A Latin term meaning "above this point" or "earlier in this written work/document/instrument." In a case citation, it usually means that the case was previously referred to or the citation was previously given in the text of the decision or judgment.

Suspension Clause

A withdrawal clause placed in international trade preference agreements. The purpose of such a clause is to allow a party to the international trade agreement to suspend operation of the agreement and withdraw a preference as a punishment for the other party committing related human rights violations, such as forced labor, slavery, child labor, and violations of the right to association.

Systematic Attacks/Violations

Human rights violations that occur in a definite organized pattern, with consistent frequency, indicating an intentional, concerted, planned action to commit such acts. The concept of systematic and widespread attacks constituting crimes against humanity is found in international criminal law. The usual legal threshold for atrocious acts against a civilian population to rise to the level of a crime against humanity is that the attacks/violations must be widespread and systematic, not just isolated or random incidents. Customary international law has defined systematic attacks as following a regular pattern on the basis of a common policy and involving substantial public or private resources. This concept is included in the definition and threshold of crimes against humanity in the ICC Statute, article 7. *See* Appendix C.

The idea is that only crimes that endanger the international community or shock the conscience of mankind, by their magnitude and savagery or by their large number, warrant intervention by states other than the one on whose territory the acts are committed and should rise to the level of international crimes, such as crimes against humanity. Systematic attacks/violations are considered to be those that have the potential to undermine global or regional peace and security.

Systematic Human Rights Education

Education in human rights that starts with persons at the earliest levels of formal schooling, continues throughout primary and secondary schooling, and continues throughout life through informal sources and modes of education, such as NGOs and CBOs, so that all members of society are educated in human rights.

Technical Cooperation (and Advisory Services)

A mechanism of an international intergovernmental organization, such as the United Nations, that aims to improve the effective enjoyment of human rights through concrete projects designed to strengthen regional and national human rights infrastructures. This includes measures to nationally modify laws and government practices and is accomplished, e.g., by sending experts to a state to help examine and assist local human rights mechanisms; providing translations of human rights conventions; and possibly by offering scholarships and seminars, training personnel and judges, and establishing law faculties.

The IGO offers technical cooperation with states that request it or sometimes upon referral when a state is under scrutiny for human rights violations.

Ter (Draft Articles: Bis, Ter, Quater)
[Latin, lit.: third]

1. Draft treaty* article: A Latin numerical adverb used to identify a certain proposed draft article of a proposed treaty*. In the drafting of an international instrument, different parties often will submit various draft articles or alternative wordings for consideration. Each of these drafts is accorded a sequential Latin designation. The second proposed draft is given the designation "bis," meaning the second proposed draft, e.g., "article 5 bis." The next proposed article 5 is designated "ter" (third), and the next is "quater" (fourth), e.g., "article 5 ter," "article 5 *quater*." The drafting states will negotiate and deliberate over which proposal to adopt as the authentic treaty* text. This helps identify the various proposals for reference, correctness, and ease of negotiation.

2. Generally: Ter can also be used generally in other contexts to refer to a third one of something. Example: "Trial Chamber I ter" refers to a third trial court chamber, such as when one chamber has been divided into three separate chambers resulting in the designation of

Trial Chamber I, Trial Chamber I bis, and trial Chamber I ter.

TERMINATION OF TREATY*

The process of states parties to a treaty* voluntarily terminating the legal validity and existence of the treaty* and extinguishing all legal obligations of states parties after termination. Every treaty* can be terminated if the states parties to it so agree and follow the procedure set forth in the treaty*. Some treaties* have a termination clause, which sets forth the procedure for terminating the treaty*. Most human rights treaties* do not include such a clause.

TERMS OF REFERENCE (OF A BODY/ ORGAN/FORUM/OFFICIAL)

The specific written resolutions, statutes, instructions, and legal instruments setting forth the permissible activities and parameters of action of a body, organ, forum, or official. The terms of reference help define what conduct of a human rights body, etc., is lawfully permitted or how a given action should be conducted. It is the reference source to determine whether a body, etc., is competent and authorized to handle certain issues and to perform certain acts and to decide how these should be accomplished. Simply stated, the terms of reference tell us what a body/organ/forum/official is authorized and required to do. Conversely, a body, etc., is not permitted to do anything that is not included within the terms of reference.

TERRITORIAL APPLICATION/ SCOPE (OF TREATY* NORM)

The geographical area in which an international treaty* norm has legal effect. Normally, when a state ratifies* a human rights treaty*, it takes on international legal obligations, which are applicable in all territory under the jurisdiction of the state. Sometimes a state's treaty* obligations may go beyond a state's borders, and sometimes a state can limit the territorial scope, such as only to its metropolitan territory. Sometimes a state can act beyond its borders, a so-called extraterritorial act; such acts can result in a human rights violation by that state.

Example: the territorial application/ scope of the ICCPR would apply not only to the territory of a state party but to any place under the effective control of a state party, such as Guantanamo, Cuba, where POWs are under U.S. detention in 2003.

In Latin this term is often stated as application or scope *ratione loci*.

TERRITORIAL INTEGRITY (PRINCIPLE)

A general principle of international law that provides that a state has the sovereign inherent right to retain and protect all the territory over which it has dominion/sovereignty. UNCH uses this term in article 2(4) where it prohibits "the threat or use of force against the territorial integrity of any state."

It is closely related to, but not the same as, sovereignty. Territorial integrity seeks to protect the physical, geographical, territorial space of the state, which includes airspace and territorial waters.

TERRITORIAL PRINCIPLE (CRIMINAL COMPETENCE/JURISDICTION)

The principle of international criminal law that states that a state can exercise jurisdiction to define and to proscribe as a crime any act that takes place within the territory of the state. The territory of the state usually includes ships at sea under its flag, its aircraft, and diplomatic properties. This is the most accepted and undisputed one of five possible bases for legally permissible criminal law jurisdiction under international law.

Territorial Sovereignty (Principle)

A general principle of international law that describes the authority a state exercises over persons and things found within its geographical territory to the exclusion of all other states' jurisdiction.

Territorial State (ICC Competence/Jurisdiction)

The state in whose territory acts constituting a crime are committed. Every state has, with few exceptions, the right to exercise criminal jurisdiction over acts that take place on its territory.

In the 1998 Rome ICC Statute, jurisdiction of the International Criminal Court exists over crimes that take place on the territory of a state party to that treaty. Any state in which such a crime occurs is called the territorial state. This is found in article 12.2 of the ICC Statute.

Terrorism

A term not defined in international law or politics as of the date of this book, but some states have attempted to define it in national law. There is much disagreement on what constitutes terrorism. The problem with defining terrorism is that it runs up against the political/geopolitical sensitivities of different states or groups. The same violent act can be perceived and described by one person as an act of terrorism but by another person as an act of freedom fighting for independence of a people exercising its human right to self determination. The key element to the concept of terrorism is that the subject acts cause general public terror that makes people feel insecure and in danger for their life or physical well-being.

One reference to terrorism in the UN is that it refers to criminal acts intended or calculated to provoke a state of terror in the general public, a group of persons or particular persons, for political purposes. One U.S. statute defines it as "premeditated, politically motivated violence perpetrated against noncombatant targets" (22 U.S. Code section 2656f). The United States has defined terrorism in section 18 of the U.S. Code as to both domestic and international terrorism as follows:

1. International terrorism means terrorism involving the citizens or territories of more than one country (18 USC section 2656f) and "Activities that (A) involve violent acts or acts dangerous to human life that are a violation of the laws of the United States or of any state, or that would be a criminal violation if committed within the jurisdiction of the United States or of any state; (B) appear to be intended (i) to intimidate or coerce a civilian population; (ii) to influence the policy of a government by intimidation or coercion; or (iii) to affect the conduct of a government by mass destruction, assassination, or kidnapping; and (C) occur primarily outside the territorial jurisdiction of the United States, or transcend national boundaries in terms of the means by which they are accomplished, the persons they appear intended to intimidate or coerce,

or the locale in which their perpetrators operate or seek asylum." (18 USC section 2331)

2. Domestic terrorism means "Activities that (A) involve acts dangerous to human life that are a violation of the criminal laws of the United States or of any state; (B) appear to be intended (i) to intimidate or coerce a civilian population; (ii) to influence the policy of a government by intimidation or coercion; or (iii) to affect the conduct of a government by mass destruction, assassination, or kidnapping; and (C) occur primarily within the territorial jurisdiction of the United States." (18 USC section 2331)

This definition has no legal force outside of the U.S. legal system and is solely a part of its domestic law.

TEXTUAL MANDATE

The specific powers and duties contained within the express wording of a text that establishes an organ, such as a treaty-based supervisory body like the HRC, or an individual mandate, such as a special rapporteur. Textual mandates can be very full and complete and detailed or very limited, affecting the scope of power and activity of the organ or person involved. The textual mandate serves as the basis of all authority to act.

THEMATIC PROCEDURES / REPORTS / MECHANISMS (VS. COUNTRY-SPECIFIC PROCEDURES ETC.)

A term describing an international intergovernmental organization procedure, report, or mechanism for implementing human rights norms that focuses on particular themes and topics and not on an individual state's human rights practice.

Thematic procedures, reports, or mechanisms of IGO bodies, such as the UN Commission on Human Rights, deal, e.g., with subject matters such as religious intolerance, discrimination against women, torture, and indigenous peoples.

Thematic procedures, etc., are contrasted with "country-specific" procedures, etc., which focus on the human rights record or issues of specific states. Thematic reports/procedures/mechanisms usually look at the practice of all states in relation to the thematic subject. Examples of thematic procedures within the UN Commission on Human Rights would be the Special Rapporteur on Torture and the Working Group on Arbitrary Detention.

THIRD GENERATION (HUMAN) RIGHTS (AKA SOLIDARITY RIGHTS)

A term formerly used to describe a class of human rights that are historically newer rights, although the term "generation" does not necessarily connote any chronological difference or hierarchy of human rights. It is simply a political, legal, and conceptual categorization. Civil and political human rights were known as first generation human rights, and economic, social, and cultural rights were known as second generation human rights. All human rights are indivisible, interrelated, and interdependent.

Human rights formerly known as Third Generation rights are also known as "solidarity rights" or "rights of solidarity." These latter terms should not be confused with the so-called "Right to Solidarity," which is itself one of the Third Generation rights. They are complex, ill-defined conceptually and collective. Their very validity as human rights is highly disputed. In theory, they are rights that can only be realized through the concerted and good faith efforts of all actors in the international scene: states, NGOs, individuals, IGOS, and other public and private bodies, that is, the international community as a whole. Their genesis and advancement was rather political and ideological, coming mostly from cold war eastern bloc and third world/developing states.

Most scholars consider these claimed rights to constitute *lex ferenda* at best, and not yet *lex lata*, although some may argue such status for the right to development. Third Generation human rights are said include the following separate rights: right to development, right to peace, right to a clean environment, right to humanitarian assistance, right to a common heritage, and right to solidarity.

Caveat: The idea and use of the term "generation" has come into disuse, and the terms first, second, and third generation should no longer be used to describe human rights because they breed conceptual confusion.

THIRD-PARTY EFFECT (OF NORMATIVE OBLIGATIONS) (AKA HORIZONTAL EFFECT/ HORIZONTALITY/*DRITTWIRKUNG*)

See Horizontal Effect/Horizontality; *Drittwirkung.*

THIRD WORLD

A group of international states known during the Cold War as "nonaligned states," who allied themselves with neither the United States nor the USSR. Most were in Asia, Africa, and Latin America, and most were also developing nations.

THRESHOLD (CLAUSE) (ICC)

A treaty* clause that sets forth the minimum level of seriousness or extent of criminal conduct over which the criminal court/tribunal is competent to exercise jurisdiction and render a decision.

The purpose of a threshold clause is to set a minimum threshold of matters that the court may handle so as to keep it from becoming overburdened from too many cases that are not deemed to be of international concern. In the ICC Statute the preamble states that the court is to exercise jurisdiction "only over the most serious crimes of concern to the international community," and article 1 states that the court may bring persons to justice "for the most serious crimes of international concern." In the ICC Statute certain crimes such as crimes against humanity may have thresholds. For crimes against humanity the threshhold required is either that the attacks against a civilian population be "widespread" or "systematic" before rising to the level of such crimes as come within the ICC's competence. *See* article 7.1, ICC Statute, Appendix C.

Used generally, threshold refers to a certain starting point when something goes into effect, a certain specified level of activity or action, or injury or damage, necessary to engage something else, such as the applicability of certain human rights norms or implementation mechanisms.

TOKYO RULES (UN STANDARD MINIMUM RULES FOR NONCUSTODIAL MEASURES)

A name used to describe a set of proposed specific rules drafted by the UN states to use as basic, minimum, common-denominator standards for the imposition by government authorities (police, etc.) of noncustodial measures in lieu of prison/jail. These were adopted in Tokyo in 1990 and are not legally binding, but states are encouraged to transform them into domestic law.

Tolerance (vs. Intolerance)

The attitude of accepting, bearing, or putting up with the differences of others, such as race, religion, color, political opinion, or ethnic background. Tolerance is accepting others as they are and refraining from any acts of intolerance that communicate to them that their racial, etc., differences are unacceptable. Tolerance is considered a necessary prerequisite for respecting human rights.

Torture

Generally speaking, torture is the purposeful infliction or threat of infliction of severe pain or suffering on a detainee by public officials, or with their complicity or collusion. The UN Convention against Torture and Other Cruel, Inhuman or Degrading Treatment or Punishment (1984) defines torture as

> any act by which severe pain or suffering, whether physical or mental, is intentionally inflicted on a person for such purposes as obtaining from him or a third person information or a confession, punishing him for an act he or a third person has committed or is suspected of having committed, or intimidating or coercing him or a third person, or for any reason based on discrimination of any kind, when such pain or suffering is inflicted by or at the instigation of or with the consent or acquiescence of a public official or

other person acting in an official capacity. It does not include pain or suffering arising only from, inherent in or incidental to lawful sanctions.

This convention definition is the most cited and authoritative definition and is considered binding as a matter of customary international law. The parameters of this norm are complex and controversial. Many national and international judicial and quasi-judicial bodies have decided cases involving torture. Some scholars, such as Nigel Rodley, argue that acts of cruel, inhuman, or degrading treatment or punishment committed by public officials, or with their complicity or collusion, will be elevated to acts constituting torture where such acts are committed for any of the specific purposes set forth in the above definition of torture.

Torture is prohibited under international human rights law and the LOAC, under the UDHR, ICCPR, Torture Convention, ECHR, IACHR, ACHPR, Geneva Conventions of 1949 and P I and II, and as a matter of Customary International Law.

Freedom from torture is an absolute right, is nonderogable, and is a *jus cogens* norm. It is an international crime to commit torture, and those responsible for such acts are subject to universal jurisdiction of all states. It is a crime within the jurisdiction of the ICC.

Totalitarianism

Authoritarian control by the state over individuals and organizations so that all activity is harmonized with the policies and goals of the governing regime. It is characterized by the government's domination of all political, social, and economic activities of a state, i.e., virtually all aspects of life. Usually, a totalitarian regime is an oppressive form of government with a large number of national security, police, and intelligence agents.

TRAFFICKING IN HUMAN BEINGS/PERSONS

The selling and/or transporting of human beings in a way inconsistent with the human dignity of the victims. Trafficking in human beings is a violation of human rights and an exploitation of human beings, and is being increasingly condemned by the international community. In 2000 the UN General Assembly adopted a Convention against Transnational Organized Crime and two optional Protocols. One Protocol concerns trafficking in persons and calls for its criminalization in states parties. That Protocol provided the following definition of trafficking in persons:

> The recruitment, transportation, transfer, harbouring or receipt of persons, by means of the threat or use of force or other forms of coercion, of abduction, of fraud, of deception, of the abuse of power or of a position of vulnerability or of the giving or receiving of payments or benefits to achieve the consent of a person having control over another person, for the purpose of exploitation. Exploitation shall include, at a minimum, the exploitation of the prostitution of others or other forms of sexual exploitation, forced labour or services, slavery or practices similar to slavery, servitude or the removal of organs.

TRANSFORMATION (OF NORMS)

The process of changing (transforming) international law into domestic (national) law via a state's constitutional processes. For example, passage of implementing legislation by the U.S. Congress on a ratified* treaty would constitute the transformation of that treaty's* norms into domestic/municipal U.S. law.

TRANSFORMATIVE HUMAN RIGHTS EDUCATION

Human rights education that has the effect of not only teaching *about* human rights but also *for* human rights, with the ultimate goal of empowering individuals to take action to protect their own human rights and promote their own full human development, and equally to take action to do the same thing in the lives of others. It is education that is not just cognitive, but creates a human rights conscience and consciousness in the learner and the will to act for human rights.

TRANSNATIONAL ACTIVISTS

Human rights activists who are engaged in human rights in more than one state. (*See* Activist, supra.)

TRANSNATIONAL CORPORATION (TNC)

A corporation that engages in business in two or more states in the world. One formerly used the term "multinational corporation" (MNC), but this description is now less seen and used, and TNC is used more in the field of human rights.

Human rights norms normally bind only states, not private corporations. Because TNCs have a powerful influence in the world and in particular states, the international human rights movement is attempting to get TNCs to act in a way consistent with human rights norms. This is so that those working and involved with them will see human rights respected by business, and the state in which they operate may be influenced in a positive way as to human rights compliance. This is done primarily by getting the TNCs to accept to conduct themselves according to a business code of conduct that is consistent with human rights. TNCs are sometimes nonstate actors in international affairs and are subject to certain international laws.

TRANSNATIONAL CRIME

A crime that has one or more of its elements happening in more than one state. A crime involving two or more states. If for example, one were to stand on the border of a state, shoot a gun at, and kill a person in the other state, that would be a transnational crime. The elements of the mental act of trying to shoot or kill someone and the physical act of shooting occur in one state, and the wounding or killing occurs in another state. Some human rights violations involving international criminal responsibility, such as genocide or crimes against humanity, could be transnational in character and engage international criminal responsibility. This concept is important for determining the appropriate jurisdiction for prosecuting the crimes. A crime could be both a transnational and an international crime.

The September 11, 2000, World Trade Center crashes would constitute a transnational crime (a crime against humanity) if they involved elements committed both in a foreign state (e.g., planning, conspiracy) and in the U.S. (carrying out the attack).

TRANSNATIONAL HUMAN RIGHTS NETWORK

A partially autonomous issue-specific political life form, which consists of diverse, overlapping entities of domestic NGOs,

private agencies and foundations, church groups both domestic and international, and agents of state governments. They are connected by shared values, a common discourse, dense exchange of information, and services.

Some have said that the start of the twenty-first century saw the rise of such networks in response to human rights abuses all over the globe.

TRANSNATIONAL HUMAN RIGHTS OBLIGATIONS

The relatively new idea that a state may have responsibility under international human rights law for its actions, which cause effects to persons in the territory of other states. Some scholars have defined it as implying the possibility that states may have legal obligations relating to the human rights effects of their external activities, such as trade, development cooperation, participation in international organizations, and security activities. Generally stated, states have an obligation, a duty, under international law to act in their international operations in a way that people in a foreign state do not suffer as a result of the first state's action.

Although most human rights work involves the human rights activity of a state to people within its own borders, the concept of transnational human rights obligations looks to the human rights effects on persons in the territory of another state. Examples would be the sending by one state of its agents into another state to assassinate someone, or a state causing a massive forced exodus of persons into another state where they are mistreated. This concept focuses on the cross boundary effects of one state's acts but does not necessarily require that agents of the actor state cross into the territory of the state where the victim is deprived of human rights. Many of the issues involved in this concept will involve the direct effects of transnational activity of a state into another state.

TRANSPARENCE / TRANSPARENT (GOVERNMENT)

The quality of a state government that is open to monitoring, scrutiny, and examination in all its activities, subject usually to national security interest so that the governed feel that their government is accessible, accountable, fair, honest, and operating within the rule of law. When a government's operations are characterized by transparence, its faults, such as human rights violations or financial malfeasance, can be detected, brought to public attention, and corrected. Transparence helps to ensure the accountability of those making up the government and of the civil servants and lessens the chance of impunity for persons who commit human rights violations or other wrongful acts.

Transparence is necessary for openness in resolving public issues so as to avoid the people's suspicion and mistrust especially in critical matters affecting the public interest. Transparence usually leads to public confidence, trust, and support of the state system.

Transparence is not just seen as applying only to states. It can also be applied to any social or political system, such as an IGO or an NGO.

TRAVAUX PRÉPARATOIRES (AKA PREPARATORY WORKS / LEGISLATIVE HISTORY / TPS)
[French, lit.: preparatory works]

A French term that is translated in English as "preparatory works" and is some-times referred to as the "legislative history" of a treaty*.

The *Travaux Préparatoires* is the collected written record of the diplomatic work (negotiations) that went into the drafting and establishment (adoption) of a treaty*. Sometimes it is resorted to as an aid in the interpretation of the treaty* text when an issue arises under the instrument. It contains the legislative history, deliberations, and discussions of the negotiating parties during the treaty*-making negotiations.

Sometimes this term is simply referred to as "the *travaux*," or it can be seen in its abbreviated form: TPS.

TREATY* (INTERNATIONAL LEGAL INSTRUMENT)

In a general sense, a treaty* is a negotiated contract, set forth in writing between two or more political authorities (as states or sovereigns), formally signed by representatives, duly authorized, and ratified* by the lawmaking authority of the states.

The Vienna Convention, article 1(a), defines treaty* as "an international agreement concluded between states in written form and governed by international law, whether embodied in a single instrument or in two or more related instruments and whatever its particular designation."

This word "Treaty"* is both the generic word applicable to all types of international legal instruments, i.e., conventions, covenants, pacts, agreements, protocols, and sometimes charters and statutes, and may itself be the title designation of a particular treaty, i.e.: "Treaty of Friendship Commerce and Navigation between State A and State B."

A treaty* is intended to have a legally

obligatory character and effect because it is deemed to be subject to the international law principle of *pacta sunt servanda*, meaning that "agreements must be kept."

Treaty*-Based (Organ/ Body/Procedure/Mechanism) (vs. Non-Treaty-Based/Charter Based Organ, etc.)

A term meaning that the source of the legal authority for the establishment of the body, organ procedure, or mechanism is in a treaty* instrument. A treaty*-based mechanism is often called a "treaty* body." This is distinguished from a "non-treaty-based" organ, etc., which is also known as a "charter-based" organ, etc., because it has been established under a constitution or charter.

The UN Human Rights Committee and the European Court of Human Rights are examples of treaty*-based bodies.

Treaty *Erge Omnes* (Obligation)

An *erge omnes* norm that has its basis in a human rights treaty*. *Erge omnes* is a doctrine of international law, which says that certain norms are binding on all states and are peremptory norms from which no derogation or limitation is permissible. There are two kinds of *erge omnes* norms: customary *erge omnes* and treaty *erge omnes*. Customary *erge omnes* norms bind every state. Genocide is a customary *erge omnes* norm. Every state has a right to scrutinize the action of every other state as to acts of genocide. In treaty *erge omnes* the obligation runs from each state party to every other state party to the treaty*, so that each state party has the right to scrutinize the acts of each other state party as to the norms of that treaty*. For example, for all states that are parties to the Torture Convention there exists a treaty *erge omnes* obligation between and among all states parties, arising from the Convention.

Treaty* (Monitoring/ Supervising) Body

A judicial organ (court/tribunal) or quasi-judicial organ (commission/committee) established by and within a treaty*, under an international intergovernmental organization to supervise and monitor compliance of states parties to the treaty* norms. They work to assure state compliance with the norms by looking for areas and incidents of noncompliance, and they promote the carrying out of implementation measures by states parties, such as through reporting and complaint* systems according to their particular terms of reference. The UN Human Rights Committee, which was established under article 28 of the ICCPR, is an example of a treaty* monitoring/supervising body.

Trial Monitoring/Observation

A type of on-site observation and monitoring of a court trial of political/human rights significance by representatives from other states or NGOs, or even by private parties, in order to ensure respect by the trial forum for internationally recognized rights to a fair and open/public trial by an independent and impartial judiciary.

Usually the out-of-state representatives are lawyers knowledgeable about the international due process/fair trial standards. This process, usually occurring in the presence of expert observers, makes the international community's concern for a fair trial known to the forum and the forum state, thereby making it more likely that the defendant will get a fair trial. The monitoring representatives give the defendant and defense attorney a sense of international support and solidarity and demonstrate the sponsor's concern by sending the monitors.

Strictly speaking, trial observation and monitoring do not have to take place in a foreign state but may take place in the monitor's/observer's own state.

Truth Commission

A body of individuals selected by a government usually from different segments of society to establish a forum to uncover the truth concerning major social turmoil, such as civil war or a violent or oppressive racist regime. The purpose of the commission is to establish exactly what happened during the subject time by answering such questions as who murdered whom and on whose orders, who disappeared, who ordered the disappearance and where is the victim now, who belonged to the death squad, who assassinated the government official, where are the mass graves, who arrested the human rights defenders?

Truth commissions are sometimes used as a post–social trauma mechanism to obtain testimony and evidence from all sides of a situation in order to provide the public with the most comprehensive information regarding what really happened behind the scenes and to which individuals or groups responsibility should be assigned. It is often used when criminal prosecution and civil remedies against all unlawful acts committed during the subject situation are impos-

sible or impractical or otherwise undesirable. Such commissions can be set up either along with or in place of criminal prosecutions. The incentive offered to a wrongdoer to come forward and tell the truth is usually a grant of immunity or amnesty, an offer for forgiveness of the wrongdoing.

The truth commission established in post-apartheid South Africa is a classic example of a fully operating truth commission.

History has born out that such commissions can result in a general sense that justice is being done, which promotes the society's healing through reunification, rebuilding, and moving past traumas, while fully revealing and owning up to what really happened.

Tu Quoque (Criminal Defense)
[Latin, lit.: and you also]

A legal defense used in international war crimes trials under the LOAC. This defense is raised by persons accused of committing war crimes. The defense essentially asserts that the accusing/prosecuting party/state(s) cannot seek to prosecute the accused defendant where the prosecuting party was itself also guilty of committing the same criminal acts during the conflict. The idea is that it is inequitable and unjust to prosecute someone else for the same offenses the accuser committed and for which the accuser is not being prosecuted. This defense was asserted in the Nuremberg Trials. And it was because of this anticipated defense, for example, that the victorious allies did not prosecute the Nazis responsible for the buzz-bombing air attacks on London because the allies had done similar acts to German cities, such as the firebombings in Dresden and Leipzig, and no allied soldiers were being prosecuted for those similar crimes.

Turku Abo Principles (loac)

The name of principles set forth in a document produced by a conference on human rights and humanitarian law applicable in noninternational armed conflicts, especially those conflicts not rising to the level of the Geneva Convention, Common Article 3, or Protocol II. The conference was held at Turku Abo, Finland, in 1990. The document was entitled *Minimum Humanitarian Standards Applicable in Noninternational Conflicts*.

These principles are an expanded codification/amplification of existing and proposed norms to cover a gray area of the loac involving noninternational armed conflict situations. It is a mix of classic peacetime human rights and human rights in international humanitarian law as they apply in armed conflicts.

Tyranny/Tyrant

A type of government in which absolute power is held by a single person, a tyrant, who is unrestrained by law or constitution and who usually rules oppressively, unjustly, and arbitrarily without accountability to anyone and with impunity for his actions.

udhr

An acronym for the Universal Declaration of Human Rights adopted by the United Nations in 1948.

Ultra Vires
[Latin, lit.: beyond [its] powers]

Action in excess of one's lawful powers. If an organ/forum/body/official commits an act that is beyond/outside the specific powers expressed in a charter, constitution, statute, or regulation that specifies its "mandate" or "terms of reference," then such an act is characterized as an ultra vires act.

Actions that are ultra vires are illegal or do not fall lawfully within the terms of reference or mandate because they are done without any legal authority. Such acts can be nullified but may also, in some instances, be ratified* by the parent body/organization so as to legitimize them.

Unalienable Rights
(aka Inalienable Rights)

Describes rights that, at least in theory, cannot be voluntarily or involuntarily transferred, surrendered, or waived by the holder/bearer of the rights and cannot be taken away or annulled by another person or group or even by the state. This is so because human rights are natural, intrinsic attributes of the human personality. They inhere in human beings because human beings possess inherent human dignity, which can never be lost or taken away.

"Unalienable" is the adjective used in the famous American Declaration of Independence of July 4, 1776 ("and endowed with certain unalienable rights"). The term now most commonly used is "Inalienable Rights" (*see* supra). Both terms have the same meaning.

un Charter (unch)

The un Charter (unch) is the international legal instrument (treaty*) adopted in San Francisco on June 26, 1945, that established, defined, and provided the mandate of the United Nations, an international intergovernmental organization.

This instrument sets forth its purposes, goals, functions, organs, and responsibilities. All member states of the UN have become member states by ratifying* the charter and are legally bound by its provisions, including those relating to human rights.

UNDERSTANDING
(TREATY*, INSTRUMENT OF)
(AKA INTERPRETATION)

An international legal instrument submitted by a state at the time of ratification* of a treaty*, wherein the state party expresses how it interprets or understands a particular article, clause, or term in a treaty*. This sometimes happens when a state feels the article, etc., is ambiguous or vague or where it needs to be understood in light of the state party's constitution or high court decisions. It is also called an "instrument of interpretation," but the official term is an "instrument of understanding." Sometimes referred to simply as a state party's "Understanding."

Often an instrument of understanding is submitted along with the state's "Reservations" and "Declarations," if any (*see* supra). These are abbreviated as RDUS.

UNDERTAKE (TREATY* OBLIGATIONS)

A verb used in human rights treaty* instruments as the operative word of the legal obligation that a state party accepts upon ratification*. In essence, it means that the state engages itself to respect and to take steps to guarantee the substantive rights in the treaty*, that it takes upon itself solemnly or expressly to place itself under legal obligation to perform or execute, to covenant, and to assume responsibility for compliance with the instru-

ment. Usually the term is found shortly after the preamble. *See* ICCPR, article 2.1.

UNILATERAL INTERVENTION

The act of one state, without prior UN authorization, to forcibly intervene in the internal affairs, or on the territory of another state to stop breaches of the peace, threats to the peace, or acts of military aggression, or for any other reason. This is contrasted with a multilateral or collective intervention, which is one authorized by the Security Council under Chapter VII.

UNILATERALISM (VS. MULTILATERALISM)

The conduct of a single state acting in the international arena all by itself and on its own initiative, largely without concern for the position of other states. There exists an international community of states that has established international institutions for the purpose of concerted multilateral action to deal with issues, conflicts, and problems at the international level. The intent of the international community is that collective action, not self help, is the best way to resolve conflicts and that unilateral action is unwise and subject to abuse and danger.

The charge of unilateralism is most often raised against the U.S. for its taking actions on its own outside of the United Nations collective process. The multilateral approach is the international norm.

UNIPOLAR MOMENT

In the context of this post Cold War era, this term refers to the fact that the U.S. has emerged as the sole true global super power, which characterizes and affects all international relations. The U.S. is unrivaled in many ways, particularly as to the hard power of military might and economic power of its national economy, and the soft power of its human rights history and activity. This has led to a perceived U.S. attitude and action characterized as unilateralist or exceptionalist. The U.S. has the unrivaled power to accomplish its national and international political objectives, including human rights at home or abroad thanks to this power arising from this so-called unipolar moment.

Universal (Human Rights)

Generally, "Universal" means applicable everywhere in the world and applicable to all persons. Human rights are universal attributes of the human personality. Universal means that all human beings are the holders or bearers of these rights. They are held by all citizens of all states and stateless persons.

The state of a characteristic, such as human dignity, that exists throughout the whole world with little or no variation.

Universal Declaration of Human Rights (udhr)

The fountainhead document of international human rights adopted by the resolution of the United Nations on December 10, 1948. It set forth for the first time a list of specific, substantive human rights recognized by most states. Initially adopted as a declaration of human rights principles, it was not intended to be a legally binding instrument. However, most scholars say that over the past fifty years it has been referred to and followed by the bulk of state practice so that it has now become binding ("ripened" or "crystallized") as a matter of customary inter-

national law and is therefore binding upon all states. Some say that only some of its substantive rights (the "hard core" rights) are binding on that basis, e.g., regarding torture, slavery, right to life.

Universality (of Human Rights) (vs. Cultural Relativism)

A doctrine/theory of human rights that says that all human rights are held by all persons in all states and societies regardless of race, color, nationality, religion, language, or ethnic traits and must be applied and interpreted in the same way in all states and regions, regardless of the legal system or political ideology.

The doctrine of universality is opposed by those who believe in "Cultural Relativism," a doctrine that claims that human rights are applied and interpreted differently in different societies based on various "Particularities" or "Specificities," such as race, religion, and culture.

The universality doctrine is now the predominantly accepted view.

Universalization of Human Rights

The idea and process of human rights coming to be considered applicable to all human beings of every country and nation in all political societies.

Universal Jurisdiction (International Criminal Law) (Principle)

A term describing the domestic (national) legal power (competence) of courts in every state in the world to exercise jurisdiction to prosecute an alleged perpetrator of certain international crimes. Some international crimes, such as genocide, war crimes, and torture, allow for universal jurisdiction of all states because these crimes are considered to be committed against the whole human race. Therefore, every state has the right to prosecute and punish those who commit these international crimes, and universal jurisdiction encourages and facilitates this universal goal.

Universal Suffrage

The human right of every adult citizen to vote for the principal elective institutions and agents of government. The right to vote is a basic political human right and a requisite to a participatory democracy. States have an obligation to allow every eligible member of society to vote and to make the voting process accessible to the electorate.

There is no human right of noncitizens to vote in the elections of another state, although a state or political subdivision of a state may choose to allow voting by noncitizen resident members of that society. In a human rights culture all members of a society should have a meaningful say in the shaping and direction of the government.

Unlawful Combatant (aka Illegal Combatant or Unprivileged Combatant / Belligerent) (loac)

An outdated term meant to describe the legal status of a person engaged in armed conflict but who does not qualify as a combatant entitled to pow status if captured. This term is not accepted as legitimate under the loac. It is most commonly known and used in the U.S., particularly as applied to the Taliban/Al-Qaeda detainees held in Guantanamo, Cuba and intended to mean that they have no legal protection under the Third Geneva Convention of 1949 and can be treated as common criminals. This basically denies such detainees most legal rights and any access to courts to determine the legality of detention or conditions of detention.

This position, and the use of the term unlawful or illegal combatant, is not accepted by the icrc, which supervises compliance and development of international humanitarian law. Under the loac there are only combatants and noncombatants, also called civilians. There is no such person as an unlawful or illegal combatant. There are, however, a couple of types of persons who would otherwise be lawful combatants but who are denied combatant status and protection, such as spies, saboteurs, and mercenaries.

The loac creates a legal presumption that when there is a question as to the legal status of a person as to being a combatant or noncombatant, the person is presumed to be a combatant and subject to loac as a pow if captured, and that where any uncertainty exists about one's status this should be determined by a competent court, which presumes access by the detainee to a court to seek a determination of such status. Treating such a person as an unlawful combatant and depriving him of his rights as a pow is a violation of his human rights and a breach of humanitarian law. Human rights applies to military persons as well to civilians, although with some differences inherent in their status and occupation. *See also* Illegal Combatant, supra.

Unnecessary Suffering (Principle) (loac)

A principle found in international humanitarian law to describe a belligerent's infliction of physical or mental suffering to an extent that exceeds what was necessary to neutralize an adversary, regardless of the weapons used or tactics employed. It is prohibited to use methods or means in armed conflict that would cause unnecessary suffering, which is most often done to terrorize an adversary, and is not a matter of military necessity. An example would be the indiscriminate use of napalm or dumdum bullets. It is a principle of humanity under humanitarian law. It is closely related to "Superfluous Injury" (*see* supra).

UNPRIVILEGED BELLIGERENT/ COMBATANT (AKA ILLEGAL COMBATANT/UNLAWFUL COMBATANT)

See Illegal Combatant or Unlawful Combatant, supra.

URGENT ACTION

A process or procedure for responding to human rights violations as immediately as possible where the nature of the violations is such that grave or irreparable harm is imminent and only urgent action can prevent or mitigate the violation. Examples where such urgent action would be warranted would be an imminent extra-judicial execution, a forced disappearance, or an imminent deportation or expulsion from a state to a place where serious harm will occur, or fear of imminent torture of a prisoner.

Such term is used by certain human rights organizations such as Amnesty International, which seeks to mobilize immediate and expedient activist activity to incite the international community to take action to resolve the problem.

Such term is also used to describe procedures within the UN extra-conventional mechanisms, where a communication to one of these mechanisms contains information that a serious human rights violation is about to be committed. In such cases the particular mechanism, for example, the Working Group on Enforced or Involuntary Disappearances, can take urgent action, for example, by immediately contacting (e.g., fax or telegram) the government concerned and asking for it to stop the subject action and ensure the protection of the human rights of the victim. This can also be done by some special rapporteurs who receive information of such imminent violation, if within the scope of their terms of reference mandate. Such urgent actions have a preventative character. The criteria for such interventions vary from one mandate to another and are described in the methods of work of the respective mechanisms.

USAGE (CUSTOMARY INTERNATIONAL LAW)

In international law it refers to the consistent, recurring practice of states in a certain matter, over the course of time, indicating the acceptable and expected conduct of states. Usage is one of two requisite elements for the creation of a norm of customary international law. It is the objective element. The other element is the subjective element, the existence of *opinio juris*. *See* Customary International Law, supra.

UTILITY (PRINCIPLE OF)

A principle that approves or disapproves of every human action whatsoever, according to the tendency that it appears to have to augment or diminish the happiness of the party whose interest is in question; or to promote or oppose that happiness. This principle was espoused by philosophers such as Jeremy Bentham in the late 1700s as part of the philosophy of utilitarianism.

VEL NON
[Latin, lit.: or not]

A Latin term that is used most often in legal language to mean "whether or not" something is legally or factually so. Example: "The court must first determine the issue of the complainant's standing, *vel non*"—meaning whether the complainant has or does not have standing (the legal right/capacity) to file the complaint*.

VICTIM (OF A VIOLATION)

A person or group that has been harmed by the state's violation of a human rights norm. Normally, only "victims" of a violation have standing to file formal written complaints* against a state in a human rights forum. Victims can be direct or indirect, such as a person summarily executed or the murder of that person's spouse. Some complaint* systems permit nonvictims, such as NGOs, to file complaints*.

VIENNA CONVENTION ON CONSULAR RELATIONS (UN 1963)

A multilateral international treaty setting forth the legal rights of states in the realm of consular affairs, which is the relation of a state's government to its citizens found in other states. Article 36 of this convention requires a state to expressly notify an arrested alien that he has the right to contact his own state's consulate to seek its assistance with regard to any

criminal proceedings, so as to assure that his due process-fair trial rights are protected in the foreign forum.

Many issues involving foreign nationals on death row who were not informed of their consular contact rights under this convention have arisen regarding the U.S.

VIENNA CONVENTION ON THE LAW OF TREATIES (UN1969) (AKA "THE VIENNA CONVENTION"/ "THE TREATY ON TREATIES")

A 1969 UN treaty that entered into force in 1980, setting forth norms about treaty* making, treaty* obligations, and treaty* interpretation. It is also called the "Treaty on Treaties" and often is simply referred to as the Vienna Convention. It is the treaty most resorted to in determining international legal obligations in treaties* and for the rules of application and interpretation of treaty* texts. This treaty is now largely accepted as declaratory of customary international law and thus is binding upon all states, whether or not they are states parties to the Vienna Convention of 1969 itself. Caveat: Do not confuse this 1969 Vienna Convention, which is a treaty, with the Vienna Declaration and Programme of Action (UN 1993; *see* infra), which is not a treaty.

VIENNA DECLARATION AND PROGRAMME OF ACTION (UN 1993)

The concluding declaration of the member states of the United Nations present at the 1993 UN Vienna World Conference on Human Rights. The Declaration and Programme of Action was drafted as the articulation of the consensus of the states resulting from their "Stocktaking" of UN human rights activity, with a view toward rationalizing all UN procedures/mechanisms for maximum efficiency and cost effectiveness. The declaration also includes the consensus on certain key human right issues, such as "Universality" of human rights; it set the direction and tone of subsequent UN human rights activity for years to come.

VIEWS (HRC)

The term used to describe the decisions of the UN Human Rights Committee arising from complaints (communications) filed by individuals or states against a state alleged to have violated the ICCPR. Because the HRC is a quasi-judicial body, its decisions cannot be called judgments. (*See* ICCPR, article 42.) The term "views" was chosen by the drafters of the ICCPR because certain states were worried about the legal affect and status of the results of HRC deliberations and decisions on the merits of complaints. Most scholars hold that views are not legally binding even as to the parties to the dispute, including the subject respondent state.

Although the term "views" does not even sound legally binding, the written views of the HRC do follow a judicial pattern and are effectively decisions on the merits. They have come to be generally respected and followed by the offending state. These views include a determination of the admissibility of the communication and "considerations" upon which the Committee based its decision, and the views of the HRC on the obligation of a violating state in light of the HRC's findings. The compilation of its "views" is known as the jurisprudence of the HRC.

VIOLATION (OF A NORM/TREATY*)

The failure of a state to act in a manner consistent with legally binding human rights obligations. The UN Training Manual on Human Rights Monitoring states that human rights violations

> include governmental transgressions of the rights guaranteed by national, regional and international human rights law and acts and omissions directly attributable to the state involving failure to implement legal obligations derived from human rights standards. Violations occur when a law, policy or practice deliberately contravenes or ignores obligations held by the state concerned or when the state fails to achieve a required standard of conduct or result.

Human rights are legal rights found primarily in international treaties* and in customary international law. These rights create legal norms, or standards of conduct of government, which a state must meet in order to respect human rights and fulfill its legal obligations. There are four obligations upon states regarding human rights: respect, protect, ensure, and fulfill. Failure to fulfill any of these constitutes a violation of human rights.

A violation gives rise to domestic or international remedies for such state conduct. The result of violations is that certain legal measures can and should be taken, usually as set forth in a human rights treaty*, to stop and to redress the violations. These measures are normally taken before courts, commissions, committees, and other permanent or ad hoc bodies set up for that purpose. Human rights violations are acts of a state that violate the human dignity of an individual subject to its jurisdiction. They are the legitimate concern of all people of all states.

It is used somewhat interchangeably with the term "breach" of an obligation.

Violence against Women

Any act of gender-based violence that results in, or is likely to result in, physical, sexual, or psychological harm or suffering to women, including threats of such acts, coercion, or arbitrary deprivation of liberty, whether occurring in public or in a woman's private life.

Vis-à-Vis
[French, lit.: face to face]

A French phrase meaning "as it relates to," "in relation to," "as regards," or "toward." Example: "Human rights are rights held by individuals vis-à-vis the state"; or "children have certain rights vis-à-vis their parents."

Void ab Initio
[Latin, lit.: empty/invalid from the beginning]

A Latin legal expression that means that a legal act such as a law, international instrument, or contractual agreement was invalid from the very moment it was made (*ab initio*), because of an underlying rule that invalidated it. This is sometimes used in reference to peremptory norms of international law and their legal effect on national laws or on other international agreements. Generally speaking, where a peremptory norm of international law exists, for example, the prohibition against torture, any international

agreement between states that said that torture would be legal would be an agreement deemed *void ab initio*. This is to say that at the very moment it was entered into, it was legally null and void because no such agreement permitting torture is legally permissible under international law.

No state may enter into any agreement with any other state or conclude any multilateral treaty that contravenes peremptory human rights norms, such as slavery, genocide, and torture. Such agreements would be *void ab initio* under international law. *See* the Vienna Convention on the Law of Treaties, article 53.

Voluntary Trust (un)

A trust fund established by the un to receive voluntary contributions of money from anyone, such as an ngo, community group, corporation, private group of individuals, or an individual interested in advancing and supporting a program/project that cannot be funded under the regular budget or for supplementing an existing budgetary allocation.

War (loac) (State of)

A formal legal state or condition of armed hostilities between states that is governed by the international laws of war, the "Law of Armed Conflict," such as the 1899 and 1907 Hague Rules and the four gcs of 1949. While a "state of war"—the legal status of a relationship between two or more states—is usually accompanied by acts of armed violence, such violence may take place either before or after the declaration of war is made. War can exist without any violent hostilities taking

274 · *Definitions of Terms*

place. War is a legal status, not the fact of armed violence.

The more commonly used term today is "Armed Conflict," a term that includes not only international but noninternational armed conflicts as well.

War Crimes (loac)

These are criminal offenses against the law(s) of war, now more commonly called the "Law of Armed Conflict," that are set forth within the particular body of international law known as "Humanitarian Law" (known in Latin as the *jus in bello*). These are crimes in violation of international law committed by individuals, military or civilian, during an armed conflict and that involve individual criminal responsibility and universal jurisdiction.

War crimes can be based on Humanitarian Law as found both in treaty* law, such as the grave breaches of the four GCs of 1949 and P I of 1977, and in customary international law, known as the "Laws and Customs of War," as found in Hague Law and most particularly in the Hague IV Regulations of 1907. The "Laws and Customs of War" were later set forth in the Nuremberg Charter, which is considered declaratory of customary international law.

War crimes are now one of the international crimes within the inherent/automatic jurisdiction of the International Criminal Court.

In addition to war crimes created by grave breaches of the four GCs (*see* GC I, article 50; GC II, article 51; GC III, article 130; GC IV, article 147; P I, article 85), some of the acts that would constitute war crimes include murder, torture, physical mutilation, medical experimentation, inhumane treatment of civilians or POWs, taking hostages, rape, plunder of public or private property, wanton destruction of property not justified by military necessity, and deportation.

Classically, war crimes applied only in international armed conflicts. Now it is said that war crimes can occur in noninternational armed conflicts by virtue of Common Article 3 of the four GCs, P II, and the extension of the Laws and Customs of War, i.e., as a matter of customary international law.

Weak Cultural Relativism

The concept that holds that culture may be an important source of the validity of a moral right or rule.

Weapons of Mass Destruction (wmd) (loac)

Weapons that by their very nature cause widespread and indiscriminate damage and loss of life, such as nuclear bombs, and chemical and biological weapons. These are also known as NBC weapons (nuclear, biological, chemical).

Military weapons must be designed to be able to be directed only at military persons and objects and to not cause collateral damage to civilians and civilian objects The LOAC requires that states use weapons of such quality and in such a way to prevent disproportionate collateral damage. "All-out war," wherein a belligerent state attempts to wipe out all parts of an enemy state, military and civilian, is no longer legally permissible under international law. Weapons of mass destruction have the likely result of not being able to cause legally permissible damage to an enemy. This is because, by their very nature, their impact is large scale and indiscriminate. They cannot be targeted only against enemy military combatants and military objects. As such, weapons of mass destruction may, and in most situations would, violate the LOAC and Human Rights Law, depending on their use. They are subject to the LOAC principle that parties to an armed conflict do not have unlimited choice of the methods and means of combat.

The International Court of Justice in a 1996 advisory opinion ruled that the use of nuclear weapons would only possibly be legal under international law if they were absolutely necessary to preserve the very existence of a state and there were absolutely no other means of protecting the state's existence, and that, even then, they would be subject to international human rights and humanitarian law norms.

In the international arena weapons of mass destruction (WMDs) are dealt with largely under the rubric of, and in the international institutions involved with, the "law of disarmament." This is because certain major states, particularly those possessing such weapons, have not allowed them to be governed solely under the LOAC and Human Rights Law where their use would likely be prohibited per se and *in toto*.

WELTANSCHAUUNG
[German, lit.: a worldview]

A worldview or reason based on one's perception of how the world works and what is true. A worldview is most often the basis of a person, group, or state's policy and action, including as to respect for human rights and fundamental freedoms.

WIDESPREAD ATTACKS / VIOLATIONS

Human rights violations that occur regularly and broadly against many people in a state, indicating an intentional, concerted planned action to commit such acts. The concept of widespread attacks against a civilian population constituting a crime against humanity is found in international criminal law. The usual legal threshold for atrocious acts against a civilian population to rise to the level of a crime against humanity is that the acts must be widespread and systematic, not just isolated incidents. This concept is included in the definition of crimes against humanity in the ICC Statute, article 7.1. Under the ICC Statute such crime need only meet the threshold of either a widespread *or* systematic attack to constitute a crime against humanity.

Customary international law has defined "widespread" as massive, frequent, large-scale action, carried out collectively with considerable seriousness and directed against a multitude of victims.

The idea is that only crimes that endanger the peace and stability of the international community or shock the conscience of mankind, by their magnitude and savagery or by their large number, warrant intervention by states other than the one on whose territory the act is committed. When they do, they rise to the level of international crimes such as crimes against humanity.

WOMEN'S (HUMAN) RIGHTS

A term referring to all human rights either directly related to, or related as applied to, the female gender, such as gender-based discrimination, rape, reproduction, economic rights, etc. The locus classicus of women's rights is the UN Convention on the Elimination of Discrimination against Women (1979).

WORKING GROUP

A group of persons chosen and mandated by an organization to deal with a specific limited matter. Often they are chosen from among the members of the principal organization as a subgroup that usually meets periodically between sessions of the principle organization. The group can address human rights matters as mandated by the organization, e.g., specific issues in certain states, themes such as disappearances, or the admissibility of written complaints* received by the organization. Example: The UN Working Group on Enforced Disappearances, which is under the Commission on Human Rights.

WORKING LANGUAGES

The different particular language or languages used officially at an international conference, meeting, or session, or in a draft text. Many meetings of international or regional, intergovernmental organizations are given using only a few different languages in which to conduct their business. Such events cannot practically allow every language to be used, largely due to the cost and time involved. The working languages are selected to make the work go more efficiently.

Very often in the world of human rights, one finds that the conferences, sessions, meetings, and official documents are in the specified working languages. Usually, the working languages at the global level are French and English. There may, and most often are, simultaneous translations going on in many languages during the actual conferences, sessions, or meetings, so that those involved who do not speak one of the working languages can understand what is going on.

WORLD TRADE ORGANIZATION (WTO)

The member driven international treaty system that is successor to the GATT Agreement process, dealing with international trade, particularly tariff barriers. Because the WTO activities were perceived by the international human rights movement, especially certain human rights NGOs, as having a negative impact on human rights, particularly in developing states, there has been a lot of protest and political activity to get the WTO states to become more human rights sensitive.

WORLDVIEW

A set of beliefs and opinions regarding the important issues of life. One's worldview determines one's responses to and decisions regarding the various ethical and moral questions encountered in everyday living. A worldview is sometimes referred to as a "philosophy of life."

The distinguishing characteristic between human beings and animals is the ability to process rational thought and view the world as a whole and develop a sense of how everything works. Using that ability well is the key to living a fruitful personal life as well as functioning positively in society at large. A person's worldview is the combination of beliefs regarding life's most serious and basic questions. These questions include: Where do I come from (e.g., Is there a creator/God and if so, in what form?), or am I part of a random evolutionary process? What is my purpose in life? How do

I respond to other people, and do I owe anything to my fellow human beings? How should society be run? Is there such a thing as absolute right and wrong, or is all truth relative?

The history of the world includes the process of people forming their opinions on these various questions and manifesting them in their lifestyles. One's worldview can be expressed in various theistic belief systems, such as Islam, Christianity, Judaism, and Hinduism. A worldview can also be based on various nontheistic systems, such as those embodied in existentialism, nihilism, humanism, and atheism. A society's worldview will affect its perception, interpretation, and application of human rights norms.

XENOPHOBIA
[Greek, lit.: fear of foreigners]

The fear of foreigners or persons from other countries. This fear often comes from the existing population's belief that the foreigners will harm the state, culture, or dominant ethnic group through criminal actions; by taking away jobs; by trying to change the culture, language, or political structure of the society; or by becoming an economic burden on the state.

Xenophobia is an attitude inconsistent with respect for the human dignity and equality of every human being, and all states are under an obligation to eradicate it because history has shown that, if left unchallenged, it can lead to intolerance, discrimination, marginalization, violence, and even armed conflict against the foreigners.

ZEITGEIST
[German, lit.: the spirit of the times]

The prevailing, acceptable idea or attitude of the present time. The common moral intuition of peoples in general, at a given time.

THE FOLLOWING are the substantive human rights that you hold, which are found in the first three of the four following international human rights instruments that comprise the *International Bill of Rights*:
- Universal Declaration of Human Rights (UDHR)
- International Covenant on Economic, Social and Cultural Rights (ICESCR)
- International Covenant on Civil and Political Rights (ICCPR)
- Optional Protocol to the International Covenant on Civil and Political Rights (ICCPR-OP)

Some sources include the Second Optional Protocol to the ICCPR, abolishing the death penalty, as one of the human rights instruments that form the *International Bill of Rights*. Because this is not generally accepted, this instrument will not be reflected in the following list of human rights. These rights have been transposed by the present writer into second person declarative sentences so as to reinforce the reader's sense of ownership of these human rights.

SUBSTANTIVE RIGHTS

You have the right to the exercise of all the following rights without discrimination based on your race, religion, color, sex, language, political or other opinion, national or social origin, property, birth, or other status.

You have the right to life.

You have the right to liberty and security of person.

You have the right to be free from slavery and forced labor.

You have the right to be free from torture, cruel, inhuman, or degrading treatment or punishment.

You have the right to recognition as a legal person before the law.

You have the right to equal protection (equality) of the law.

You have the right to access to effective domestic legal remedies for human rights violations.

You have the right to be free from arbitrary arrest or detention.

You have the right to a fair public hearing/trial before a competent, independent, impartial judiciary.

You have the right to be presumed innocent against criminal charges and to all procedural due process rights.

You have the right to be free from retroactive (*ex post facto*) criminal laws and from double jeopardy.

You have the right, if you are a detained person, to be treated with humanity (humanely) and respect for your human dignity.

You have the right to be free from interference with privacy, home, and family.

You have the right to be free from imprisonment for the inability to pay debts.

You have the right to freedom of movement, choice of residence, and to leave a country.

You have the right to seek asylum from persecution.

You have the right to have a nationality.

You have the right to own property.

You have the right, as a man and a woman of marriageable age, to marry and have (found) a family.

You have the right, if you are in motherhood or a childhood, to special protection.

You have the right, if you are an alien, to freedom from arbitrary expulsion from a country.

You have the right to freedom of thought, conscience, and religion.

You have the right to freedom of expression, opinion, and the press.

You have the right to freedom from propaganda advocating war or inciting national, racial, or religious hatred.

You have the right to free peaceful assembly and association.

You have the right to participate in the political life of the society.

You have the right, if you are a member of an ethnic, religious, or linguistic minority, to enjoy your own culture, use your own language, and practice your own religion.

You have the right to an adequate standard of living, including housing, clothing, and food.

You have the right to the highest attainable standard of physical and mental health.

You have the right to an education.

You have the right to social security.

You have the right to work, under just and favorable conditions.

You have the right to form and participate in trade unions.

You have the right to participate in the cultural life of your society.

You have the right to enjoy the benefits of scientific progress.

You have the collective right as "peoples" to self-determination (to determine your own political status; pursue economic and cultural development; and use your own natural wealth and resources).

You have the right to a social and international order necessary to allow you to realize these rights.

You have the right to adequate rest and leisure.

(In situations of armed conflict, you would have legal protection under human rights law and also under international humanitarian law.)

1. Universal Declaration of Human Rights; (UN 1948)
2. International Covenant on Civil and Political Rights (UN 1966)
3. First Optional Protocol to the International Covenant on Civil and Political Rights (UN 1966)
4. Second Optional Protocol to the International Covenant on Civil and Political Rights (UN 1989) [1]
5. International Covenant on Economic, Social and Cultural Rights (UN 1966)
(The full text of these and many other human rights instruments can be found at the following electronic address: www.umn.edu/humanrts and www.un.org/rights, and in the reference texts cited in the Bibliography)

1. *UNIVERSAL DECLARATION OF HUMAN RIGHTS*
GA RES. 217A (III), UN DOC A/810 AT 71 (1948).

PREAMBLE

Whereas recognition of the inherent dignity and of the equal and inalienable rights of all members of the human family is the foundation of freedom, justice and peace in the world,

Whereas disregard and contempt for human rights have resulted in barbarous acts which have outraged the conscience of mankind, and the advent of a world in which human beings shall enjoy freedom of speech and belief and freedom from fear and want has been proclaimed as the highest aspiration of the common people,

Whereas it is essential, if man is not to be compelled to have recourse, as a last resort, to rebellion against tyranny and oppression, that human rights should be protected by the rule of law,

---

[1] Some authorities do not accept the Second Optional Protocol to the ICCPR, on abolition of the death penalty, as part of the official canon of the International Bill of Rights. The present author does, and so has added this Second Protocol to the International Bill of Rights.

Whereas it is essential to promote the development of friendly relations between nations,

Whereas the peoples of the United Nations have in the Charter reaffirmed their faith in fundamental human rights, in the dignity and worth of the human person and in the equal rights of men and women and have determined to promote social progress and better standards of life in larger freedom,

Whereas Member States have pledged themselves to achieve, in co-operation with the United Nations, the promotion of universal respect for and observance of human rights and fundamental freedoms,

Whereas a common understanding of these rights and freedoms is of the greatest importance for the full realization of this pledge,

Now therefore,

The General Assembly Proclaims this Universal Declaration of Human Rights as a common standard of achievement for all peoples and all nations, to the end that every individual and every organ society, keeping this Declaration constantly in mind, shall strive by teaching and education to promoted respect for these rights and freedoms and by progressive measures, national and international, to secure their universal and effective recognition and observance, both among the peoples of Member States themselves and among the peoples of territories under their jurisdiction.

ARTICLE 1

All human beings are born free and equal in dignity and rights. They are endowed with reason and conscience and should act towards one another in a spirit of brotherhood.

ARTICLE 2

Everyone is entitled to all the rights and freedoms set forth in this Declaration, without distinction of any kind, such as race, colour, sex, language, religion, political or other opinion, national or social origin, property, birth, or other status. Furthermore, no distinction shall be made on the basis of the political, jurisdictional or international status of the country or territory to which a person belongs, whether it be independent, trust, non-self-governing or under any other limitation of sovereignty.

ARTICLE 3

Everyone has the right to life, liberty and the security of person.

ARTICLE 4

No one shall be held in slavery or servitude; slavery and the slave trade shall be prohibited in all their forms.

ARTICLE 5

No one shall be subjected to torture or to cruel, inhuman or degrading treatment or punishment.

ARTICLE 6

Everyone has the right to recognition everywhere as a person before the law.

ARTICLE 7

All are equal before the law and are entitled without any discrimination to equal protection against any discrimination in violation of this Declaration and against any incitement to such discrimination.

ARTICLE 8

Everyone has the right to an effective remedy by the competent national tribunals for acts violating the fundamental rights granted him by the constitution or by law.

ARTICLE 9

No one shall be subjected to arbitrary arrest, detention or exile.

ARTICLE 10

Everyone is entitled in full equality to a fair and public hearing by an independent and impartial tribunal, in the determination of his rights and obligations and of any criminal charge against him.

ARTICLE 11

1. Everyone charged with a penal offence has the right to be presumed innocent until proved guilty according to law in a public trial at which he has had all the guarantees necessary for his defense.
2. No one shall be held guilty of any penal offence on account of any act or omission which did not constitute a penal offence, under national or international law, at the time when it was committed. Nor shall a heavier penalty be imposed than the one that was applicable at the time the penal offence was committed.

ARTICLE 12

No one shall be subjected to arbitrary interference which his privacy, family, home or correspondence, nor to attacks upon his honour and reputation. Everyone has the right to the protection of the law against such interference or attacks.

ARTICLE 13

1. Everyone has the right to freedom of movement and residence within the borders of each State.
2. Everyone has the right to leave any country, including his own, and to return to his country.

ARTICLE 14

1. Everyone has the right to seek and to enjoy in other countries asylum from persecution.
2. This right may not be invoked in the case of prosecutions genuinely arising from non-political crimes or from acts contrary to the purposes and principles of the United Nations.

ARTICLE 15

1. Everyone has the right to a nationality.
2. No one shall be arbitrarily deprived of his nationality nor denied the right to change his nationality.

ARTICLE 16

1. Men and women of full age, without any limitation due to race, nationality or religion, have the right to marry and to found a family. They are entitled to equal rights as to marriage, during marriage and at its dissolution.
2. Marriage shall be entered into only with the free and full consent of the intending spouses.
3. The family is the natural and fundamental group unit of society and is entitled to protection by society and the State.

ARTICLE 17

1. Everyone has the right to own property alone as well as in association with others.
2. No one shall be arbitrarily deprived of his property.

ARTICLE 18

Everyone has the right to freedom of thought, conscience and religion; this right includes freedom to change his religion or belief, and freedom, either alone or in community with others and in public or private, to manifest his religion or belief in teaching, practice, worship and observance.

ARTICLE 19

Everyone has the right to freedom of opinion and expression; this right includes freedom to hold opinions without interference and to seek, receive and impart information and ideas through any media and regardless of frontiers.

ARTICLE 20

1. Everyone has the right to freedom of peaceful assembly and association.
2. No one may be compelled to belong to an association.

ARTICLE 21

1. Everyone has the right to take part in the government of his country, directly or through freely chosen representatives.
2. Everyone has the right of equal access to public service in his country.
3. The will of the people shall be the basis of the authority of government; this will shall be expressed in periodic and genuine elections which shall be by universal and equal suffrage and shall be held by secret vote or by equivalent free voting procedures.

ARTICLE 22

Everyone, as a member of society, has the right to social security and is entitled to realization, through national effort and international co-operation and in accordance with the organization and resources of each State, of the economic, social and cultural rights indispensable for his dignity and the free development of his personality.

ARTICLE 23

1. Everyone has the right to work, to free choice of employment, to just and favorable conditions of work and to protection against unemployment.
2. Everyone without any discrimination, has the right to equal pay for equal work.
3. Everyone who works has the right to just and favorable remuneration ensuring for himself and his family an existence worthy of human dignity, and supplement if necessary, by other means of social protection.
4. Everyone has the right to form and to join trade unions for the protection of his interests.

ARTICLE 24

Everyone has the right to rest and leisure, including reasonable limitation of working hours and periodic holidays with pay.

ARTICLE 25

1. Everyone has the right to a standard of living adequate for the health and well-being of himself and of his family, including food, clothing, housing and medical care and necessary social services, and the right to security in the event of unemployment, sickness, disability, widowhood, old age or other lack of livelihood in circumstances beyond his control.
2. Motherhood and childhood are entitled to special care and assistance. All children, whether born in or out of wedlock, shall enjoy the same social protection.

ARTICLE 26

1. Everyone has the right to education. Education shall be free at least in the elementary and fundamental stages. Elementary education shall be compulsory. Techni-

cal and professional education shall be made generally available and higher education shall be equally accessible to all on the basis of merit.

2. Education shall be directed to the full development of the human personality and to the strengthening of respect for human rights and fundamental freedoms. It shall promote understanding, tolerance and friendship among all nations, racial or religious groups, and shall further the activities of the United Nations for the maintenance of peace.

3. Parents have a prior right to choose the kind of education that shall be given to their children.

ARTICLE 27

1. Everyone has the right freely to participate in the cultural life of the community, to enjoy the arts and to share in scientific advancement and its benefits.

2. Everyone has the right to the protection of the moral and material interests resulting from any scientific, literary or artistic production of which he is the author.

ARTICLE 28

Everyone is entitled to a social and international order in which the rights and freedoms set forth in this Declaration can be fully realized.

ARTICLE 29

1. Everyone has duties to the community in which alone the free and full development of his personality is possible.

2. In the exercise of his rights and freedoms, everyone shall be subject only to such limitations as are determined by law solely for the purpose of securing due recognition and respect for the rights and freedoms of others and of meeting the just requirements of morality, public order and the general welfare in a democratic society.

3. These rights and freedoms may in no case be exercised contrary to the purposes and principles of the United Nations.

ARTICLE 30

Nothing in this Declaration may be interpreted as implying for any State, group or person any right or engage in any activity or to perform any act aimed at the destruction of any of the rights and freedoms set forth herein.

2. *INTERNATIONAL COVENANT ON CIVIL AND POLITICAL RIGHTS*
GA RES. 2200A (XXI), 21 UN GAOR SUPP. (NO. 16) AT 52,
UN DOC. A/6316 (1966), 999 UNTS 171,
ENTERED INTO FORCE MAR. 23, 1976.

PREAMBLE

The States Parties to the present Covenant,
Considering that, in accordance with the principles proclaimed in the Charter of

the United Nations, recognition of the inherent dignity and of the equal and inalienable rights of all members of the human family is the foundation of freedom, justice and peace in the world,

Recognizing that these rights derive from the inherent dignity of the human person,

Recognizing that, in accordance with the Universal Declaration of Human Rights, the ideal of free human beings enjoying civil and political freedom and freedom from fear and want can only be achieved if conditions are created whereby everyone may enjoy his civil and political rights, as well as his economic, social and cultural rights,

Considering the obligation of States under the Charter of the United Nations to promote universal respect for, and observance of, human rights and freedoms,

Realizing that the individual, having duties to other individuals and to the community to which he belongs, is under a responsibility to strive for the promotion and observance of the rights recognized in the present Covenant,

Agree upon the following articles:

PART I

ARTICLE 1

1. All peoples have the right of self-determination. By virtue of that right they freely determine their political status and freely pursue their economic, social and cultural development.
2. All peoples may, for their own ends, freely dispose of their natural wealth and resources without prejudice to any obligations arising out of international economic co-operation, based upon the principle of mutual benefit, and international law. In no case may a people be deprived of its own means of subsistence.
3. The States Parties to the present Covenant, including those having responsibility for the administration of Non-Self-Governing and Trust Territories, shall promote the realization of the right of self-determination, and shall respect that right, in conformity with the provisions of the Charter of the United Nations.

PART II

ARTICLE 2

1. Each State Party to the present Covenant undertakes to respect and to ensure to all individuals within its territory and subject to its jurisdiction the rights recognized in the present Covenant, without distinction of any kind, such as race, colour, sex, language, religion, political or other opinion, national or social origin, property, birth or other status.
2. Where not already provided for by existing legislative or other measures, each State Party to the present Covenant undertakes to take the necessary steps, in accordance with its constitutional processes and with the provisions of the present Covenant, to adopt such other measures as may be necessary to give effect to the rights recognized in the present Covenant.

3. Each State Party to the present Covenant undertakes:
   (a) To ensure that any person whose rights or freedoms as herein recognized are violated shall have an effective remedy, notwithstanding that the violation has been committed by persons acting in an official capacity;
   (b) To ensure that any person claiming such a remedy shall have his right thereto determined by competent judicial, administrative or legislative authorities, or by any other competent authority provided for by the legal system of the State, and to develop the possibilities of judicial remedy;
   (c) To ensure that the competent authorities shall enforce such remedies when granted.

ARTICLE 3

The States Parties to the present Covenant undertake to ensure the equal right of men and women to the enjoyment of all civil and political rights set forth in the present Covenant.

ARTICLE 4

1. In time of public emergency which threatens the life of the nation and the existence of which is officially proclaimed, the States Parties to the present Covenant may take measures derogating from their obligations under the present Covenant to the extent strictly required by the exigencies of the situation, provided that such measures are not inconsistent with their other obligations under international law and do not involve discrimination solely on the ground of race, colour, sex, language, religion or social origin.
2. No derogation from Articles 6, 7, 8 (paragraphs 1 and 2), 11, 15, 16 and 18 may be made under this provision.
3. Any State Party to the present Covenant availing itself of the right of derogation shall immediately inform the other States Parties to the present Covenant, through the intermediary of the Secretary-General of the United Nations, of the provisions from which it has derogated and of the reasons by which it was actuated. A further communication shall be made, through the same intermediary, on the date on which it terminates such derogation.

ARTICLE 5

1. Nothing in the present Covenant may be interpreted as implying for any State, group or person any right to engage in any activity or perform any act aimed at the destruction of any of the rights and freedoms recognized herein or at their limitation to a greater extent than is provided for in the present Covenant.
2. There shall be no restriction upon or derogation from any of the fundamental human rights recognized or existing in any State Party to the present Covenant pursuant to law, conventions, regulations or custom on the pretext that the present Covenant does not recognize such rights or that it recognizes them to a lesser extent.

PART III

ARTICLE 6

1. Every human being has the inherent right to life. This right shall be protected by law. No one shall be arbitrarily deprived of his life.
2. In countries which have not abolished the death penalty, sentence of death may be imposed only for the most serious crimes in accordance with the law in force at the time of the commission of the crime and not contrary to the provisions of the present Covenant and to the Convention on the Prevention and Punishment of the Crime of Genocide. This penalty can only be carried out pursuant to a final judgement rendered by a competent court.
3. When deprivation of life constitutes the crime of genocide, it is understood that nothing in this article shall authorize any State Party to the present Covenant to derogate in any way from any obligation assumed under the provisions of the Convention on the Prevention and Punishment of the Crime of Genocide.
4. Anyone sentenced to death shall have the right to seek pardon or commutation of the sentence. Amnesty, pardon or commutation of the sentence of death may be granted in all cases.
5. Sentence of death shall not be imposed for crimes committed by persons below eighteen years of age and shall not be carried out on pregnant women.
6. Nothing in this article shall be invoked to delay or to prevent the abolition of capital punishment by any State Party to the present Covenant.

ARTICLE 7

No one shall be subjected to torture or to cruel, inhuman or degrading treatment or punishment. In particular, no one shall be subjected without his free consent to medical or scientific experimentation.

ARTICLE 8

1. No one shall be held in slavery; slavery and the slave-trade in all their forms shall be prohibited.
2. No one shall be held in servitude.
3. (a) No one shall be required to perform forced or compulsory labour;
   (b) Paragraph 3 (a) shall not be held to preclude, in countries where imprisonment with hard labour may be imposed as a punishment for a crime, the performance of hard labour in pursuance of a sentence to such punishment by a competent court;
   (c) For the purpose of this paragraph the term "forced or compulsory labour" shall not include:
      (i) Any work or service, not referred to in subparagraph (b), normally required of a person who is under detention in consequence of a lawful order of a court, or of a person during conditional release from such detention;

(ii) Any service of a military character and, in countries where conscientious objection is recognized, any national service required by law of conscientious objectors;

(iii) Any service exacted in cases of emergency or calamity threatening the life or well-being of the community;

(iv) Any work or service which forms part of normal civil obligations.

ARTICLE 9

1. Everyone has the right to liberty and security of person. No one shall be subjected to arbitrary arrest or detention. No one shall be deprived of his liberty except on such grounds and in accordance with such procedure as are established by law.

2. Anyone who is arrested shall be informed, at the time of arrest, of the reasons for his arrest and shall be promptly informed of any charges against him.

3. Anyone arrested or detained on a criminal charge shall be brought promptly before a judge or other officer authorized by law to exercise judicial power and shall be entitled to trial within a reasonable time or to release. It shall not be the general rule that persons awaiting trial shall be detained in custody, but release may be subject to guarantees to appear for trial, at any other stage of the judicial proceedings, and, should occasion arise, for execution of the judgement.

4. Anyone who is deprived of his liberty by arrest or detention shall be entitled to take proceedings before a court, in order that court may decide without delay on the lawfulness of his detention and order his release if the detention is not lawful.

5. Anyone who has been the victim of unlawful arrest or detention shall have an enforceable right to compensation.

ARTICLE 10

1. All persons deprived of their liberty shall be treated with humanity and with respect for the inherent dignity of the human person.

2. (a) Accused persons shall, save in exceptional circumstances, be segregated from convicted persons and shall be subject to separate treatment appropriate to their status as unconvicted persons;

(b) Accused juvenile persons shall be separated from adults and brought as speedily as possible for adjudication.

3. The penitentiary system shall comprise treatment of prisoners the essential aim of which shall be their reformation and social rehabilitation. Juvenile offenders shall be segregated from adults and be accorded treatment appropriate to their age and legal status.

ARTICLE 11

No one shall be imprisoned merely on the ground of inability to fulfill a contractual obligation.

ARTICLE 12

1. Everyone lawfully within the territory of a State shall, within that territory, have the right to liberty of movement and freedom to choose his residence.
2. Everyone shall be free to leave any country, including his own.
3. The above-mentioned rights shall not be subject to any restrictions except those which are provided by law, are necessary to protect national security, public order (ordre public), public health or morals or the rights and freedoms of others, and are consistent with the other rights recognized in the present Covenant.
4. No one shall be arbitrarily deprived of the right to enter his own country.

ARTICLE 13

An alien lawfully in the territory of a State Party to the present Covenant may be expelled therefrom only in pursuance of a decision reached in accordance with law and shall, except where compelling reasons of national security otherwise require, be allowed to submit the reasons against his expulsion and to have his case reviewed by, and be represented for the purpose before, the competent authority or a person or persons especially designated by the competent authority.

ARTICLE 14

1. All persons shall be equal before the courts and tribunals. In the determination of any criminal charge against him, or of his rights and obligations in a suit at law, everyone shall be entitled to a fair and public hearing by a competent, independent and impartial tribunal established by law. The press and the public may be excluded from all or part of a trial for reasons of morals, public order (ordre public) or national security in a democratic society, or when the interest of the private lives of the parties so requires, or to the extent strictly necessary in the opinion of the court in special circumstances where publicity would prejudice the interests of justice; but any judgement rendered in a criminal case or in a suit at law shall be made public except where the interest of juvenile persons otherwise requires or the proceedings concern matrimonial disputes or the guardianship of children.
2. Everyone charged with a criminal offence shall have the right to be presumed innocent until proved guilty according to law.
3. In the determination of any criminal charge against him, everyone shall be entitled to the following minimum guarantees, in full equality:
    (a) To be informed promptly and in detail in a language which he understands of the nature and cause of the charge against him;
    (b) To have adequate time and facilities for the preparation of his defence and to communicate with counsel of his own choosing;
    (c) To be tried without undue delay;
    (d) To be tried in his presence, and to defend himself in person or through legal assistance of his own choosing; to be informed, if he does not have legal as-

sistance, of this right; and to have legal assistance assigned to him, in any case where the interests of justice so require, and without payment by him in any such case if he does not have sufficient means to pay for it;

(e) To examine, or have examined, the witnesses against him and to obtain the attendance and examination of witnesses on his behalf under the same conditions as witnesses against him;

(f) To have the free assistance of an interpreter if he cannot understand or speak the language used in court;

(g) Not to be compelled to testify against himself or to confess guilt.

4. In the case of juvenile persons, the procedure shall be such as will take account of their age and the desirability of promoting their rehabilitation.

5. Everyone convicted of a crime shall have the right to his conviction and sentence being reviewed by a higher tribunal according to law.

6. When a person has by a final decision been convicted of a criminal offence and when subsequently his conviction has been reversed or he has been pardoned on the ground that a new or newly discovered fact shows conclusively that there has been a miscarriage of justice, the person who has suffered punishment as a result of such conviction shall be compensated according to law, unless it is proved that the non-disclosure of the unknown fact in time is wholly or partly attributable to him.

7. No one shall be liable to be tried or punished again for an offence for which he has already been finally convicted or acquitted in accordance with the law and penal procedure of each country.

ARTICLE 15

1. No one shall be held guilty of any criminal offence on account of any act or omission which did not constitute a criminal offence, under national or international law, at the time when it was committed. Nor shall a heavier penalty be imposed than the one that was applicable at the time when the criminal offence was committed. If, subsequent to the commission of the offence, provision is made by law for the imposition of the lighter penalty, the offender shall benefit thereby.

2. Nothing in this article shall prejudice the trial and punishment of any person for any act or omission which, at the time when it was committed, was criminal according to the general principles of law recognized by the community of nations.

ARTICLE 16

Everyone shall have the right to recognition everywhere as a person before the law.

ARTICLE 17

1. No one shall be subjected to arbitrary or unlawful interference with his privacy, family, home or correspondence, nor to unlawful attacks on his honour and reputation.

2. Everyone has the right to the protection of the law against such interference or attacks.

ARTICLE 18

1. Everyone shall have the right to freedom of thought, conscience and religion. This right shall include freedom to have or to adopt a religion or belief of his choice, and freedom, either individually or in community with others and in public or private, to manifest his religion or belief in worship, observance, practice and teaching.
2. No one shall be subject to coercion which would impair his freedom to have or to adopt a religion or belief of his choice.
3. Freedom to manifest one's religion or beliefs may be subject only to such limitations as are prescribed by law and are necessary to protect public safety, order, health, or morals or the fundamental rights and freedoms of others. 4. The States Parties to the present Covenant undertake to have respect for the liberty of parents and, when applicable, legal guardians to ensure the religious and moral education of their children in conformity with their own convictions.

ARTICLE 19

1. Everyone shall have the right to hold opinions without interference.
2. Everyone shall have the right to freedom of expression; this right shall include freedom to seek, receive and impart information and ideas of all kinds, regardless of frontiers, either orally, in writing or in print, in the form of art, or through any other media of his choice.
3. The exercise of the rights provided for in paragraph 2 of this article carries with it special duties and responsibilities. It may therefore be subject to certain restrictions, but these shall only be such as are provided by law and are necessary:
    (a) For respect of the rights or reputations of others;
    (b) For the protection of national security or of public order (ordre public), or of public health or morals.

ARTICLE 20

1. Any propaganda for war shall be prohibited by law.
2. Any advocacy of national, racial or religious hatred that constitutes incitement to discrimination, hostility or violence shall be prohibited by law.

ARTICLE 21

The right of peaceful assembly shall be recognized. No restrictions may be placed on the exercise of this right other than those imposed in conformity with the law and which are necessary in a democratic society in the interests of national security or public safety, public order (ordre public), the protection of public health or morals or the protection of the rights and freedoms of others.

ARTICLE 22

1. Everyone shall have the right to freedom of association with others, including the right to form and join trade unions for the protection of his interests.

2. No restrictions may be placed on the exercise of this right other than those which are prescribed by law and which are necessary in a democratic society in the interests of national security or public safety, public order (ordre public), the protection of public health or morals or the protection of the rights and freedoms of others. This article shall not prevent the imposition of lawful restrictions on members of the armed forces and of the police in their exercise of this right.

3. Nothing in this article shall authorize States Parties to the International Labour Organisation Convention of 1948 concerning Freedom of Association and Protection of the Right to Organize to take legislative measures which would prejudice, or to apply the law in such a manner as to prejudice, the guarantees provided for in that Convention.

ARTICLE 23

1. The family is the natural and fundamental group unit of society and is entitled to protection by society and the State.

2. The right of men and women of marriageable age to marry and to found a family shall be recognized.

3. No marriage shall be entered into without the free and full consent of the intending spouses.

4. States Parties to the present Covenant shall take appropriate steps to ensure equality of rights and responsibilities of spouses as to marriage, during marriage and at its dissolution. In the case of dissolution, provision shall be made for the necessary protection of any children.

ARTICLE 24

1. Every child shall have, without any discrimination as to race, colour, sex, language, religion, national or social origin, property or birth, the right to such measures of protection as are required by his status as a minor, on the part of his family, society and the State.

2. Every child shall be registered immediately after birth and shall have a name.

3. Every child has the right to acquire a nationality.

ARTICLE 25

Every citizen shall have the right and the opportunity, without any of the distinctions mentioned in article 2 and without unreasonable restrictions:

(a) To take part in the conduct of public affairs, directly or through freely chosen representatives;

(b) To vote and to be elected at genuine periodic elections which shall bee by universal and equal suffrage and shall be held by secret ballot; guaranteeing the free expression of the will of the electors;

(c) To have access, on general terms of equality, to public service in his country.

ARTICLE 26

All persons are equal before the law and are entitled without any discrimination to the equal protection of the law. In this respect, the law shall prohibit any discrimination and guarantee to all persons equal and effective protection against discrimination on any ground such as race, colour, sex, language, religion, political or other opinion, national or social origin, property, birth or other status.

ARTICLE 27

In those States in which ethnic, religious or linguistic minorities exist, persons belonging to such minorities shall not be denied the right, in community with the other members of their group, to enjoy their own culture, to profess and practice their own religion, or to use their own language.

PART IV

ARTICLE 28

1. There shall be established a Human Rights Committee (hereafter referred to in the present Covenant as the Committee). It shall consist of eighteen members and shall carry out the functions hereinafter provided.
2. The Committee shall be composed of nationals of the States Parties to the present Covenant who shall be persons of high moral character and recognized competence in the field of human rights, consideration being given to the usefulness of the participation of some persons having legal experience.
3. The members of the Committee shall be elected and shall serve in their personal capacity.

ARTICLE 29

1. The members of the Committee shall be elected by secret ballot from a list of persons possessing the qualifications prescribed in Article 28 and nominated for the purpose by the States Parties to the present Covenant.
2. Each State Party to the present Covenant may nominate not more than two persons. These persons shall be nationals of the nominating State.
3. A person shall be eligible for renomination.

ARTICLE 30

1. The initial election shall be held no later than six months after the date of the entry into force of the present Covenant.
2. At least four months before the date of each election to the Committee, other than an election to fill a vacancy declared in accordance with Article 34, the Secretary-General of the United Nations shall address a written invitation to the States Par-

ties to the present Covenant to submit their nominations for membership of the Committee within three months.

3. The Secretary-General of the United Nations shall prepare a list in alphabetical order of all the persons thus nominated, with an indication of the States Parties which have nominated them, and shall submit it to the States Parties to the present Covenant no later than one month before the date of each election.

4. Elections of the members of the Committee shall be held at a meeting of the States Parties to the present Covenant convened by the Secretary General of the United Nations at the Headquarters of the United Nations. At that meeting, for which two thirds of the States Parties to the present Covenant shall constitute a quorum, the persons elected to the Committee shall be those nominees who obtain the largest number of votes and an absolute majority of the votes of the representatives of States Parties present and voting.

ARTICLE 31

1. The Committee may not include more than one national of the same State.

2. In the election of the Committee, consideration shall be given to equitable geographical distribution of membership and to the representation of the different forms of civilization and of the principal legal systems.

ARTICLE 32

1. The members of the Committee shall be elected for a term of four years. They shall be eligible for re-election if renominated. However, the terms of nine of the members elected at the first election shall expire at the end of two years; immediately after the first election, the names of these nine members shall be chosen by lot by the Chairman of the meeting referred to in Article 30, paragraph 4.

2. Elections at the expiry of office shall be held in accordance with the preceding articles of this part of the present Covenant.

ARTICLE 33

1. If, in the unanimous opinion of the other members, a member of the Committee has ceased to carry out his functions for any cause other than absence of a temporary character, the Chairman of the Committee shall notify the Secretary-General of the United Nations, who shall then declare the seat of that member to be vacant.

2. In the event of the death or the resignation of a member of the Committee, the Chairman shall immediately notify the Secretary-General of the United Nations, who shall declare the seat vacant from the date of death or the date on which the resignation takes effect.

ARTICLE 34

1. When a vacancy is declared in accordance with article 33 and if the term of office of the member to be replaced does not expire within six months of the declaration

of the vacancy, the Secretary-General of the United Nations shall notify each of the States Parties to the present Covenant, which may within two months submit nominations in accordance with article 29 for the purpose of filling the vacancy.

2. The Secretary-General of the United Nations shall prepare a list in alphabetical order of the persons thus nominated and shall submit it to the States Parties to the present Covenant. The election to fill the vacancy shall then take place in accordance with the relevant provisions of this part of the present Covenant.

3. A member of the Committee elected to fill a vacancy declared in accordance with article 33 shall hold office for the remainder of the term of the member who vacated the seat on the Committee under the provisions of that article.

ARTICLE 35

The members of the Committee shall, with the approval of the General Assembly of the United Nations, receive emoluments from United Nations resources on such terms and conditions as the General Assembly may decide, having regard to the importance of the Committee's responsibilities.

ARTICLE 36

The Secretary-General of the United Nations shall provide the necessary staff and facilities for the effective performance of the functions of the Committee under the present Covenant.

ARTICLE 37

1. The Secretary-General of the United Nations shall convene the initial meeting of the Committee at the Headquarters of the United Nations.

2. After its initial meeting, the Committee shall meet at such times as shall be provided in its rules of procedure.

3. The Committee shall normally meet at the Headquarters of the United Nations or at the United Nations Office at Geneva.

ARTICLE 38

Every member of the Committee shall, before taking up his duties, make a solemn declaration in open committee that he will perform his functions impartially and conscientiously.

ARTICLE 39

1. The Committee shall elect its officers for a term of two years. They may be re-elected.

2. The Committee shall establish its own rules of procedure, but these rules shall provide, inter alia, that:

(a) Twelve members shall constitute a quorum;

(b) Decisions of the Committee shall be made by a majority vote of the members present.

ARTICLE 40

1. The States Parties to the present Covenant undertake to submit reports on the measures they have adopted which give effect to the rights recognized herein and on the progress made in the enjoyment of those rights:
   (a) Within one year of the entry into force of the present Covenant for the States Parties concerned;
   (b) Thereafter whenever the Committee so requests.
2. All reports shall be submitted to the Secretary-General of the United Nations, who shall transmit them to the Committee for consideration. Reports shall indicate the factors and difficulties, if any, affecting the implementation of the present Covenant.
3. The Secretary-General of the United Nations may, after consultation with the Committee, transmit to the specialized agencies concerned copies of such parts of the reports as may fall within their field of competence.
4. The Committee shall study the reports submitted by the States Parties to the present Covenant. It shall transmit its reports, and such general comments as it may consider appropriate, to the States Parties. The Committee may also transmit to the Economic and Social Council these comments along with the copies of the reports it has received from States Parties to the present Covenant.
5. The States Parties to the present Covenant may submit to the Committee observations on any comments that may be made in accordance with paragraph 4 of this Article.

ARTICLE 41

1. A State Party to the present Covenant may at any time declare under this article that it recognizes the competence of the Committee to receive and consider communications to the effect that a State Party claims that another State Party is not fulfilling its obligations under the present Covenant. Communications under this Article may be received and considered only if submitted by a State Party which has made a declaration recognizing in regard to itself the competence of the Committee. No communication shall be received by the Committee if it concerns a State Party which has not made such a declaration. Communications received under this Article shall be dealt with in accordance with the following procedure:
   (a) If a State Party to the present Covenant considers that another State Party is not giving effect to the provisions of the present Covenant, it may, by written communication, bring the matter to the attention of that State Party. Within three months after the receipt of the communication the receiving State shall afford the State which sent the communication an explanation, or any other statement in writing clarifying the matter which should include, to the extent possible and pertinent, reference to domestic procedures and remedies taken, pending, or available in the matter;

(b) If the matter is not adjusted to the satisfaction of both States Parties concerned within six months after the receipt by the receiving State of the initial communication, either State shall have the right to refer the matter to the Committee, by notice given to the Committee and to the other State;

(c) The Committee shall deal with a matter referred to it only after it has ascertained that all available domestic remedies have been invoked and exhausted in the matter, in conformity with the generally recognized principles of international law. This shall not be the rule where the application of the remedies is unreasonably prolonged;

(d) The Committee shall hold closed meetings when examining communications under this Article;

(e) Subject to the provisions of subparagraph (c), the Committee shall make available its good offices to the States Parties concerned with a view to a friendly solution of the matter on the basis of respect for human rights and fundamental freedoms as recognized in the present Covenant;

(f) In any matter referred to it, the Committee may call upon the States Parties concerned, referred to in subparagraph (b), to supply any relevant information;

(g) The States Parties concerned, referred to in subparagraph (b), shall have the right to be represented when the matter is being considered in the Committee and to make submissions orally and/or in writing;

(h) The Committee shall, within twelve months after the date of receipt of notice under subparagraph (b), submit a report:

(i) If a solution within the terms of subparagraph (e) is reached, the Committee shall confine its report to a brief statement of the facts and of the solution reached;

(j) If a solution within the terms of subparagraph (e) is not reached, the Committee shall confine its report to a brief statement of the facts; the written submissions and record of the oral submissions made by the States Parties concerned shall be attached to the report. In every matter, the report shall be communicated to the States Parties concerned.

2. The provisions of this Article shall come into force when ten States Parties to the present Covenant have made declarations under paragraph I of this Article. Such declarations shall be deposited by the States Parties with the Secretary-General of the United Nations, who shall transmit copies thereof to the other States Parties. A declaration may be withdrawn at any time by notification to the Secretary-General. Such a withdrawal shall not prejudice the consideration of any matter which is the subject of a communication already transmitted under this Article; no further communication by any State Party shall be received after the notification of withdrawal of the declaration has been received by the Secretary-General, unless the State Party concerned has made a new declaration.

ARTICLE 42

1. (a) If a matter referred to the Committee in accordance with article 41 is not resolved to the satisfaction of the States Parties concerned, thee Committee may,

with the prior consent of the States Parties concerned, appoint an ad hoc Conciliation Commission (hereinafter referred to as the Commission). The good offices of the Commission shall be made available to the States Parties concerned with a view to an amicable solution of the matter on the basis of respect for the present Covenant;

(b) The Commission shall consist of five persons acceptable to the States Parties concerned. If the States Parties concerned fail to reach agreement within three months on all or part of the composition of the Commission, the members of the Commission concerning whom no agreement has been reached shall be elected by secret ballot by a two-thirds majority vote of the Committee from among its members.

2. The members of the Commission shall serve in their personal capacity. They shall not be nationals of the States Parties concerned, or of a State not Party to the present Covenant, or of a State Party which has not made a declaration under Article 41.

3. The Commission shall elect its own Chairman and adopt its own rules of procedure.

4. The meetings of the Commission shall normally be held at the Headquarters of the United Nations or at the United Nations Office at Geneva. However, they may be held at such other convenient places as the Commission may determine in consultation with the Secretary-General of the United Nations and the States Parties concerned.

5. The secretariat provided in accordance with Article 36 shall also service the commissions appointed under this Article.

6. The information received and collated by the Committee shall be made available to the Commission and the Commission may call upon the States Parties concerned to supply any other relevant information.

7. When the Commission has fully considered the matter, but in any event not later than twelve months after having been seized of the matter, it shall submit to the Chairman of the Committee a report for communication to the States Parties concerned:

(a) If the Commission is unable to complete its consideration of the matter within twelve months, it shall confine its report to a brief statement of the status of its consideration of the matter;

(b) If an amicable solution to the matter on tie basis of respect for human rights as recognized in the present Covenant is reached, the Commission shall confine its report to a brief statement of the facts and of the solution reached;

(c) If a solution within the terms of subparagraph (b) is not reached, the Commission's report shall embody its findings on all questions of fact relevant to the issues between the States Parties concerned, and its views on the possibilities of an amicable solution of the matter. This report shall also contain the written submissions and a record of the oral submissions made by the States Parties concerned;

(d) If the Commission's report is submitted under subparagraph (c), the States Parties concerned shall, within three months of the receipt of the report, notify the

Chairman of the Committee whether or not they accept the contents of the report of the Commission.

8. The provisions of this article are without prejudice to the responsibilities of the Committee under Article 41.

9. The States Parties concerned shall share equally all the expenses of the members of the Commission in accordance with estimates to be provided by the Secretary-General of the United Nations.

10. The Secretary-General of the United Nations shall be empowered to pay the expenses of the members of the Commission, if necessary, before reimbursement by the States Parties concerned, in accordance with paragraph 9 of this Article.

ARTICLE 43

The members of the Committee, and of the ad hoc conciliation commissions which may be appointed under article 42, shall be entitled to the facilities, privileges and immunities of experts on mission for the United Nations as laid down in the relevant sections of the Convention on the Privileges and Immunities of the United Nations.

ARTICLE 44

The provisions for the implementation of the present Covenant shall apply without prejudice to the procedures prescribed in the field of human rights by or under the constituent instruments and the conventions of the United Nations and of the specialized agencies and shall not prevent the States Parties to the present Covenant from having recourse to other procedures for settling a dispute in accordance with general or special international agreements in force between them.

ARTICLE 45

The Committee shall submit to the General Assembly of the United Nations, through the Economic and Social Council, an annual report on its activities.

PART V

ARTICLE 46

Nothing in the present Covenant shall be interpreted as impairing the provisions of the Charter of the United Nations and of the constitutions of the specialized agencies which define the respective responsibilities of the various organs of the United Nations and of the specialized agencies in regard to the matters dealt with in the present Covenant.

ARTICLE 47

Nothing in the present Covenant shall be interpreted as impairing the inherent right of all peoples to enjoy and utilize fully and freely their natural wealth and resources.

PART VI

ARTICLE 48

1. The present Covenant is open for signature by any State Member of the United Nations or member of any of its specialized agencies, by any State Party to the Statute of the International Court of Justice, and by any other State which has been invited by the General Assembly of the United Nations to become a Party to the present Covenant.
2. The present Covenant is subject to ratification. Instruments of ratification shall be deposited with the Secretary-General of the United Nations.
3. The present Covenant shall be open to accession by any State referred to in paragraph 1 of this Article.
4. Accession shall be effected by the deposit of an instrument of accession with the Secretary-General of the United Nations.
5. The Secretary-General of the United Nations shall inform all States which have signed this Covenant or acceded to it of the deposit of each instrument of ratification or accession.

ARTICLE 49

1. The present Covenant shall enter into force three months after the date of the deposit with the Secretary-General of the United Nations of the thirty-fifth instrument of ratification or instrument of accession.
2. For each State ratifying the present Covenant or acceding to it after the deposit of the thirty-fifth instrument of ratification or instrument of accession, the present Covenant shall enter into force three months after the date of the deposit of its own instrument of ratification or instrument of accession.

ARTICLE 50

The provisions of the present Covenant shall extend to all parts of federal States without any limitations or exceptions.

ARTICLE 51

1. Any State Party to the present Covenant may propose an amendment and file it with the Secretary-General of the United Nations. The Secretary-General of the United Nations shall thereupon communicate any proposed amendments to the States Parties to the present Covenant with a request that they notify him whether they favour a conference of States Parties for the purpose of considering and voting upon the proposals. In the event that at least one third of the States Parties favours such a conference, the Secretary-General shall convene the conference under the auspices of the United Nations. Any amendment adopted by a majority of the States Parties present and voting at the conference shall be submitted to the General Assembly of the United Nations for approval.

2. Amendments shall come into force when they have been approved by the General Assembly of the United Nations and accepted by a two-thirds majority of the States Parties to the present Covenant in accordance with their respective constitutional processes.

3. When amendments come into force, they shall be binding on those States Parties which have accepted them, other States Parties still being bound by the provisions of the present Covenant and any earlier amendment which they have accepted.

ARTICLE 52

Irrespective of the notifications made under article 48, paragraph 5, the Secretary-General of the United Nations shall inform all States referred to in paragraph I of the same article of the following particulars:
(a) Signatures, ratifications and accessions under article 48;
(b) The date of the entry into force of the present Covenant under Article 49 and the date of the entry into force of any amendments under Article 51.

ARTICLE 53

1. The present Covenant, of which the Chinese, English, French, Russian and Spanish texts are equally authentic, shall be deposited in the archives of the United Nations.

2. The Secretary-General of the United Nations shall transmit certified copies of the present Covenant to all States referred to in Article 48.

3. *FIRST OPTIONAL PROTOCOL TO THE INTERNATIONAL COVENANT ON CIVIL AND POLITICAL RIGHTS* GA RES. 2200A (XXI), 21 UN GAOR SUPP. (NO. 16) AT 59, UN DOC. A/6316 (1966), 999 UNTS 302, ENTERED INTO FORCE MARCH 23, 1976.

The States Parties to the present Protocol,

Considering that in order further to achieve the purposes of the International Covenant on Civil and Political Rights (herein after referred to as the Covenant) and the implementation of its provisions it would be appropriate to enable the Human Rights Committee set up in Part IV of the Covenant (hereinafter referred to as the Committee) to receive and consider, as provided in the present Protocol, communications from individuals claiming to be victims of violations of any of the rights set forth in the Covenant.

Have agreed as follows:

ARTICLE I

A State Party to the Covenant that becomes a Party to the present Protocol recognizes the competence of the Committee to receive and consider communications from individuals subject to its jurisdiction who claim to be victims of a violation by that State Party of any of the rights set forth in the Covenant. No communication shall be received by the Committee if it concerns a State Party to the Covenant which is not a Party to the present Protocol.

ARTICLE 2

Subject to the provisions of Article 1, individuals who claim that any of their rights enumerated in the Covenant have been violated and who have exhausted all available domestic remedies may submit a written communication to the Committee for consideration.

ARTICLE 3

The Committee shall consider inadmissible any communication under the present Protocol which is anonymous, or which it considers to be an abuse of the right of submission of such communications or to be incompatible with the provisions of the Covenant.

ARTICLE 4

1. Subject to the provisions of Article 3, the Committee shall bring any communications submitted to it under the present Protocol to the attention of the State Party to the present Protocol alleged to be violating any provision of the Covenant.
2. Within six months, the receiving State shall submit to the Committee written explanations or statements clarifying the matter and the remedy, if any, that may have been taken by that State.

ARTICLE 5

1. The Committee shall consider communications received under the present Protocol in the light of all written information made available to it by the individual and by the State Party concerned.
2. The Committee shall not consider any communication from an individual unless it has ascertained that:
   (a) The same matter is not being examined under another procedure of international investigation or settlement;
   (b) The individual has exhausted all available domestic remedies. This shall not be the rule where the application of the remedies is unreasonably prolonged.
3. The Committee shall hold closed meetings when examining communications under the present Protocol.
4. The Committee shall forward its views to the State Party concerned and to the individual.

ARTICLE 6

The Committee shall include in its annual report under Article 45 of the Covenant a summary of its activities under the present Protocol.

ARTICLE 7

Pending the achievement of the objectives of resolution 1514 (XV) adopted by the General Assembly of the United Nations on 14 December 1960 concerning the Declaration on the Granting of Independence to Colonial Countries and Peoples, the provisions of the present Protocol shall in no way limit the right of petition granted to these peoples by the Charter of the United Nations and other international conventions and instruments under the United Nations and its specialized agencies.

ARTICLE 8

1. The present Protocol is open for signature by any State which has signed the Covenant.
2. The present Protocol is subject to ratification by any State which has ratified or acceded to the Covenant. Instruments of ratification shall be deposited with the Secretary-General of the United Nations.
3. The present Protocol shall be open to accession by any State which has ratified or acceded to the Covenant.
4. Accession shall be effected by the deposit of an instrument of accession with the Secretary-General of the United Nations.
5. The Secretary-General of the United Nations shall inform all States which have signed the present Protocol or acceded to it of the deposit of each instrument of ratification or accession.

ARTICLE 9

1. Subject to the entry into force of the Covenant, the present Protocol shall enter into force three months after the date of the deposit with the Secretary-General of the United Nations of the tenth instrument of ratification or instrument of accession.
2. For each State ratifying the present Protocol or acceding to it after the deposit of the tenth instrument of ratification or instrument of accession, the present Protocol shall enter in to force three months after the date of the deposit of its own instrument of ratification or instrument of accession.

ARTICLE 10

The provisions of the present Protocol shall extend to all parts of federal States without any limitations or exceptions.

ARTICLE 11

1. Any State Party to the present Protocol may propose an amendment and file it with the Secretary-General of the United Nations. The Secretary-General shall thereupon communicate any proposed amendments to the States Parties to the present Protocol with a request that they notify him whether they favour a conference of States Parties for the purpose of considering and voting upon the proposal. In the event that at least one third of the States Parties favours such a conference, the

Secretary-General shall convene the conference under the auspices of the United Nations. Any amendment adopted by a majority of the States Parties present and voting at the conference shall be submitted to the General Assembly of the United Nations for approval.

2. Amendments shall come into force when they have been approved by the General Assembly of the United Nations and accepted by a two-thirds majority of the States Parties to the present Protocol in accordance with their respective constitutional processes.

3. When amendments come into force, they shall be binding on those States Parties which have accepted them, other States Parties still being bound by the provisions of the present Protocol and any earlier amendment which they have accepted.

ARTICLE 12

1. Any State Party may denounce the present Protocol at any time by written notification addressed to the Secretary-General of the United Nations. Denunciation shall take effect three months after the date of receipt of the notification by the Secretary-General.

2. Denunciation shall be without prejudice to the continued application of the provisions of the present Protocol to any communication submitted under Article 2 before the effective date of denunciation.

ARTICLE 13

Irrespective of the notifications made under Article 8, paragraph 5, of the present Protocol, the Secretary-General of the United Nations shall inform all States referred to in Article 48, paragraph 1, of the Covenant of the following particulars:

(a) Signatures, ratifications and accessions under Article 8;

(b) The date of the entry into force of the present Protocol under Article 9 and the date of the entry into force of any amendments under Article 11;

(c) Denunciations under Article 12.

ARTICLE 14

1. The present Protocol, of which the Chinese, English, French, Russian and Spanish texts are equally authentic, shall be deposited in the archives of the United Nations.

2. The Secretary-General of the United Nations shall transmit certified copies of the present Protocol to all States referred to in Article 48 of the Covenant.

4. *SECOND OPTIONAL PROTOCOL TO THE INTERNATIONAL COVENANT ON CIVIL AND POLITICAL RIGHTS, AIMING AT THE ABOLITION OF THE DEATH PENALTY* GA RES. 44/128, ANNEX, 44 UN GAOR SUPP. (NO. 49) AT 207, UN DOC. A/44/49 (1989), ENTERED INTO FORCE JULY 11, 1991.

The States Parties to the present Protocol,

Believing that abolition of the death penalty contributes to enhancement of human dignity and progressive development of human rights,

Recalling Article 3 of the Universal Declaration of Human Rights, adopted on 10 December 1948, and Article 6 of the International Covenant on Civil and Political Rights, adopted on 16 December 1966,

Noting that Article 6 of the International Covenant on Civil and Political Rights refers to abolition of the death penalty in terms that strongly suggest that abolition is desirable,

Convinced that all measures of abolition of the death penalty should be considered as progress in the enjoyment of the right to life,

Desirous to undertake hereby an international commitment to abolish the death penalty,

Have agreed as follows:

ARTICLE 1

1. No one within the jurisdiction of a State Party to the present Protocol shall be executed.
2. Each State Party shall take all necessary measures to abolish the death penalty within its jurisdiction.

ARTICLE 2

1. No reservation is admissible to the present Protocol, except for a reservation made at the time of ratification or accession that provides for the application of the death penalty in time of war pursuant to a conviction for a most serious crime of a military nature committed during wartime.
2. The State Party making such a reservation shall at the time of ratification or accession communicate to the Secretary-General of the United Nations the relevant provisions of its national legislation applicable during wartime.
3. The State Party having made such a reservation shall notify the Secretary-General of the United Nations of any beginning or ending of a state of war applicable to its territory.

ARTICLE 3

The States Parties to the present Protocol shall include in the reports they submit to the Human Rights Committee, in accordance with Article 40 of the Covenant, information on the measures that they have adopted to give effect to the present Protocol.

ARTICLE 4

With respect to the States Parties to the Covenant that have made a declaration under Article 41, the competence of the Human Rights Committee to receive and consider communications when a State Party claims that another State Party is not fulfilling its obligations shall extend to the provisions of the present Protocol, unless that State Party concerned has made a statement to the contrary at the moment of ratification or accession.

ARTICLE 5

With respect to the States Parties to the first Optional Protocol to the International Covenant on Civil and Political Rights adopted on 16 December 1966, the competence of the Human Rights Committee to receive and consider communications from individuals subject to its jurisdiction shall extend to the provisions of the present Protocol, unless the State Party concerned has made a statement to the contrary at the moment of ratification or accession.

ARTICLE 6

1. The provisions of the present Protocol shall apply as additional provisions to the covenant.
2. Without prejudice to the possibility of a reservation under Article 2 of the present Protocol, the right guaranteed in Article 1, paragraph 1, of the present Protocol shall not be subject to any derogation under Article 4 of the Covenant.

ARTICLE 7

1. The present Protocol is open for signature by any State that has signed the Covenant.
2. The present Protocol is subject to ratification by any State that has ratified the Covenant or acceded to it. Instruments of ratification shall be deposited with the Secretary-General of the United Nations.
3. The present Protocol shall be open to accession by any State that has ratified the Covenant or acceded to it.
4. Accession shall be effected by the deposit of an instrument of accession with the Secretary-General of the United Nations.
5. The Secretary-General of the United Nations shall inform all States that have signed the present Protocol or acceded to it of the deposit of each instrument of ratification or accession.

ARTICLE 8

1. The present Protocol shall enter into force three months after the date of the deposit with the Secretary-General of the United Nations of the tenth instrument of ratification or accession.
2. For each State ratifying the present Protocol or acceding to it after the deposit of the tenth instrument of ratification or accession, the present Protocol shall enter into

force three months after the date of the deposit of its own instrument of ratification or accession.

ARTICLE 9

The provisions of the present Protocol shall extend to all parts of federal States without any limitations or exceptions.

ARTICLE 10

The Secretary-General of the United Nations shall inform all States referred to in Article 48, paragraph 1, of the Covenant of the following particulars:
   (a) Reservations, communications and notifications under Article 2 of the present Protocol;
   (b) Statements made under Articles 4 or 5 of the present Protocol;
   (c) Signatures, ratifications and accessions under Article 7 or the present Protocol;
   (d) The date of the entry into force of the present Protocol under Article 8 thereof.

ARTICLE 11

1. The present Protocol, of which the Arabic, Chinese, English, French, Russian and Spanish texts are equally authentic, shall be deposited in the archives of the United Nations.
2. The Secretary-General of the United Nations shall transmit certified copies of the present Protocol to all States referred to in Article 48 of the Covenant.

5. *INTERNATIONAL COVENANT ON ECONOMIC, SOCIAL AND CULTURAL RIGHTS* GA RES. 2200A (XXI), 21 UN GAOR SUPP. (NO. 16) AT 49, UN DOC. A/6316 (1966), 993 UNTS 3, ENTERED INTO FORCE JAN. 3, 1976.

PREAMBLE

The States Parties to the present Covenant, considering that, in accordance with the principles proclaimed in the Charter of the United Nations, recognition of the inherent dignity and of the equal and inalienable rights of all members of the human family is the foundation of freedom, justice and peace in the world.

Recognizing that these rights derive from the inherent dignity of the human person.

Recognizing that, in accordance with the Universal Declaration of Human Rights, the ideal of free human beings enjoying freedom fro fear and want can only be achieved if conditions are created whereby everyone may enjoy his economic, social and cultural rights, as well as his civil and political rights.

Considering the obligation of States under the Charter of the United Nations to promote universal respect for, and observance of, human rights and freedoms,

Realizing that the individual, having duties to other individuals and to the community to which he belongs, is under a responsibility to strive for the promotion and observance of the rights recognized in the present Covenant,

Agree upon the following articles:

PART I

ARTICLE 1

1. All peoples have the right of self-determination. By virtue of that right they freely determine their political status and freely pursue their economic, social and cultural development.
2. All peoples may, for their own ends, freely dispose of their natural wealth and resources without prejudice to any obligations arising out of international economic cooperation, based upon the principle of mutual benefit, and international law. In no case may people be deprived of its own means of subsistence.
3. The States Parties of the present Covenant, including those having responsibility for the administration of Non-Self-Governing and Trust Territories, shall promote the realization of the right of self-determination, and shall respect that right, in conformity with the provisions of the Charter of The United Nations.

PART II

ARTICLE 2

1. Each State Party to the present Covenant undertakes to take steps, individually and through international assistance and cooperation, especially economic and technical, to the maximum of its available resources, with a view to achieving progressively the full realization of the rights recognized in the present Covenant by all appropriate means, including particularly the adoption of legislative measures.
2. The States Parties to the present Covenant undertake to guarantee that the rights enunciated in the present Covenant will be exercised without discrimination of any kind as to race, colour, sex, language, religion, political or other opinion, national or social origin, property, birth or other status.
3. Developing countries, with due regard to human rights and their national economy, may determine to what extent they would guarantee the economic rights recognized in the present Covenant to non-nationals.

ARTICLE 3

The States Parties to the present Covenant undertake to ensure the equal right of men and women to the enjoyment of all economic, social and cultural rights set forth in the present Covenant.

ARTICLE 4

The States Parties to the present Covenant recognize that, in the enjoyment of those rights provided by the State in conformity with the present Covenant, the State may subject such rights only to such limitations as are determined by law only in so far as this may be compatible with the nature of these rights and solely for the purpose of promoting the general welfare in a democratic society.

ARTICLE 5

1. Nothing in the present Covenant may be interpreted as implying for any State, group or person any right to engage in any activity or to perform any act aimed at the destruction of any of the rights or freedoms recognized herein, or at their limitation to a greater extent than is provided for in the present Covenant.
2. No restriction upon or derogation from any of the fundamental human rights recognized or existing in any country in virtue of law, conventions, regulations or custom shall be admitted on the pretext that the present Covenant does not recognize such rights or that it recognizes them to a lesser extent.

PART III

ARTICLE 6

1. The States Parties to the present Covenant recognize the right to work, which includes the right of everyone to the opportunity to gain his living by work which he freely chooses or accepts, and will take appropriate steps to safeguard this right.
2. The steps to be taken by a Sate Party to the present Covenant to achieve the full realization of this right shall include technical and vocational guidance and training programmes, policies and techniques to achieve steady economic, social and cultural development and full and productive employment under conditions safeguarding fundamental political and economic freedoms to the individual.

ARTICLE 7

The States Parties to the present Covenant recognize the right of everyone to the enjoyment of just and favourable conditions of work which ensure, in particular:
(a) Remuneration which provides all workers, as a minimum, with:
  (i) Fair wages and equal remuneration for work of equal value with distinction of any kind, in particular women being guaranteed conditions of work not inferior to those enjoyed by men, with equal pay for equal work;
  (ii) A decent living for themselves and their families in accordance with the provisions of the present Covenant;
(b) Safe and healthy working conditions;
(c) Equal opportunity for everyone to be promoted in his employment to an appropriate higher level, subject to no considerations other than those of seniority and competence;
(d) Rest, leisure and reasonable limitation of working hours and periodic holidays with pay, as well as remuneration for public holidays.

ARTICLE 8

1. The States Parties to the present Covenant undertake to ensure:
    (a) The right of everyone to form trade unions and join the trade union of his choice, subject only to the rules of the organization convened, for the promotion and protection of his economic and social interests. No restrictions may be placed on the exercise of this right other than those prescribed by law and which are necessary in a democratic society in the interest of national security or public order or for the protection of the rights and freedoms of others;
    (b) The right of trade unions to establish national federations or confederations and the right of the latter to form or join international trade-union organizations;
    (c) The right of trade unions to function freely subject to no limitations other than those prescribed by law and which are necessary in a democratic society in the interests of national security or public order or for the protection of the rights and freedoms of others;
    (d) The right to strike, provided that it is exercised in conformity with the laws of the particular country.
2. This Article shall not prevent the imposition of lawful restrictions on the exercise of these rights by members of the armed forces or of the police or of the administration of the State.
3. Nothing in this Article shall authorize States Parties to the International Labour Organization Convention of 1948 convening Freedom of Association and Protection of the Right to Organize to take legislative measures which would prejudice, or apply the law in such a manner as would prejudice, the guarantees provided for in that Convention.

ARTICLE 9

The States Parties to the present Covenant recognize the right of everyone to social security, including social insurance.

ARTICLE 10

The States Parties to the present Covenant recognize that:
1. The widest possible protection and assistance should be accorded to the family, which is the natural and fundamental group unit of society, particularly for its establishment and while it is responsible for the care and education of dependent children. Marriage must be entered into with the free consent of the intending spouses.
2. Special protection should be accorded to mothers during a reasonable period before and after childbirth. During such period working mothers should be accorded paid leave or leave with adequate social security benefits.
3. Special measures of protection and assistance should be taken on behalf of all children and young persons without any discrimination for reasons of parentage or other conditions. Children and young persons should be protected from economic

and social exploitation. Their employment in work harmful to their morals or health or dangerous to life or likely to hamper their normal development should be punishable by law. States should also set age limits below which the paid employment of child labour should be prohibited and punishable by law.

ARTICLE 11

1. The States Parties to the present Covenant recognize the right of everyone to an adequate standard of living for himself and his family, including adequate food, clothing and housing, and to the continuous improvement of living conditions. The States Parties will take appropriate steps to ensure the realization of this right, recognizing to this effect the essential importance of international cooperation based on free consent.
2. The States Parties to the present Covenant, recognizing the fundamental right of everyone to be free from hunger, shall take, individually and through international cooperation, the measures, including specific programmes, which are needed:
   (a) To improve methods of production, conservation and distribution of food by making full use of technical and scientific knowledge, by disseminating knowledge of the principles of nutrition and by developing or reforming agrarian systems in such a way as to achieve the most efficient development and utilization of natural resources;
   (b) Taking into account the problems of both food-importing and food-exporting countries, to ensure an equitable distribution of world food supplies in relation to need.

ARTICLE 12

1. The States Parties to the present Covenant recognize the right of everyone to the enjoyment of the highest attainable standard of physical and mental health.
2. The steps to be taken by the States Parties to the present Covenant to achieve the full realization of this right shall include those necessary for:
   (a) The provision for the reduction of the stillbirth-rate and of infant mortality and for the healthy development of the child;
   (b) The improvement of all aspects of environmental and industrial hygiene;
   (c) The prevention, treatment and control of epidemic, endemic, occupational and other diseases;
   (d) The creation of conditions which would assure to all medical service and medical attention in the event of sickness.

ARTICLE 13

1. The States Parties to the present Covenant recognize the right of everyone to education. They agree that education shall be directed to the full development of the human personality and the sense of its dignity, and shall strengthen the respect for human rights and fundamental freedoms. They further agree that education shall

enable all persons to participate effectively in a free society, promote understanding, tolerance and friendship among all nations and all racial, ethnic or religious groups, and further the activities of the United Nations for the maintenance of peace.

2. The States Parties to the present Covenant recognize that with a view to achieving the full realization of this right:

(a) Primary education shall be compulsory and available free to all;

(b) Secondary education in its different forms, including technical and vocational secondary education, shall be made generally available and accessible to all by every appropriate means, and in particular by the progressive introduction of free education;

(c) Higher education shall be made equally accessible to all, on the basis of capacity, by every appropriate means, and in particular by the progressive introduction of free education;

(d) Fundamental education shall be encouraged or intensified as far as possible for those persons who have not received or completed the whole period of their primary education;

(e) The development of a system of schools at all levels shall be actively pursued, an adequate fellowship system shall be established, and the material conditions of teaching staff shall be continuously improved.

3. The States Parties to the present Covenant undertake to have respect for the liberty of parents and, when applicable, legal guardians to choose for their children schools, other than those established by the public authorities, which conform to such minimum educational standards as may be laid down or approved by the State and to ensure the religious and moral education of their children in conformity with their own convictions.

4. No part of this article shall be construed so as to interfere with the liberty of individuals and bodies to establish and direct educational institutions, subject always to the observance of the principles set forth in paragraph I of this article and to the requirement that the education given in such institutions shall conform to such minimum standards as may be laid down by the State.

ARTICLE 14

Each State Party to the present Covenant which, at the time of becoming a Party, has not been able to secure in its metropolitan territory or other territories under its jurisdiction compulsory primary education, free of charge, undertakes, within two years, to work out and adopt a detailed plan of action for the progressive implementation, within a reasonable number of years, to be fixed in the plan, of the principle of compulsory education free of charge for all.

ARTICLE 15

1. The States Parties to the present Covenant recognize the right of everyone:

(a) To take part in cultural life;

(b) To enjoy the benefits of scientific progress and its applications;

(c) To benefit from the protection of the moral and material interests resulting from any scientific, literary or artistic production of which he is the author.

2. The steps to be taken by the States Parties to the present Covenant to achieve the full realization of this right shall include those necessary for the conservation, the development and the diffusion of science and culture.

3. The States Parties to the present Covenant undertake to respect the freedom indispensable for scientific research and creative activity.

4. The States Parties to the present Covenant recognize the benefits to be derived form the encouragement and development of international contacts and cooperation in the scientific and cultural fields.

PART IV

ARTICLE 16

1. The States Parties to the present Covenant undertake to submit in conformity with this part of the Covenant reports on the measures which they have adopted and the progress made in achieving the observance of the rights recognized herein.

2. (a) All reports shall be submitted to the Secretary-General of the United Nations, who shall transmit copies to the Economic and Social Council for consideration in accordance with the provisions of the present Covenant;

   (b) The Secretary-General of the United Nations shall also transmit to the specialized agencies copies of the reports, or any relevant parts therefrom, from States Parties to the present Covenant which are also members of these specialized agencies in so far as these reports, or parts therefrom, relate to any matters which fall within the responsibilities of the said agencies in accordance with their constitutional instruments.

ARTICLE 17

1. The States Parties to the present Covenant shall furnish their reports in stages, in accordance with a programme to be established by the Economic and Social Council within one year of the entry into force of the present Covenant after consultation with the States Parties and the specialized agencies concerned.

2. Reports may indicate factors and difficulties affecting the degree of fulfillment of obligations under the present Covenant.

3. Where relevant information has previously been furnished to the United Nations or to any specialized agency by any State Party to the present Covenant, it will not be necessary to reproduce that information, but a precise reference to the information so furnished will suffice.

ARTICLE 18

Pursuant to its responsibilities under the Charter of the United Nations in the field of human rights and fundamental freedoms, the Economic and Social Council may make arrangements with the specialized agencies in respect of their reporting to it on the progress made in achieving the observance of the provisions of the present Covenant falling within the scope of their activities. These reports may include particulars of decisions and recommendations on such implementation adopted by their competent organs.

ARTICLE 19

The Economic and Social Council may transmit to the Commission on Human Rights for study and general recommendation or, as appropriate, for information the reports concerning human rights submitted by States in accordance with Articles 16 and 17, and those concerning human rights submitted by the specialized agencies in accordance with Article 18.

ARTICLE 20

The States Parties to the present Covenant and the specialized agencies concerned may submit comments to the Economic and Social Council on any general recommendation under Article 19 or reference to such general recommendation in any report of the Commission on Human Rights or any documentation referred to therein.

ARTICLE 21

The Economic and Social Council may submit from time to time to the General Assembly reports with recommendations of a general nature and a summary of the information received from the States Parties to the present Covenant and the specialized agencies on the measures taken and the progress made in achieving general observance of the rights recognized in the present Covenant.

ARTICLE 22

The Economic and Social Council may bring to the attention of other organs of the United Nations, their subsidiary organs and specialized agencies concerned with furnishing technical assistance any matters arising out of the reports referred to in this part of the present Covenant which may assist such bodies in deciding, each within its field of competence, on the advisability of international measures likely ton contribute to the effective progressive implementation of the present Covenant.

ARTICLE 23

The States Parties to the present Covenant agree that international action for the achievement of the rights recognized in the present Covenant includes such methods as the conclusion of conventions, the adoption of recommendations, the furnishing of technical assistance and the holding of regional meetings and technical meetings for the purpose of consultation and study organized in conjunction with the Governments concerned.

ARTICLE 24

Nothing in the present Covenant shall be interpreted as impairing the provisions of the Charter of the United Nations and of the constitutions of the specialized agencies which define the respective responsibilities of the various organs of the United Nations and of the specialized agencies in regard to the matters dealt with in the present Covenant.

ARTICLE 25

Nothing in the present Covenant shall be interpreted as impairing the inherent right of all peoples to enjoy and utilize fully and freely their natural wealth and resources.

PART V

ARTICLE 26

1. The present Covenant is open for signature by any State Member of the United Nations or member of any of its specialized agencies, by any State Party to the Statute of the International Court of Justice, and by any other State which has been invited by the General Assembly of the United Nations to become a party to the present Covenant.
2. The present Covenant is subject to ratification. Instruments of ratification shall be deposited with the Secretary-General of the United Nations.
3. The present Covenant shall be open to accession by any State referred to in paragraph 1 of this Article.
4. Accession shall be effected by the deposit of an instrument of accession with the Secretary-General of the United Nations.
5. The Secretary-General of the United Nations shall inform all States which have signed the present Covenant or acceded to it of the deposit of each instrument of ratification or accession.

ARTICLE 27

1. The present Covenant shall enter into force three months after the date of the deposit with the Secretary-General of the United Nations of the thirty-fifth instrument of ratification or instrument of accession.
2. For each State ratifying the present Covenant or acceding to it after the deposit of the thirty-fifth instrument of ratification or instrument of accession, the present Covenant shall enter into force three months after the date of the deposit of its own instrument of ratification or instrument of accession.

ARTICLE 28

The provisions of the present Covenant shall extend to all parts of federal States without any limitations or exceptions.

ARTICLE 29

1. Any State Party to the present Covenant may propose an amendment and file it with the Secretary-General of the United Nations. The Secretary-General; shall thereupon communicate any proposed amendments to the States Parties to the present Covenant with a request that they notify him whether they favour a conference of States Parties for the purpose of considering and voting upon the proposals. In the event that at least one third of the States Parties favours such a conference, the Secretary-General shall convene the conference under the auspices of the United Nations. Any amendment adopted by a majority of the States Parties present and voting at the conference shall be submitted to the General Assembly of the United Nations for approval.

2. Amendments shall come into force when they have been approved by the General Assembly of the United Nations and accepted by a two-thirds majority of the States Parties to the present Covenant in accordance with their respective constitutional processes.

3. When amendments come into force they shall be binding on those States Parties which have accepted them, other States Parties still being bound by the provisions of the present Covenant and any earlier amendment which they have accepted.

ARTICLE 30

Irrespective of the notifications made under Article 26, paragraph 5, the Secretary-General of the United Nations shall inform all States referred to in paragraph I of the same Article of the following particulars:

    (a) Signatures, ratifications and accessions under Article 26;

    (b) The date of the entry into force of the present Covenant under Article 27 and the date of the entry into force of any amendments under Article 29.

ARTICLE 31

1. The present Covenant, of which the Chinese, English, French, Russian and Spanish texts are equally authentic, shall be deposited in the archives of the United Nations.

2. The Secretary-General of the United Nations shall transmit certified copies of the present Covenant to all States referred to in Article 26.

• APPENDIX C •

Excerpts from Selected International Human Rights Instruments

1. DECLARATION ON THE RIGHT AND RESPONSIBILITY OF INDIVIDUALS, GROUPS AND ORGANS OF SOCIETY TO PROMOTE AND PROTECT UNIVERSALLY RECOGNIZED HUMAN RIGHTS AND FUNDAMENTAL FREEDOMS (UNITED NATIONS GENERAL ASSEMBLY RESOLUTION 53/144, 9 DECEMBER 1998)

The General Assembly,

. . .

Recognizing the relationship between international peace and security and the enjoyment of human rights and fundamental freedoms, and mindful that the absence of international peace and security does not excuse non-compliance,

. . .

Stressing that the prime responsibility and duty to promote and protect human rights and fundamental freedoms lie with the State,

. . . *Recognizing* the right and the responsibility of individuals, groups and associations to promote respect for and foster knowledge of human rights and fundamental freedoms at the national and international levels,

Declares:

. . .

ARTICLE 14

1. The State has the responsibility to take legislative, judicial, administrative or other appropriate measures to promote the understanding by all persons under its jurisdiction of their civil, political, economic, social and cultural rights.
2. Such measures shall include, *inter alia*:
   (*a*) The publication and widespread availability of national laws and regulations and of applicable basic international human rights instruments;

ARTICLE 15

The State has the responsibility to promote and facilitate the teaching of human rights and fundamental freedoms at all levels of education and to ensure that all those responsible for training lawyers, law enforcement officers, the personnel of the armed forces and public officials include appropriate elements of human rights teaching in their training programme.

ARTICLE 16

Individuals, non-governmental organizations and relevant institutions have an important role to play in contributing to making the public more aware of questions relating to all human rights and fundamental freedoms through activities such as education, training and research in these areas to strengthen further, *inter alia*, understanding, tolerance, peace and friendly relations among nations and among all racial and religious groups, bearing in mind the various backgrounds of the societies and communities in which they carry out their activities.

2. CONVENTION ON THE PREVENTION AND PUNISHMENT OF THE CRIME OF GENOCIDE (GENOCIDE CONVENTION) 78 UNTS 277, ENTERED INTO FORCE JAN. 12, 1951.

The Contracting Parties,

Having considered the declaration made by the General Assembly of the United Nations in its resolution 96 (I) dated 11 December 1946 that genocide is a crime under international law, contrary to the spirit and aims of the United Nations and condemned by the civilized world,

Recognizing that at all periods of history genocide has inflicted great losses on humanity, and Being convinced that, in order to liberate mankind from such an odious scourge, international co-operation is required, Hereby agree as hereinafter provided:

ARTICLE 1

The Contracting Parties confirm that genocide, whether committed in time of peace or in time of war, is a crime under international law which they undertake to prevent and to punish.

ARTICLE 2

In the present Convention, genocide means any of the following acts committed with intent to destroy, in whole or in part, a national, ethnical, racial or religious group, as such:
(a) Killing members of the group;
(b) Causing serious bodily or mental harm to members of the group;
(c) Deliberately inflicting on the group conditions of life calculated to bring about its physical destruction in whole or in part;
(d) Imposing measures intended to prevent births within the group;
(e) Forcibly transferring children of the group to another group.

ARTICLE 3

The following acts shall be punishable:
(a) Genocide;
(b) Conspiracy to commit genocide;
(c) Direct and public incitement to commit genocide;
(d) Attempt to commit genocide;
(e) Complicity in genocide.

ARTICLE 4

Persons committing genocide or any of the other acts enumerated in article III shall be punished, whether they are constitutionally responsible rulers, public officials or private individuals.

ARTICLE 5

The Contracting Parties undertake to enact, in accordance with their respective Constitutions, the necessary legislation to give effect to the provisions of the present Convention, and, in particular, to provide effective penalties for persons guilty of genocide or any of the other acts enumerated in article III.

ARTICLE 6

Persons charged with genocide or any of the other acts enumerated in article III shall be tried by a competent tribunal of the State in the territory of which the act was committed, or by such international penal tribunal as may have jurisdiction with re-spect to those Contracting Parties which shall have accepted its jurisdiction.

ARTICLE 7

Genocide and the other acts enumerated in article III shall not be considered as po-litical crimes for the purpose of extradition.

The Contracting Parties pledge themselves in such cases to grant extradition in ac-cordance with their laws and treaties in force.

ARTICLE 8

Any Contracting Party may call upon the competent organs of the United Nations to take such action under the Charter of the United Nations as they consider appro-priate for the prevention and suppression of acts of genocide or any of the other acts enumerated in article III.

ARTICLE 9

Disputes between the Contracting Parties relating to the interpretation, applica-tion or fulfilment of the present Convention, including those relating to the respon-sibility of a State for genocide or for any of the other acts enumerated in article III, shall be submitted to the International Court of Justice at the request of any of the parties to the dispute.

ARTICLE 10

The present Convention, of which the Chinese, English, French, Russian and Spanish texts are equally authentic, shall bear the date of 9 December 1948.

ARTICLE 11

The present Convention shall be open until 31 December 1949 for signature on be-half of any Member of the United Nations and of any nonmember State to which an invitation to sign has been addressed by the General Assembly.

The present Convention shall be ratified, and the instruments of ratification shall be deposited with the Secretary-General of the United Nations.

After 1 January 1950, the present Convention may be acceded to on behalf of any Member of the United Nations and of any non-member State which has received an invitation as aforesaid. Instruments of accession shall be deposited with the Secretary-General of the United Nations.

ARTICLE 12

Any Contracting Party may at any time, by notification addressed to the Secretary-General of the United Nations, extend the application of the present Convention to all or any of the territories for the conduct of whose foreign relations that Contract-ing Party is responsible.

ARTICLE 13

On the day when the first twenty instruments of ratification or accession have been deposited, the Secretary-General shall draw up a procès-verbal and transmit a copy thereof to each Member of the United Nations and to each of the non-member States contemplated in article 11.

The present Convention shall come into force on the ninetieth day following the date of deposit of the twentieth instrument of ratification or accession.

Any ratification or accession effected, subsequent to the latter date shall become effective on the ninetieth day following the deposit of the instrument of ratification or accession.

ARTICLE 14

The present Convention shall remain in effect for a period of ten years as from the date of its coming into force.

It shall thereafter remain in force for successive periods of five years for such Contracting Parties as have not denounced it at least six months before the expiration of the current period.

Denunciation shall be effected by a written notification addressed to the Secretary-General of the United Nations.

ARTICLE 15

If, as a result of denunciations, the number of Parties to the present Convention should become less than sixteen, the Convention shall cease to be in force as from the date on which the last of these denunciations shall become effective.

ARTICLE 16

A request for the revision of the present Convention may be made at any time by any Contracting Party by means of a notification in writing addressed to the Secretary General.

The General Assembly shall decide upon the steps, if any, to be taken in respect of such request.

ARTICLE 17

The Secretary-General of the United Nations shall notify all Members of the United Nations and the non-member States contemplated in article XI of the following:

(a) Signatures, ratifications and accessions received in accordance with article 11;
(b) Notifications received in accordance with article 12;
(c) The date upon which the present Convention comes into force in accordance with article 13;
(d) Denunciations received in accordance with article 14;
(e) The abrogation of the Convention in accordance with article 15;
(f) Notifications received in accordance with article 16.

ARTICLE 18

The original of the present Convention shall be deposited in the archives of the United Nations.

A certified copy of the Convention shall be transmitted to each Member of the United Nations and to each of the non-member States contemplated in article XI.

ARTICLE 19

The present Convention shall be registered by the Secretary-General of the United Nations on the date of its coming into force.

3. *CONVENTION AGAINST TORTURE AND OTHER CRUEL, INHUMAN OR DEGRADING TREATMENT OR PUNISHMENT* GA RES. 39/46, ANNEX, 39 UN GAOR SUPP. (NO. 51) AT 197, UN DOC. A/39/51 (1984), ENTERED INTO FORCE JUNE 26, 1987

The States Parties to this Convention,

Considering that, in accordance with the principles proclaimed in the Charter of the United Nations, recognition of the equal and inalienable rights of all members of the human family is the foundation of freedom, justice and peace in the world,

Recognizing that those rights derive from the inherent dignity of the human person,

Considering the obligation of States under the Charter, in particular Article 55, to promote universal respect for, and observance of, human rights and fundamental freedoms,

Having regard to article 5 of the Universal Declaration of Human Rights and article 7 of the International Covenant on Civil and Political Rights, both of which provide that no one shall be subjected to torture or to cruel, inhuman or degrading treatment or punishment,

Having regard also to the Declaration on the Protection of All Persons from Being Subjected to Torture and Other Cruel, Inhuman or Degrading Treatment or Punishment, adopted by the General Assembly on 9 December 1975,

Desiring to make more effective the struggle against torture and other cruel, inhuman or degrading treatment or punishment throughout the world,

Have agreed as follows:

PART I

ARTICLE 1

1. For the purposes of this Convention, the term "torture" means any act by which severe pain or suffering, whether physical or mental, is intentionally inflicted on a person for such purposes as obtaining from him or a third person information or a confession, punishing him for an act he or a third person has committed or is suspected of having committed, or intimidating or coercing him or a third person, or

for any reason based on discrimination of any kind, when such pain or suffering is inflicted by or at the instigation of or with the consent or acquiescence of a public official or other person acting in an official capacity. It does not include pain or suffering arising only from, inherent in or incidental to lawful sanctions.

2. This Article is without prejudice to any international instrument or national legislation which does or may contain provisions of wider application.

ARTICLE 2

1. Each State Party shall take effective legislative, administrative, judicial or other measures to prevent acts of torture in any territory under its jurisdiction.
2. No exceptional circumstances whatsoever, whether a state of war or a threat of war, internal political in stability or any other public emergency, may be invoked as a justification of torture.
3. An order from a superior officer or a public authority may not be invoked as a justification of torture.

ARTICLE 3

1. No State Party shall expel, return ("refouler") or extradite a person to another State where there are substantial grounds for believing that he would be in danger of being subjected to torture.
2. For the purpose of determining whether there are such grounds, the competent authorities shall take into account all relevant considerations including, where applicable, the existence in the State concerned of a consistent pattern of gross, flagrant or mass violations of human rights.

ARTICLE 4

1. Each State Party shall ensure that all acts of torture are offences under its criminal law. The same shall apply to an attempt to commit torture and to an act by any person which constitutes complicity or participation in torture.
2. Each State Party shall make these offences punishable by appropriate penalties which take into account their grave nature.

ARTICLE 5

1. Each State Party shall take such measures as may be necessary to establish its jurisdiction over the offences referred to in Article 4 in the following cases:
   (a) When the offences are committed in any territory under its jurisdiction or on board a ship or aircraft registered in that State;
   (b) When the alleged offender is a national of that State;
   (c) When the victim is a national of that State if that State considers it appropriate.
2. Each State Party shall likewise take such measures as may be necessary to establish its jurisdiction over such offences in cases where the alleged offender is present in

any territory under its jurisdiction and it does not extradite him pursuant to Article 8 to any of the States mentioned in paragraph I of this Article.

3. This Convention does not exclude any criminal jurisdiction exercised in accordance with internal law.

ARTICLE 6

1. Upon being satisfied, after an examination of information available to it, that the circumstances so warrant, any State Party in whose territory a person alleged to have committed any offence referred to in Article 4 is present shall take him into custody or take other legal measures to ensure his presence. The custody and other legal measures shall be as provided in the law of that State but may be continued only for such time as is necessary to enable any criminal or extradition proceedings to be instituted.

2. Such State shall immediately make a preliminary inquiry into the facts.

3. Any person in custody pursuant to paragraph I of this Article shall be assisted in communicating immediately with the nearest appropriate representative of the State of which he is a national, or, if he is a stateless person, with the representative of the State where he usually resides.

4. When a State, pursuant to this article, has taken a person into custody, it shall immediately notify the States referred to in Article 5, paragraph 1, of the fact that such person is in custody and of the circumstances which warrant his detention. The State which makes the preliminary inquiry contemplated in paragraph 2 of this article shall promptly report its findings to the said States and shall indicate whether it intends to exercise jurisdiction.

ARTICLE 7

1. The State Party in the territory under whose jurisdiction a person alleged to have committed any offence referred to in Article 4 is found shall in the cases contemplated in Article 5, if it does not extradite him, submit the case to its competent authorities for the purpose of prosecution.

2. These authorities shall take their decision in the same manner as in the case of any ordinary offence of a serious nature under the law of that State. In the cases referred to in Article 5, paragraph 2, the standards of evidence required for prosecution and conviction shall in no way be less stringent than those which apply in the cases referred to in Article 5, paragraph 1.

3. Any person regarding whom proceedings are brought in connection with any of the offences referred to in Article 4 shall be guaranteed fair treatment at all stages of the proceedings.

ARTICLE 8

1. The offences referred to in Article 4 shall be deemed to be included as extraditable offences in any extradition treaty existing between States Parties. States Parties un-

dertake to include such offences as extraditable offences in every extradition treaty to be concluded between them.

2. If a State Party which makes extradition conditional on the existence of a treaty receives a request for extradition from another. State Party with which it has no extradition treaty, it may consider this Convention as the legal basis for extradition in respect of such offences. Extradition shall be subject to the other conditions provided by the law of the requested State.

3. States Parties which do not make extradition conditional on the existence of a treaty shall recognize such offences as extraditable offences between themselves subject to the conditions provided by the law of the requested State.

4. Such offences shall be treated, for the purpose of extradition between States Parties, as if they had been committed not only in the place in which they occurred but also in the territories of the States required to establish their jurisdiction in accordance with Article 5, paragraph 1.

ARTICLE 9

1. States Parties shall afford one another the greatest measure of assistance in connection with criminal proceedings brought in respect of any of the offences referred to in Article 4, including the supply of all evidence at their disposal necessary for the proceedings.

2. States Parties shall carry out their obligations under paragraph I of this Article in conformity with any treaties on mutual judicial assistance that may exist between them.

ARTICLE 10

1. Each State Party shall ensure that education and information regarding the prohibition against torture are fully included in the training of law enforcement personnel, civil or military, medical personnel, public officials and other persons who may be involved in the custody, interrogation or treatment of any individual subjected to any form of arrest, detention or imprisonment.

2. Each State Party shall include this prohibition in the rules or instructions issued in regard to the duties and functions of any such person.

ARTICLE 11

Each State Party shall keep under systematic review interrogation rules, instructions, methods and practices as well as arrangements for the custody and treatment of persons subjected to any form of arrest, detention or imprisonment in any territory under its jurisdiction, with a view to preventing any cases of torture.

ARTICLE 12

Each State Party shall ensure that its competent authorities proceed to a prompt and impartial investigation, wherever there is reasonable ground to believe that an act of torture has been committed in any territory under its jurisdiction.

ARTICLE 13

Each State Party shall ensure that any individual who alleges he has been subjected to torture in any territory under its jurisdiction has the right to complain to, and to have his case promptly and impartially examined by, its competent authorities. Steps shall be taken to ensure that the complainant and witnesses are protected against all ill-treatment or intimidation as a consequence of his complaint or any evidence given.

ARTICLE 14

1. Each State Party shall ensure in its legal system that the victim of an act of torture obtains redress and has an enforceable right to fair and adequate compensation, including the means for as full rehabilitation as possible. In the event of the death of the victim as a result of an act of torture, his dependants shall be entitled to compensation.
2. Nothing in this article shall affect any right of the victim or other persons to compensation which may exist under national law.

ARTICLE 15

Each State Party shall ensure that any statement which is established to have been made as a result of torture shall not be invoked as evidence in any proceedings, except against a person accused of torture as evidence that the statement was made.

ARTICLE 16

1. Each State Party shall undertake to prevent in any territory under its jurisdiction other acts of cruel, inhuman or degrading treatment or punishment which do not amount to torture as defined in Article 1, when such acts are committed by or at the instigation of or with the consent or acquiescence of a public official or other person acting in an official capacity. In particular, the obligations contained in Articles 10, 11, 12 and 13 shall apply with the substitution for references to torture of references to other forms of cruel, inhuman or degrading treatment or punishment.
2. The provisions of this Convention are without prejudice to the provisions of any other international instrument or national law which prohibits cruel, inhuman or degrading treatment or punishment or which relates to extradition or expulsion.

PART II

ARTICLE 17

1. There shall be established a Committee against Torture (hereinafter referred to as the Committee) which shall carry out the functions hereinafter provided. The Committee shall consist of ten experts of high moral standing and recognized competence in the field of human rights, who shall serve in their personal capacity. The experts shall be elected by the States Parties.

4. *INTERNATIONAL CONVENTION ON THE ELIMINATION OF ALL FORMS OF RACIAL DISCRIMINATION*
660 UNTS 195, ENTERED INTO FORCE JAN. 4, 1969

The States Parties to this Convention,

Considering that the Charter of the United Nations is based on the principles of the dignity and equality inherent in all human beings, and that all Member States have pledged themselves to take joint and separate action, in cooperation with the Organization, for the achievement of one of the purposes of the United Nations which is to promote and encourage universal respect for and observance of human rights and fundamental freedoms for all, without distinction as to race, sex, language or religion,

Considering that the Universal Declaration of Human Rights proclaims that all human beings are born free and equal in dignity and rights and that everyone is entitled to all the rights and freedoms set out therein, without distinction of any kind, in particular as to race, colour or national origin,

Considering that all human beings are equal before the law and are entitled to equal protection of the law against any discrimination and against any incitement to discrimination,

Considering that the United Nations has condemned colonialism and all practices of segregation and discriminated associated therewith, in whatever form and wherever they exist, and that the Declaration on the Granting of Independence to Colonial Countries and Peoples of 14 December 1960 (General Assembly resolution 1514 (XV)) has affirmed and solemnly proclaimed the necessity of bringing them to a speedy and unconditional end,

Considering that the United Nations Declaration on the Elimination of All Forms of Racial Discrimination of 20 November 1963 (General Assembly resolution 1904 (XVIII)) solemnly affirms the necessity of speedily eliminating racial discrimination throughout the world in all its forms and manifestations and of securing understanding of an respect for the dignity of the human person,

Convinced that any doctrine of superiority based on racial differentiation is scientifically false, morally condemnable, socially unjust and dangerous, and that there is no justification for racial discrimination, in theory or in practice, anywhere,

Reaffirming that discrimination between human beings on the grounds of race, colour or ethnic origin is an obstacle to friendly and peaceful relations among nations and is capable of disturbing peace and security among peoples and the harmony of persons living side by side even within one and the same State,

Convinced that the existence of racial barriers is repugnant to the ideals of any human society, alarmed by manifestations of racial discrimination still in evidence in some areas of the world and by governmental policies based on racial superiority or hatred, such as policies of apartheid, segregation or separation,

Resolved to adopt all necessary measures for speedily eliminating racial discrimination in all its forms and manifestations, and to prevent and combat racist doctrines and practices in order to promote understanding between races and to build an international community free from all forms of racial segregation and racial discrimination,

Bearing in mind the Convention International Labour Organization in 1958, and the Convention against Discrimination in Education adopted by the United Nations Educational, Scientific and Cultural Organization in 1960,

Desiring to implement the principles embodied in the United Nations Declaration on the Elimination of all Forms of Racial Discrimination and to secure the earliest adoption of practical measures to that end,

Have agreed as follows:

PART I

ARTICLE 1

1. In this Convention, the term "racial discrimination" shall mean any distinction, exclusion, restriction or preference based on race, colour, descent, or national or ethnic origin which has the purpose or effect of nullifying or impairing the recognition, enjoyment or exercise, on an equal footing, of human rights and fundamental freedoms in the political, economic, social, cultural or any other field of public life.
2. This Convention shall not apply to distinctions, exclusions, restrictions or preferences made by a State Party to this Convention between citizens and non-citizens.
3. Nothing in this Convention may be interpreted as affecting in any way the legal provisions of States Parties concerning nationality, citizen ship or naturalization, provided that such provisions do not discriminate against any particular nationality.
4. Special measures taken for the sole purpose of securing adequate advancement of certain racial or ethnic groups or individuals requiring such protection as may be necessary in order to ensure such groups or individuals equal enjoyment or exercise of human rights and fundamental freedoms shall not be deemed racial discrimination, provided, however, that such measures do not, as a consequence, lead to the maintenance of separate rights for different racial groups and that they shall not be continued after the objectives for which they were taken have been achieved.

ARTICLE 2

1. States Parties condemn racial discrimination and undertake to pursue by all appropriate means and without delay a policy of eliminating racial discrimination in all its forms and promoting understanding among all races, and, to this end:
    (a) Each State Party undertakes to engage in no act or practice of racial discrimination against persons, groups of persons or institutions and to ensure that all public authorities and public institutions, national and local, shall act in conformity with this obligation;
    (b) Each State Party undertakes not to sponsor, defend or support racial discrimination by any persons or organizations;
    (c) Each State Party shall take effective measures to review governmental, national and local policies, and to amend, rescind or nullify any laws and regulations which have the effect of creating or perpetuating racial discrimination wherever it exists;
    (d) Each State Party shall prohibit and bring to an end, by all appropriate means,

including legislation as required by circumstances, racial discrimination by any persons, group or organization;

(e) Each State Party undertakes to encourage, where appropriate, integrationist multiracial organizations and movements and other means of eliminating barriers between races, and to discourage anything which tends to strengthen racial division.

2. States Parties shall, when the circumstances so warrant, take, in the social, economic, cultural and other fields, special and concrete measures to ensure the adequate development and protection of certain racial groups or individuals belong to them, for the purpose of guaranteeing them the full and equal enjoyment of human rights and fundamental freedoms. These measures shall in no case entail as a consequence the maintenance of unequal or separate rights for different racial groups after the objectives for which they were taken have been achieved.

ARTICLE 3

States Parties particularly condemn racial segregation and apartheid and undertake to prevent, prohibit and eradicate all practices of this nature in territories under their jurisdiction.

ARTICLE 4

States Parties condemn all propaganda and all organizations which are based on ideas or theories of superiority of one race or group of persons of one colour or ethnic origin, or which attempt to justify or promote racial hatred and discrimination in any form, and undertake to adopt immediate and positive measures designed to eradicate all incitement to, or acts of, such discrimination and, to this end, with due regard to the principles embodied in the Universal Declaration of Human Rights and the rights expressly set forth in Article 5 of this Convention, *inter alia*:

(a) Shall declare an offence punishable by law all dissemination of ideas based on racial superiority or hatred, incitement to racial discrimination, as well as all race or group of persons of another colour or ethnic origin, and also the provision of any assistance to racist activities, including the financing thereof;

(b) Shall declare illegal and prohibit organizations, and also organized and all other propaganda activities, which promote and incite racial discrimination, and shall recognize participation in such organizations or activities as an offence punishable by law;

(c) Shall not permit public authorities or public institutions, national or local, to promote or incite racial discrimination.

ARTICLE 5

In compliance with the fundamental obligations laid down in Article 2 of this Convention, States Parties undertake to prohibit and to eliminate racial discrimination in all its forms and to guarantee the right of everyone, without distinction as to race, colour, or national or ethnic origin, to equality before the law, notably in the enjoyment of the following rights:

(a) The right to equal treatment before the tribunals and all other organs administering justice;

(b) The right to security of person and protection by the State against violence or bodily harm, whether inflicted by government officials or by any individual group or institution;

(c) Political rights, in particular the right to participate in elections—to vote and to stand for election—on the basis of universal and equal suffrage, to take part in the Government as well as in the conduct of public affairs at any level and to have equal access to public service;

(d) Other civil rights, in particular:

    (i) The right to freedom of movement and residence within the border of the State:

    (ii) The right to leave any country, including one's own, and to return to one's country;

    (iii) The right to nationality;

    (iv) The right to marriage and choice of spouse;

    (v) The right to own property alone as well as in association with others;

    (vi) The right to inherit;

    (vii) The right to freedom of thought, conscience and religion;

    (viii) The right to freedom of opinion and expression;

    (ix) The right to freedom of peaceful assembly and association;

(e) Economic, social and cultural rights, in particular:

    (i) The rights to work, to free choice of employment, to just and favorable conditions of work, to protection against unemployment, to equal pay for equal work, to just and favorable remuneration;

    (ii) The right to form and join trade unions;

    (iii) The right to housing;

    (iv) The right to public health, medical care, social security and social services;

    (v) The right to education and training;

    (vi) The right to equal participation in cultural activities;

    (vii) The right of access to any place or service intended for use by the general public, such as transport hotels, restaurants, cafes, theaters and parks.

ARTICLE 6

States Parties shall assure to everyone within their jurisdiction effective protection and remedies, through the competent national tribunals and other State institutions, against any acts of racial discrimination which violate his human rights and fundamental freedoms contrary to this Convention, as well as the right to seek from such tribunals just and adequate reparation or satisfaction for any damage suffered as a result of such discrimination.

ARTICLE 7

States Parties undertake to adopt immediate and effective measures, particularly in the fields of teaching, education, culture and information, with a view to combating prejudices which lead to racial discrimination and to promoting understanding, tolerance and friendship among nations and racial or ethnical groups, as well as to propagating the purposes and principles of the Charter of the United Nations, the Universal Declaration of Human Rights, the United Nations Declaration on the Elimination of All Forms of Racial Discrimination, and this Convention.

PART II

ARTICLE 8

1. There shall be established a Committee on the Elimination of Racial Discrimination (hereinafter referred to as the Committee) consisting of eighteen experts of high moral standing and acknowledged impartiality elected by States Parties from among their nationals, who shall serve in their personal capacity, consideration being given to equitable geographical distribution and to the representation of the different forms of civilization as well as of the principal legal systems.

5. *CONVENTION ON THE ELIMINATION OF ALL FORMS OF DISCRIMINATION AGAINST WOMEN,* GA RES. 34/180, 34 UN GAOR SUPP. (NO. 46) AT 193, UN DOC. A/34/46, ENTERED INTO FORCE SEPT. 3, 1981

The States Parties to the present Convention,

Noting that the Charter of the United Nations reaffirms faith in fundamental human rights, in the dignity and worth of the human person and in the equal rights of men and women,

Noting that the Universal Declaration of Human Rights affirms the principle of the inadmissibility of discrimination and proclaims that all human beings are born free and equal in dignity and rights and that everyone is entitled to all the rights and freedoms set forth therein, without distinction of any kind, including distinction based on sex,

Noting that the States Parties to the International Covenants on Human Rights have the obligation to ensure the equal rights of men and women to enjoy all economic, social, cultural, civil and political rights,

Considering the international conventions concluded under the auspices of the United Nations and the specialized agencies promoting equality of rights of men and women,

Noting also the resolutions, declarations and recommendations adopted by the United Nations and the specialized agencies promoting equality of rights of men and women,

Concerned, however, that despite these various instruments extensive discrimination against women continues to exist,

Recalling that discrimination against women violates the principles of equality of rights and respect for human dignity, is an obstacle to the participation of women, on equal terms with men, in the political, social, economic and cultural life of their countries, hampers the growth of the prosperity of society and the family and makes more difficult the full development of the potentialities of women in the service of their countries and of humanity,

Concerned that in situations of poverty women have the least access to food, health, education, training and opportunities for employment and other needs,

Convinced that the establishment of the new international economic order based on equity and justice will contribute significantly towards the promotion of equality between men and women, emphasizing that the eradication of apartheid, all forms of racism, racial discrimination, colonialism, neo-colonialism, aggression, foreign occupation and domination and interference in the internal affairs of States is essential to the full enjoyment of the rights of men and women,

Affirming that the strengthening of international peace and security, the relaxation of international tension, mutual cooperation among all States irrespective of their social and economic systems, general and complete disarmament, in particular nuclear disarmament under strict and effective international control, the affirmation of the principles of justice, equality and mutual benefit in relations among countries and the realization of the right of peoples under alien and colonial domination and foreign occupation to self-determination and independence, as well as respect for national sovereignty and territorial integrity, will promote social progress and development and as a consequence will contribute to the attainment of full equality between men and women,

Convinced that the full and complete development of a country, the welfare of the world and the cause of peace require the maximum participation of women on equal terms with men in all fields,

Bearing in mind the great contribution of women to the welfare of the family and to the development of society, so far not fully recognized, the social significance of maternity and the role of both parents in the family and in the upbringing of children, and aware that the role of women in procreation should not be a basis for discrimination but that the upbringing of children requires a sharing of responsibility between men and women and society as a whole;

Aware that a change in the traditional role of men as well as the role of women in society and in the family is needed to achieve full equality between men and women,

Determined to implement the principles set forth in the declaration on the elimination of discrimination against women and for that purpose, to adopt the measures required for the elimination of such discrimination in all its forms and manifestations,

Have agreed on the following:

PART I

ARTICLE I

For the purposes of the present Convention, the term "discrimination against women" shall mean any distinction, exclusion or restriction made on the basis of sex which has the effect or purpose of impairing or nullifying the recognition, enjoyment or exercise by women, irrespective of their marital status, on a basis of equality of men and women, of human rights and fundamental freedoms in the political, economic, social, cultural, civil or any other field.

ARTICLE 2

States Parties condemn discrimination against women in all its forms, agree to pursue by all appropriate means and without delay a policy of eliminating discrimination against women and, to this end, undertake:

(a) To embody the principle of the equality of men and women in their national constitutions or other appropriate legislation if not yet incorporated therein and to ensure, through law and other appropriate means, the practical realization of this principle;

(b) To adopt appropriate legislative and other measures, including sanctions where appropriate, prohibiting all discrimination against women;

(c) To establish legal protection of the rights of women on an equal basis with men and to ensure through competent national tribunals and other public institutions the effective protection of women against any act of discrimination;

(d) To refrain from engaging in any act or practice of discrimination against women and to ensure that public authorities and institutions shall act in conformity with this obligation;

(e) To take all appropriate measures to eliminate discrimination against women by any person, organization or enterprise;

(f) To take all appropriate measures, including legislation, to modify or abolish existing laws, regulations, customs and practices which constitute discrimination against women;

(g) To repeal all national penal provisions which constitute discrimination against women.

ARTICLE 3

States Parties shall take in all fields, in particular in the political, social, economic and cultural fields, all appropriate measures, including legislation, to ensure the full development and advancement of women, for the purpose of guaranteeing them the exercise and enjoyment of human rights and fundamental freedoms on a basis of equality with men.

ARTICLE 4

1. Adoption by States Parties of temporary special measures aimed at accelerating de facto equality between men and women shall not be considered discrimination as defined in the present Convention, but shall in no way entail as a consequence the maintenance of unequal or separate standards; these measures shall be discontinued when the objectives of equality of opportunity and treatment have been achieved.
2. Adoption by States Parties of special measures, including those measures contained

in the present Convention, aimed at protecting maternity shall not be considered discriminatory.

ARTICLE 5

States Parties shall take all appropriate measures:
(a) To modify the social and cultural patterns of conduct of men and women, with a view to achieving the elimination of prejudices and customary and all other practices which are based on the idea of the inferiority or the superiority of either of the sexes or on stereotyped roles for men and women;
(b) To ensure that family education includes a proper understanding of maternity as a social function and the recognition of the common responsibility of men and women in the upbringing and development of their children, it being understood that the interest of the children is the primordial consideration in all cases.

ARTICLE 6

States Parties shall take all appropriate measures, including legislation, to suppress all forms of traffic in women and exploitation of prostitution of women.

PART II

ARTICLE 7

States Parties shall take all appropriate measures to eliminate discrimination against women in the political and public life of the country and, in particular, shall ensure to women, on equal terms with men, the right:
(a) To vote in all elections and public referenda and to be eligible for election to all publicly elected bodies;
(b) To participate in the formulation of government policy and the implementation thereof and to hold public office and perform all public functions at all levels of government;
(c) To participate in non-governmental organizations and associations concerned with the public and political life of the country.

ARTICLE 8

States Parties shall take all appropriate measures to ensure to women, on equal terms with men and without any discrimination, the opportunity to represent their Governments at the international level and to participate in the work of international organizations.

ARTICLE 9

1. States Parties shall grant women equal rights with men to acquire, change or retain their nationality. They shall ensure in particular that neither marriage to an alien nor change of nationality by the husband during marriage shall automatically change

the nationality of the wife, render her stateless or force upon her the nationality of the husband.

2. States Parties shall grant women equal rights with men with respect to the nationality of their children.

PART III

ARTICLE 10

States Parties shall take all appropriate measures to eliminate discrimination against women in order to ensure to them equal rights with men in the field of education and in particular to ensure, on a basis of equality of men and women:

(a) The same conditions for career and vocational guidance, for access to studies and for the achievement of diplomas in educational establishments of all categories in rural as well as in urban areas; this equality shall be ensured in preschool, general, technical, professional and higher technical education, as well as in all types of vocational training;

(b) Access to the same curricula, the same examinations, teaching staff with qualifications of the same standard and school premises and equipment of the same quality;

(c) The elimination of any stereotype concept of the roles of men and women at all levels and in all forms of education by encouraging coeducation and other types of education which will help to achieve this aim and,. In particular, by the revision of textbooks and school programs and the adaptation of teaching methods;

(d) The same opportunities to benefit from scholarships and other study grants;

(e) The same opportunities for access to programs of continuing education, including adult and functional literacy programs, particularly those aimed at reducing, at the earliest possible time, any gap in education existing between men and women;

(f) The reduction of female student drop-out rates and the organization of programs for girls and women who have left school prematurely;

(g) The same opportunities to participate actively in sports and physical education;

(h) Access to specific educational information to help to ensure the health and well-being of families, including information and advice on family planning.

ARTICLE 11

1. States Parties shall take all appropriate measures to eliminate discrimination against women in the field of employment in order to ensure, on a basis of equality of men and women, the same rights, in particular:

(a) The right to work as an inalienable right of all human beings;

(b) the right to the same employment opportunities, including the application of the same criteria for selection in matters of employment;

(c) the right to free choice of profession and employment, the right to promotion,

job security and all the benefits and conditions of service and the right to receive vocational training and retraining, including apprenticeships, advanced
vocational training and recurrent training;

(d) the right to equal remuneration, including benefits, and to equal treatment in
respect of work of equal value, as well as equality of treatment n the evaluation
of the quality of work;

(e) the right to social security, particularly in cases of retirement, unemployment,
sickness, invalidity, and old age and other incapacity to work, as well as the
right to paid leave;

(f) the right to protection of health and to safety in working conditions, including
safeguarding of the function of reproduction.

2. In order to prevent discrimination against women on the grounds of marriage or
maternity and to ensure their effective right to work, States Parties shall take appropriate measures:

(a) To prohibit, subject to the imposition of sanctions, dismissal on the grounds of
pregnancy or of maternity leave and discrimination in dismissals on the basis of
marital status;

(b) To introduce maternity leave with pay or with comparable social benefits without loss of former employment, seniority or social allowances;

(c) To encourage the provision of the necessary supporting social services to enable
parents to combine family obligations with work responsibilities and participation in public life, in particular through promoting the establishment and
development of a network of child-care facilities;

(d) To provide special protection to women during pregnancy in types of work
proved to be harmful to them.

3. Protective legislation relating to matters covered in this Article shall be reviewed periodically in the light of scientific and technological knowledge and shall be revised,
repealed or extended as necessary.

ARTICLE 12

1. States Parties shall take all appropriate measures to eliminate discrimination against
women in the field of health care in order to ensure, on a basis of equality of men and
women, access to health care services, including those related to family planning.

2. Notwithstanding the provisions of paragraph 1 of this Article, States Parties shall
ensure to women appropriate services in connection with pregnancy, confinement
and the post-natal period, granting free services where necessary, as well as adequate nutrition during pregnancy and lactation.

ARTICLE 13

States Parties shall take all appropriate measures to eliminate discrimination against
women in other areas of economic and social life in order to ensure, on a basis of
equality of men and women, the same rights, in particular:

(a) The right to family benefits;

(b) The right to bank loans, mortgages and other forms of financial credit;
(c) The right to participate in recreational activities, sports and all aspects of cultural life.

ARTICLE 14

1. States Parties shall take into account the particular problems faced by rural women and the significant roles which rural women play in the economic survival of their families, including their work in the non-monetized sectors of the economy, and shall take all appropriate measures to ensure the application of the provisions of the present Convention to women in rural areas.
2. States Parties shall take all appropriate measures to eliminate discrimination against women in rural areas in order to ensure, on a basis of equality of men and women, that they participate in and benefit from rural development and, in particular, shall ensure to such women the right:
   (a) To participate in the elaboration and implementation of development planning at all levels;
   (b) To have access to adequate health care facilities, including information, counseling and services in family planning;
   (c) To benefit directly from social security programs;
   (d) To obtain all types of training and education, formal and non-formal, including that relating to functional literacy, as well as, *inter alia*, the benefit of all community and extension services, in order to increase their technical proficiency;
   (e) To organize self-help groups and cooperatives in order to obtain equal access to economic opportunities through employment or self-employment;
   (f) To participate in all community activities;
   (g) To have access to agricultural credit and loans, marketing facilities, appropriate technology and equal treatment in land and agrarian reform as well as in land resettlement schemes;
   (h) To enjoy adequate living conditions, particularly in relation to housing, sanitation, electricity and water supply, transport and communications.

PART IV

ARTICLE 15

1. States Parties shall accord to women equality with men before the law.
2. States Parties shall accord to women, in civil matters, a legal capacity identical to that of men and the same opportunities to exercise that capacity. In particular, they shall give women equal rights to conclude contracts and to administer property and shall treat them equally in all stages of procedure in courts and tribunals.
3. States Parties agree that all contracts and all other private instruments of any kind with a legal effect which is directed at restricting the legal capacity of women shall be deemed null and void.
4. States Parties shall accord to men and women the same rights with regard to the

law relating to the movement of persons and the freedom to choose their residence and domicile.

ARTICLE 16

1. States Parties shall take all appropriate measures to eliminate discrimination against women in all matters relating to marriage and family relations and in particular shall ensure, on a basis of equality of men and women:
   (a) The same right to enter into marriage;
   (b) The same right freely to choose a spouse and to enter into marriage only with their free and full consent;
   (c) The same rights and responsibilities during marriage and at its dissolution;
   (d) The same rights and responsibilities as parents, irrespective of their marital status, in matters relating to their children; in all cases the interests of the children shall be paramount;
   (e) The same rights to decide freely and responsibly on the number and spacing of their children and to have access to the information, education and means to enable them to exercise these rights;
   (f) The same rights and responsibilities with regard to guardianship, wardship, trusteeship and adoption of children, or similar institutions where these concepts exist in national legislation; in all cases the interests of the children shall be paramount;
   (g) The same personal rights as husband and wife, including the right to choose a family name, a profession and an occupation;
   (h) The same rights for both spouses in respect of the ownership, acquisition, management, administration, enjoyment and disposition of property, whether free of charge or for a valuable consideration.
2. The betrothal and the marriage of a child shall have no legal effect, and all necessary action, including legislation, shall be taken to specify a minimum age for marriage and to make the registration of marriages in an official registry compulsory.

ARTICLE 17

1. For the purpose of considering the progress made in the implementation of the present Convention, there shall be established a Committee on the Elimination of Discrimination against Women (hereinafter referred to as the Committee) consisting, at the time of entry into force of the Convention, of eighteen and, after ratification of or accession to the Convention by the thirty-fifth State Party, of twenty-three experts of high moral standing and competence in the field covered by the Convention. The experts shall be elected by States Parties from among their nationals and shall serve in their personal capacity, consideration being given to equitable geographical distribution and to the representation of the different forms of civilization as well as the principal legal systems.

6. *AMERICAN CONVENTION ON HUMAN RIGHTS*
OAS TREATY SERIES NO. 36, 1144 UNTS 123 ENTERED
INTO FORCE JULY 18, 1978, REPRINTED IN BASIC
DOCUMENTS PERTAINING TO HUMAN RIGHTS
IN THE INTER-AMERICAN SYSTEM, OEA/SER.L.V/II.82
DOC.6 REV.1 AT 25 (1992)
PREAMBLE

The American states signatory to the present Convention,

Reaffirming their intention to consolidate in this hemisphere, within the framework of democratic institutions, a system of personal liberty and social justice based on respect for the essential rights of man;

Recognizing that the essential rights of man are not derived from one's being a national of a certain state, but are based upon attributes of the human personality, and that they therefore justify international protection in the form of a convention reinforcing or complementing the protection provided by the domestic law of the American states;

Considering that these principles have been set forth in the Charter of the Organization of American States, in the American Declaration of the Rights and Duties of Man, and in the Universal Declaration of Human Rights, and that they have been reaffirmed and refined in other international instruments, worldwide as well as regional in scope;

Reiterating that, in accordance with the Universal Declaration of Human Rights, the ideal of free men enjoying freedom from fear and want can be achieved only if conditions are created whereby everyone may enjoy his economic, social, and cultural rights, as well as his civil and political rights; and

Considering that the Third Special Inter-American Conference (Buenos Aires, 1967) approved the incorporation into the Charter of the Organization itself of broader standards with respect to economic, social, and educational rights and resolved that an inter-American convention on human rights should determine the structure, competence, and procedure of the organs responsible for these matters,

Have agreed upon the following:

PART I—STATE OBLIGATIONS AND RIGHTS PROTECTED
CHAPTER I—GENERAL OBLIGATIONS

ARTICLE 1. OBLIGATION TO RESPECT RIGHTS

1. The States Parties to this Convention undertake to respect the rights and freedoms recognized herein and to ensure to all persons subject to their jurisdiction the free and full exercise of those rights and freedoms, without any discrimination for reasons of race, color, sex, language, religion, political or other opinion, national or social origin, economic status, birth, or any other social condition.
2. For the purposes of this Convention, "person" means every human being.

ARTICLE 2. DOMESTIC LEGAL EFFECTS

Where the exercise of any of the rights or freedoms referred to in Article 1 is not already ensured by legislative or other provisions, the States Parties undertake to adopt, in accordance with their constitutional processes and the provisions of this Convention, such legislative or other measures as may be necessary to give effect to those rights or freedoms.

CHAPTER II—CIVIL AND POLITICAL RIGHTS

ARTICLE 3. RIGHT TO JURIDICAL PERSONALITY

Every person has the right to recognition as a person before the law.

ARTICLE 4. RIGHT TO LIFE

1. Every person has the right to have his life respected. This right shall be protected by law and, in general, from the moment of conception. No one shall be arbitrarily deprived of his life.
2. In countries that have not abolished the death penalty, it may be imposed only for the most serious crimes and pursuant to a final judgment rendered by a competent court and in accordance with a law establishing such punishment, enacted prior to the commission of the crime. The application of such punishment shall not be extended to crimes to which it does not presently apply.
3. The death penalty shall not be reestablished in states that have abolished it.
4. In no case shall capital punishment be inflicted for political offenses or related common crimes.
5. Capital punishment shall not be imposed upon persons who, at the time the crime was committed, were under 18 years of age or over 70 years of age; nor shall it be applied to pregnant women.
6. Every person condemned to death shall have the right to apply for amnesty, pardon, or commutation of sentence, which may be granted in all cases. Capital punishment shall not be imposed while such a petition is pending decision by the competent authority.

ARTICLE 5. RIGHT TO HUMANE TREATMENT

1. Every person has the right to have his physical, mental, and moral integrity respected.
2. No one shall be subjected to torture or to cruel, inhuman, or degrading punishment or treatment. All persons deprived of their liberty shall be treated with respect for the inherent dignity of the human person.
3. Punishment shall not be extended to any person other than the criminal.
4. Accused persons shall, save in exceptional circumstances, be segregated from con-

victed persons, and shall be subject to separate treatment appropriate to their status as unconvicted persons.

5. Minors while subject to criminal proceedings shall be separated from adults and brought before specialized tribunals, as speedily as possible, so that they may be treated in accordance with their status as minors.

6. Punishments consisting of deprivation of liberty shall have as an essential aim the reform and social readaptation of the prisoners.

ARTICLE 6. FREEDOM FROM SLAVERY

1. No one shall be subject to slavery or to involuntary servitude, which are prohibited in all their forms, as are the slave trade and traffic in women.

2. No one shall be required to perform forced or compulsory labor. This provision shall not be interpreted to mean that, in those countries in which the penalty established for certain crimes is deprivation of liberty at forced labor, the carrying out of such a sentence imposed by a competent court is prohibited. Forced labor shall not adversely affect the dignity or the physical or intellectual capacity of the prisoner.

3. For the purposes of this article, the following do not constitute forced or compulsory labor:

   a. work or service normally required of a person imprisoned in execution of a sentence or formal decision passed by the competent judicial authority. Such work or service shall be carried out under the supervision and control of public authorities, and any persons performing such work or service shall not be placed at the disposal of any private party, company, or juridical person;

   b. military service and, in countries in which conscientious objectors are recognized, national service that the law may provide for in lieu of military service;

   c. service exacted in time of danger or calamity that threatens the existence or the well-being of the community; or

   d. work or service that forms part of normal civic obligations.

ARTICLE 7. RIGHT TO PERSONAL LIBERTY

1. Every person has the right to personal liberty and security.

2. No one shall be deprived of his physical liberty except for the reasons and under the conditions established beforehand by the constitution of the State Party concerned or by a law established pursuant thereto.

3. No one shall be subject to arbitrary arrest or imprisonment.

4. Anyone who is detained shall be informed of the reasons for his detention and shall be promptly notified of the charge or charges against him.

5. Any person detained shall be brought promptly before a judge or other officer authorized by law to exercise judicial power and shall be entitled to trial within a reasonable time or to be released without prejudice to the continuation of the proceedings. His release may be subject to guarantees to assure his appearance for trial.

6. Anyone who is deprived of his liberty shall be entitled to recourse to a competent

court, in order that the court may decide without delay on the lawfulness of his arrest or detention and order his release if the arrest or detention is unlawful. In States Parties whose laws provide that anyone who believes himself to be threatened with deprivation of his liberty is entitled to recourse to a competent court in order that it may decide on the lawfulness of such threat, this remedy may not be restricted or abolished. The interested party or another person in his behalf is entitled to seek these remedies.

7. No one shall be detained for debt. This principle shall not limit the orders of a competent judicial authority issued for non-fulfillment of duties of support.

ARTICLE 8. RIGHT TO A FAIR TRIAL

1. Every person has the right to a hearing, with due guarantees and within a reasonable time, by a competent, independent, and impartial tribunal, previously established by law, in the substantiation of any accusation of a criminal nature made against him or for the determination of his rights and obligations of a civil, labor, fiscal, or any other nature.

2. Every person accused of a criminal offense has the right to be presumed innocent so long as his guilt has not been proven according to law. During the proceedings, every person is entitled, with full equality, to the following minimum guarantees:

   a. the right of the accused to be assisted without charge by a translator or interpreter, if he does not understand or does not speak the language of the tribunal or court;
   b. prior notification in detail to the accused of the charges against him;
   c. adequate time and means for the preparation of his defense;
   d. the right of the accused to defend himself personally or to be assisted by legal counsel of his own choosing, and to communicate freely and privately with his counsel;
   e. the inalienable right to be assisted by counsel provided by the state, paid or not as the domestic law provides, if the accused does not defend himself personally or engage his own counsel within the time period established by law;
   f. the right of the defense to examine witnesses present in the court and to obtain the appearance, as witnesses, of experts or other persons who may throw light on the facts;
   g. the right not to be compelled to be a witness against himself or to plead guilty; and
   h. the right to appeal the judgment to a higher court.

3. A confession of guilt by the accused shall be valid only if it is made without coercion of any kind.

4. An accused person acquitted by a non-appealable judgment shall not be subjected to a new trial for the same cause.

5. Criminal proceedings shall be public, except insofar as may be necessary to protect the interests of justice.

Article 9. Freedom from Ex Post Facto Laws

No one shall be convicted of any act or omission that did not constitute a criminal offense, under the applicable law, at the time it was committed. A heavier penalty shall not be imposed than the one that was applicable at the time the criminal offense was committed. If subsequent to the commission of the offense the law provides for the imposition of a lighter punishment, the guilty person shall benefit therefrom.

Article 10. Right to Compensation

Every person has the right to be compensated in accordance with the law in the event he has been sentenced by a final judgment through a miscarriage of justice.

Article 11. Right to Privacy

1. Everyone has the right to have his honor respected and his dignity recognized.
2. No one may be the object of arbitrary or abusive interference with his private life, his family, his home, or his correspondence, or of unlawful attacks on his honor or reputation.
3. Everyone has the right to the protection of the law against such interference or attacks.

Article 12. Freedom of Conscience and Religion

1. Everyone has the right to freedom of conscience and of religion. This right includes freedom to maintain or to change one's religion or beliefs, and freedom to profess or disseminate one's religion or beliefs, either individually or together with others, in public or in private.
2. No one shall be subject to restrictions that might impair his freedom to maintain or to change his religion or beliefs.
3. Freedom to manifest one's religion and beliefs may be subject only to the limitations prescribed by law that are necessary to protect public safety, order, health, or morals, or the rights or freedoms of others.
4. Parents or guardians, as the case may be, have the right to provide for the religious and moral education of their children or wards that is in accord with their own convictions.

Article 13. Freedom of Thought and Expression

1. Everyone has the right to freedom of thought and expression. This right includes freedom to seek, receive, and impart information and ideas of all kinds, regardless of frontiers, either orally, in writing, in print, in the form of art, or through any other medium of one's choice.
2. The exercise of the right provided for in the foregoing paragraph shall not be sub-

ject to prior censorship but shall be subject to subsequent imposition of liability, which shall be expressly established by law to the extent necessary to ensure:

   a. respect for the rights or reputations of others; or

   b. the protection of national security, public order, or public health or morals.

3. The right of expression may not be restricted by indirect methods or means, such as the abuse of government or private controls over newsprint, radio broadcasting frequencies, or equipment used in the dissemination of information, or by any other means tending to impede the communication and circulation of ideas and opinions.

4. Notwithstanding the provisions of paragraph 2 above, public entertainments may be subject by law to prior censorship for the sole purpose of regulating access to them for the moral protection of childhood and adolescence.

5. Any propaganda for war and any advocacy of national, racial, or religious hatred that constitute incitements to lawless violence or to any other similar action against any person or group of persons on any grounds including those of race, color, religion, language, or national origin shall be considered as offenses punishable by law.

ARTICLE 14. RIGHT OF REPLY

1. Anyone injured by inaccurate or offensive statements or ideas disseminated to the public in general by a legally regulated medium of communication has the right to reply or to make a correction using the same communications outlet, under such conditions as the law may establish.

2. The correction or reply shall not in any case remit other legal liabilities that may have been incurred.

3. For the effective protection of honor and reputation, every publisher, and every newspaper, motion picture, radio, and television company, shall have a person responsible who is not protected by immunities or special privileges.

ARTICLE 15. RIGHT OF ASSEMBLY

The right of peaceful assembly, without arms, is recognized. No restrictions may be placed on the exercise of this right other than those imposed in conformity with the law and necessary in a democratic society in the interest of national security, public safety or public order, or to protect public health or morals or the rights or freedom of others.

ARTICLE 16. FREEDOM OF ASSOCIATION

1. Everyone has the right to associate freely for ideological, religious, political, economic, labor, social, cultural, sports, or other purposes.

2. The exercise of this right shall be subject only to such restrictions established by law as may be necessary in a democratic society, in the interest of national security, public safety or public order, or to protect public health or morals or the rights and freedoms of others.

3. The provisions of this article do not bar the imposition of legal restrictions, including even deprivation of the exercise of the right of association, on members of the armed forces and the police.

ARTICLE 17. RIGHTS OF THE FAMILY

The family is the natural and fundamental group unit of society and is entitled to protection by society and the state.

2. The right of men and women of marriageable age to marry and to raise a family shall be recognized, if they meet the conditions required by domestic laws, insofar as such conditions do not affect the principle of nondiscrimination established in this Convention.
3. No marriage shall be entered into without the free and full consent of the intending spouses.
4. The States Parties shall take appropriate steps to ensure the equality of rights and the adequate balancing of responsibilities of the spouses as to marriage, during marriage, and in the event of its dissolution. In case of dissolution, provision shall be made for the necessary protection of any children solely on the basis of their own best interests.
5. The law shall recognize equal rights for children born out of wedlock and those born in wedlock.

ARTICLE 18. RIGHT TO A NAME

Every person has the right to a given name and to the surnames of his parents or that of one of them. The law shall regulate the manner in which this right shall be ensured for all, by the use of assumed names if necessary.

ARTICLE 19. RIGHTS OF THE CHILD

Every minor child has the right to the measures of protection required by his condition as a minor on the part of his family, society, and the state.

ARTICLE 20. RIGHT TO NATIONALITY

1. Every person has the right to a nationality.
2. Every person has the right to the nationality of the state in whose territory he was born if he does not have the right to any other nationality.
3. No one shall be arbitrarily deprived of his nationality or of the right to change it.

ARTICLE 21. RIGHT TO PROPERTY

1. Everyone has the right to the use and enjoyment of his property. The law may subordinate such use and enjoyment to the interest of society.

2. No one shall be deprived of his property except upon payment of just compensation, for reasons of public utility or social interest, and in the cases and according to the forms established by law.
3. Usury and any other form of exploitation of man by man shall be prohibited by law.

ARTICLE 22. FREEDOM OF MOVEMENT AND RESIDENCE

1. Every person lawfully in the territory of a State Party has the right to move about in it, and to reside in it subject to the provisions of the law.
2. Every person has the right to leave any country freely, including his own.
3. The exercise of the foregoing rights may be restricted only pursuant to a law to the extent necessary in a democratic society to prevent crime or to protect national security, public safety, public order, public morals, public health, or the rights or freedoms of others.
4. The exercise of the rights recognized in paragraph 1 may also be restricted by law in designated zones for reasons of public interest.
5. No one can be expelled from the territory of the state of which he is a national or be deprived of the right to enter it.
6. An alien lawfully in the territory of a State Party to this Convention may be expelled from it only pursuant to a decision reached in accordance with law.
7. Every person has the right to seek and be granted asylum in a foreign territory, in accordance with the legislation of the state and international conventions, in the event he is being pursued for political offenses or related common crimes.
8. In no case may an alien be deported or returned to a country, regardless of whether or not it is his country of origin, if in that country his right to life or personal freedom is in danger of being violated because of his race, nationality, religion, social status, or political opinions.
9. The collective expulsion of aliens is prohibited.

ARTICLE 23. RIGHT TO PARTICIPATE IN GOVERNMENT

1. Every citizen shall enjoy the following rights and opportunities:
   a. to take part in the conduct of public affairs, directly or through freely chosen representatives;
   b. to vote and to be elected in genuine periodic elections, which shall be by universal and equal suffrage and by secret ballot that guarantees the free expression of the will of the voters; and
   c. to have access, under general conditions of equality, to the public service of his country.
2. The law may regulate the exercise of the rights and opportunities referred to in the preceding paragraph only on the basis of age, nationality, residence, language, education, civil and mental capacity, or sentencing by a competent court in criminal proceedings.

ARTICLE 24. RIGHT TO EQUAL PROTECTION

All persons are equal before the law. Consequently, they are entitled, without discrimination, to equal protection of the law.

ARTICLE 25. RIGHT TO JUDICIAL PROTECTION

1. Everyone has the right to simple and prompt recourse, or any other effective recourse, to a competent court or tribunal for protection against acts that violate his fundamental rights recognized by the constitution or laws of the state concerned or by this Convention, even though such violation may have been committed by persons acting in the course of their official duties.
2. The States Parties undertake:
   a. to ensure that any person claiming such remedy shall have his rights determined by the competent authority provided for by the legal system of the state;
   b. to develop the possibilities of judicial remedy; and
   c. to ensure that the competent authorities shall enforce such remedies when granted.

CHAPTER III—ECONOMIC, SOCIAL, AND CULTURAL RIGHTS

ARTICLE 26. PROGRESSIVE DEVELOPMENT

The States Parties undertake to adopt measures, both internally and through international cooperation, especially those of an economic and technical nature, with a view to achieving progressively, by legislation or other appropriate means, the full realization of the rights implicit in the economic, social, educational, scientific, and cultural standards set forth in the Charter of the Organization of American States as amended by the Protocol of Buenos Aires.

CHAPTER IV—SUSPENSION OF GUARANTEES, INTERPRETATION, AND APPLICATION

ARTICLE 27. SUSPENSION OF GUARANTEES

1. In time of war, public danger, or other emergency that threatens the independence or security of a State Party, it may take measures derogating from its obligations under the present Convention to the extent and for the period of time strictly required by the exigencies of the situation, provided that such measures are not inconsistent with its other obligations under international law and do not involve discrimination on the ground of race, color, sex, language, religion, or social origin.
2. The foregoing provision does not authorize any suspension of the following articles: Article 3 (Right to Juridical Personality), Article 4 (Right to Life), Article 5

(Right to Humane Treatment), Article 6 (Freedom from Slavery), Article 9 (Freedom from Ex Post Facto Laws), Article 12 (Freedom of Conscience and Religion), Article 17 (Rights of the Family), Article 18 (Right to a Name), Article 19 (Rights of the Child), Article 20 (Right to Nationality), and Article 23 (Right to Participate in Government), or of the judicial guarantees essential for the protection of such rights.

3. Any State Party availing itself of the right of suspension shall immediately inform the other States Parties, through the Secretary General of the Organization of American States, of the provisions the application of which it has suspended, the reasons that gave rise to the suspension, and the date set for the termination of such suspension.

Article 28. Federal Clause

1. Where a State Party is constituted as a federal state, the national government of such State Party shall implement all the provisions of the Convention over whose subject matter it exercises legislative and judicial jurisdiction.

2. With respect to the provisions over whose subject matter the constituent units of the federal state have jurisdiction, the national government shall immediately take suitable measures, in accordance with its constitution and its laws, to the end that the competent authorities of the constituent units may adopt appropriate provisions for the fulfillment of this Convention.

3. Whenever two or more States Parties agree to form a federation or other type of association, they shall take care that the resulting federal or other compact contains the provisions necessary for continuing and rendering effective the standards of this Convention in the new state that is organized.

Article 29. Restrictions Regarding Interpretation

No provision of this Convention shall be interpreted as:
   a. permitting any State Party, group, or person to suppress the enjoyment or exercise of the rights and freedoms recognized in this Convention or to restrict them to a greater extent than is provided for herein;
   b. restricting the enjoyment or exercise of any right or freedom recognized by virtue of the laws of any State Party or by virtue of another convention to which one of the said states is a party;
   c. precluding other rights or guarantees that are inherent in the human personality or derived from representative democracy as a form of government; or
   d. excluding or limiting the effect that the American Declaration of the Rights and Duties of Man and other international acts of the same nature may have.

Article 30. Scope of Restrictions

The restrictions that, pursuant to this Convention, may be placed on the enjoyment or exercise of the rights or freedoms recognized herein may not be applied except in accordance with laws enacted for reasons of general interest and in accordance with the purpose for which such restrictions have been established.

ARTICLE 31. RECOGNITION OF OTHER RIGHTS

Other rights and freedoms recognized in accordance with the procedures established in Articles 76 and 77 may be included in the system of protection of this Convention.

CHAPTER V—PERSONAL RESPONSIBILITIES

ARTICLE 32. RELATIONSHIP BETWEEN DUTIES AND RIGHTS

1. Every person has responsibilities to his family, his community, and mankind.
2. The rights of each person are limited by the rights of others, by the security of all, and by the just demands of the general welfare, in a democratic society.

PART II—MEANS OF PROTECTION
CHAPTER VI—COMPETENT ORGANS

ARTICLE 33

The following organs shall have competence with respect to matters relating to the fulfillment of the commitments made by the States Parties to this Convention:
   a. the Inter-American Commission on Human Rights, referred to as "The Commission;" and
   b. the Inter-American Court of Human Rights, referred to as "The Court."

7. AFRICAN [BANJUL] CHARTER
ON HUMAN AND PEOPLES' RIGHTS
ADOPTED JUNE 27, 1981, OAU DOC. CAB/LEG/67/3
REV. 5, 21 ILM 58 (1982), ENTERED INTO
FORCE OCT. 21, 1986

Preamble

The African States members of the Organization of African Unity, parties to the present convention entitled "African Charter on Human and Peoples' Rights",

Recalling Decision 115 (XVI) of the Assembly of Heads of State and Government at its Sixteenth Ordinary Session held in Monrovia, Liberia, from 17 to 20 July 1979 on the preparation of a "preliminary draft on an African Charter on Human and Peoples' Rights providing *inter alia* for the establishment of bodies to promote and protect human and peoples' rights";

Considering the Charter of the Organization of African Unity, which stipulates that "freedom, equality, justice and dignity are essential objectives for the achievement of the legitimate aspirations of the African peoples";

Reaffirming the pledge they solemnly made in Article 2 of the said Charter to eradicate all forms of colonialism from Africa, to coordinate and intensify their cooperation and efforts to achieve a better life for the peoples of Africa and to promote international cooperation having due regard to the Charter of the United Nations and the Universal Declaration of Human Rights;

Taking into consideration the virtues of their historical tradition and the values of African civilization which should inspire and characterize their reflection on the concept of human and peoples' rights;

Recognizing on the one hand, that fundamental human rights stem from the attributes of human beings which justifies their national and international protection and on the other hand that the reality and respect of peoples rights should necessarily guarantee human rights;

Considering that the enjoyment of rights and freedoms also implies the performance of duties on the part of everyone;

Convinced that it is henceforth essential to pay a particular attention to the right to development and that civil and political rights cannot be dissociated from economic, social and cultural rights in their conception as well as universality and that the satisfaction of economic, social and cultural rights is a guarantee for the enjoyment of civil and political rights;

Conscious of their duty to achieve the total liberation of Africa, the peoples of which are still struggling for their dignity and genuine independence, and undertaking to eliminate colonialism, neo-colonialism, apartheid, Zionism and to dismantle aggressive foreign military bases and all forms of discrimination, particularly those based on race, ethnic group, color, sex. language, religion or political opinions;

Reaffirming their adherence to the principles of human and peoples' rights and freedoms contained in the declarations, conventions and other instrument adopted by the Organization of African Unity, the Movement of Non-Aligned Countries and the United Nations;

Firmly convinced of their duty to promote and protect human and people' rights and freedoms taking into account the importance traditionally attached to these rights and freedoms in Africa;

Have agreed as follows:

PART I: RIGHTS AND DUTIES
CHAPTER I—HUMAN AND PEOPLES' RIGHTS

ARTICLE 1

The Member States of the Organization of African Unity parties to the present Charter shall recognize the rights, duties and freedoms enshrined in this Chapter and shall undertake to adopt legislative or other measures to give effect to them.

ARTICLE 2

Every individual shall be entitled to the enjoyment of the rights and freedoms recognized and guaranteed in the present Charter without distinction of any kind such as race, ethnic group, color, sex, language, religion, political or any other opinion, national and social origin, fortune, birth or other status.

ARTICLE 3

1. Every individual shall be equal before the law.
2. Every individual shall be entitled to equal protection of the law.

ARTICLE 4

Human beings are inviolable. Every human being shall be entitled to respect for his life and the integrity of his person. No one may be arbitrarily deprived of this right.

ARTICLE 5

Every individual shall have the right to the respect of the dignity inherent in a human being and to the recognition of his legal status. All forms of exploitation and degradation of man particularly slavery, slave trade, torture, cruel, inhuman or degrading punishment and treatment shall be prohibited.

ARTICLE 6

Every individual shall have the right to liberty and to the security of his person. No one may be deprived of his freedom except for reasons and conditions previously laid down by law. In particular, no one may be arbitrarily arrested or detained.

ARTICLE 7

1. Every individual shall have the right to have his cause heard. This comprises:
   (a) the right to an appeal to competent national organs against acts of violating his fundamental rights as recognized and guaranteed by conventions, laws, regulations and customs in force;
   (b) the right to be presumed innocent until proved guilty by a competent court or tribunal;
   (c) the right to defence, including the right to be defended by counsel of his choice;
   (d) the right to be tried within a reasonable time by an impartial court or tribunal.
2. No one may be condemned for an act or omission which did not constitute a legally punishable offence at the time it was committed. No penalty may be inflicted for an offence for which no provision was made at the time it was committed. Punishment is personal and can be imposed only on the offender.

ARTICLE 8

Freedom of conscience, the profession and free practice of religion shall be guaranteed. No one may, subject to law and order, be submitted to measures restricting the exercise of these freedoms.

ARTICLE 9

1. Every individual shall have the right to receive information. 2. Every individual shall have the right to express and disseminate his opinions within the law.

ARTICLE 10

1. Every individual shall have the right to free association provided that he abides by the law.
2. Subject to the obligation of solidarity provided for in 29 no one may be compelled to join an association.

ARTICLE 11

Every individual shall have the right to assemble freely with others. The exercise of this right shall be subject only to necessary restrictions provided for by law in particular those enacted in the interest of national security, the safety, health, ethics and rights and freedoms of others.

ARTICLE 12

1. Every individual shall have the right to freedom of movement and residence within the borders of a State provided he abides by the law.
2. Every individual shall have the right to leave any country including his own, and to return to his country. This right may only be subject to restrictions, provided for by law for the protection of national security, law and order, public health or morality.
3. Every individual shall have the right, when persecuted, to seek and obtain asylum in other countries in accordance with laws of those countries and international conventions.
4. A non-national legally admitted in a territory of a State Party to the present Charter, may only be expelled from it by virtue of a decision taken in accordance with the law.
5. The mass expulsion of non-nationals shall be prohibited. Mass expulsion shall be that which is aimed at national, racial, ethnic or religious groups.

ARTICLE 13

1. Every citizen shall have the right to participate freely in the government of his country, either directly or through freely chosen representatives in accordance with the provisions of the law.
2. Every citizen shall have the right of equal access to the public service of his country.
3. Every individual shall have the right of access to public property and services in strict equality of all persons before the law.

ARTICLE 14

The right to property shall be guaranteed. It may only be encroached upon in the interest of public need or in the general interest of the community and in accordance with the provisions of appropriate laws.

ARTICLE 15

Every individual shall have the right to work under equitable and satisfactory conditions, and shall receive equal pay for equal work.

ARTICLE 16

1. Every individual shall have the right to enjoy the best attainable state of physical and mental health.
2. States Parties to the present Charter shall take the necessary measures to protect the health of their people and to ensure that they receive medical attention when they are sick.

ARTICLE 17

1. Every individual shall have the right to education.
2. Every individual may freely, take part in the cultural life of his community.
3. The promotion and protection of morals and traditional values recognized by the community shall be the duty of the State.

ARTICLE 18

1. The family shall be the natural unit and basis of society. It shall be protected by the State which shall take care of its physical health and moral.
2. The State shall have the duty to assist the family which is the custodian of morals and traditional values recognized by the community.
3. The State shall ensure the elimination of every discrimination against women and also ensure the protection of the rights of the woman and the child as stipulated in international declarations and conventions.
4. The aged and the disabled shall also have the right to special measures of protection in keeping with their physical or moral needs.

ARTICLE 19

All peoples shall be equal; they shall enjoy the same respect and shall have the same rights. Nothing shall justify the domination of a people by another.

ARTICLE 20

1. All peoples shall have the right to existence. They shall have the unquestionable and inalienable right to self-determination. They shall freely determine their polit-

ical status and shall pursue their economic and social development according to the policy they have freely chosen.

2. Colonized or oppressed peoples shall have the right to free themselves from the bonds of domination by resorting to any means recognized by the international community.

3. All peoples shall have the right to the assistance of the States parties to the present Charter in their liberation struggle against foreign domination, be it political, economic or cultural.

ARTICLE 21

1. All peoples shall freely dispose of their wealth and natural resources. This right shall be exercised in the exclusive interest of the people. In no case shall a people be deprived of it.

2. In case of spoliation the dispossessed people shall have the right to the lawful recovery of its property as well as to an adequate compensation.

3. The free disposal of wealth and natural resources shall be exercised without prejudice to the obligation of promoting international economic cooperation based on mutual respect, equitable exchange and the principles of international law.

4. States parties to the present Charter shall individually and collectively exercise the right to free disposal of their wealth and natural resources with a view to strengthening African unity and solidarity.

5. States parties to the present Charter shall undertake to eliminate all forms of foreign economic exploitation particularly that practiced by international monopolies so as to enable their peoples to fully benefit from the advantages derived from their national resources.

ARTICLE 22

1. All peoples shall have the right to their economic, social and cultural development with due regard to their freedom and identity and in the equal enjoyment of the common heritage of mankind.

2. States shall have the duty, individually or collectively, to ensure the exercise of the right to development.

ARTICLE 23

1. All peoples shall have the right to national and international peace and security. The principles of solidarity and friendly relations implicitly affirmed by the Charter of the United Nations and reaffirmed by that of the Organization of African Unity shall govern relations between States.

2. For the purpose of strengthening peace, solidarity and friendly relations, States parties to the present Charter shall ensure that:

(a) any individual enjoying the right of asylum under 12 of the present Charter shall not engage in subversive activities against his country of origin or any other State party to the present Charter;

(b) their territories shall not be used as bases for subversive or terrorist activities against the people of any other State party to the present Charter.

ARTICLE 24

All peoples shall have the right to a general satisfactory environment favorable to their development.

ARTICLE 25

States parties to the present Charter shall have the duty to promote and ensure through teaching, education and publication, the respect of the rights and freedoms contained in the present Charter and to see to it that these freedoms and rights as well as corresponding obligations and duties are understood.

ARTICLE 26

States parties to the present Charter shall have the duty to guarantee the independence of the Courts and shall allow the establishment and improvement of appropriate national institutions entrusted with the promotion and protection of the rights and freedoms guaranteed by the present Charter.

CHAPTER II—DUTIES

ARTICLE 27

1. Every individual shall have duties towards his family and society, the State and other legally recognized communities and the international community.
2. The rights and freedoms of each individual shall be exercised with due regard to the rights of others, collective security, morality and common interest.

ARTICLE 28

Every individual shall have the duty to respect and consider his fellow beings without discrimination, and to maintain relations aimed at promoting, safeguarding and reinforcing mutual respect and tolerance.

ARTICLE 29

The individual shall also have the duty:

1. to preserve the harmonious development of the family and to work for the cohesion and respect of the family; to respect his parents at all times, to maintain them in case of need;

2. To serve his national community by placing his physical and intellectual abilities at its service;
3. Not to compromise the security of the State whose national or resident he is;
4. To preserve and strengthen social and national solidarity, particularly when the latter is threatened;
5. To preserve and strengthen the national independence and the territorial integrity of his country and to contribute to its defence in accordance with the law;
6. To work to the best of his abilities and competence, and to pay taxes imposed by law in the interest of the society;
7. to preserve and strengthen positive African cultural values in his relations with other members of the society, in the spirit of tolerance, dialogue and consultation and, in general, to contribute to the promotion of the moral well being of society;
8. To contribute to the best of his abilities, at all times and at all levels, to the promotion and achievement of African unity.

PART II: MEASURES OF SAFEGUARD
CHAPTER I—ESTABLISHMENT AND ORGANIZATION OF THE AFRICAN COMMISSION ON HUMAN AND PEOPLES' RIGHTS

ARTICLE 30

An African Commission on Human and Peoples' Rights, hereinafter called "the Commission", shall be established within the Organization of African Unity to promote human and peoples' rights and ensure their protection in Africa.

8. *EUROPEAN CONVENTION FOR THE PROTECTION OF HUMAN RIGHTS AND FUNDAMENTAL FREEDOMS* 213 UNTS 222, ENTERED INTO FORCE SEPT. 3, 1953, AS AMENDED BY PROTOCOLS NOS 3, 5, 8, AND 11 WHICH ENTERED INTO FORCE ON 21 SEPTEMBER 1970, 20 DECEMBER 1971, 1 JANUARY 1990, AND 1 NOVEMBER 1998 RESPECTIVELY. (PROTOCOLS NOT INCLUDED)

"The text of the Convention had been amended according to the provisions of Protocol No. 3 (ETS No. 45), which entered into force on 21 September 1970, of Protocol No. 5 (ETS No. 55), which entered into force on 20 December 1971 and of Protocol No. 8 (ETS No. 118), which entered into force on 1 January 1990, and comprised also the text of Protocol No. 2 (ETS No. 44) which, in accordance with Article 5, paragraph 3 thereof, had been an integral part of the Convention since its entry into force on 21 September 1970. All provisions which had been amended or added by these Protocols are replaced by Protocol No. 11 (ETS No. 155), as from the date of its entry into force on 1 November 1998. As from that date, Protocol n° 9 (ETS No. 140), which entered into force on 1 October 1994, is repealed and Protocol n° 10 (ETS No. 146), which has not entered into force, has lost its purpose."

The governments signatory hereto, being members of the Council of Europe,

Considering the Universal Declaration of Human Rights proclaimed by the General Assembly of the United Nations on 10th December 1948;

Considering that this Declaration aims at securing the universal and effective recognition and observance of the Rights therein declared;

Considering that the aim of the Council of Europe is the achievement of greater unity between its members and that one of the methods by which that aim is to be pursued is the maintenance and further realisation of human rights and fundamental freedoms;

Reaffirming their profound belief in those fundamental freedoms which are the foundation of justice and peace in the world and are best maintained on the one hand by an effective political democracy and on the other by a common understanding and observance of the human rights upon which they depend;

Being resolved, as the governments of European countries which are like-minded and have a common heritage of political traditions, ideals, freedom and the rule of law, to take the first steps for the collective enforcement of certain of the rights stated in the Universal Declaration,

Have agreed as follows:

ARTICLE 1— OBLIGATION TO RESPECT HUMAN RIGHTS

The High Contracting Parties shall secure to everyone within their jurisdiction the rights and freedoms defined in Section I of this Convention.

SECTION I—RIGHTS AND FREEDOMS

ARTICLE 2 — RIGHT TO LIFE

1 Everyone's right to life shall be protected by law. No one shall be deprived of his life intentionally save in the execution of a sentence of a court following his conviction of a crime for which this penalty is provided by law.
2 Deprivation of life shall not be regarded as inflicted in contravention of this article when it results from the use of force which is no more than absolutely necessary:
   a. in defence of any person from unlawful violence;
   b. in order to effect a lawful arrest or to prevent the escape of a person lawfully detained;
   c. in action lawfully taken for the purpose of quelling a riot or insurrection.

ARTICLE 3 — PROHIBITION OF TORTURE

No one shall be subjected to torture or to inhuman or degrading treatment or punishment.

ARTICLE 4 — PROHIBITION OF SLAVERY AND FORCED LABOUR

1 No one shall be held in slavery or servitude.
2 No one shall be required to perform forced or compulsory labour.

3 For the purpose of this article the term "forced or compulsory labour" shall not include:

a. any work required to be done in the ordinary course of detention imposed according to the provisions of Article 5 of this Convention or during conditional release from such detention;

b. any service of a military character or, in case of conscientious objectors in countries where they are recognised, service exacted instead of compulsory military service;

c. any service exacted in case of an emergency or calamity threatening the life or well-being of the community;

d. any work or service which forms part of normal civic obligations.

Article 5 — Right to Liberty and Security

1 Everyone has the right to liberty and security of person. No one shall be deprived of his liberty save in the following cases and in accordance with a procedure prescribed by law:

a. the lawful detention of a person after conviction by a competent court;

b. the lawful arrest or detention of a person for non- compliance with the lawful order of a court or in order to secure the fulfillment of any obligation prescribed by law;

c. the lawful arrest or detention of a person effected for the purpose of bringing him before the competent legal authority on reasonable suspicion of having committed an offence or when it is reasonably considered necessary to prevent his committing an offence or fleeing after having done so;

d. the detention of a minor by lawful order for the purpose of educational supervision or his lawful detention for the purpose of bringing him before the competent legal authority;

e. the lawful detention of persons for the prevention of the spreading of infectious diseases, of persons of unsound mind, alcoholics or drug addicts or vagrants;

f. the lawful arrest or detention of a person to prevent his effecting an unauthorised entry into the country or of a person against whom action is being taken with a view to deportation or extradition.

2 Everyone who is arrested shall be informed promptly, in a language, which he understands, of the reasons for his arrest and of any charge against him.

3 Everyone arrested or detained in accordance with the provisions of paragraph 1.c of this article shall be brought promptly before a judge or other officer authorised by law to exercise judicial power and shall be entitled to trial within a reasonable time or to release pending trial. Release may be conditioned by guarantees to appear for trial.

4 Everyone who is deprived of his liberty by arrest or detention shall be entitled to take proceedings by which the lawfulness of his detention shall be decided speedily by a court and his release ordered if the detention is not lawful.

5 Everyone who has been the victim of arrest or detention in contravention of the provisions of this article shall have an enforceable right to compensation.

ARTICLE 6 — RIGHT TO A FAIR TRIAL

1 In the determination of his civil rights and obligations or of any criminal charge against him, everyone is entitled to a fair and public hearing within a reasonable time by an independent and impartial tribunal established by law. Judgment shall be pronounced publicly but the press and public may be excluded from all or part of the trial in the interests of morals, public order or national security in a democratic society, where the interests of juveniles or the protection of the private life of the parties so require, or to the extent strictly necessary in the opinion of the court in special circumstances where publicity would prejudice the interests of justice.

2 Everyone charged with a criminal offence shall be presumed innocent until proved guilty according to law.

3 Everyone charged with a criminal offence has the following minimum rights:

    a. to be informed promptly, in a language which he understands and in detail, of the nature and cause of the accusation against him;

    b. to have adequate time and facilities for the preparation of his defence;

    c. to defend himself in person or through legal assistance of his own choosing or, if he has not sufficient means to pay for legal assistance, to be given it free when the interests of justice so require;

    d. to examine or have examined witnesses against him and to obtain the attendance and examination of witnesses on his behalf under the same conditions as witnesses against him;

    e. to have the free assistance of an interpreter if he cannot understand or speak the language used in court.

ARTICLE 7 — NO PUNISHMENT WITHOUT LAW

1 No one shall be held guilty of any criminal offence on account of any act or omission which did not constitute a criminal offence under national or international law at the time when it was committed. Nor shall a heavier penalty be imposed than the one that was applicable at the time the criminal offence was committed.

2 This article shall not prejudice the trial and punishment of any person for any act or omission which, at the time when it was committed, was criminal according to the general principles of law recognised by civilised nations.

ARTICLE 8 — RIGHT TO RESPECT FOR PRIVATE AND FAMILY LIFE

1 Everyone has the right to respect for his private and family life, his home and his correspondence.

2 There shall be no interference by a public authority with the exercise of this right except such as is in accordance with the law and is necessary in a democratic soci-

ety in the interests of national security, public safety or the economic well-being of the country, for the prevention of disorder or crime, for the protection of health or morals, or for the protection of the rights and freedoms of others.

Article 9—Freedom of Thought, Conscience and Religion

1 Everyone has the right to freedom of thought, conscience and religion; this right includes freedom to change his religion or belief and freedom, either alone or in community with others and in public or private, to manifest his religion or belief, in worship, teaching, practice and observance.

2 Freedom to manifest one's religion or beliefs shall be subject only to such limitations as are prescribed by law and are necessary in a democratic society in the interests of public safety, for the protection of public order, health or morals, or for the protection of the rights and freedoms of others.

Article 10—Freedom of Expression

1 Everyone has the right to freedom of expression. This right shall include freedom to hold opinions and to receive and impart information and ideas without interference by public authority and regardless of frontiers.
This article shall not prevent States from requiring the licensing of broadcasting, television or cinema enterprises.

2 The exercise of these freedoms, since it carries with it duties and responsibilities, may be subject to such formalities, conditions, restrictions or penalties as are prescribed by law and are necessary in a democratic society, in the interests of national security, territorial integrity or public safety, for the prevention of disorder or crime, for the protection of health or morals, for the protection of the reputation or rights of others, for preventing the disclosure of information received in confidence, or for maintaining the authority and impartiality of the judiciary.

Article 11—Freedom of Assembly and Association

1 Everyone has the right to freedom of peaceful assembly and to freedom of association with others, including the right to form and to join trade unions for the protection of his interests.

2 No restrictions shall be placed on the exercise of these rights other than such as are prescribed by law and are necessary in a democratic society in the interests of national security or public safety, for the prevention of disorder or crime, for the protection of health or morals or for the protection of the rights and freedoms of others.
This article shall not prevent the imposition of lawful restrictions on the exercise of these rights by members of the armed forces, of the police or of the administration of the State.

ARTICLE 12 — RIGHT TO MARRY

Men and women of marriageable age have the right to marry and to found a family, according to the national laws governing the exercise of this right.

ARTICLE 13 — RIGHT TO AN EFFECTIVE REMEDY

Everyone whose rights and freedoms as set forth in this Convention are violated shall have an effective remedy before a national authority notwithstanding that the violation has been committed by persons acting in an official capacity.

ARTICLE 14 — PROHIBITION OF DISCRIMINATION

The enjoyment of the rights and freedoms set forth in this Convention shall be secured without discrimination on any ground such as sex, race, colour, language, religion, political or other opinion, national or social origin, association with a national minority, property, birth or other status.

ARTICLE 15 — DEROGATION IN TIME OF EMERGENCY

1 In time of war or other public emergency threatening the life of the nation any High Contracting Party may take measures derogating from its obligations under this Convention to the extent strictly required by the exigencies of the situation, provided that such measures are not inconsistent with its other obligations under international law.
2 No derogation from Article 2, except in respect of deaths resulting from lawful acts of war, or from Articles 3, 4 (paragraph 1) and 7 shall be made under this provision.
3 Any High Contracting Party availing itself of this right of derogation shall keep the Secretary General of the Council of Europe fully informed of the measures which it has taken and the reasons therefore It shall also inform the Secretary General of the Council of Europe when such measures have ceased to operate and the provisions of the Convention are again being fully executed.

ARTICLE 16 — RESTRICTIONS ON POLITICAL ACTIVITY OF ALIENS

Nothing in Articles 10, 11 and 14 shall be regarded as preventing the High Contracting Parties from imposing restrictions on the political activity of aliens.

ARTICLE 17 — PROHIBITION OF ABUSE OF RIGHTS

Nothing in this Convention may be interpreted as implying for any State, group or person any right to engage in any activity or perform any act aimed at the destruction of any of the rights and freedoms set forth herein or at their limitation to a greater extent than is provided for in the Convention.

ARTICLE 18—LIMITATION ON USE OF RESTRICTIONS ON RIGHTS

The restrictions permitted under this Convention to the said rights and freedoms shall not be applied for any purpose other than those for which they have been prescribed.

SECTION II—EUROPEAN COURT OF HUMAN RIGHTS

ARTICLE 19—ESTABLISHMENT OF THE COURT

To ensure the observance of the engagements undertaken by the High Contracting Parties in the Convention and the Protocols thereto, there shall be set up a European Court of Human Rights, hereinafter referred to as "the Court". It shall function on a permanent basis.

ARTICLE 20—NUMBER OF JUDGES

The Court shall consist of a number of judges equal to that of the High Contracting Parties.

ARTICLE 21—CRITERIA FOR OFFICE

1 The judges shall be of high moral character and must either possess the qualifications required for appointment to high judicial office or be jurisconsults of recognised competence.
2 The judges shall sit on the Court in their individual capacity.
3 During their term of office the judges shall not engage in any activity which is incompatible with their independence, impartiality or with the demands of a full-time office; all questions arising from the application of this paragraph shall be decided by the Court.

ARTICLE 22—ELECTION OF JUDGES

1 The judges shall be elected by the Parliamentary Assembly with respect to each High Contracting Party by a majority of votes cast from a list of three candidates nominated by the High Contracting Party.
2 The same procedure shall be followed to complete the Court in the event of the accession of new High Contracting Parties and in filling casual vacancies.

ARTICLE 23—TERMS OF OFFICE

1 The judges shall be elected for a period of six years. They may be re-elected. However, the terms of office of one-half of the judges elected at the first election shall expire at the end of three years.
2 The judges whose terms of office are to expire at the end of the initial period of three years shall be chosen by lot by the Secretary General of the Council of Europe immediately after their election.

3 In order to ensure that, as far as possible, the terms of office of one-half of the judges are renewed every three years, the Parliamentary Assembly may decide, before proceeding to any subsequent election, that the term or terms of office of one or more judges to be elected shall be for a period other than six years but not more than nine and not less than three years.

4 In cases where more than one term of office is involved and where the Parliamentary Assembly applies the preceding paragraph, the allocation of the terms of office shall be effected by a drawing of lots by the Secretary General of the Council of Europe immediately after the election.

5 A judge elected to replace a judge whose term of office has not expired shall hold office for the remainder of his predecessor's term.

6 The terms of office of judges shall expire when they reach the age of 70.

7 The judges shall hold office until replaced. They shall, however, continue to deal with such cases as they already have under consideration.

ARTICLE 24—DISMISSAL

No judge may be dismissed from his office unless the other judges decide by a majority of two-thirds that he has ceased to fulfill the required conditions.

ARTICLE 25—REGISTRY AND LEGAL SECRETARIES

The Court shall have a registry, the functions and organisation of which shall be laid down in the rules of the Court. The Court shall be assisted by legal secretaries.

ARTICLE 26—PLENARY COURT

The plenary Court shall
   a. elect its President and one or two Vice-Presidents for a period of three years; they may be re-elected;
   b. set up Chambers, constituted for a fixed period of time;
   c. elect the Presidents of the Chambers of the Court; they may be re-elected;
   d. adopt the rules of the Court, and
   e. elect the Registrar and one or more Deputy Registrars.

ARTICLE 27—COMMITTEES, CHAMBERS AND GRAND CHAMBER

1 To consider cases brought before it, the Court shall sit in committees of three judges, in Chambers of seven judges and in a Grand Chamber of seventeen judges. The Court's Chambers shall set up committees for a fixed period of time.

2 There shall sit as an ex officio member of the Chamber and the Grand Chamber the judge elected in respect of the State Party concerned or, if there is none or if he is unable to sit, a person of its choice who shall sit in the capacity of judge.

3 The Grand Chamber shall also include the President of the Court, the Vice-Presidents, the Presidents of the Chambers and other judges chosen in accordance

with the rules of the Court. When a case is referred to the Grand Chamber under Article 43, no judge from the Chamber which rendered the judgment shall sit in the Grand Chamber, with the exception of the President of the Chamber and the judge who sat in respect of the State Party concerned.

ARTICLE 28 — DECLARATIONS OF INADMISSIBILITY BY COMMITTEES

A committee may, by a unanimous vote, declare inadmissible or strike out of its list of cases an application submitted under Article 34 where such a decision can be taken without further examination. The decision shall be final.

ARTICLE 29 — DECISIONS BY CHAMBERS ON ADMISSIBILITY AND MERITS

1 If no decision is taken under Article 28, a Chamber shall decide on the admissibility and merits of individual applications submitted under Article 34.
2 A Chamber shall decide on the admissibility and merits of inter-State applications submitted under Article 33.
3 The decision on admissibility shall be taken separately unless the Court, in exceptional cases, decides otherwise.

ARTICLE 30 — RELINQUISHMENT OF JURISDICTION TO THE GRAND CHAMBER

Where a case pending before a Chamber raises a serious question affecting the interpretation of the Convention or the protocols thereto, or where the resolution of a question before the Chamber might have a result inconsistent with a judgment previously delivered by the Court, the Chamber may, at any time before it has rendered its judgment, relinquish jurisdiction in favour of the Grand Chamber, unless one of the parties to the case objects.

ARTICLE 31 — POWERS OF THE GRAND CHAMBER

The Grand Chamber shall
   a. determine applications submitted either under Article 33 or Article 34 when a Chamber has relinquished jurisdiction under Article 30 or when the case has been referred to it under Article 43; and
   b. consider requests for advisory opinions submitted under Article 47.

ARTICLE 32 — JURISDICTION OF THE COURT

1 The jurisdiction of the Court shall extend to all matters concerning the interpretation and application of the Convention and the protocols thereto which are referred to it as provided in Articles 33, 34 and 47.
2 In the event of dispute as to whether the Court has jurisdiction, the Court shall decide.

ARTICLE 33 — INTER-STATE CASES

Any High Contracting Party may refer to the Court any alleged breach of the provisions of the Convention and the protocols thereto by another High Contracting Party.

ARTICLE 34 — INDIVIDUAL APPLICATIONS

The Court may receive applications from any person, non-governmental organisation or group of individuals claiming to be the victim of a violation by one of the High Contracting Parties of the rights set forth in the Convention or the protocols thereto. The High Contracting Parties undertake not to hinder in any way the effective exercise of this right.

ARTICLE 35 — ADMISSIBILITY CRITERIA

1 The Court may only deal with the matter after all domestic remedies have been exhausted, according to the generally recognised rules of international law, and within a period of six months from the date on which the final decision was taken.
2 The Court shall not deal with any application submitted under Article 34 that
   a. is anonymous; or
   b. is substantially the same as a matter that has already been examined by the Court or has already been submitted to another procedure of international investigation or settlement and contains no relevant new information.
3 The Court shall declare inadmissible any individual application submitted under Article 34 which it considers incompatible with the provisions of the Convention or the protocols thereto, manifestly ill-founded, or an abuse of the right of application.
4 The Court shall reject any application which it considers inadmissible under this Article. It may do so at any stage of the proceedings.

ARTICLE 36 — THIRD PARTY INTERVENTION

1 In all cases before a Chamber or the Grand Chamber, a High Contracting Party one of whose nationals is an applicant shall have the right to submit written comments and to take part in hearings.
2 The President of the Court may, in the interest of the proper administration of justice, invite any High Contracting Party which is not a party to the proceedings or any person concerned who is not the applicant to submit written comments or take part in hearings.

ARTICLE 37 — STRIKING OUT APPLICATIONS

1 The Court may at any stage of the proceedings decide to strike an application out of its list of cases where the circumstances lead to the conclusion that
   a. the applicant does not intend to pursue his application; or
   b. the matter has been resolved; or

368 • *Appendix

c. for any other reason established by the Court, it is no longer justified to continue the examination of the application.

However, the Court shall continue the examination of the application if respect for human rights as defined in the Convention and the protocols thereto so requires.

2 The Court may decide to restore an application to its list of cases if it considers that the circumstances justify such a course.

ARTICLE 38 — EXAMINATION OF THE CASE AND FRIENDLY SETTLEMENT PROCEEDINGS

1 If the Court declares the application admissible, it shall
   a. pursue the examination of the case, together with the representatives of the parties, and if need be, undertake an investigation, for the effective conduct of which the States concerned shall furnish all necessary facilities;
   b. place itself at the disposal of the parties concerned with a view to securing a friendly settlement of the matter on the basis of respect for human rights as defined in the Convention and the protocols thereto.
2 Proceedings conducted under paragraph 1.b shall be confidential.

ARTICLE 39 — FINDING OF A FRIENDLY SETTLEMENT

If a friendly settlement is effected, the Court shall strike the case out of its list by means of a decision, which shall be confined to a brief statement of the facts and of the solution reached.

ARTICLE 40 — PUBLIC HEARINGS AND ACCESS TO DOCUMENTS

1 Hearings shall be in public unless the Court in exceptional circumstances decides otherwise.
2 Documents deposited with the Registrar shall be accessible to the public unless the President of the Court decides otherwise.

ARTICLE 41 — JUST SATISFACTION

If the Court finds that there has been a violation of the Convention or the protocols thereto, and if the internal law of the High Contracting Party concerned allows only partial reparation to be made, the Court shall, if necessary, afford just satisfaction to the injured party.

ARTICLE 42 — JUDGMENTS OF CHAMBERS

Judgments of Chambers shall become final in accordance with the provisions of Article 44, paragraph 2.

Article 43 — Referral to the Grand Chamber

1 Within a period of three months from the date of the judgment of the Chamber, any party to the case may, in exceptional cases, request that the case be referred to the Grand Chamber.
2 A panel of five judges of the Grand Chamber shall accept the request if the case raises a serious question affecting the interpretation or application of the Convention or the protocols thereto, or a serious issue of general importance.
3 If the panel accepts the request, the Grand Chamber shall decide the case by means of a judgment.

Article 44 — Final Judgments

1 The judgment of the Grand Chamber shall be final.
2 The judgment of a Chamber shall become final
    a. when the parties declare that they will not request that the case be referred to the Grand Chamber; or
    b. three months after the date of the judgment, if reference of the case to the Grand Chamber has not been requested; or
    c. when the panel of the Grand Chamber rejects the request to refer under Article 43.
3 The final judgment shall be published.

Article 45 — Reasons for Judgments and Decisions

1 Reasons shall be given for judgments as well as for decisions declaring applications admissible or inadmissible.
2 If a judgment does not represent, in whole or in part, the unanimous opinion of the judges, any judge shall be entitled to deliver a separate opinion.

Article 46 — Binding Force and Execution of Judgments

1 The High Contracting Parties undertake to abide by the final judgment of the Court in any case to which they are parties.
2 The final judgment of the Court shall be transmitted to the Committee of Ministers, which shall supervise its execution.

Article 47 — Advisory Opinions

1 The Court may, at the request of the Committee of Ministers, give advisory opinions on legal questions concerning the interpretation of the Convention and the protocols thereto.
2 Such opinions shall not deal with any question relating to the content or scope of the rights or freedoms defined in Section I of the Convention and the protocols thereto, or with any other question which the Court or the Committee of Minis-

ters might have to consider in consequence of any such proceedings as could be instituted in accordance with the Convention.

3 Decisions of the Committee of Ministers to request an advisory opinion of the Court shall require a majority vote of the representatives entitled to sit on the Committee.

ARTICLE 48—ADVISORY JURISDICTION OF THE COURT

The Court shall decide whether a request for an advisory opinion submitted by the Committee of Ministers is within its competence as defined in Article 47.

ARTICLE 49—REASONS FOR ADVISORY OPINIONS

1 Reasons shall be given for advisory opinions of the Court.

2 If the advisory opinion does not represent, in whole or in part, the unanimous opinion of the judges, any judge shall be entitled to deliver a separate opinion.

3 Advisory opinions of the Court shall be communicated to the Committee of Ministers.

ARTICLE 50—EXPENDITURE ON THE COURT

The expenditure on the Court shall be borne by the Council of Europe.

ARTICLE 51—PRIVILEGES AND IMMUNITIES OF JUDGES

The judges shall be entitled, during the exercise of their functions, to the privileges and immunities provided for in Article 40 of the Statute of the Council of Europe and in the agreements made thereunder.

SECTION III—MISCELLANEOUS PROVISIONS

ARTICLE 52—INQUIRIES BY THE SECRETARY GENERAL

On receipt of a request from the Secretary General of the Council of Europe any High Contracting Party shall furnish an explanation of the manner in which its internal law ensures the effective implementation of any of the provisions of the Convention.

ARTICLE 53—SAFEGUARD FOR EXISTING HUMAN RIGHTS

Nothing in this Convention shall be construed as limiting or derogating from any of the human rights and fundamental freedoms which may be ensured under the laws of any High Contracting Party or under any other agreement to which it is a Party.

ARTICLE 54—POWERS OF THE COMMITTEE OF MINISTERS

Nothing in this Convention shall prejudice the powers conferred on the Committee of Ministers by the Statute of the Council of Europe.

ARTICLE 55 — EXCLUSION OF OTHER MEANS OF DISPUTE SETTLEMENT

The High Contracting Parties agree that, except by special agreement, they will not avail themselves of treaties, conventions or declarations in force between them for the purpose of submitting, by way of petition, a dispute arising out of the interpretation or application of this Convention to a means of settlement other than those provided for in this Convention.

ARTICLE 56 — TERRITORIAL APPLICATION

1 Any State may at the time of its ratification or at any time thereafter declare by notification addressed to the Secretary General of the Council of Europe that the present Convention shall, subject to paragraph 4 of this Article, extend to all or any of the territories for whose international relations it is responsible.

2 The Convention shall extend to the territory or territories named in the notification as from the thirtieth day after the receipt of this notification by the Secretary General of the Council of Europe.

3 The provisions of this Convention shall be applied in such territories with due regard, however, to local requirements.

4 Any State which has made a declaration in accordance with paragraph 1 of this article may at any time thereafter declare on behalf of one or more of the territories to which the declaration relates that it accepts the competence of the Court to receive applications from individuals, non-governmental organisations or groups of individuals as provided by Article 34 of the Convention.

ARTICLE 57 — RESERVATIONS

1 Any State may, when signing this Convention or when depositing its instrument of ratification, make a reservation in respect of any particular provision of the Convention to the extent that any law then in force in its territory is not in conformity with the provision. Reservations of a general character shall not be permitted under this article.

2 Any reservation made under this article shall contain a brief statement of the law concerned.

ARTICLE 58 — DENUNCIATION

1 A High Contracting Party may denounce the present Convention only after the expiry of five years from the date on which it became a party to it and after six months' notice contained in a notification addressed to the Secretary General of the Council of Europe, who shall inform the other High Contracting Parties.

2 Such a denunciation shall not have the effect of releasing the High Contracting Party concerned from its obligations under this Convention in respect of any act which, being capable of constituting a violation of such obligations, may have been performed by it before the date at which the denunciation became effective.

3 Any High Contracting Party which shall cease to be a member of the Council of Europe shall cease to be a Party to this Convention under the same conditions.

4 The Convention may be denounced in accordance with the provisions of the preceding paragraphs in respect of any territory to which it has been declared to extend under the terms of Article 56.

ARTICLE 59 — SIGNATURE AND RATIFICATION

1 This Convention shall be open to the signature of the members of the Council of Europe. It shall be ratified. Ratifications shall be deposited with the Secretary General of the Council of Europe.

2 The present Convention shall come into force after the deposit of ten instruments of ratification.

3 As regards any signatory ratifying subsequently, the Convention shall come into force at the date of the deposit of its instrument of ratification.

4 The Secretary General of the Council of Europe shall notify all the members of the Council of Europe of the entry into force of the Convention, the names of the High Contracting Parties who have ratified it, and the deposit of all instruments of ratification which may be effected subsequently.

Done at Rome this 4th day of November 1950, in English and French, both texts being equally authentic, in a single copy which shall remain deposited in the archives of the Council of Europe. The Secretary General shall transmit certified copies to each of the signatories.

9. *ROME STATUTE OF THE INTERNATIONAL CRIMINAL COURT*
UN DOC. A/CONF 183/9 (1998)

PREAMBLE

The States Parties to this Statute,

Conscious that all peoples are united by common bonds, their cultures pieced together in a shared heritage, and concerned that this delicate mosaic may be shattered at any time,

Mindful that during this century millions of children, women and men have been victims of unimaginable atrocities that deeply shock the conscience of humanity,

Recognizing that such grave crimes threaten the peace, security and well-being of the world,

Affirming that the most serious crimes of concern to the international community as a whole must not go unpunished and that their effective prosecution must be ensured by taking measures at the national level and by enhancing international cooperation,

Determined to put an end to impunity for the perpetrators of these crimes and thus to contribute to the prevention of such crimes,

Recalling that it is the duty of every State to exercise its criminal jurisdiction over those responsible for international crimes,

Reaffirming the Purposes and Principles of the Charter of the United Nations, and in particular that all States shall refrain from the threat or use of force against the territorial integrity or political independence of any State, or in any other manner inconsistent with the Purposes of the United Nations,

Emphasizing in this connection that nothing in this Statute shall be taken as authorizing any State Party to intervene in an armed conflict or in the internal affairs of any State,

Determined to these ends and for the sake of present and future generations, to establish an independent permanent International Criminal Court in relationship with the United Nations system, with jurisdiction over the most serious crimes of concern to the international community as a whole,

Emphasizing that the International Criminal Court established under this Statute shall be complementary to national criminal jurisdictions,

Resolved to guarantee lasting respect for and the enforcement of international justice,

Have agreed as follows

PART 1. ESTABLISHMENT OF THE COURT

ARTICLE 1

The Court
An International Criminal Court ("the Court") is hereby established. It shall be a permanent institution and shall have the power to exercise its jurisdiction over persons for the most serious crimes of international concern, as referred to in this Statute, and shall be complementary to national criminal jurisdictions. The jurisdiction and functioning of the Court shall be governed by the provisions of this Statute.

ARTICLE 2

Relationship of the Court with the United Nations
The Court shall be brought into relationship with the United Nations through an agreement to be approved by the Assembly of States Parties to this Statute and thereafter concluded by the President of the Court on its behalf.

ARTICLE 3

Seat of the Court
1. The seat of the Court shall be established at The Hague in the Netherlands ("the host State").
2. The Court shall enter into a headquarters agreement with the host State, to be approved by the Assembly of States Parties and thereafter concluded by the President of the Court on its behalf.
3. The Court may sit elsewhere, whenever it considers it desirable, as provided in this Statute.

ARTICLE 4

Legal status and powers of the Court
1. The Court shall have international legal personality. It shall also have such legal capacity as may be necessary for the exercise of its functions and the fulfilment of its purposes.
2. The Court may exercise its functions and powers, as provided in this Statute, on the territory of any State Party and, by special agreement, on the territory of any other State.

PART 2. JURISDICTION, ADMISSIBILITY AND APPLICABLE LAW

ARTICLE 5

Crimes within the jurisdiction of the Court
1. The jurisdiction of the Court shall be limited to the most serious crimes of concern to the international community as a whole. The Court has jurisdiction in accordance with this Statute with respect to the following crimes:
   (a) The crime of genocide;
   (b) Crimes against humanity;
   (c) War crimes;
   (d) The crime of aggression.
2. The Court shall exercise jurisdiction over the crime of aggression once a provision is adopted in accordance with articles 121 and 123 defining the crime and setting out the conditions under which the Court shall exercise jurisdiction with respect to this crime. Such a provision shall be consistent with the relevant provisions of the Charter of the United Nations.

ARTICLE 6

Genocide
   For the purpose of this Statute, "genocide" means any of the following acts committed with intent to destroy, in whole or in part, a national, ethnical, racial or religious group, as such:
   (a) Killing members of the group;
   (b) Causing serious bodily or mental harm to members of the group;
   (c) Deliberately inflicting on the group conditions of life calculated to bring about its physical destruction in whole or in part;
   (d) Imposing measures intended to prevent births within the group;
   (e) Forcibly transferring children of the group to another group.

ARTICLE 7

Crimes against humanity
1. For the purpose of this Statute, "crime against humanity" means any of the fol-

lowing acts when committed as part of a widespread or systematic attack directed against any civilian population, with knowledge of the attack:

(a) Murder;

(b) Extermination;

(c) Enslavement;

(d) Deportation or forcible transfer of population;

(e) Imprisonment or other severe deprivation of physical liberty in violation of fundamental rules of international law;

(f) Torture;

(g) Rape, sexual slavery, enforced prostitution, forced pregnancy, enforced sterilization, or any other form of sexual violence of comparable gravity;

(h) Persecution against any identifiable group or collectivity on political, racial, national, ethnic, cultural, religious, gender as defined in paragraph 3, or other grounds that are universally recognized as impermissible under international law, in connection with any act referred to in this paragraph or any crime within the jurisdiction of the Court;

(i) Enforced disappearance of persons;

(j) The crime of apartheid;

(k) Other inhumane acts of a similar character intentionally causing great suffering, or serious injury to body or to mental or physical health.

2. For the purpose of paragraph 1:

(a) "Attack directed against any civilian population" means a course of conduct involving the multiple commission of acts referred to in paragraph 1 against any civilian population, pursuant to or in furtherance of a State or organizational policy to commit such attack;

(b) "Extermination" includes the intentional infliction of conditions of life, *inter alia* the deprivation of access to food and medicine, calculated to bring about the destruction of part of a population;

(c) "Enslavement" means the exercise of any or all of the powers attaching to the right of ownership over a person and includes the exercise of such power in the course of trafficking in persons, in particular women and children;

(d) "Deportation or forcible transfer of population" means forced displacement of the persons concerned by expulsion or other coercive acts from the area in which they are lawfully present, without grounds permitted under international law;

(e) "Torture" means the intentional infliction of severe pain or suffering, whether physical or mental, upon a person in the custody or under the control of the accused; except that torture shall not include pain or suffering arising only from, inherent in or incidental to, lawful sanctions;

(f) "Forced pregnancy" means the unlawful confinement of a woman forcibly made pregnant, with the intent of affecting the ethnic composition of any population or carrying out other grave violations of international law. This definition shall not in any way be interpreted as affecting national laws relating to pregnancy;

(g) "Persecution" means the intentional and severe deprivation of fundamental rights contrary to international law by reason of the identity of the group or collectivity;

(h) "The crime of apartheid" means inhumane acts of a character similar to those referred to in paragraph 1, committed in the context of an institutionalized regime of systematic oppression and domination by one racial group over any other racial group or groups and committed with the intention of maintaining that regime;

(i) "Enforced disappearance of persons" means the arrest, detention or abduction of persons by, or with the authorization, support or acquiescence of, a State or a political organization, followed by a refusal to acknowledge that deprivation of freedom or to give information on the fate or whereabouts of those persons, with the intention of removing them from the protection of the law for a prolonged period of time.

3. For the purpose of this Statute, it is understood that the term "gender" refers to the two sexes, male and female, within the context of society. The term "gender" does not indicate any meaning different from the above.

ARTICLE 8

War crimes

1. The Court shall have jurisdiction in respect of war crimes in particular when committed as part of a plan or policy or as part of a large-scale commission of such crimes.

2. For the purpose of this Statute, "war crimes" means:

(a) Grave breaches of the Geneva Conventions of 12 August 1949, namely, any of the following acts against persons or property protected under the provisions of the relevant Geneva Convention:
    (i) Wilful killing;
    (ii) Torture or inhuman treatment, including biological experiments;
    (iii) Wilfully causing great suffering, or serious injury to body or health;
    (iv) Extensive destruction and appropriation of property, not justified by military necessity and carried out unlawfully and wantonly;
    (v) Compelling a prisoner of war or other protected person to serve in the forces of a hostile Power;
    (vi) Wilfully depriving a prisoner of war or other protected person of the rights of fair and regular trial;
    (vii) Unlawful deportation or transfer or unlawful confinement;
    (viii) Taking of hostages.

(b) Other serious violations of the laws and customs applicable in international armed conflict, within the established framework of international law, namely, any of the following acts:
    (i) Intentionally directing attacks against the civilian population as such or against individual civilians not taking direct part in hostilities;
    (ii) Intentionally directing attacks against civilian objects, that is, objects which are not military objectives;

(iii) Intentionally directing attacks against personnel, installations, material, units or vehicles involved in a humanitarian assistance or peacekeeping mission in accordance with the Charter of the United Nations, as long as they are entitled to the protection given to civilians or civilian objects under the international law of armed conflict;

(iv) Intentionally launching an attack in the knowledge that such attack will cause incidental loss of life or injury to civilians or damage to civilian objects or widespread, long-term and severe damage to the natural environment which would be clearly excessive in relation to the concrete and direct overall military advantage anticipated;

(v) Attacking or bombarding, by whatever means, towns, villages, dwellings or buildings which are undefended and which are not military objectives;

(vi) Killing or wounding a combatant who, having laid down his arms or having no longer means of defence, has surrendered at discretion;

(vii) Making improper use of a flag of truce, of the flag or of the military insignia and uniform of the enemy or of the United Nations, as well as of the distinctive emblems of the Geneva Conventions, resulting in death or serious personal injury;

(viii) The transfer, directly or indirectly, by the Occupying Power of parts of its own civilian population into the territory it occupies, or the deportation or transfer of all or parts of the population of the occupied territory within or outside this territory;

(ix) Intentionally directing attacks against buildings dedicated to religion, education, art, science or charitable purposes, historic monuments, hospitals and places where the sick and wounded are collected, provided they are not military objectives;

(x) Subjecting persons who are in the power of an adverse party to physical mutilation or to medical or scientific experiments of any kind which are neither justified by the medical, dental or hospital treatment of the person concerned nor carried out in his or her interest, and which cause death to or seriously endanger the health of such person or persons;

(xi) Killing or wounding treacherously individuals belonging to the hostile nation or army;

(xii) Declaring that no quarter will be given;

(xiii) Destroying or seizing the enemy's property unless such destruction or seizure be imperatively demanded by the necessities of war;

(xiv) Declaring abolished, suspended or inadmissible in a court of law the rights and actions of the nationals of the hostile party;

(xv) Compelling the nationals of the hostile party to take part in the operations of war directed against their own country, even if they were in the belligerent's service before the commencement of the war;

(xvi) Pillaging a town or place, even when taken by assault;

(xvii) Employing poison or poisoned weapons;

(xviii) Employing asphyxiating, poisonous or other gases, and all analogous liquids, materials or devices;

(xix) Employing bullets which expand or flatten easily in the human body, such as bullets with a hard envelope which does not entirely cover the core or is pierced with incisions;

(xx) Employing weapons, projectiles and material and methods of warfare which are of a nature to cause superfluous injury or unnecessary suffering or which are inherently indiscriminate in violation of the international law of armed conflict, provided that such weapons, projectiles and material and methods of warfare are the subject of a comprehensive prohibition and are included in an annex to this Statute, by an amendment in accordance with the relevant provisions set forth in articles 121 and 123;

(xxi) Committing outrages upon personal dignity, in particular humiliating and degrading treatment;

(xxii) Committing rape, sexual slavery, enforced prostitution, forced pregnancy, as defined in article 7, paragraph 2 (f), enforced sterilization, or any other form of sexual violence also constituting a grave breach of the Geneva Conventions;

(xxiii) Utilizing the presence of a civilian or other protected person to render certain points, areas or military forces immune from military operations;

(xxiv) Intentionally directing attacks against buildings, material, medical units and transport, and personnel using the distinctive emblems of the Geneva Conventions in conformity with international law;

(xxv) Intentionally using starvation of civilians as a method of warfare by depriving them of objects indispensable to their survival, including wilfully impeding relief supplies as provided for under the Geneva Conventions;

(xxvi) Conscripting or enlisting children under the age of fifteen years into the national armed forces or using them to participate actively in hostilities.

(c) In the case of an armed conflict not of an international character, serious violations of article 3 common to the four Geneva Conventions of 12 August 1949, namely, any of the following acts committed against persons taking no active part in the hostilities, including members of armed forces who have laid down their arms and those placed hors de combat by sickness, wounds, detention or any other cause:

(i) Violence to life and person, in particular murder of all kinds, mutilation, cruel treatment and torture;

(ii) Committing outrages upon personal dignity, in particular humiliating and degrading treatment;

(iii) Taking of hostages;

(iv) The passing of sentences and the carrying out of executions without previous judgment pronounced by a regularly constituted court, affording all judicial guarantees which are generally recognized as indispensable.

(d) Paragraph 2 (c) applies to armed conflicts not of an international character and thus does not apply to situations of internal disturbances and tensions, such as riots, isolated and sporadic acts of violence or other acts of a similar nature.

(e) Other serious violations of the laws and customs applicable in armed conflicts not of an international character, within the established framework of international law, namely, any of the following acts:

(i) Intentionally directing attacks against the civilian population as such or against individual civilians not taking direct part in hostilities;

(ii) Intentionally directing attacks against buildings, material, medical units and transport, and personnel using the distinctive emblems of the Geneva Conventions in conformity with international law;

(iii) Intentionally directing attacks against personnel, installations, material, units or vehicles involved in a humanitarian assistance or peacekeeping mission in accordance with the Charter of the United Nations, as long as they are entitled to the protection given to civilians or civilian objects under the international law of armed conflict;

(iv) Intentionally directing attacks against buildings dedicated to religion, education, art, science or charitable purposes, historic monuments, hospitals and places where the sick and wounded are collected, provided they are not military objectives;

(v) Pillaging a town or place, even when taken by assault;

(vi) Committing rape, sexual slavery, enforced prostitution, forced pregnancy, as defined in article 7, paragraph 2 (f), enforced sterilization, and any other form of sexual violence also constituting a serious violation of article 3 common to the four Geneva Conventions;

(vii) Conscripting or enlisting children under the age of fifteen years into armed forces or groups or using them to participate actively in hostilities;

(viii) Ordering the displacement of the civilian population for reasons related to the conflict, unless the security of the civilians involved or imperative military reasons so demand;

(ix) Killing or wounding treacherously a combatant adversary;

(x) Declaring that no quarter will be given;

(xi) Subjecting persons who are in the power of another party to the conflict to physical mutilation or to medical or scientific experiments of any kind which are neither justified by the medical, dental or hospital treatment of the person concerned nor carried out in his or her interest, and which cause death to or seriously endanger the health of such person or persons;

(xii) Destroying or seizing the property of an adversary unless such destruction or seizure be imperatively demanded by the necessities of the conflict;

(f) Paragraph 2 (e) applies to armed conflicts not of an international character and thus does not apply to situations of internal disturbances and tensions, such as riots, isolated and sporadic acts of violence or other acts of a similar nature. It applies to armed conflicts that take place in the territory of a State when there is protracted armed conflict between governmental authorities and organized armed groups or between such groups.

3. Nothing in paragraph 2 (c) and (e) shall affect the responsibility of a Government to maintain or re-establish law and order in the State or to defend the unity and territorial integrity of the State, by all legitimate means.

ARTICLE 9

Elements of Crimes

1. Elements of Crimes shall assist the Court in the interpretation and application of articles 6, 7 and 8. They shall be adopted by a two-thirds majority of the members of the Assembly of States Parties.
2. Amendments to the Elements of Crimes may be proposed by:
    (a) Any State Party;
    (b) The judges acting by an absolute majority;
    (c) The Prosecutor.
    Such amendments shall be adopted by a two-thirds majority of the members of the Assembly of States Parties.
3. The Elements of Crimes and amendments thereto shall be consistent with this Statute.

ARTICLE 10

Nothing in this Part shall be interpreted as limiting or prejudicing in any way existing or developing rules of international law for purposes other than this Statute.

ARTICLE 11

Jurisdiction ratione temporis

1. The Court has jurisdiction only with respect to crimes committed after the entry into force of this Statute.
2. If a State becomes a Party to this Statute after its entry into force, the Court may exercise its jurisdiction only with respect to crimes committed after the entry into force of this Statute for that State, unless that State has made a declaration under article 12, paragraph 3.

ARTICLE 12

Preconditions to the exercise of jurisdiction

1. A State which becomes a Party to this Statute thereby accepts the jurisdiction of the Court with respect to the crimes referred to in article 5.
2. In the case of article 13, paragraph (a) or (c), the Court may exercise its jurisdiction if one or more of the following States are Parties to this Statute or have accepted the jurisdiction of the Court in accordance with paragraph 3:
    (a) The State on the territory of which the conduct in question occurred or, if the crime was committed on board a vessel or aircraft, the State of registration of that vessel or aircraft;
    (b) The State of which the person accused of the crime is a national.
3. If the acceptance of a State which is not a Party to this Statute is required under paragraph 2, that State may, by declaration lodged with the Registrar, accept the exercise of jurisdiction by the Court with respect to the crime in question. The ac-

cepting State shall cooperate with the Court without any delay or exception in accordance with Part 9.

ARTICLE 13

Exercise of jurisdiction

The Court may exercise its jurisdiction with respect to a crime referred to in article 5 in accordance with the provisions of this Statute if:

  (a) A situation in which one or more of such crimes appears to have been committed is referred to the Prosecutor by a State Party in accordance with article 14;

  (b) A situation in which one or more of such crimes appears to have been committed is referred to the Prosecutor by the Security Council acting under Chapter VII of the Charter of the United Nations; or

  (c) The Prosecutor has initiated an investigation in respect of such a crime in accordance with article 15.

ARTICLE 14

Referral of a situation by a State Party

1. A State Party may refer to the Prosecutor a situation in which one or more crimes within the jurisdiction of the Court appear to have been committed requesting the Prosecutor to investigate the situation for the purpose of determining whether one or more specific persons should be charged with the commission of such crimes.

2. As far as possible, a referral shall specify the relevant circumstances and be accompanied by such supporting documentation as is available to the State referring the situation.

ARTICLE 15

Prosecutor

1. The Prosecutor may initiate investigations *proprio motu* on the basis of information on crimes within the jurisdiction of the Court.

2. The Prosecutor shall analyse the seriousness of the information received. For this purpose, he or she may seek additional information from States, organs of the United Nations, intergovernmental or non-governmental organizations, or other reliable sources that he or she deems appropriate, and may receive written or oral testimony at the seat of the Court.

3. If the Prosecutor concludes that there is a reasonable basis to proceed with an investigation, he or she shall submit to the Pre-Trial Chamber a request for authorization of an investigation, together with any supporting material collected. Victims may make representations to the Pre-Trial Chamber, in accordance with the Rules of Procedure and Evidence.

4. If the Pre-Trial Chamber, upon examination of the request and the supporting material, considers that there is a reasonable basis to proceed with an investigation, and that the case appears to fall within the jurisdiction of the Court, it shall au-

382 • *Appendix C*

thorize the commencement of the investigation, without prejudice to subsequent determinations by the Court with regard to the jurisdiction and admissibility of a case.

5. The refusal of the Pre-Trial Chamber to authorize the investigation shall not preclude the presentation of a subsequent request by the Prosecutor based on new facts or evidence regarding the same situation.

6. If, after the preliminary examination referred to in paragraphs 1 and 2, the Prosecutor concludes that the information provided does not constitute a reasonable basis for an investigation, he or she shall inform those who provided the information. This shall not preclude the Prosecutor from considering further information submitted to him or her regarding the same situation in the light of new facts or evidence.

ARTICLE 16

Deferral of investigation or prosecution

No investigation or prosecution may be commenced or proceeded with under this Statute for a period of 12 months after the Security Council, in a resolution adopted under Chapter VII of the Charter of the United Nations, has requested the Court to that effect; that request may be renewed by the Council under the same conditions.

ARTICLE 17

Issues of admissibility

1. Having regard to paragraph 10 of the Preamble and article 1, the Court shall determine that a case is inadmissible where:

   (a) The case is being investigated or prosecuted by a State which has jurisdiction over it, unless the State is unwilling or unable genuinely to carry out the investigation or prosecution;

   (b) The case has been investigated by a State which has jurisdiction over it and the State has decided not to prosecute the person concerned, unless the decision resulted from the unwillingness or inability of the State genuinely to prosecute;

   (c) The person concerned has already been tried for conduct which is the subject of the complaint, and a trial by the Court is not permitted under article 20, paragraph 3;

   (d) The case is not of sufficient gravity to justify further action by the Court.

2. In order to determine unwillingness in a particular case, the Court shall consider, having regard to the principles of due process recognized by international law, whether one or more of the following exist, as applicable:

   (a) The proceedings were or are being undertaken or the national decision was made for the purpose of shielding the person concerned from criminal responsibility for crimes within the jurisdiction of the Court referred to in article 5;

   (b) There has been an unjustified delay in the proceedings which in the circumstances is inconsistent with an intent to bring the person concerned to justice;

   (c) The proceedings were not or are not being conducted independently or impartially, and they were or are being conducted in a manner which, in the circumstances, is inconsistent with an intent to bring the person concerned to justice.

3. In order to determine inability in a particular case, the Court shall consider whether, due to a total or substantial collapse or unavailability of its national judicial system, the State is unable to obtain the accused or the necessary evidence and testimony or otherwise unable to carry out its proceedings.

ARTICLE 18

Preliminary rulings regarding admissibility

1. When a situation has been referred to the Court pursuant to article 13 (a) and the Prosecutor has determined that there would be a reasonable basis to commence an investigation, or the Prosecutor initiates an investigation pursuant to articles 13 (c) and 15, the Prosecutor shall notify all States Parties and those States which, taking into account the information available, would normally exercise jurisdiction over the crimes concerned. The Prosecutor may notify such States on a confidential basis and, where the Prosecutor believes it necessary to protect persons, prevent destruction of evidence or prevent the absconding of persons, may limit the scope of the information provided to States.

2. Within one month of receipt of that notification, a State may inform the Court that it is investigating or has investigated its nationals or others within its jurisdiction with respect to criminal acts which may constitute crimes referred to in article 5 and which relate to the information provided in the notification to States. At the request of that State, the Prosecutor shall defer to the State's investigation of those persons unless the Pre-Trial Chamber, on the application of the Prosecutor, decides to authorize the investigation.

3. The Prosecutor's deferral to a State's investigation shall be open to review by the Prosecutor six months after the date of deferral or at any time when there has been a significant change of circumstances based on the State's unwillingness or inability genuinely to carry out the investigation.

4. The State concerned or the Prosecutor may appeal to the Appeals Chamber against a ruling of the Pre-Trial Chamber, in accordance with article 82. The appeal may be heard on an expedited basis.

5. When the Prosecutor has deferred an investigation in accordance with paragraph 2, the Prosecutor may request that the State concerned periodically inform the Prosecutor of the progress of its investigations and any subsequent prosecutions. States Parties shall respond to such requests without undue delay.

6. Pending a ruling by the Pre-Trial Chamber, or at any time when the Prosecutor has deferred an investigation under this article, the Prosecutor may, on an exceptional basis, seek authority from the Pre-Trial Chamber to pursue necessary investigative steps for the purpose of preserving evidence where there is a unique opportunity to obtain important evidence or there is a significant risk that such evidence may not be subsequently available.

7. A State which has challenged a ruling of the Pre-Trial Chamber under this article

may challenge the admissibility of a case under article 19 on the grounds of additional significant facts or significant change of circumstances.

ARTICLE 19

Challenges to the jurisdiction of the Court or the admissibility of a case

1. The Court shall satisfy itself that it has jurisdiction in any case brought before it. The Court may, on its own motion, determine the admissibility of a case in accordance with article 17.
2. Challenges to the admissibility of a case on the grounds referred to in article 17 or challenges to the jurisdiction of the Court may be made by:
   (a) An accused or a person for whom a warrant of arrest or a summons to appear has been issued under article 58;
   (b) A State which has jurisdiction over a case, on the ground that it is investigating or prosecuting the case or has investigated or prosecuted; or
   (c) A State from which acceptance of jurisdiction is required under article 12.
3. The Prosecutor may seek a ruling from the Court regarding a question of jurisdiction or admissibility. In proceedings with respect to jurisdiction or admissibility, those who have referred the situation under article 13, as well as victims, may also submit observations to the Court.
4. The admissibility of a case or the jurisdiction of the Court may be challenged only once by any person or State referred to in paragraph 2. The challenge shall take place prior to or at the commencement of the trial. In exceptional circumstances, the Court may grant leave for a challenge to be brought more than once or at a time later than the commencement of the trial. Challenges to the admissibility of a case, at the commencement of a trial, or subsequently with the leave of the Court, may be based only on article 17, paragraph 1 (c).
5. A State referred to in paragraph 2 (b) and (c) shall make a challenge at the earliest opportunity.
6. Prior to the confirmation of the charges, challenges to the admissibility of a case or challenges to the jurisdiction of the Court shall be referred to the Pre-Trial Chamber. After confirmation of the charges, they shall be referred to the Trial Chamber. Decisions with respect to jurisdiction or admissibility may be appealed to the Appeals Chamber in accordance with article 82.
7. If a challenge is made by a State referred to in paragraph 2 (b) or (c), the Prosecutor shall suspend the investigation until such time as the Court makes a determination in accordance with article 17.
8. Pending a ruling by the Court, the Prosecutor may seek authority from the Court:
   (a) To pursue necessary investigative steps of the kind referred to in article 18, paragraph 6;
   (b) To take a statement or testimony from a witness or complete the collection and examination of evidence which had begun prior to the making of the challenge; and
   (c) In cooperation with the relevant States, to prevent the absconding of persons

in respect of whom the Prosecutor has already requested a warrant of arrest under article 58.

9. The making of a challenge shall not affect the validity of any act performed by the Prosecutor or any order or warrant issued by the Court prior to the making of the challenge.

10. If the Court has decided that a case is inadmissible under article 17, the Prosecutor may submit a request for a review of the decision when he or she is fully satisfied that new facts have arisen which negate the basis on which the case had previously been found inadmissible under article 17.

11. If the Prosecutor, having regard to the matters referred to in article 17, defers an investigation, the Prosecutor may request that the relevant State make available to the Prosecutor information on the proceedings.

That information shall, at the request of the State concerned, be confidential. If the Prosecutor thereafter decides to proceed with an investigation, he or she shall notify the State to which deferral of the proceedings has taken place.

· APPENDIX D ·

Official Citations for Human Rights and Related Instruments (Treaty * and Non Treaty Instruments)

African [Banjul] Charter on Human and Peoples' Rights, OAU Doc. CAB/LEG/67/3 rev. 5, 21 ILM 58 (1982), entered into force 21 October 1986.

Agreement for the Prosecution and Punishment of the Major War Criminals of the European Axis, 58 Stat. 1544, EAS. No. 472, 82 UNTS.

American Convention on Human Rights, 22 November 1969, OAS Treaty Series no. 36, at 1, OEA/Ser.L./V/II.23 doc. rev.2, 1144 UNTS 123, entered into force July 18, 1978, reprinted in *Basic Documents Pertaining to Human Rights in the Inter-American System*, OEA/Ser.LV/II. 82, doc. 6, rev. 1 (1992).

American Declaration of the Rights and Duties of Man, OAS Res. XXX, adopted by the Ninth International Conference of American States (1948), reprinted in *Basic Documents Pertaining to Human Rights in the Inter-American System*, OEA/Ser.LV/II. 82, doc. 6, rev. 1 (1992).

[Proposed] American Declaration on the Rights of Indigenous Peoples, approved by the Inter-American Commission on Human Rights on February 26, 1997, at its 1333rd session, 95th Regular Session, OEA/Ser/L/V/.II.95 Doc.6 (1997).

Arab Charter on Human Rights, Council of the League of Arab States, 102nd Session, Resolution 5437, 15 September 1994, not yet entered into force.

Beijing Declaration and Platform for Action, Fourth World Conference on Women, A/CONF.177/20 (1995) and A/CONF.177/20/Add. 1.

Body of Principles for the Protection of All Persons under Any Form of Detention or Imprisonment, GA res. 43/173, 43 UN GAOR, Supp. no. 49, UN Doc. A/43/49 (1988).

Charter of Fundamental Rights of the European Union, 7 December 2000. Official Journal of the European Communities, C 364/1, December 18, 2000.

Charter of the Organization of African Unity, 479 UNTS 39, entered into force 13 September 1963.

Charter of the Organization of American States, 119 UNTS 3, entered into force 13 December 1951, amended 721 UNTS 324, entered into force 27 February 1970.

Convention against Discrimination in Education, 429 UNTS 43, entered into force 22 May 1962.

Convention against Torture and Other Cruel. Inhuman or Degrading Treatment or Punishment, GA. rs. 39/46, 39 GAOR Supp. (no. 51) at 197, UN Doc. A/39/51 (1985), entered into force 26 June 1987.

Convention Concerning Indigenous and Tribal Peoples in Independent Countries (ILO no. 169), 72 ILO Official Bull. 59, entered into force 5 September 1991.

Convention Governing Specific Aspects of Refugee Problems in Africa, 1000 UNTS 46, entered into force 20 June 1974.

Convention on the Elimination of All Forms of Discrimination against Women, GA. res. 34/180, 34 UN GAOR, Supp. no. 46, UN Doc. A/Res/34/180 (1981), entered into force 3 September 1981.

Convention on the Rights of the Child, GA res. 44/25, annex, 44 UN GAOR Supp. (no. 49) at 167, UN Doc. A/44/49 (1989), entered into force 2 September 1990.

Convention Relating to the Status of Refugees, 189 UNTS 137, entered into force 22 April 1954.

Covenant on Civil and Political Rights, GA. res. 2200A (XXI), 21 UN GAOR Supp. (no. 16) at 52, UN Doc. A/6316 (1966), entered into force 23 March 1976.

Covenant on Economic, Social, and Cultural Rights, GA res. 2200A (XXI), 21 UN GAOR Supp. (no. 16) at 49, UN Doc. A/6316 (1966), 993 UNTS 3, entered into force 3 January 1976.

Declaration on Fact-finding by the UN in the Field of the Maintenance of international Peace and Security, *Annex,* UN Doc. A/RES/46/59 (1992).

Declaration on the Elimination of All Forms of Intolerance and Discrimination Based on Religion or Belief, GA res. 36/55 1981.

Declaration on the Elimination of Violence against Women, GA Res. 104, UN GAOR, 48th Sess, UN Doc. A/48/629 (1993).

Declaration on the Protection of All Persons Belonging to National or Ethnic, Religious, or Linguistic Minorities, GA res. 47/135, 18 December 1992.

Declaration on the Protection of All Persons from Enforced Disappearances on December 18, 1992. GA res. 47/133, 47 UN GAOR Supp. (no. 49) at 207, UN Doc. A/47/49 (1992).

Declaration on the Right and Responsibility of Individuals, Groups, and Organs of Society to Promote and Protect Universally Recognized Human Rights and Fundamental Freedoms, GA res. 53/144 Annex.

Declaration on the Right to Development, (GA res. 41/128, Annex, 41, UN GAOR Supp. (no. 53). UN Doc. A/41/53 (1986).

Declaration on the Rights of Disabled Persons, GA res. 3447 (XXX), 30 UN GAOR Supp. (no. 34), UN Doc. A/10034 (1975).

Draft Declaration on the Rights of Indigenous Peoples, E/CN,4/Sub.2/1994/2/Add. I (1994).

Durban Declaration and Programme of Action, World Conference against Racism, Racial Discrimination, Xenophobia, and Related Intolerance, A/CONF.189/5 (2001).

(European) Convention for the Protection of Human Rights and Fundamental Freedoms, 213 UNTS 222 (1950), entered into force 3 September 1953.

European Social Charter, ETS no. 35, entered into force 26 February 1965.

European Social Charter (Revised), ETS no. 163, entered into force 1 July 1999.

Final Act of the Conference on Security and Cooperation in Europe. Adopted at Helsinki 1 August 1975–73 U.S. DEPT. OF STATE BULL. 323, 14 ILM 1292, 70 AM. J. INT'L L. 41 (1976).

Geneva Conventions of 1949, Conventions I-IV. 6 UST 3114, 3217, 3316, 3516; TIAS no. 3362-3365; 75 UNTS 31, 85, 135,287, entered into force 21 October 1950.

(ILO) Convention Concerning Forced or Compulsory Labour (ILO no. 29), 39 UNTS 55, entered into force 1 May 1932.

(ILO) Convention Concerning Minimum Age for Admission to Employment (ILO no. 138), 1015 UNTS 297XX, entered into force 19 June 1976.

(ILO) Convention Concerning the Prohibition and Immediate Action for the Elimination of the Worst Forms of Child Labour ((ILO no. 182), 38 ILM 1207 (1999), entered into force 19 November 2000.

Inter-American Convention on Forced Disappearance of Persons, 33 ILM 1429 (1994), entered into force 28 March 1996.

Inter-American Convention on the Prevention, Punishment, and Eradication of Violence against Women, 33 ILM 1534 (1994), entered into force 5 March 1995, 589.

International Convention on the Elimination of All Forms of Racial Discrimination, 660 UNTS 195, entered into force 4 January 1969, 164-66, 671.

International Convention on the Prevention and Punishment of the Crime of Genocide, 78 UNTS 277, entered into force 12 January 1951, 539, 544.

International Convention on the Protection of the Rights of All Migrant Workers and Their Families, GA res. 45/158, Annex, 45 UN GAOR Supp. (no. 49A) at 262, UN Doc. A/45/49 (1990), not yet entered into force.

International Covenant on Civil and Political Rights, GA res. 2200A, (XXI), 16 December 1966, 21 UN GAOR Supp. (no. 16) at 52, UN Doc. A/6316 (1966), 999 UNTS 1ll, entered into force 23 March 1976, 91 n.9, 10.3, 156, 603, 674, 709, 936.

International Covenant on Economic, Social, and Cultural Rights, CA, res. 2200A (XXI), 21 UN GAOR Supp. (no. 16) at 49, UN Doc. A16316(1966), 993 UNTS 3, entered into force 3 January 1976.

Optional Protocol to the Convention on the Rights of the Child on the Involvement of Children in Armed Conflict, GA res. 54/263, Annex I, 54 UN GAOR Supp. (no. 49), UN Doc. A/54/49(2000), entered into force 2 February 2002.

Optional Protocol to the Convention on the Rights of the Child on the Sale of Children Child Prostitution and Child Pornography, GA res. 54/263, Annex II, 54 UN GAOR Supp. (no. 49), UN Doc. A/54/49(2000), entered into force 8 January 2002.

Optional Protocol (First) to the Covenant on Civil and Political Rights, GA res. 2200A (XXI), 21 UN GAOR, Supp. (no. 16), UN Doc. A/6316 (1966), 99 UNTS 302, entered into force 23 March 1976.

Optional Protocol (Second) to the Covenant on Civil and Political Rights, Aiming at Abolition of the Death Penalty, GA res. 44/128, 44 UN GAOR, Supp. no. 49, UN Doc. A/44/49 (1989), entered into force 11 July 1991.

Principles and Guidelines on Human Rights and Trafficking, UN High Commissioner for Human Rights, E/2002/6/Add.1 (2002).

Protocol Amending the Slavery Convention, 182 UNTS 51, entered into force 7 July 1955.

Protocol I Additional to the Geneva Conventions of 1949, 1125 UNTS 3, entered into force 7 December 1978.

Protocol II Additional to the Geneva Conventions of 1949, 1125 UNTS 609, entered into force 7 December 1978.

Protocol of 1967 Relating to the Status of Refugees, 606 UNTS 267, entered into force 4 October 1967.

Protocol of Amendment to the Charter of the Organization of American States, "Protocol of Buenos Aires," OAS Treaty Series no. 1-A, entered into force 27 February 1970.

Protocol No. 12 to the 1950 European Convention for the Protection of Human Rights and Fundamental Freedoms, (ETS no. 177), open for signature 11 April 2000, not yet in force.

Protocol to the African Charter on Human and Peoples' Rights on the Establishment of an African Court on Human and Peoples' Rights, OAU Doc. OAU/LEG/EXP/AFCHPR/PROT(III) (1998), not yet in force.

Safeguards Guaranteeing Protection of the Rights of Those Facing the Death Penalty, ESC 1984/50, 1984 UN ESCOR, Supp. no. 1, annex, UN Doc. E/1984/184 (1984).

Slavery Convention 60 UNTS 253, entered into force 9 March 1927.

Standard Minimum Rules for the Treatment of Prisoners, adopted 30 August 1955, by the First
United Nations Congress on the Prevention of Crime and the Treatment of Offenders,
UN Doc. AJCONF/6/1, Annex I, A (1956); adopted 31 July 1957, by Economic and Social
Council, ESC res. 663C 24 UN ESCOR Supp. (no. I), UN Doc. E/3048 (1957), amended
ESC res. 2076, 62 UN ESCOR Supp. (no. 1), UN Doc. E/5988 (1977) (adding Article 95);
18586.

Statute of the International Court of Justice, 17 UNTS III, entered into force 24 October 1945.

Statute of the International Criminal Court, UN Doc. A/CONF 183/9 (1998), entered into force
1 July 2002.

Supplementary Convention on the Abolition of Slavery, the Slave Trade, and Institutions and Prac-
tices Similar to Slavery, 226 UNTS 3, entered into force 30 April 1957.

Treaty Establishing the European Economic Community, 298 UNTS II, entered into force 1 January 1958.

Treaty on European Union, 7 February 1992, o.1, (C 224/1).

UN Charter, *59 Stat. 1031, T.S. 993, 3 Bevans 1153, entered into force 24 October 1945.*

United Nations Standard Minimum Rules for the Administration of Juvenile Justice ("The Beijing
Rules"), GA res. 4O/33~ 40 UN GAOR Supp. (no. 53), annex, UN Doc. A/40/53 (1985).

Universal Declaration of Human Rights, (GA res. 217 A (III), adopted by the UN Doc. A/8lo,
10 December 1948.

Vienna Convention on Consular Relations, 596 UNTS 261, 21 UST 77, TIAS no. 6820, entered into
force 19 March 1967.

Vienna Convention on Diplomatic Relations, 23 UST 3227, TIAS no. 7502, 500 UNTS 95, entered
into force 18 April 1961.

Vienna Convention on the Law of Treaties, 1155 UNTS 331, TS no. 58 (1980), 8 ILM 679 (1979),
entered into force 27 January 1980.

Vienna Declaration and Programme of Action, A/CONF 157/23, 25 June 1993

• BIBLIOGRAPHY •

TERMINOLOGY-RELATED REFERENCES

Amnesty International Handbook. 7th ed. New York: Amnesty International, 1992. (Glossary at pp. 127 and 139–42.)

Black's Law Dictionary. 7th ed. St. Paul: West, 2000.

Bledsoe, R., and B. Boczek. *The International Law Dictionary.* Santa Barbara CA: ABC-Clio, 1987.

Caccia, I. *Human Rights Thesaurus.* Ottawa: Human Rights Research & Education Centre and Human Rights Internet, 1993.

Condé, H., and R. Cartwright. *Human Rights in the United States: A Dictionary and Documents.* Santa Barbara CA: ABC-Clio, 2000. (Human rights terminology from a U.S. historical-legal-political perspective.)

Encyclopedia of Human Rights, ed. E. Lawson. 2d ed. New York: Taylor & Francis, 1997. (Contains a seventy-two-term glossary in Appendix B.)

Encyclopedia of Public International Law, ed. R. Bernhardt. Amsterdam: North-Holland, 1985.

European Parliament, Terminology Office. *Terminology of Human Rights (Terminologie des Droits de L'Homme).* Brussels: European Parliament, 1976. PE 43.330.

Freeman, C. *The Diplomat's Dictionary,* rev. ed. Washington DC: U.S. Institute of Peace Press, 1997.

Gamboa, M. *A Dictionary of International Law and Diplomacy.* Dobbs Ferry NY: Oceans Publications, 1973.

Garner, B. *The Dictionary of Modern Legal Usage.* 2d ed. New York: Oxford University Press, 1995.

Gibson, J. *Dictionary of International Human Right Law.* Lanham MD: Scarecrow Press, 1996. (Contains definitions of the substantive human rights, e.g., freedom of expression, freedom of religion.)

Marie, J. B. *Glossary of Human Rights: Basic Terms in Universal and Regional Instruments.* Paris: Editions de La Maison des Sciences de l'Homme, 1981.

Oxford Dictionary of Law, 5th ed. Oxford / New York: Oxford University Press, 2002.

Parry, C., and J. Grant. *Encyclopaedic Dictionary of International Law.* Dobbs Ferry NY: Oceana Publications, 1986.

Plano, A., and R. Olton. *The International Relations Dictionary.* 4th ed. Santa Barbara CA: ABC-Clio, 1990.

Premont, D. *Terms and Concepts Relating to Human Rights, Women's Rights, and Children's Rights.* Geneva: International Training Centre on Human Rights and Peace Teaching, 1992.

Robertson, D. *A Dictionary of Human Rights.* Philadelphia: Taylor & Francis, 1998.

Stormorken, B., and L. Zwaak. *Human Rights Terminology in International Law: A Thesaurus.* Dordrecht: Martinus Nijhoff, 1988.

Verri, P. *Dictionary of the International Law of Armed Conflict.* Geneva: International Committee of the Red Cross, 1992.

Walker, D. M. *The Oxford Companion to Law.* Oxford: Clarendon Press, 1980.

Webster's New Collegiate Dictionary. Springfield MA: Merriam-Webster, 1977.

Ziring, L., J. Piano, and R. Olton. *International Relations: A Political Dictionary.* 5th ed. Santa Barbara CA: ABC-Clio, 1995.

TEXTS OF HUMAN RIGHTS INSTRUMENTS

Basic Documents Pertaining to Human Rights in the Inter-American System. Washington DC: General Secretariat of the Organization of American States, OAS Doc. no. 31 OAE/Ser.L/V/II.92 Doc. 31 rev. 3 (1996).

Brownlie, I., ed. *Basic Documents on Human Rights.* 3d ed. Oxford: Clarendon 1992.

Council of Europe. *Human Rights in International Law: Basic Texts.* 2d ed. Strasbourg: Council of Europe Press, Directorate of Human Rights, 1992.

Council of Europe. *Human Rights Today: European Legal Texts.* Strasbourg: Council of Europe Pub., 1999.

International Protection of Human Rights Texts. Strasbourg: International Institute of Human Rights, Annual Study Session, 2002.

Office of the UNHCHR. *Human Rights: A Compilation of International Instruments.* UN Doc. ST/HR/1/Rev. 4, UN Sales no. E.94.XV.1(1994) and UN Doc. ST/HR/1/Rev. 5 (1997). New York: United Nations, 1994.

Sarnoff, I., ed. *International Instruments of the United Nations: A Compilation of Agreements, Charters, Conventions, Declarations, Principles, Proclamations, Protocols, Treaties adopted by the General Assembly of the United Nations, 1945–1995.* New York: United Nations, 1997.

Weissbrodt, D., et al., eds. *Selected International Human Rights Instruments and Bibliography for Research on International Human Rights Law.* 3d ed. Cincinnati OH: Anderson, 2001.

Wallace, R. *International Human Rights Texts and Materials.* London: Sweet & Maxwell, 1997.

Weston, B., et al., eds. *Basic Documents in International Law and World Order.* 2d ed., St. Paul: West Publishing, 1990.

University of Minnesota Human Rights Center. Human Rights Library [website], <www.umn.edu/humanrts>. (Where all global, regional, and other human rights instruments can be found.)

For ratification status of treaties (i.e., which countries have ratified and whether the treaty* has entered into force) see Jean Bernard Marie. *International Instruments Relating to Human Rights/Classification and Status of Ratifications,* in *Human Rights Law Journal,* Vol. 23, No. 1–4, 30 September 2002, Kehl (Germany): N.P. Engel, and for yearly updates once a year.

TEXT BOOKS

Buergenthal, T., D. Shelton, and J. Stewart. *International Human Rights in a Nutshell,* 3d ed. St. Paul: West, 2002.

Buergenthal, T., T. Norris, and D. Shelton. *Protecting Human Rights in the Americas: Selected Problems*. 4th ed. Kehl, Germany: N.P. Engel, 1995.

Hanski, R., and M. Suksi, eds. *An Introduction to the International Protection of Human Rights: A Textbook*. 2d ed. Turku Åbo: Åbo Akademi University, 2000.

Henkin, L., G. Neuman, D. Orentlicher, and D. Leebron. *Human Rights*. New York: Foundation Press, Casebook Series, 1999.

Martin, F. et al., eds. *International Human Rights Law and Practice: Cases, Treaties, and Materials*. The Hague: Kluwer Law International, 1997. (Comes with Documentary supplement of human rights instruments.)

Steiner, H., and P. Alston. *International Human Rights in Context: Law, Politics, Morals*. 2d ed. Oxford: Clarendon Press, 2001.

Weissbrodt, D., J. Fitzpatrick, and F. Newman. *International Human Rights: Law Policy and Process*. 3d ed. Cincinnati OH: Anderson Pub, 2001. (Includes an excellent supplement containing a compilation of "*Selected International Human Rights Instruments*" and an exhaustive "*Bibliography for Research on International Human Rights Law*.")

LAW OF ARMED CONFLICT

International Committee of the Red Cross. *The Geneva Conventions of August 12, 1949*. Geneva: ICRC, 1987.

International Committee of the Red Cross. *Protocols Additional to the Geneva Conventions of August 12, 1949*. Geneva: ICRC, 1987.

Roberts, A., and R. Guelff, eds. *Documents on the Laws of War*. 3d ed. Oxford: Clarendon Press, 2000.

INTERNATIONAL CRIMINAL LAW

Paust, J., M. Bassiouni, et al. *International Criminal Law*. 2d ed. Durham NC: Carolina Academic Press, 2000, with accompanying *Human Rights Module*.

IN THE HUMAN RIGHTS IN
INTERNATIONAL PERSPECTIVE SERIES